D0418810

5000 FANTASTIC FACTS

Published by Alligator Publishing Limited
Gadd House, Arcadia Avenue, London N3 2JU
Printed in China 0041

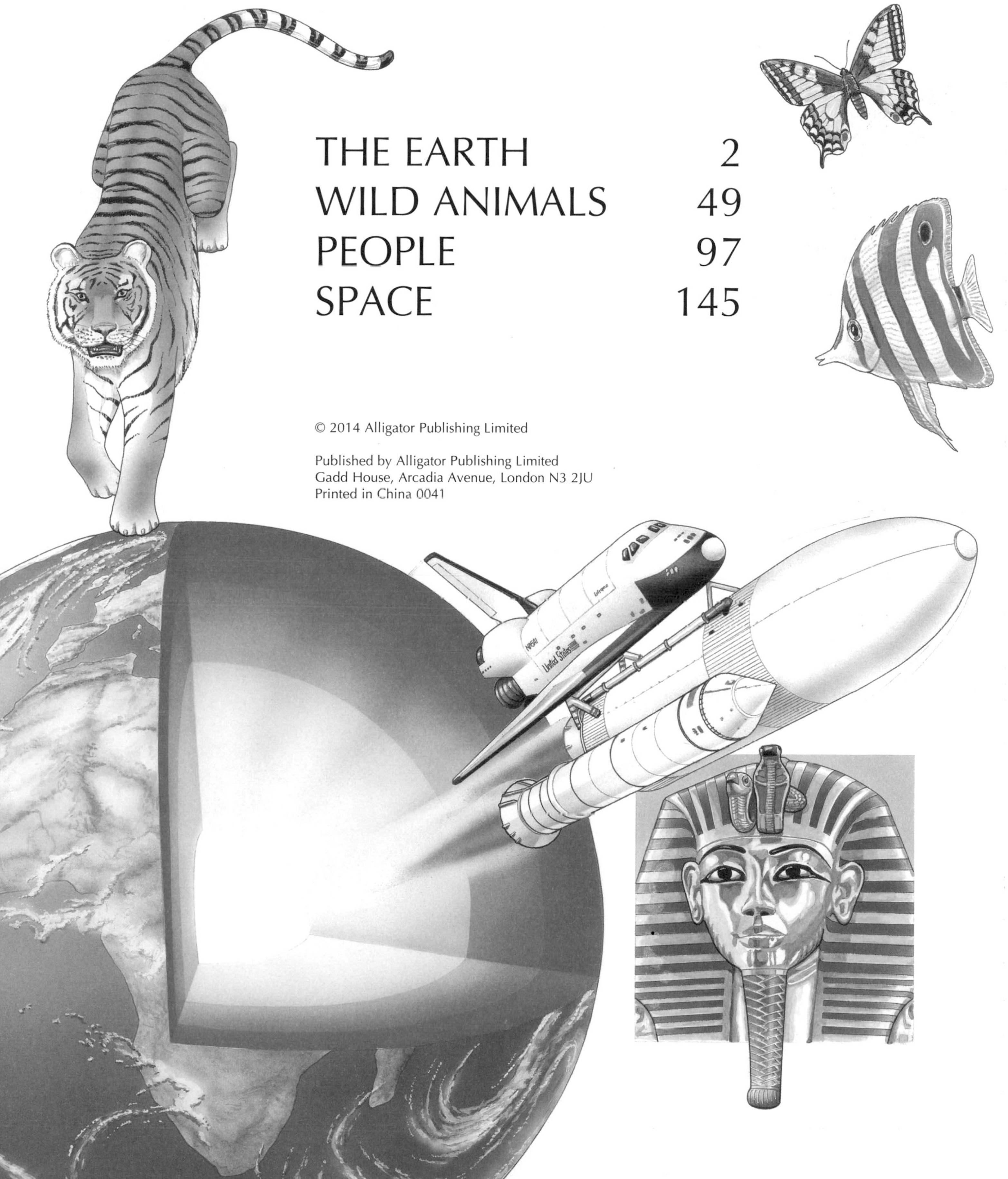

To help you pick out the things you want to read about in this book, some key words are printed in bold type like this: **volcano**.

Look out too for spot facts (which start with a •), strange-but-true facts in their special boxes, and mini-facts at the top of each page. At the end of each Part, you'll find lists of records and an index.

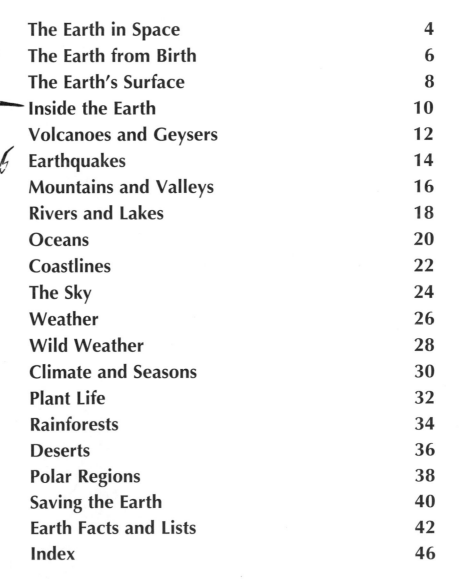

Part One

THE EARTH

Introduction

Welcome to our world! Here you can find out all about planet Earth, and how scientists think it came to be formed.

At the bottom of the Earth's crust, the rocks are red-hot. At the centre of the Earth, the temperature could be 45 times hotter than the temperature of boiling water.

Mountain-building takes millions of years. Volcanoes and earthquakes continue to change the shape of the Earth's surface. Did you know that there can be more than 20 volcanic eruptions (mostly under the sea) and a similar number of large earthquakes each year?

Places like rainforests, deserts and the polar regions have very different plants and creatures. Antarctica is the coldest and windiest place on Earth. Although birds, whales and seals live around its coast, the largest animal to be found inland is a fly!

The Earth's oceans make up 97 per cent of the water on the planet.

The world's weather ranges from burning sunshine and beautiful rainbows to fierce thunderstorms, hurricanes and tornadoes. Some tornadoes can even lift a train into the air.

The Earth in Space

Life on Earth depends on these four things:

Water

Our world is a **planet** travelling through Space. It journeys around a giant ball of fiery hot gases called the **Sun**.

The Sun is a **star**. It produces **light** and **heat** which reach the Earth.

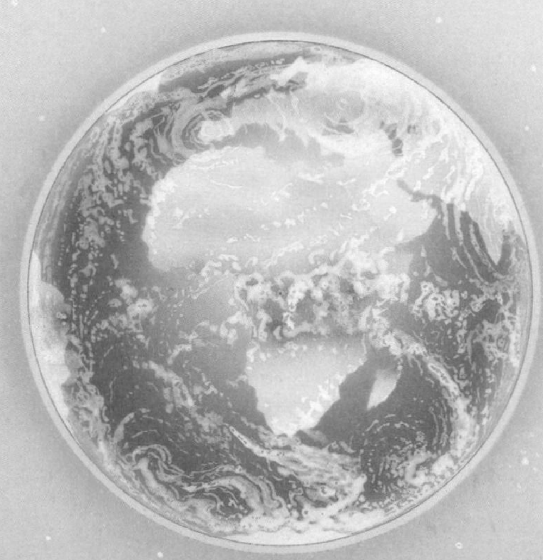

The Earth is the only known planet that has **life** on it. It is ideal for living things because it has **water** and **air**.

The Solar System

The Earth is part of the **Solar System**, a group of nine planets that travel through Space around the Sun.

• The Earth takes one year to travel round the Sun, a distance of 958 million km.

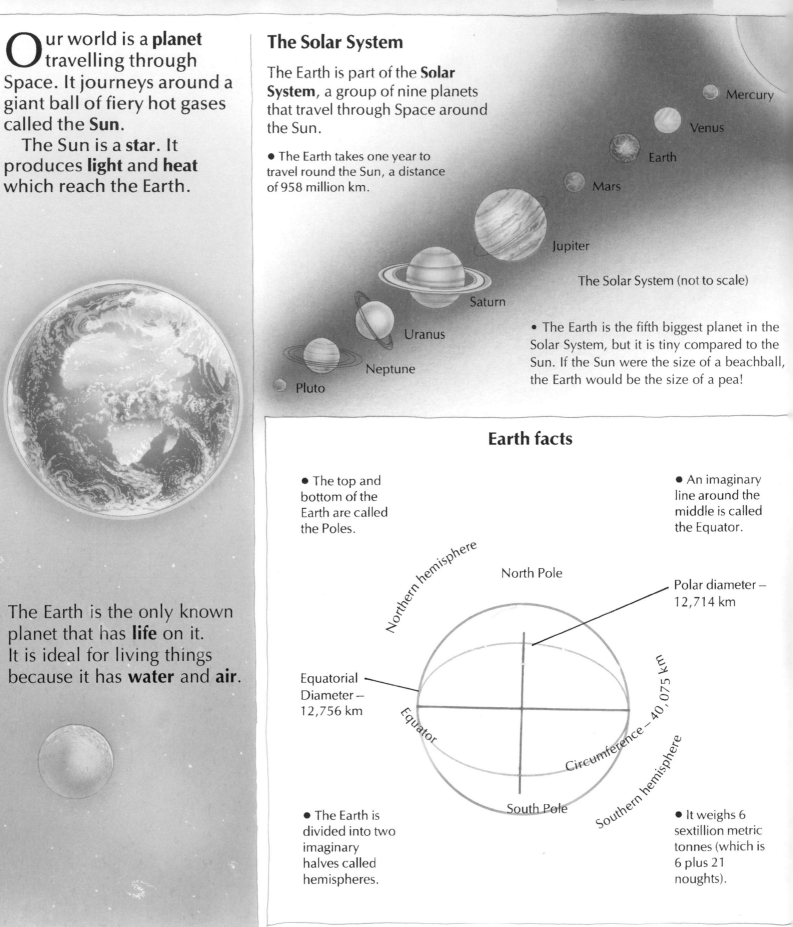

Mercury
Venus
Earth
Mars
Jupiter
Saturn
Uranus
Neptune
Pluto

The Solar System (not to scale)

• The Earth is the fifth biggest planet in the Solar System, but it is tiny compared to the Sun. If the Sun were the size of a beachball, the Earth would be the size of a pea!

Earth facts

• The top and bottom of the Earth are called the Poles.

• An imaginary line around the middle is called the Equator.

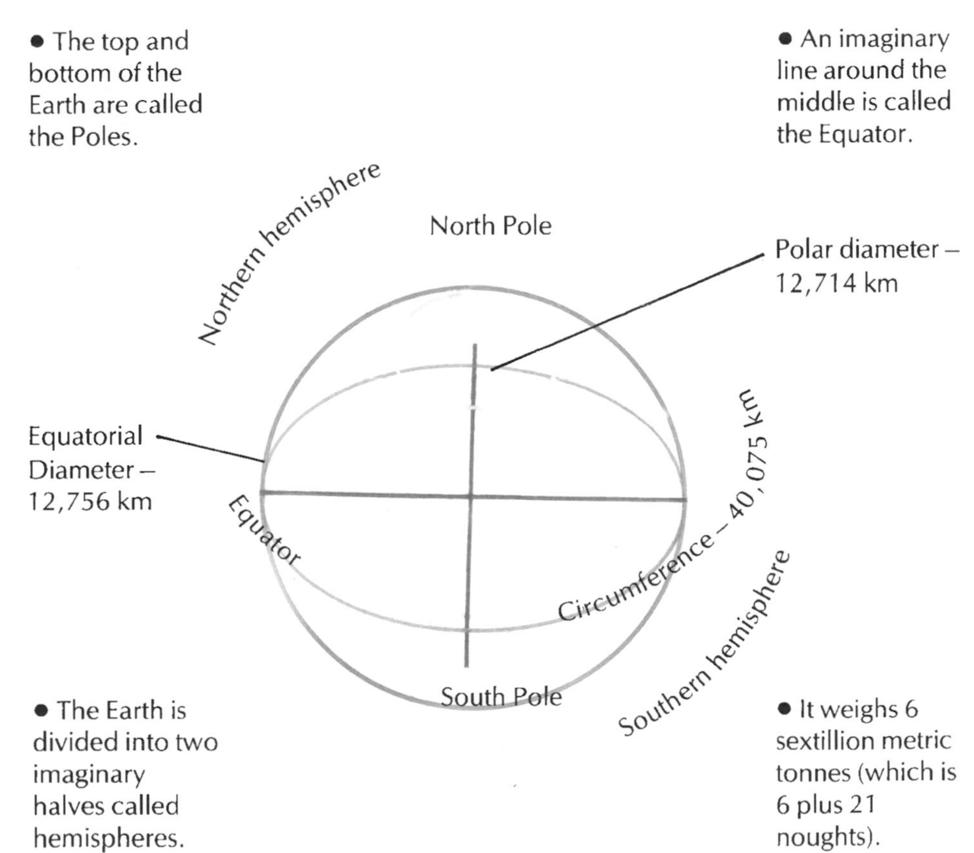

• The Earth is divided into two imaginary halves called hemispheres.

• It weighs 6 sextillion metric tonnes (which is 6 plus 21 noughts).

Air

Plants
(they produce oxygen)

The Sun's heat

Earth's orbit

The Earth's path around the Sun is called its **orbit**. It travels in a long oval shape called an **ellipse**. As it travels through Space it spins around on its **axis**, an imaginary line through the centre of the planet from Pole to Pole.

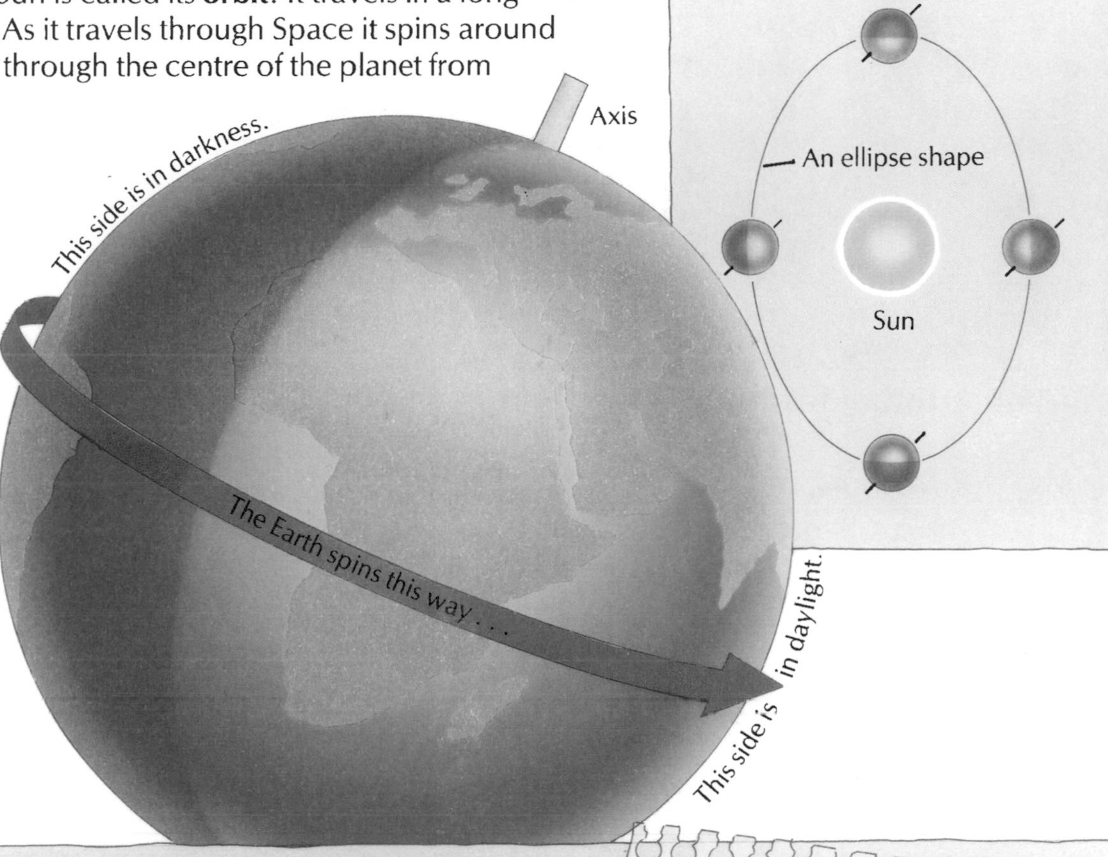

- The Earth spins on its axis once a day. When your part of the Earth turns away from the Sun, darkness falls.
- As the Earth travels round, your home begins to face the Sun again and daylight arrives.
- During the day the Sun looks as if it is moving across the sky. In fact, it is the Earth that is moving, not the Sun.

The Moon

The Moon is a **satellite** of the Earth, which means it orbits around our planet. It orbits once every 27 days, 7 hours, 43.25 minutes.

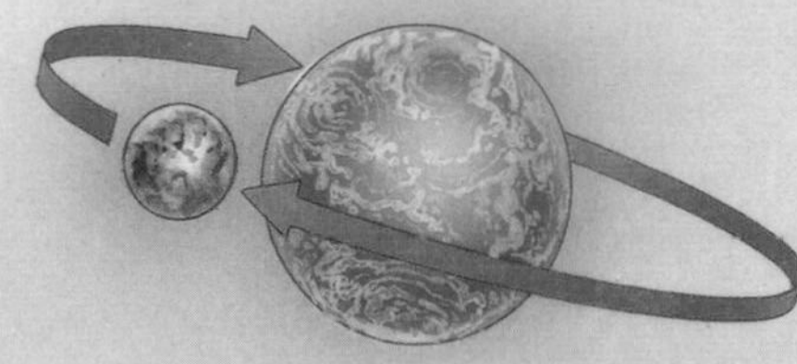

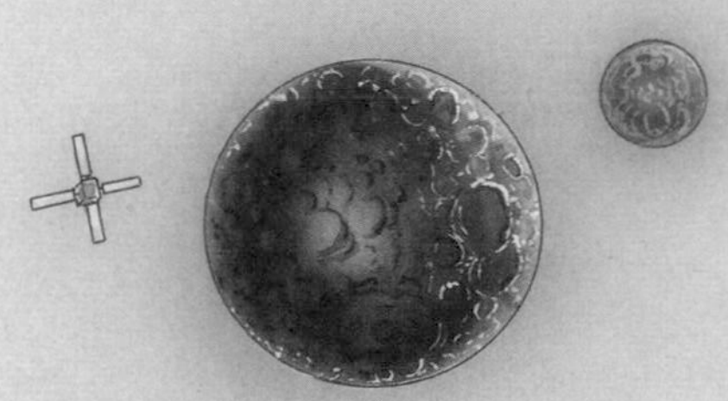

- Half of the Moon always faces away from the Sun, so it is constantly in shadow. This dark side cannot be seen from the Earth but it has been photographed by spaceships.
- Some scientists think that the Moon was once part of the Earth. It may have been broken off when a huge asteroid collided with our planet billions of years ago.

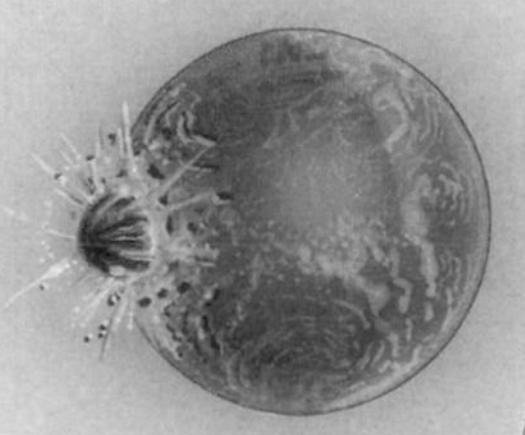

Strange but true

- The ancient Greeks thought that stars were lamps hanging above the Earth.
- For centuries people believed that the Sun orbited the Earth.

- People used to believe that the Earth was flat. They thought that ships would fall over the edge.
- The Earth gets heavier each year because it picks up dust from space.

The Earth from Birth

Here are some examples of the very first plants and animals on Earth:

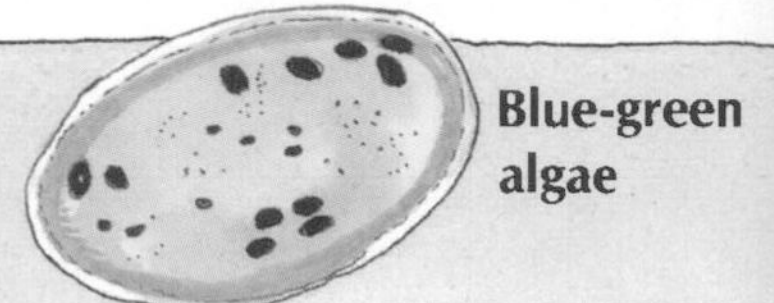

The Solar System was probably formed about **4.5 billion years** ago from a huge cloud of gas and dust, perhaps caused by the explosion of a giant star.

The gas and dust began to spin around the Sun, which formed in the middle of the cloud. Gradually the remaining dust may have joined together to form the **planets**.

The **Earth** probably began as a mass of rock which was surrounded by a thick mist of gases. It is at least 3000 million years old, and it may be much older. Since its birth it has changed in many ways.

Strange but true

- Fossilized footprints of early humans have been discovered in rocks.
- One of the biggest dinosaurs was Supersaurus. It weighed as much as 15 elephants.
- People once thought that fossils were the remains of dragons and giants.
- The Stegosaurus was 9 metres long, but had a brain the size of a walnut.

Earth's beginnings

The development of the Earth is divided into five lengths of time called **Eras**. The first two Eras, the **Archeozoic** and the **Proterozoic**, lasted for four billion years, which is almost **80%** of the Earth's history.

- During the Archeozoic Era the Earth was born. Water and gases such as oxygen were formed. Tiny and very simple creatures called bacteria developed about 3.2 billion years ago, along with tiny algae plants.

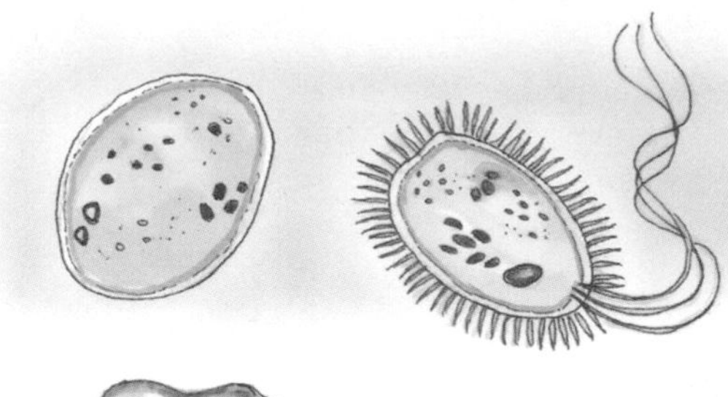

- During the Proterozoic Era, about 700 million years ago, the first animals appeared in the sea. They were simple animals without backbones, such as worms and jellyfish.

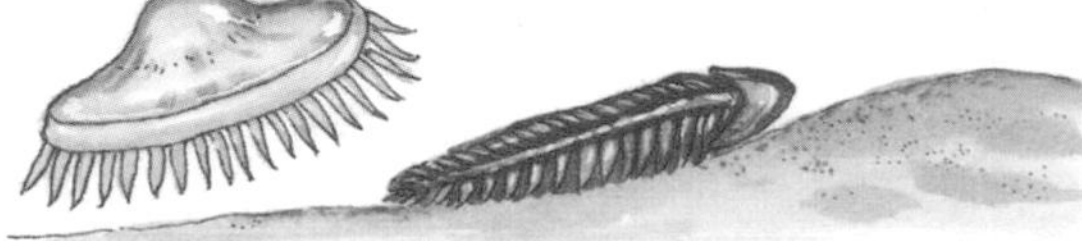

- The Paleozoic Era lasted from about 570 million years ago to 245 million years ago. During this time the Earth was covered in swamps. Larger plants, fish and amphibians appeared.

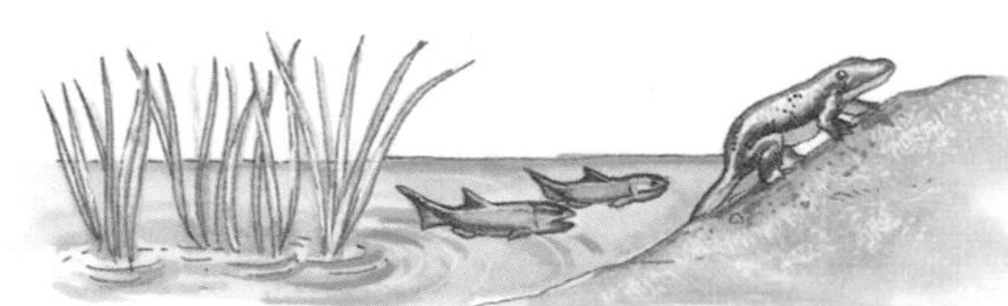

- The Mesozoic Era lasted from about 245 million years ago to 66 million years ago. In this period many animals developed, including giant reptiles called dinosaurs. The first mammals and birds also appeared.

- The Cenozoic Era began about 66 million years ago and is still going on. The plants and animals we know today developed during this time.

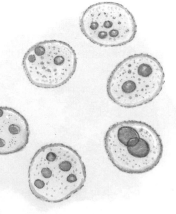

Microscopic plants called algae were amongst the first life forms.

How life began

When the Earth was young, a mixture of different chemicals covered its surface. The Sun's radiation acted on the chemicals and they formed new materials called **amino acids** and **sugars**.

The amino acids and sugars linked up and eventually living **cells** were created. Cells are the smallest units of life, from which all living things are made.

Jellyfish

Spriggina worms

Dickinsonia worms

Sea-pen corals

Fossils

Scientists can tell what early plants and animals were like by looking at **fossils**. A fossil is the hardened remains or shape of an animal or plant preserved in rock.

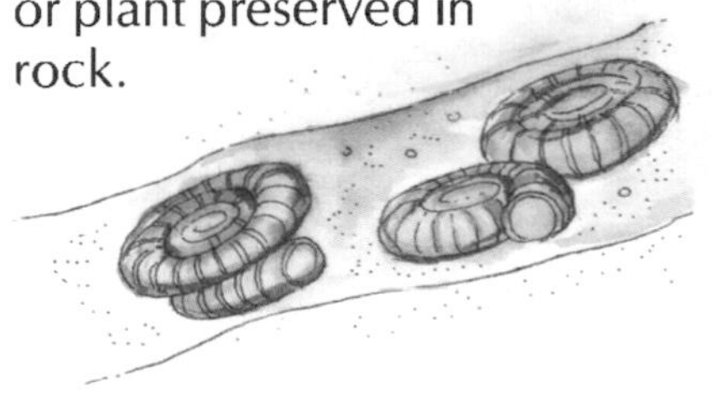

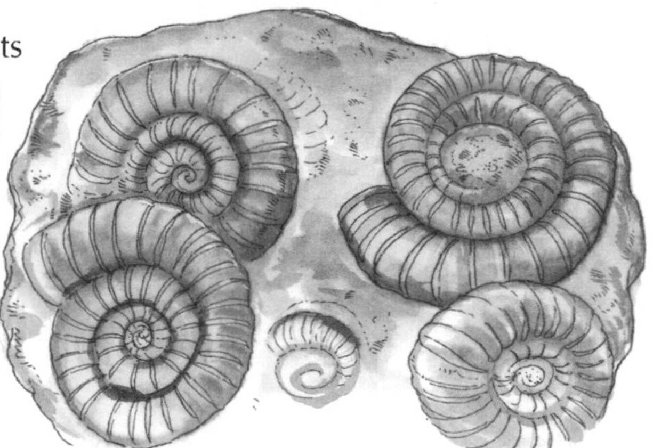

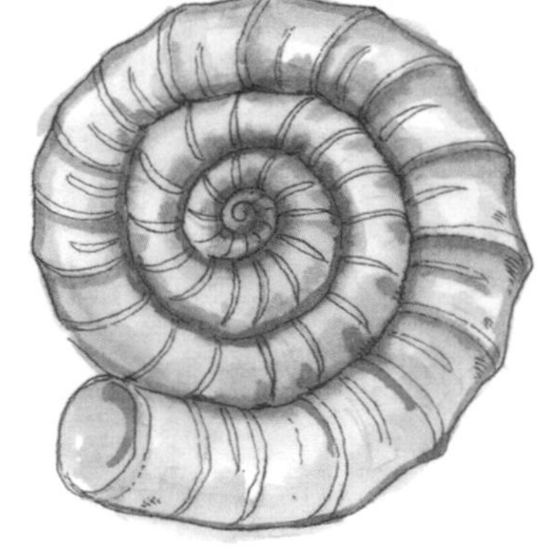

• A fossil forms when a dead animal, for example, gets covered in mud or clay.

• The soft parts of the body decay, leaving the hard parts such as bone.

• Over thousands of years, the mud hardens into rock, preserving the animal.

• Some animal and plant fossils have been found in pieces of amber, a fossilized resin which oozed from pine trees millions of years ago and then hardened.

Fossil in amber.

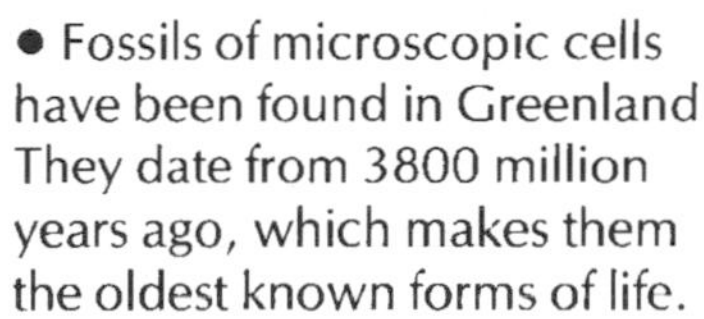

• Fossils of microscopic cells have been found in Greenland. They date from 3800 million years ago, which makes them the oldest known forms of life.

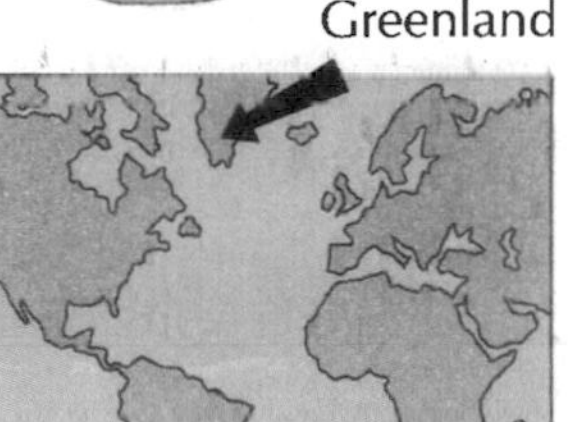

Evolution

Evolution is the theory that animals and plants have gradually changed shape and form over millions of years, to enable them to survive in their surroundings. For instance, human beings may have evolved from apes.

Dinosaurs

Dinosaurs were the biggest animals that ever lived. They were reptiles with scaly skins.

• Plant-eating dinosaurs were huge. Brachiosaurus and Diplodocus were some of the largest, up to 30 metres in length.

• Meat-eating dinosaurs were smaller and ran on hind legs. The largest was Tyrannosaurus, which stood about 5 metres tall.

The dinosaurs disappeared about 65 million years ago. No-one knows exactly why. They may have died out because:

• An asteroid hit the Earth, throwing up so much dust that the Sun's rays were blocked out, leading to the death of plants and some of the biggest animals.

• The Earth's temperature heated up and became too warm for the dinosaurs.

• The mammal population grew bigger and took most of the dinosaurs' food.

The Earth's Surface

Here are the seven continents:

Australia
8 million sq km

Asia
44 million sq km

The Earth has an outer shell called the **crust**. It is divided into 20 huge pieces called **plates** that fit together rather like a jigsaw. They float on top of hot, partly molten rock.

On top of the crust there is **land** and **ocean**. The land is split into seven parts called **continents**.

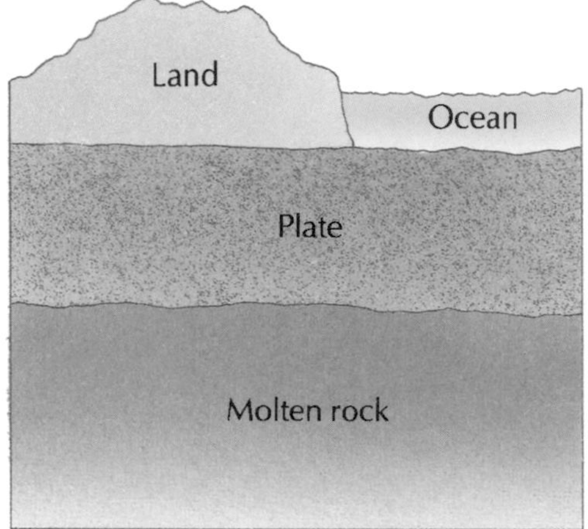

The Earth's plates

The Earth's **plates** move around very slowly as they float on top of hot rock. As they move, they carry the land and the ocean floor with them. Sometimes the plates:

- Collide, pushing up mountains or creating deep ocean trenches and volcanoes (see p12 and p20).
- Slide slowly past each other, producing so much strain that they cause earthquakes (see p14).
- Move apart so the ocean floor splits between them and molten rock rises up through cracks.

Volcanoes

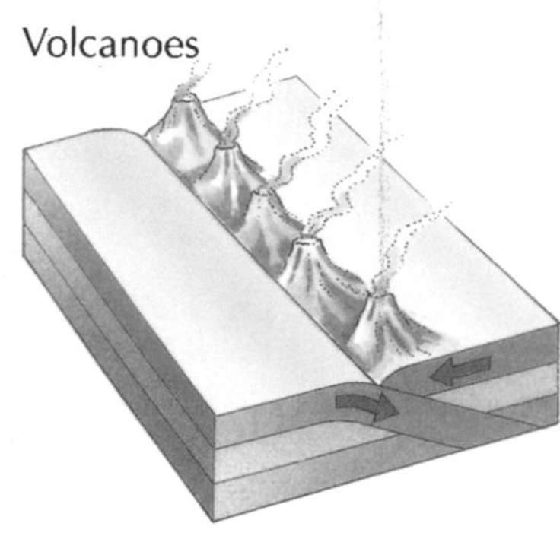

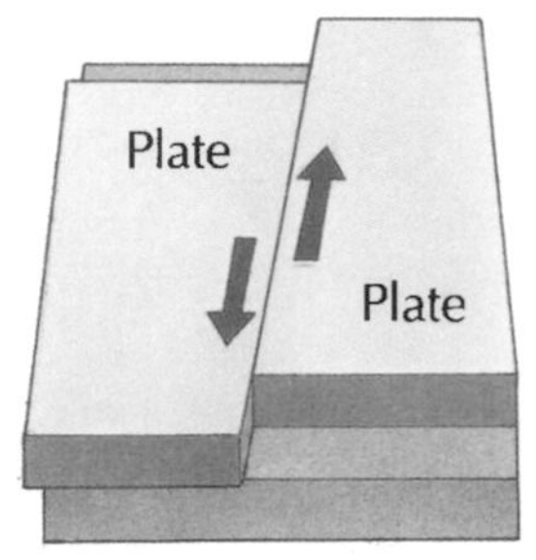

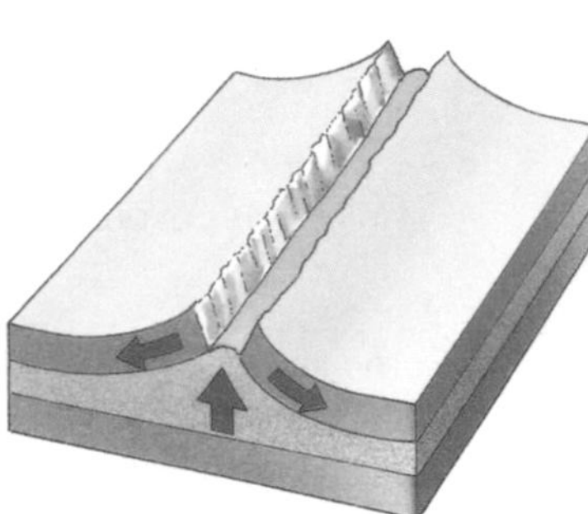

Floor spreads apart

Strange but true

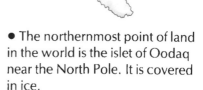

- In the past people thought that the oceans and continents were a result of Noah's flood.
- The Earth's plates move between 1.3 cm and 10 cm a year.
- The world's oceans are widening by between 1 cm and 10 cm a year.
- Pangaea comes from an ancient Greek word meaning 'whole Earth'.

Earth facts

- Greenland is the largest island in the world. It may possibly be several islands covered by a sheet of ice.

Greenland

- The northernmost point of land in the world is the islet of Oodaq near the North Pole. It is covered in ice.

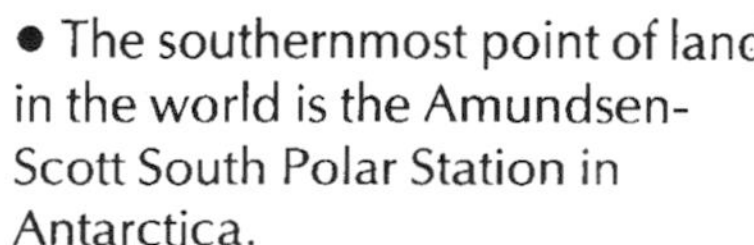

- The southernmost point of land in the world is the Amundsen-Scott South Polar Station in Antarctica.

- The highest point of land in the world is Mount Everest in the Himalayan mountain-range.

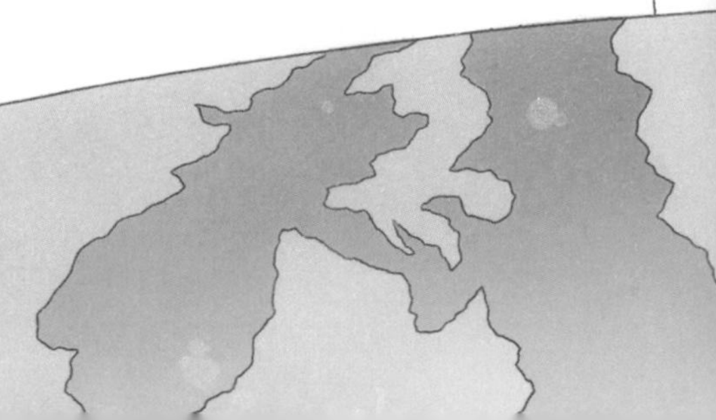

Africa 30 million sq km

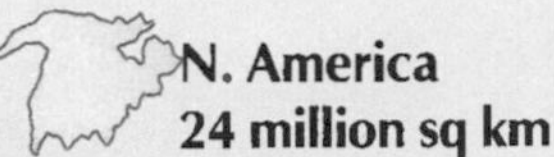
N. America 24 million sq km

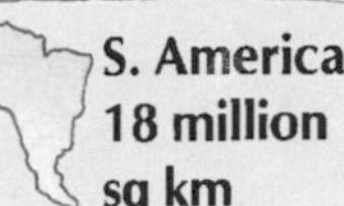
S. America 18 million sq km

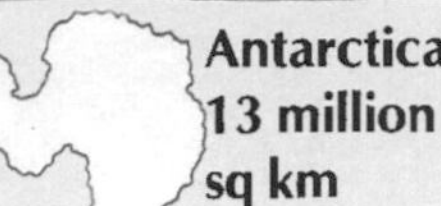
Antarctica 13 million sq km

Europe 10 million sq km

The continents

The Earth's **continents** move around on top of the plates that float beneath them. The movement is very slow; it has taken millions of years for the continents to reach where they are today.

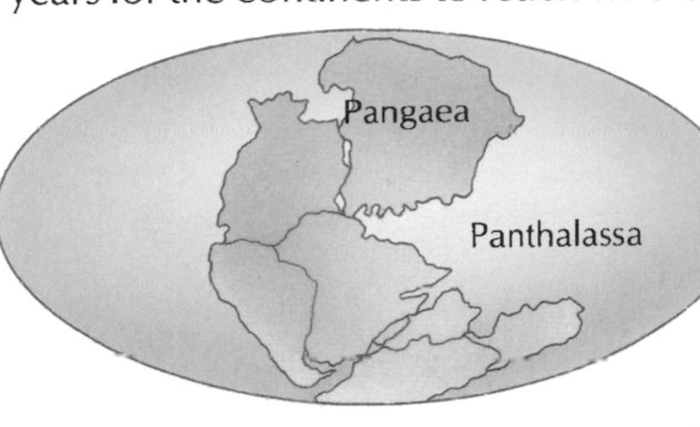

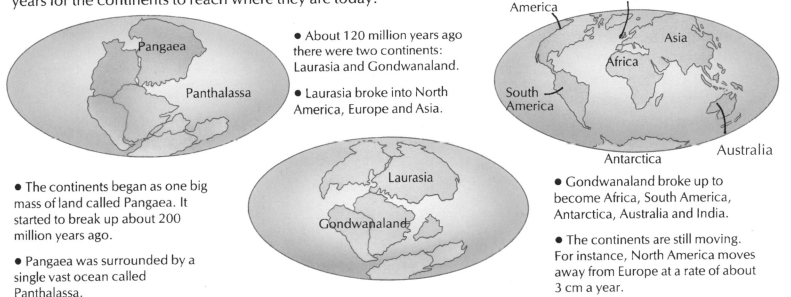

- About 120 million years ago there were two continents: Laurasia and Gondwanaland.
- Laurasia broke into North America, Europe and Asia.

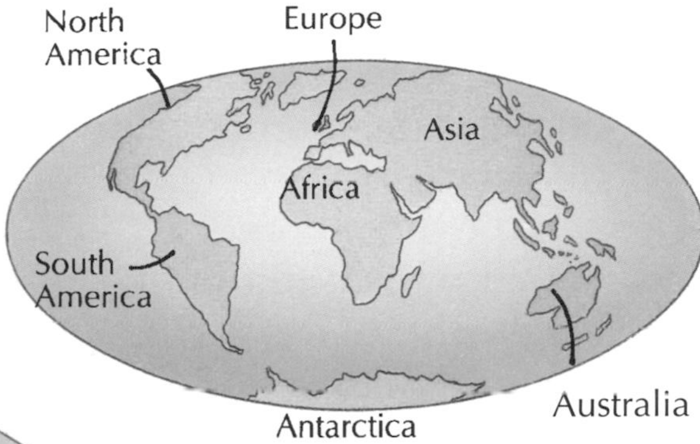

- The continents began as one big mass of land called Pangaea. It started to break up about 200 million years ago.
- Pangaea was surrounded by a single vast ocean called Panthalassa.

- Gondwanaland broke up to become Africa, South America, Antarctica, Australia and India.
- The continents are still moving. For instance, North America moves away from Europe at a rate of about 3 cm a year.

The past and the future.

Here are some examples of the shape of continents in the **past**:

- The eastern coast of South America and the western coast of Africa were joined. Their modern shapes could fit together like a jigsaw.
- The continents of Africa and Antarctica were also joined. There is proof of this because fossilized remains of tropical African plants and animals have been found in modern Antarctica.

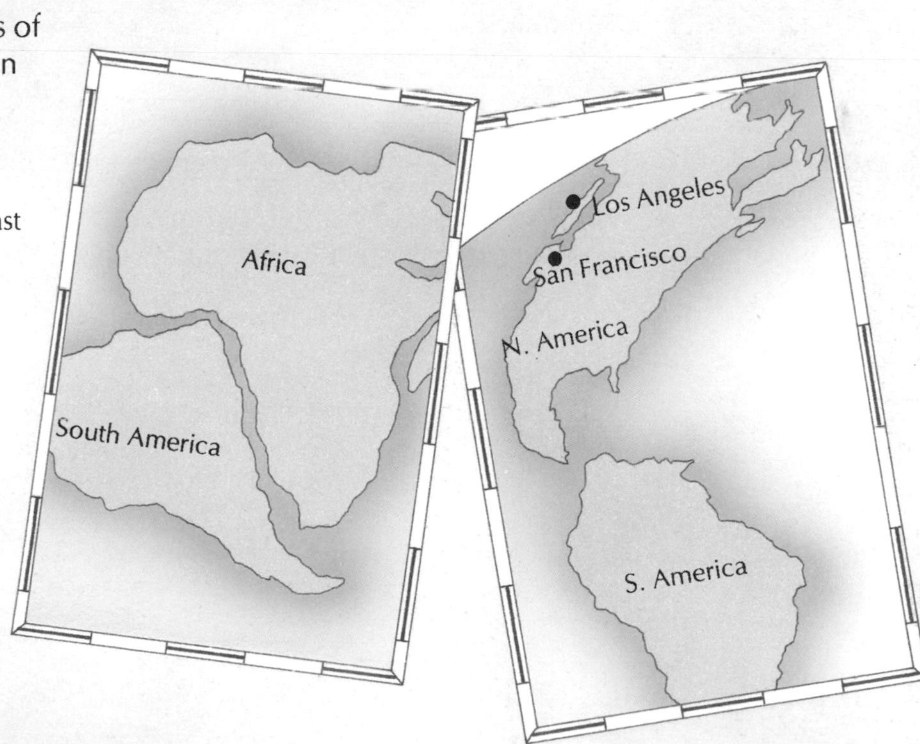

Here are some examples of what may occur in **50 million years** time:

- The two American continents will have broken apart.
- Africa and Asia will have broken apart.
- Part of California, including the city of Los Angeles, will have broken off from America. It will float north, past San Francisco on the mainland.

Inside the Earth

Here are the four most precious gems to be found beneath the Earth:

Ruby

The Earth is made up of four different layers. The layer of hot, partly-molten rock beneath the **crust** layer is called the **mantle.**

Beneath the mantle there is a layer of liquid metal called the **outer core.**

Beneath the liquid metal, in the centre of the Earth, there is a ball of very hot solid metal called the **inner core.**

Crust

Mantle

Outer core

Inner core

The Earth's layers

Scientists have worked out what is likely to be inside the Earth by analyzing **rocks** and by studying the **shock waves** that travel up to the surface during earthquakes (see p14/15).

- The temperature in the middle of the Earth is thought to be about 4500° C, which is 45 times hotter than the temperature of boiling water!

- New crust is being made all the time, as molten rock bubbles up through huge cracks between plates in the ocean floor.

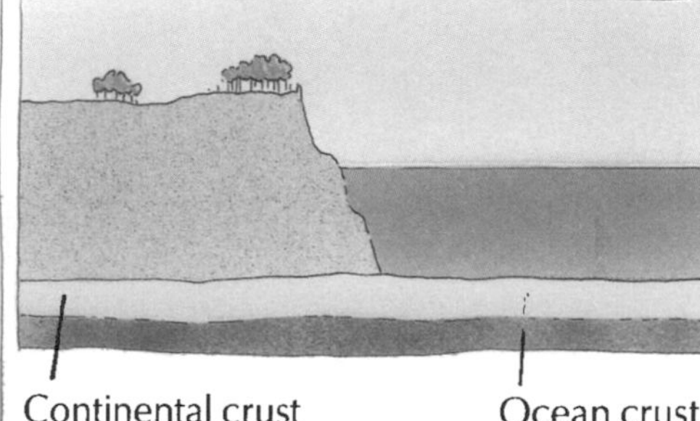

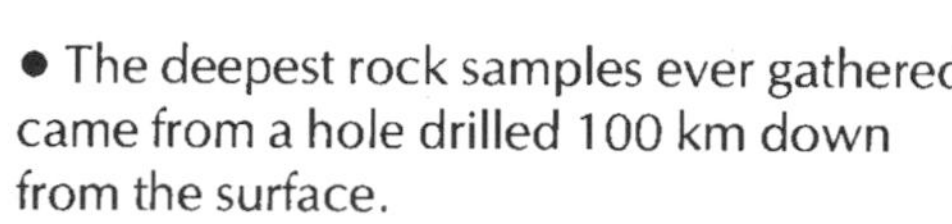

- There are two kinds of Earth crust – ocean crust beneath the seas and continental crust beneath the land.

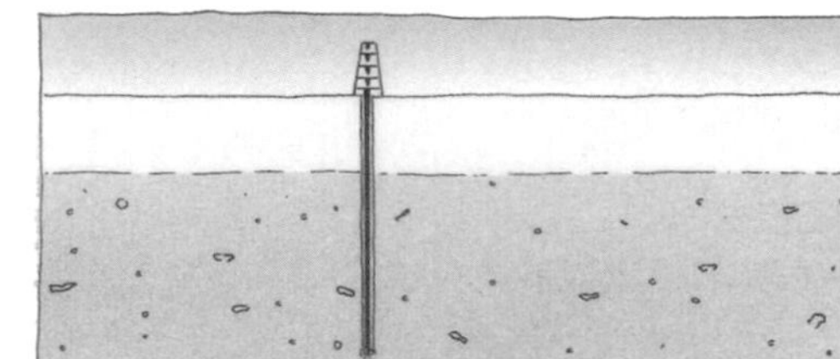

- The deepest rock samples ever gathered came from a hole drilled 100 km down from the surface.

Strange but true

- Diamond is harder than any other natural substance.

- Children playing on a beach made the first discovery of a South African diamond.

- The largest diamond ever found weighed over half a kilogram.

- Diamonds are made of carbon, the same material as coal soot.

Rocks

There are three different types of rock on Earth. They are given the names **igneous**, **sedimentary** and **metamorphic**.

- Igneous rocks are formed when hot molten material called magma bubbles up from beneath the crust and hardens.

- Some sedimentary rocks are made from pieces of other rock types that are pushed down under the Earth's surface and altered by pressure.

- Other sedimentary rocks form from layers of dead animals and plants on the seabed. The layers harden over many millions of years.

- Metamorphic rocks are formed deep beneath the Earth's crust, where igneous or sedimentary rocks are changed by heat and pressure.

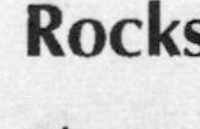

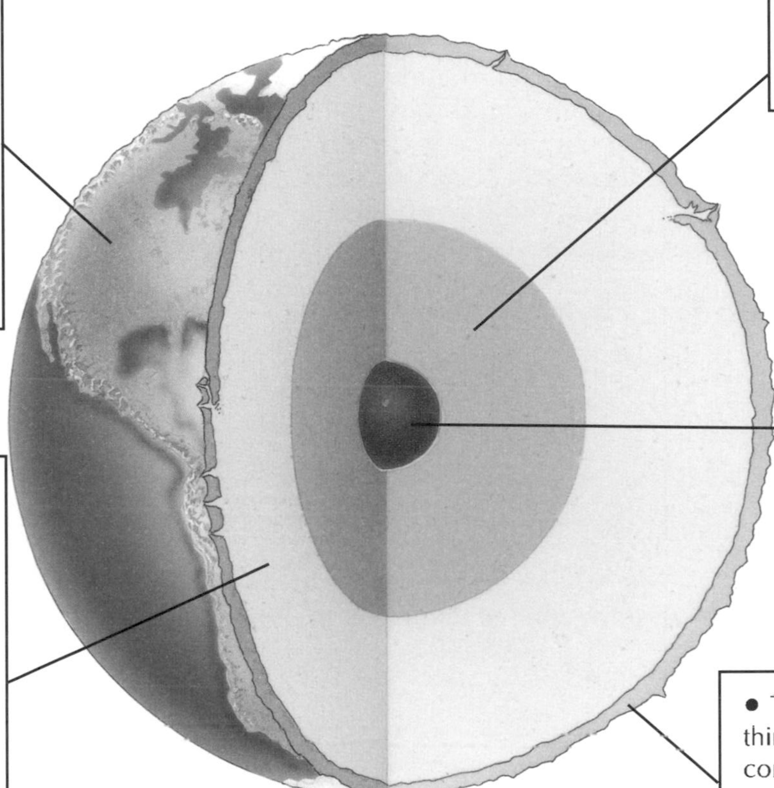

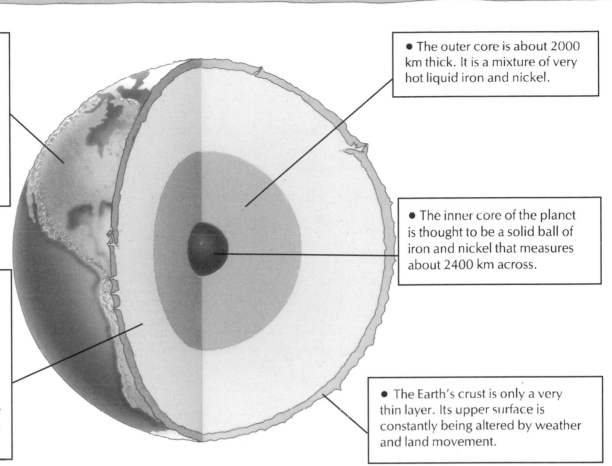

• The Earth's crust stretches about 40 km below the surface. It is made of light rock. The temperature of the crustal rock increases by about 30°C for every kilometre downwards. At the bottom of the crust, the rocks are red-hot.

• The outer core is about 2000 km thick. It is a mixture of very hot liquid iron and nickel.

• The inner core of the planet is thought to be a solid ball of iron and nickel that measures about 2400 km across.

• The Earth's mantle is about 2900 km thick. At the top it is made of solid rock. Deeper down it is so hot that the rock melts and becomes molten. The rock in the mantle layer is composed mainly of iron and magnesium.

There is a definite boundary line between the crust and the mantle.

• The Earth's crust is only a very thin layer. Its upper surface is constantly being altered by weather and land movement.

Riches from the Earth

Our main sources of **heat and power** come from beneath the Earth's surface. Oil, gas and coal are called **fossil fuels**.

• Oil is made from the bodies of tiny sea creatures that lived millions of years ago. The bodies gathered on the seabed and they were gradually squeezed down under rocks that formed above them. Eventually they turned into oil.

Ocean oil platform

• Coal is made from trees that died millions of years ago. Layers of the dead plant material were squeezed down until they turned into carbon.

• Natural gas is made when animal and plant bodies decompose. It is usually found in the same place as oil.

Gemstones

Precious stones are mined from beneath the Earth's surface.

• Gems form as crystals in igneous rock. They vary in colour, shape and size. Because they are rare, they have been prized for centuries.

• The rarest diamonds are blue or pink. Rubies are the rarest gems of all. The finest ones come from Myanmar (Burma).

• The best sapphires come from Burma, Kashmir and Montana, USA.

• The finest emeralds come from Colombia in South America.

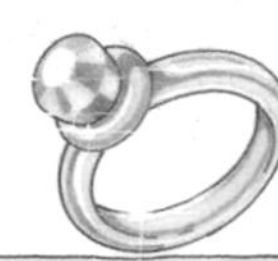

Volcanoes and Geysers

Here are some goods that often contain crushed volcanic stone:

Toothpaste

Volcanoes occur when hot rock seeps up through cracks in the Earth's crust. Most volcanoes are found where two **plates** are pushing against each other or moving apart (see p8).

Volcanoes that erupt are called active. Many are found in an area around the Pacific Ocean called the '**Pacific Ring of Fire**'.

Volcanoes in the Pacific Ring of Fire

Volcanoes that might erupt are **dormant**. Volcanoes that have stopped erupting are **extinct**.

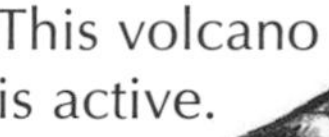

This volcano is active.

How a volcano forms

Pressure builds up underground and pushes molten liquid rock up from a chamber beneath the surface. It spews out of a crack in the ground as **lava**.

- Ash, lava and rocks build up to form a hill with a crater on top. Sometimes the lava comes out through side exits called domes.
- Gas, lava and pieces of solid rock (called tephra) spew out. Large molten lumps of tephra are called volcanic bombs.

Hot springs and geysers

Hot springs occur when underground water is heated up by hot rocks beneath the Earth's surface. The boiling water rises up through cracks in the ground.

Geysers are hot springs that spout water and steam at regular intervals.

- Yellowstone Park in the USA has over 2500 geysers, including a world-famous one nicknamed 'Old Faithful'.
- New Zealand and Iceland are the other main areas of geyser activity.
- A fumarole is a crack in the ground that releases more acid gases than water. These often occur on volcano slopes.

A fumarole

Make-up

Bath cleaner

Road surfacing material

Volcano shapes

A volcano shape depends on the type of eruption that caused it and the sort of material that comes out.

• Shield volcanoes (left) are shaped like upturned saucers, with gentle slopes.

• Cinder cone volcanoes are high, with steep slopes.

• Stratovolcanoes (left) are cone-shaped mountains.

Types of eruption

Eruptions are given different names, depending on how strong they are.

• Hawaiian eruptions are not very violent. They pour out liquid lava in fiery rivers.

• Strombolian eruptions produce thicker lava, but not too violently. They erupt continuously.

• Vulcanian eruptions produce violent explosions and throw out tephra, dust, gas and ash.

• Peléean eruptions are huge explosions which throw out a massive cloud of gas and lava.

Strange but true

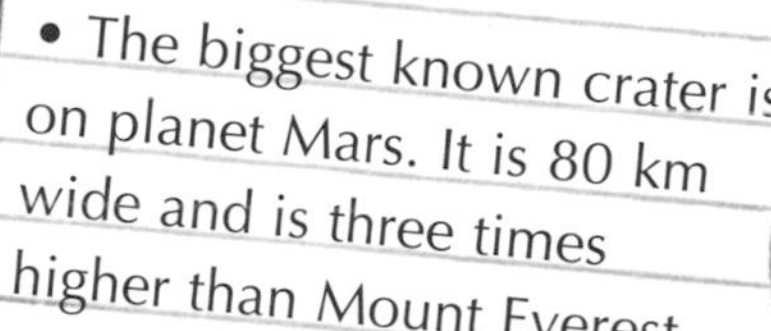

• In 1783 an Icelandic eruption threw up enough dust to temporarily block out the Sun over Europe.

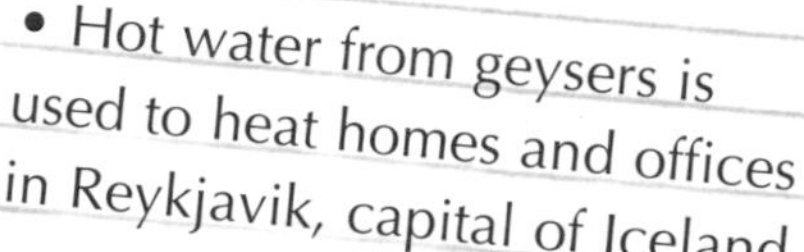

• The biggest known crater is on planet Mars. It is 80 km wide and is three times higher than Mount Everest.

• Hot water from geysers is used to heat homes and offices in Reykjavik, capital of Iceland.

• About 20 to 30 volcanoes erupt each year, mostly under the sea.

Volcanic islands

Many **ocean islands** have been formed by volcanic eruptions beneath the sea. First, ash is blown above the water and then a pile of rock and lava builds up until it appears above the waves.

• In 1963 the volcanic island of Surtsey appeared near Iceland. It took three weeks to rise from the waves.

• In 1883 the volcanic island of Krakatoa, near Java, blew up. Rock blasted 80 km into the air.

Pompeii

In AD 79 the Italian volcano Vesuvius erupted and buried the Roman cities of Pompeii and Herculaneum.

• The cities were hidden for nearly seventeen centuries, until a farmer discovered some ruins in 1748.

• Vesuvius is still an active volcano. If it erupted in the future the nearby city of Naples would have to be evacuated.

Earthquakes

These animals warn of approaching earthquakes by behaving strangely

Earthquakes are severe shocks that happen when powerful **vibrations** pass from underground up to the surface through solid rock. The ground shakes violently and huge cracks may appear, sometimes wide enough to swallow cars.

Earthquakes happen where two of the Earth's **plates** meet. The pressure of the plates pushing against each other causes deep cracks in the rock line called **fault lines**.

The rocks on either side of a fault line sometimes slide up or sideways. This makes them bend and shatter, causing earthquake **shock waves.**

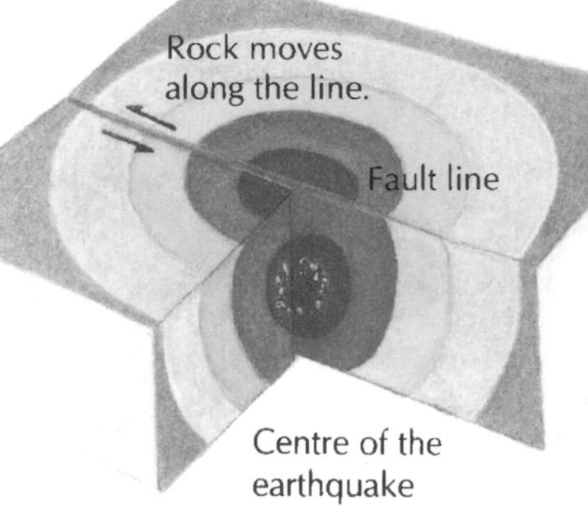

Earthquake profile

An earthquake begins beneath the ground at the point where the rocks move.

The movement creates **waves of energy** which travel up to the surface.

Shock waves

- The point where the earthquake begins underground is called the focus.
- The point on the surface above the focus is called the epicentre.

- There may be lots more minor earthquakes called aftershocks after the first earthquake. These occur because the rocks beneath are falling back into place.

Focus

Earthquake areas

- Most earthquakes happen around the edges of the Pacific Ocean or in mountainous areas such as the Himalayas and the Alps.
- The San Andreas Fault runs down California. In 1906 the rocks on one side of the fault moved 4.6 metres, causing an earthquake.

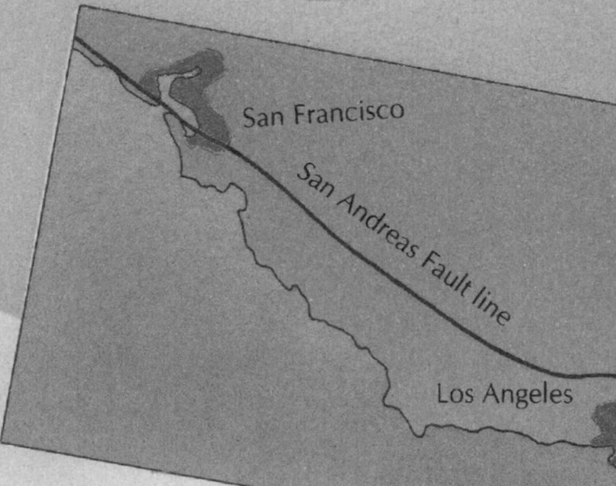

Earthquake buildings

- Earthquake-proof buildings are built with reinforced steel or concrete frames on a solid platform. Many skyscrapers in San Francisco are built this way.

Earthquake effects

An earthquake can cause:

- A series of gigantic fast-moving waves called tsunami. The biggest one ever seen was 67 metres tall, the height of about 9 houses!
- Dangerous mud and rock avalanches that engulf the surrounding land.
- Fires set off by broken gas pipes and electrical cables.

Measuring earthquakes

Earthquakes are measured using the **Richter Scale** or the **Mercalli Scale**. The Richter Scale has 8 numbers that measure earthquake energy. Each number denotes 10 times more energy than the number before. The Mercalli Scale has 12 numbers measuring the effect of an earthquake on objects and buildings.

Examples of Richter numbers:

1·2	5	7	8
Barely noticeable	Some damage	Like a nuclear bomb	Total devastation

Examples of Mercalli numbers

II	V	VII	XII
Lamps swing and windows shake.	Dishes smash	Walls collapse	Total damage

Earthquake instruments

Seismograph

Instruments called seismographs are used to measure earthquakes.

- A seismograph uses a pen attached to a frame to draw a line on a drum. The line shows the force of the earthquake.
- The very first seismograph was manufactured in China in AD 50. It was a pot with dragon heads sticking out. Tremors made balls fall from the dragons' jaws into the mouths of frogs below. The side that the balls fell showed the direction of the quake epicentre.

Ball falling.

The quake is coming from this way.

Predicting earthquakes

Scientists monitor earthquake areas to predict tremors. There are **monitoring stations** all over the world that measure Earth movement. Some early signs of earthquakes are shown below:

- A radioactive gas called radon is released from rocks. Scientists monitor well water to detect increases in radon traces.
- Small tremors called foreshocks happen just before an earthquake. The ground swells up and cracks.
- Animals behave oddly. They are often very sensitive to tremors.

Strange but true

- The longest earthquake known lasted for 38 days.

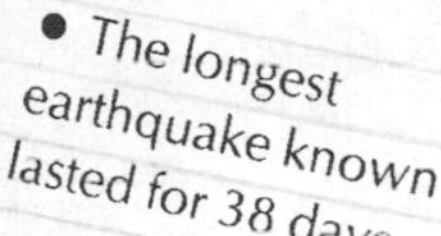

- There are thousands of earthquakes a year. Only 20 to 30 are large ones.
- In 1975 the Chinese city of Haicheng was evacuated 2 hours before an earthquake because people noticed their animals behaving oddly.

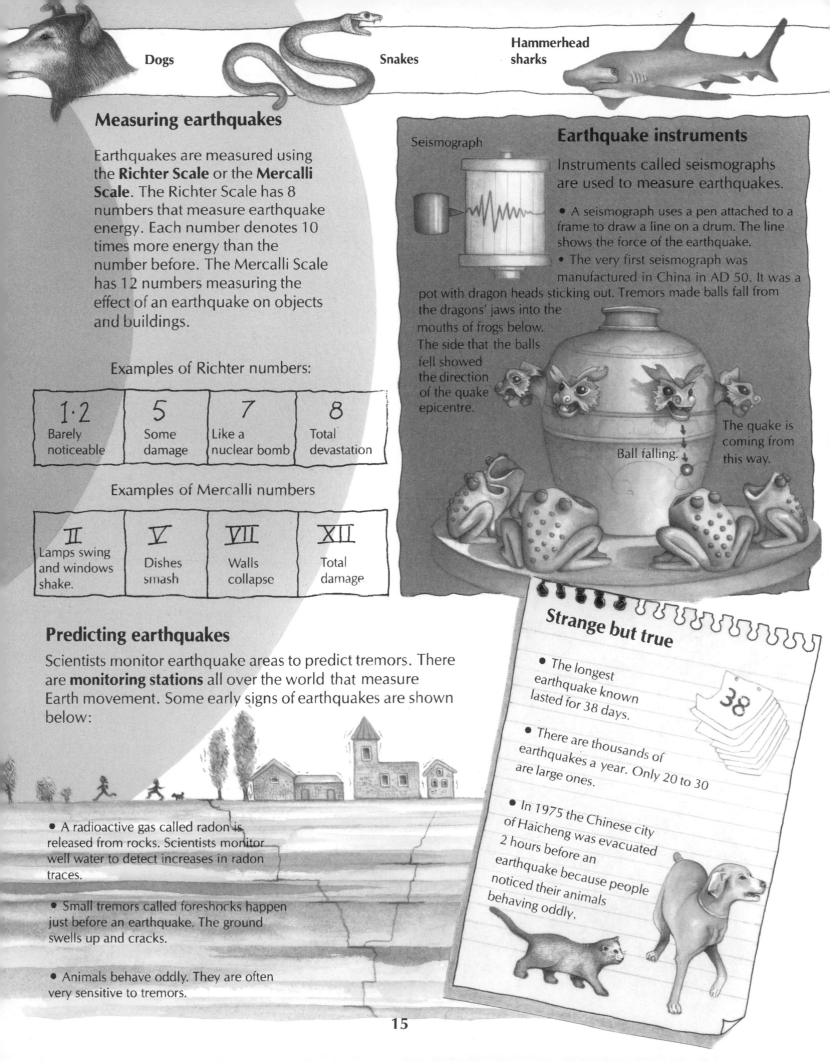

Mountains and Valleys

Here are the highest land mountains, in order of height:

Mt. Everest Himalayas 8863 metres

Mountains are masses of rock that are at least 600 metres high. They are usually found in groups called **ranges** or **chains**. They cover about one quarter of the Earth's surface.

A mountain range

Most of the world's tallest mountain ranges were built when two of the Earth's plates collided with each other, slowly pushing up the rock above. Mountain building takes millions of years. It is still going on today.

Mountains pushed up

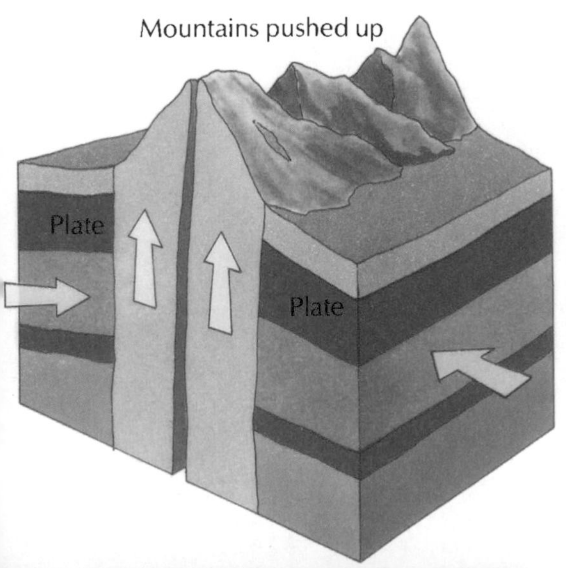

Types of mountain

There are four different types of mountain, called **fold**, **block**, **volcanic** and **dome**.

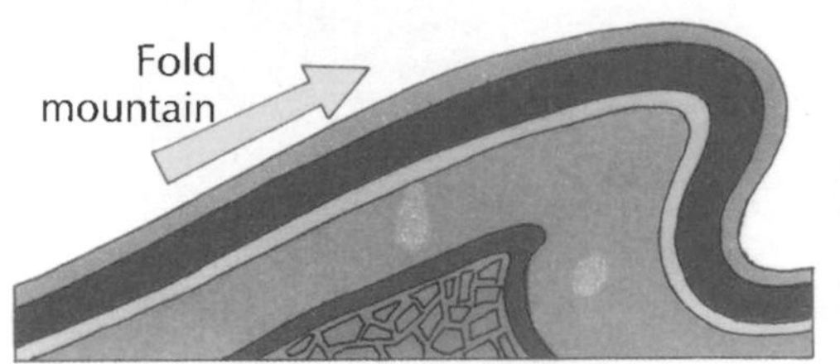

• Fold mountains occur when two of the Earth's plates push against each other. The rock in the middle is pushed up in folds.

• Sometimes two faults (deep rock cracks) run alongside each other. Pressure heaves up the block of land in the middle.

• A volcanic mountain grows when lava, dust and ashes gradually build up in a cone shape around an eruption.

• Dome mountains are created when hot volcanic material rises upwards from deep in the Earth and pushes the rocks above into a dome shape.

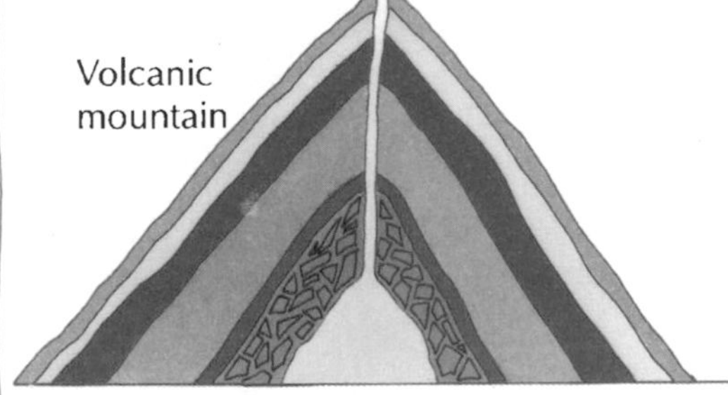

Mountain areas

There are **mountain ranges** all over the world. The largest ones are shown below.

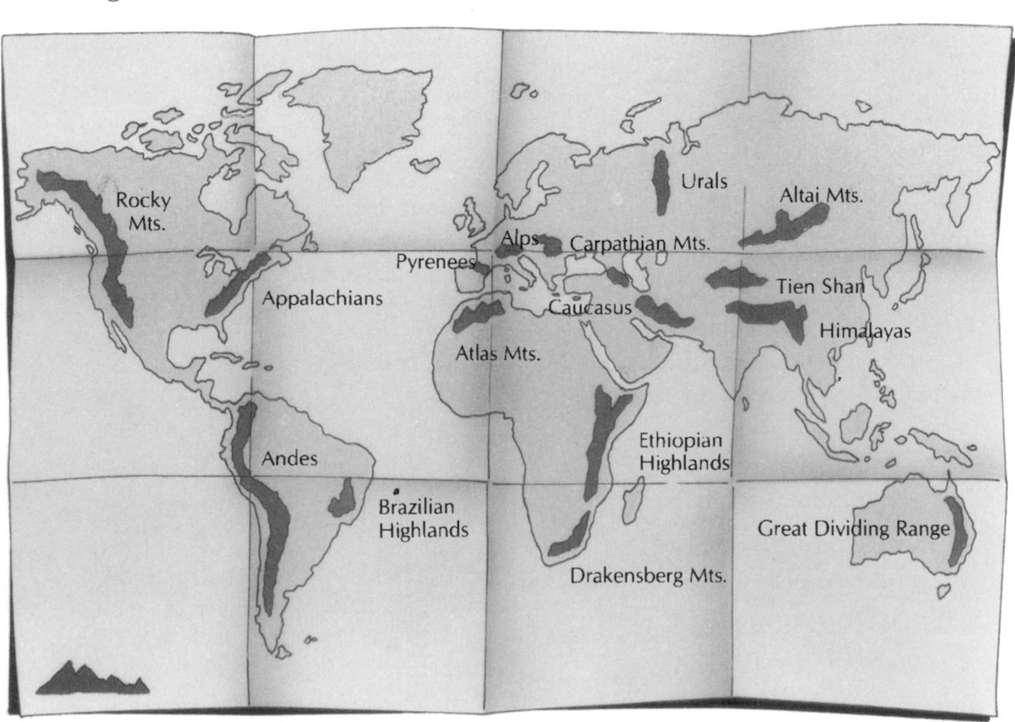

K2
Himalayas
8611 metres

Kangchenjunga
Himalayas
8586 metres

Makalu
Himalayas
8475 metres

Dhaulagiri
Himalayas
8172 metres

Mountain profile

At the bottom of a mountain there may be a forest of **deciduous trees**, which lose their leaves in winter. In warm areas there may be a **rainforest**.

Further up, there are likely to be **coniferous trees**, which keep their needles all year round.

The place where the trees stop growing is called the **tree line**. Above this line only hardy alpine plants, grasses and mosses grow.

Finally, the temperature gets too cold for plants to grow. On the top of high mountains it is so cold that there is snow all year round. Below this the snow will melt in summer. The line between the two areas is called the **snow line**.

Strange but true

- The Andes and the Himalayas are still rising upwards.
- The lowest officially-named hill stands 4.5 metres high on a golf course in Brunei.
- Mount Everest is 20 times higher than the world's tallest building, the Petronas Twin Towers in Kuala Lumpur, Malaysia.

Glaciers and valleys

A **glacier** is a huge mass of ice that travels down a mountainside. A glacier:

- Carves out a U-shaped valley as it travels along.
- Moves along very slowly.

Sometimes a **river** forms when summer snow melts on a mountainside. A river:

- Carves out a V-shaped valley as it travels.
- May carve a steep-sided valley called a gorge.

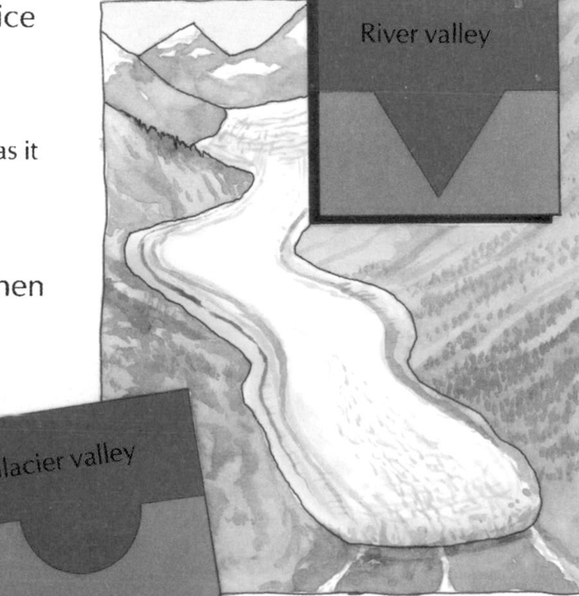

Rivers and Lakes

Here are the world's four longest rivers, in order of size:

Nile
Africa
6695 km long

Rivers begin high up on mountains and run downhill to the sea. They start from **underground springs** or **melting glaciers**.

A river's route is divided into three parts. The first part is called the upper course, where the river flows steeply downhill and the current is fast. The water carries sand, gravel and rocks down with it.

In the **middle course** the river flows along a gentler slope. It travels more slowly but it still wears away rock and sand from its banks.

In the **lower course** the river slows down and gets wider. The sand and rock it has been carrying are now worn down to tiny particles called **silt**.

River profile

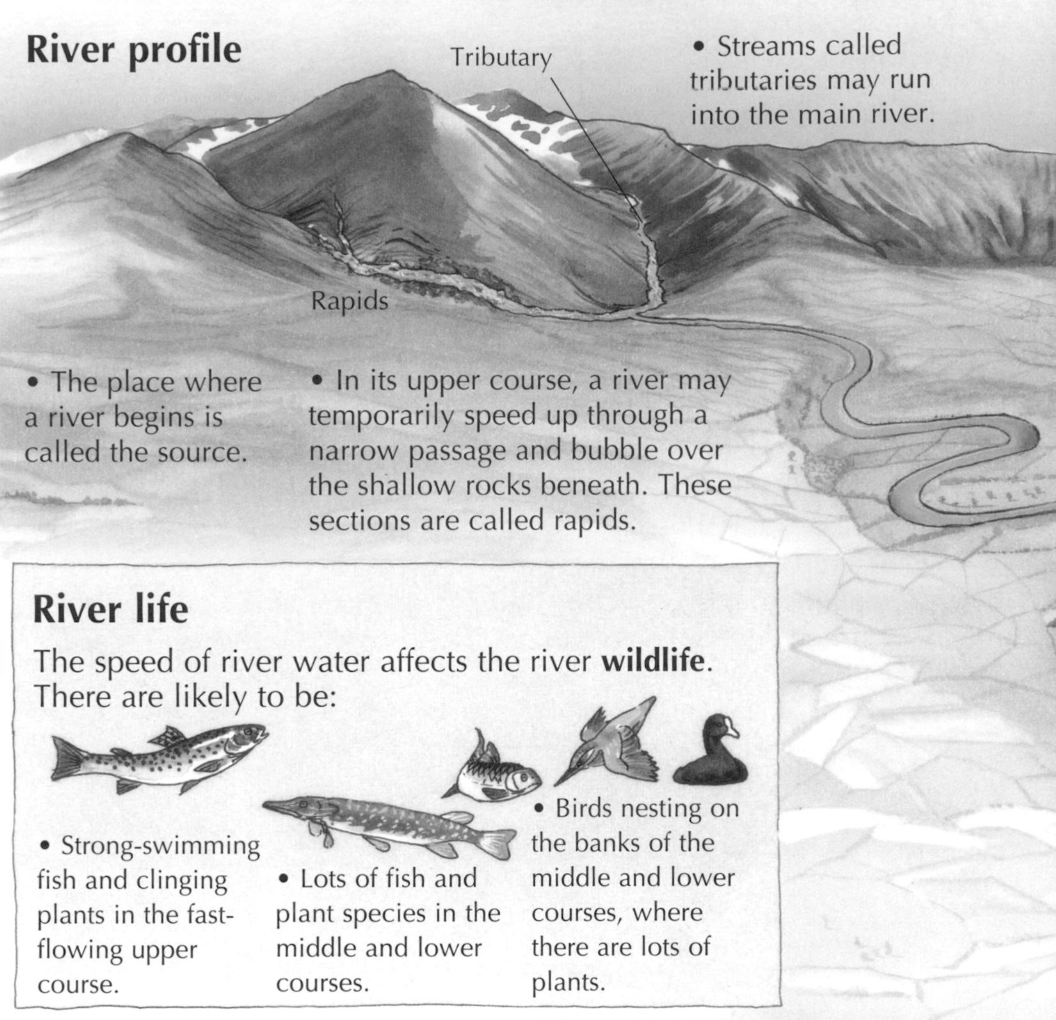

- Streams called tributaries may run into the main river.
- The place where a river begins is called the source.
- In its upper course, a river may temporarily speed up through a narrow passage and bubble over the shallow rocks beneath. These sections are called rapids.

River life

The speed of river water affects the river **wildlife**. There are likely to be:

- Strong-swimming fish and clinging plants in the fast-flowing upper course.
- Lots of fish and plant species in the middle and lower courses.
- Birds nesting on the banks of the middle and lower courses, where there are lots of plants.

Lakes

A **lake** is a large area of water that has collected in a valley. It may be caused by rainwater, melted snow or an underground stream. Lakes can be:

- Very large. The world's biggest freshwater lake is Lake Superior in the USA and Canada. It covers a vast area of over 82,000 sq km.
- Very deep. The world's deepest lake is Lake Baikal in Russia. Its deepest crevice goes down 1940 metres.

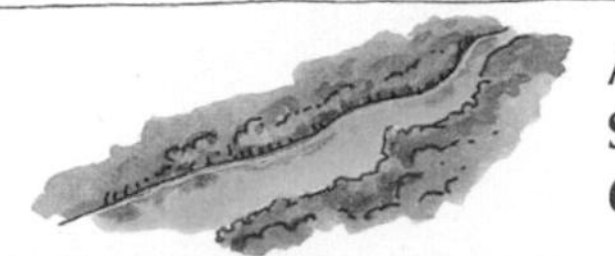

Amazon
S. America
6570 km long

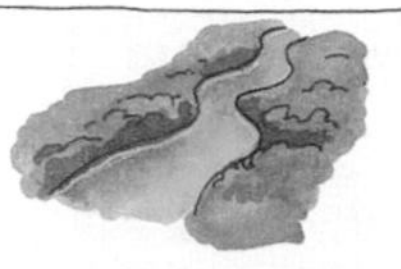

Mississippi
N. America
6020 km long

Yangtze
Asia
5530 km long

• A river joins the sea at its mouth. Here there is an area where freshwater and seawater mix, called an estuary.

• In its middle course a river slows down and travels around bends called meanders.

• As the river cuts through a valley it may leave shelves, called river terraces, on either side.

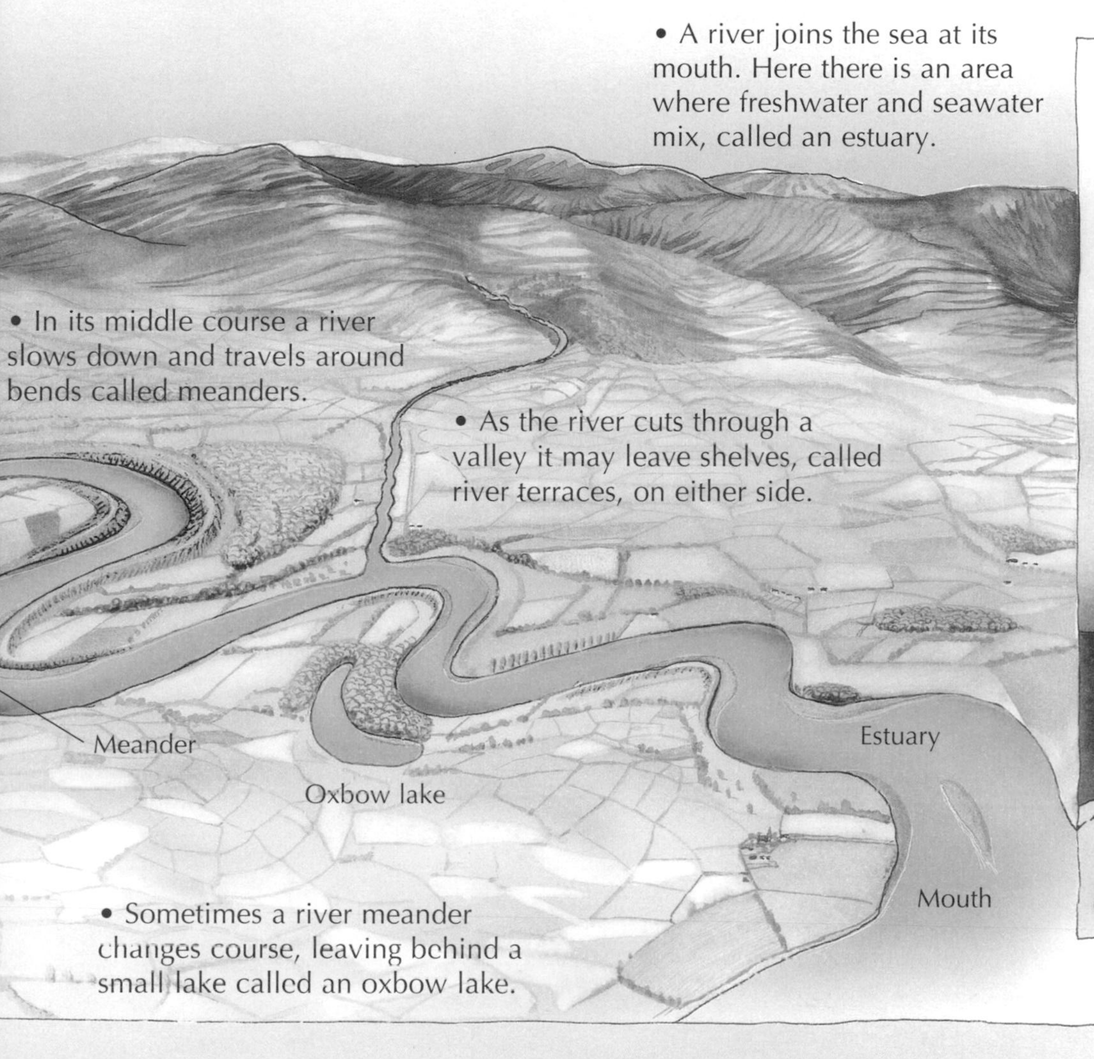

• Sometimes a river meander changes course, leaving behind a small lake called an oxbow lake.

Deltas

When a river reaches its mouth it is moving very slowly. Sometimes it is carrying lots of mud and silt which may pile up in the river mouth to form areas of land called deltas.

• The Ganges and the Brahmaputra Rivers meet in India and Bangladesh to form the world's largest delta. It is 480 km long and 160 km wide.

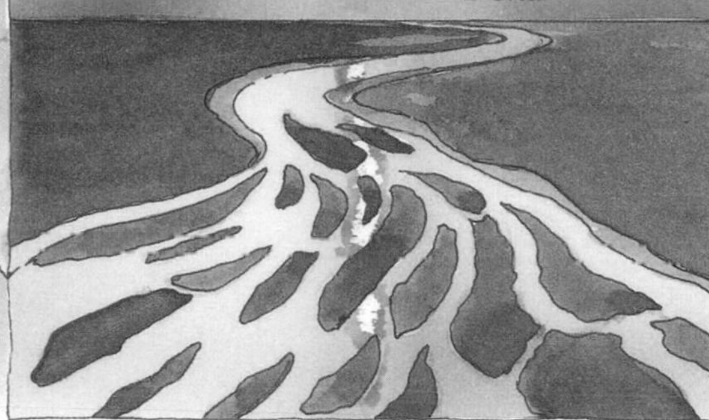

Waterfalls

Waterfalls occur when a hard band of rock crosses under a river. The water cannot wear the hard rock down, but it wears down soft rock further on. Eventually this creates a steep drop.

• The world's highest waterfall is the Salto Angel Falls in Venezuela. It plunges down a cliff 807 metres high.

Strange but true

• A huge underground river runs underneath the Nile, with six times more water than the river below.

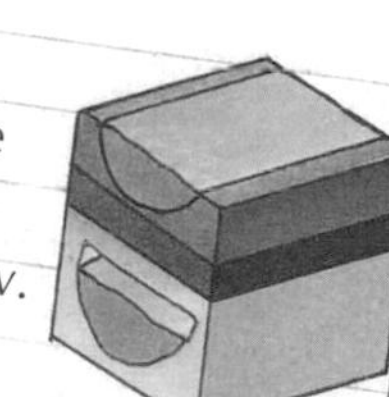

• Lake Bosumtwi in Ghana formed in a hollow made by a meteorite.

• Beaver Lake, in Yellowstone Park, USA, was artificially created by beaver damming.

• The world's shortest river with a name is the Roe River, Montana, USA. It is 61 metres long.

Oceans

Here are the world's four largest oceans, in order of size:

Pacific
166,241,000 sq km

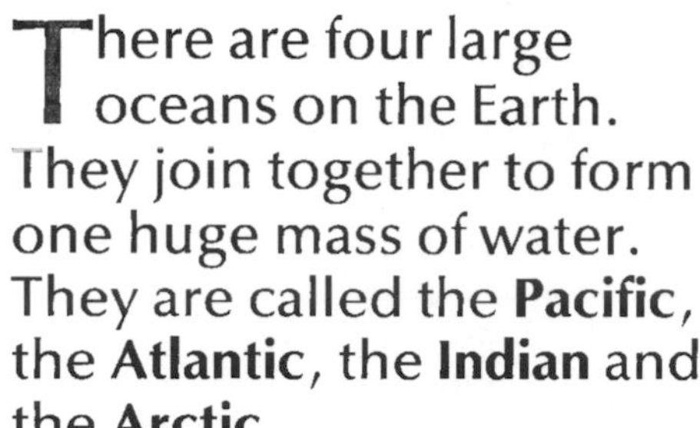

There are four large oceans on the Earth. They join together to form one huge mass of water. They are called the **Pacific**, the **Atlantic**, the **Indian** and the **Arctic**.

Parts of the oceans are divided into smaller areas called **seas**. These are mostly around coastlines and islands.

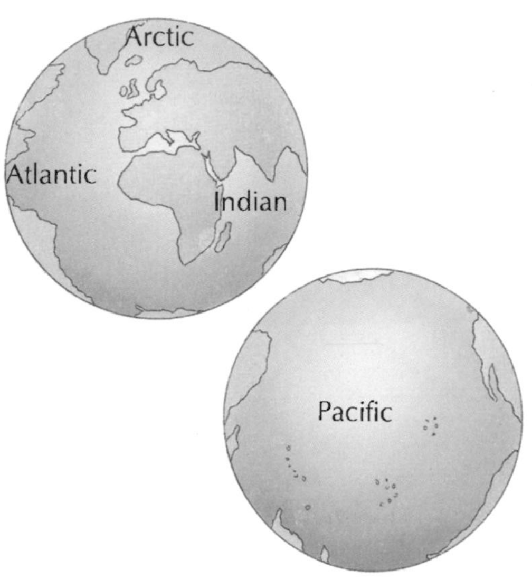

The **temperature** of seawater varies across the world. For instance, most of the water in the Arctic is permanently frozen, whereas in hot tropical areas the sea can reach the temperature of a warm bath.

Ocean floor profile

If you were able to look beneath the ocean surface you would see:

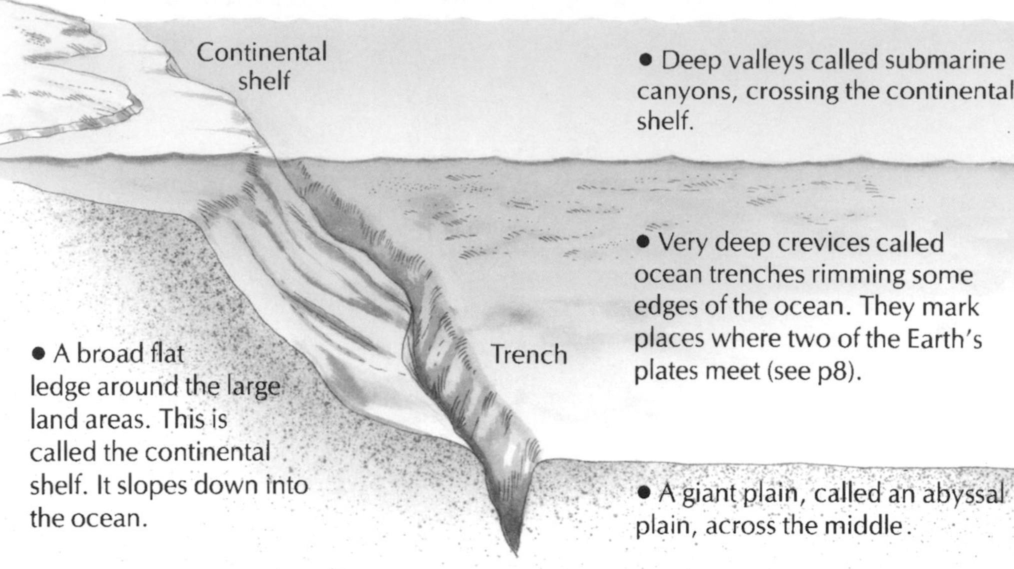

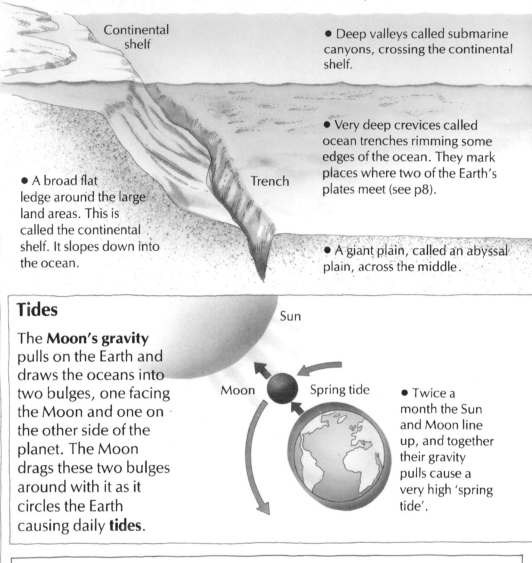

- Deep valleys called submarine canyons, crossing the continental shelf.
- Very deep crevices called ocean trenches rimming some edges of the ocean. They mark places where two of the Earth's plates meet (see p8).
- A broad flat ledge around the large land areas. This is called the continental shelf. It slopes down into the ocean.
- A giant plain, called an abyssal plain, across the middle.

Tides

The **Moon's gravity** pulls on the Earth and draws the oceans into two bulges, one facing the Moon and one on the other side of the planet. The Moon drags these two bulges around with it as it circles the Earth causing daily **tides**.

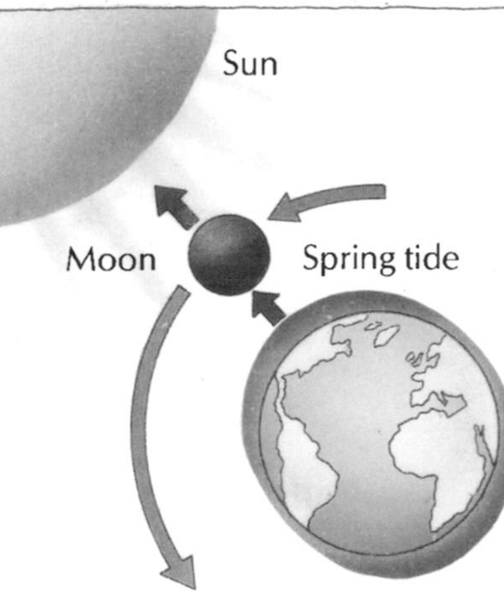

- Twice a month the Sun and Moon line up, and together their gravity pulls cause a very high 'spring tide'.

Coral reefs

Coral reefs are found in warm shallow seas. They are built by tiny animals called **polyps**. Each polyp builds a small stone cup to live in. When a polyp dies, it leaves its cup behind. New polyps build on top and gradually the reef grows.

Fringe reef

- Fringe reefs grow around the shores of continents or islands.

Barrier reef

- Barrier reefs grow several kilometres offshore. The Australian Great Barrier Reef is the biggest example.

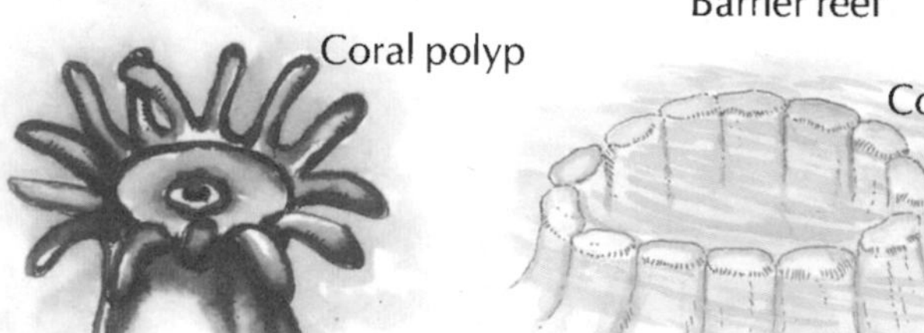

- A coral atoll is a broken ring of coral islands with water in the middle.

Atlantic
82,217,000 sq km

Indian
73,481,000 sq km

Arctic
14,056,000 sq km

- A range of volcanic mountains called an oceanic ridge, running along the middle of the abyssal plain.

- Sometimes old volcanoes called seamounts are dotted around the abyssal plain.

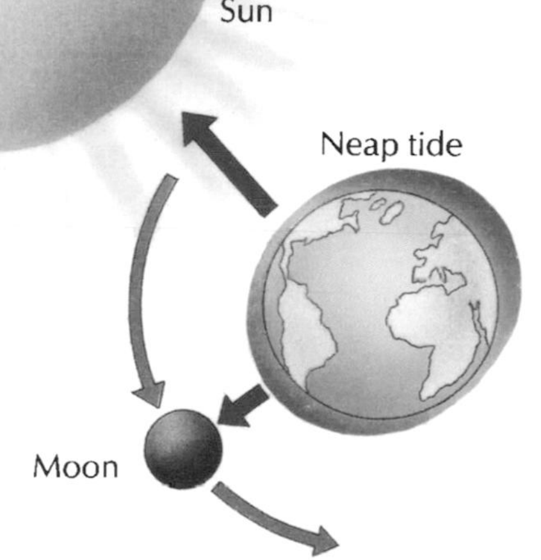

- When the Moon and Sun are at right angles the Sun opposes the Moon's gravity pull, causing a very low 'neap tide'.

Currents

Ocean water travels around the world in regular paths called **currents**. They are caused by **winds** and by **warm water** moving away from the Equator and **cold water** flowing in from polar regions to take its place.

- The world's largest current is the West Wind Drift, which flows between America and Antarctica.

Strange but true

- Off the coast of Florida there is an underwater hotel. Guests have to dive to the entrance.
- There are 4 grammes of gold in every million tonnes of seawater.
- The biggest storm wave ever recorded was 34 metres high from crest to trough.
- The biggest iceberg ever seen had a bigger surface area than the country of Belgium.

Sea riches

- Oysters, seaweed and fish can be farmed in the sea. Some scientists have managed to build artificial reef 'farms' and colonize them with lobsters and shellfish.
- Underwater communities could be built for marine farm workers. Some experiments have already been carried out using prototype underwater houses.
- On the deep ocean floor there are millions of rock lumps called manganese nodules. Manganese is used for hardening steel.

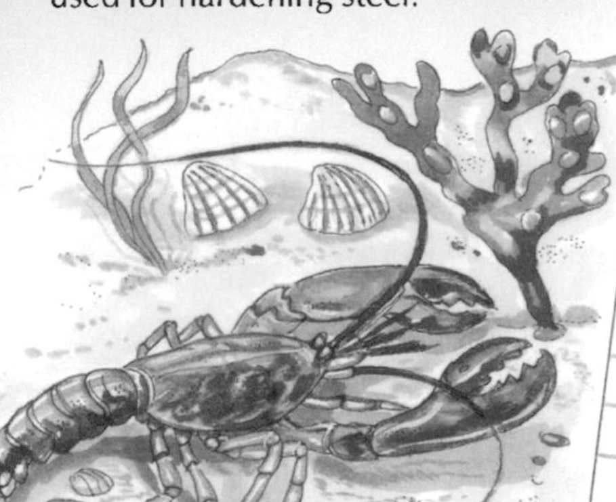

Coastlines

Here are some of the world's most beautiful shells:

Thatcheria mirabilis Japan

Lambis chiragra Sri Lanka

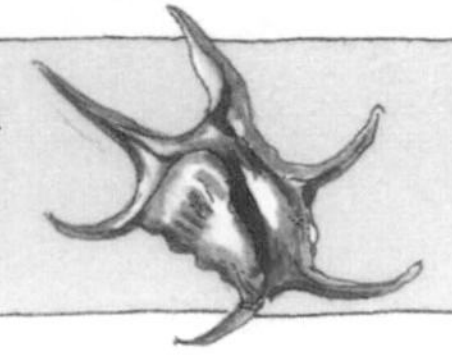

A **coastline** is the place where the land meets the ocean. Coastlines vary in shape and they have different features – for instance, one coastline might have gentle sloping **beaches**, whereas another might have rocky **cliffs** and **caves**.

Coastal features

Coastlines do not always stay the same shape. As the sea pounds against the shore it gradually wears down the rock to form features such as **caves** and **arches**.

• If there is a crack in a cliff, seawater will get into it and gradually hollow out a cave.

• Sometimes waves pound both sides of a headland and wear away an arch in the middle.

• Eventually arches collapse, leaving isolated rocks called stacks.

• Sometimes waves enlarge a cave so much that a crack appears in the roof. In rough weather water sprays out of the crack, called a blowhole.

Strange but true

• The mudskipper fish can climb up a mangrove tree and hang from a branch to wait for the tide to come in.

• The level of the sea is rising by about 30 cm every 100 years.

• Venice in Italy is built on 118 sea islets joined by 400 bridges. It is gradually sinking into the water.

Beaches

The sea gathers loose rocks and stones as it wears away at the coastline. The waves grind them into tiny particles and then drop them onto the shore, forming **beaches**.

• The Hawaiian Islands have beaches made of black sand, formed by pieces of volcanic lava.

• The Bermuda Islands have pale pink beaches. The sand is made from fragments of red shell.

• The dazzling white beaches of Barbados are made of tiny shell fragments worn down by the sea.

• A stretch of beach on the Namibian coast in Africa provides the world's best supply of loose diamonds. They are hidden amongst the sand and gravel.

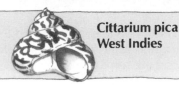

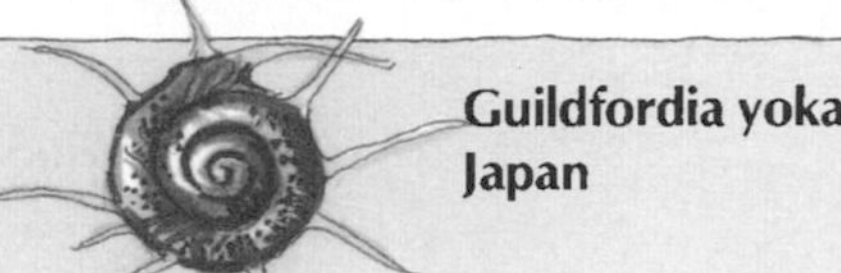
Guildfordia yoka
Japan

Cittarium pica
West Indies

Conus textile
Indo-Pacific

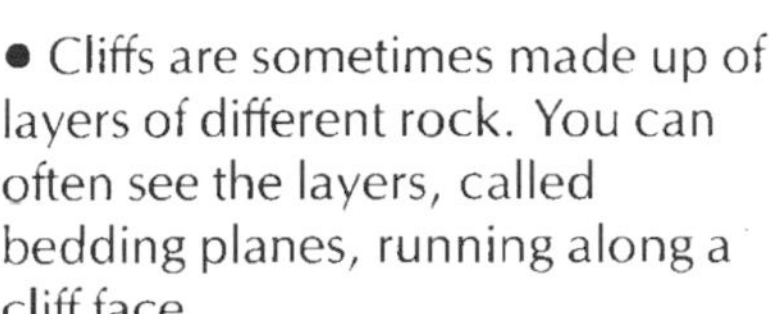

• Cliffs are sometimes made up of layers of different rock. You can often see the layers, called bedding planes, running along a cliff face.

Marshes and estuaries

• Where a river meets the sea there may be an area of muddy plain called an estuary. The sea washes over the plain, creating mudflats, creeks and salty marshes. Seabirds like to nest here.

• In hot tropical places the coastal marshes are often swamps filled with mangrove trees. They can survive in salty water because their roots are partly above the ground and can absorb oxygen from the air.

Coastal life

Beaches provide a home for lots of different **animals** and **plants**. You might find:

• Seaweed, which is a plant without roots or a stem. It is made up of fronds and a root-like 'holdfast' at the bottom for anchoring the seaweed firmly on to rocks.

Holdfast

Worm casts

• Worm casts, which are small piled-up cones of wet sand. They are made by lugworms that burrow beneath the surface. The tiny worms swallow sand and digest the minute particles of food mixed up with it. Then they push out the waste, making casts on the sand surface.

• A bubble in the sand. Underneath, there may be a cockleshell. It burrows down and then it sticks two tiny siphons above the surface. One takes in seawater along with food particles. The other expels the waste water, creating the bubble that you can see.

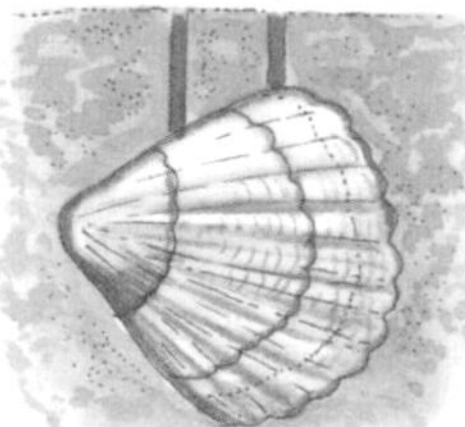

A cockleshell

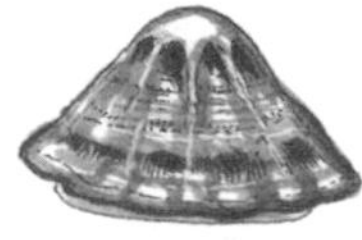

A limpet shell

• Limpets anchored firmly to the rocks. A limpet has a very powerful foot which works like a suction cup and clamps the shell firmly to the rock surface.

• Marram grasses and other hardy salt-tolerating plants. They grow on sand dunes, which are blown into sloping shapes by the wind.

Marram grasses

The Sky

Wind strength is measured on the Beaufort Scale, which goes from 1 to 12. Here are some examples:

Force 1 – wind vanes do not move

The Earth is surrounded by a blanket of **gases** called the **atmosphere**. It is made up of five main layers. Each layer is a different **temperature** and is made up of a mixture of different gases.

The boundaries between the different layers are not clear-cut.

In the air

The atmosphere is made up of:

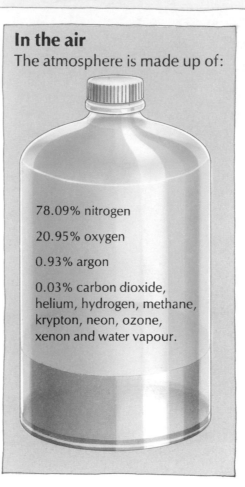

78.09% nitrogen

20.95% oxygen

0.93% argon

0.03% carbon dioxide, helium, hydrogen, methane, krypton, neon, ozone, xenon and water vapour.

Sky colours

Sunlight is made up of different **light waves**. The visible ones are red, orange, yellow, green, blue, indigo and violet. These colours are called the **spectrum**. You can see them in a rainbow, or if you pass light through a specially shaped piece of glass called a prism. The spectrum causes:

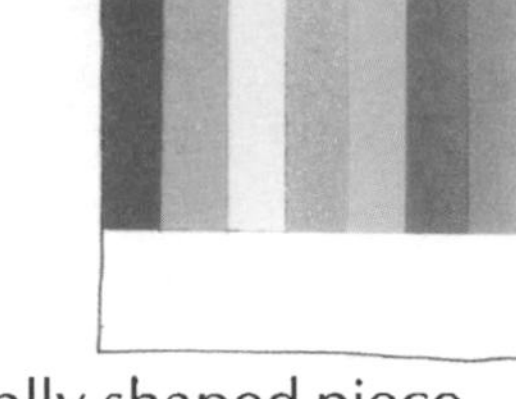

- Blue skies. When the Sun's rays reach the Earth's atmosphere, the blue light waves scatter in all directions. Provided the light is not obscured by cloud, it shows across the sky.
- Red sunrises and sunsets, when blue light waves are blocked out by dust in the air and only red light waves get through. Dust tends to be most common in the morning and evening.

Strange but true

- Some early hot-air balloons were so heavy that the passengers stripped off to help keep the weight down.
- The Ancient Egyptians worshipped a sky goddess called Nut.
- The world's windiest place is Commonwealth Bay, Antarctica.
- In 1934 a gust of wind three times as strong as Beaufort Scale 12 was measured on Mt. Washington, USA.

Air pressure

The layers of gases around the Earth press down on the surface. This force is called **air pressure**. It is strongest at ground level and gets weaker with height.

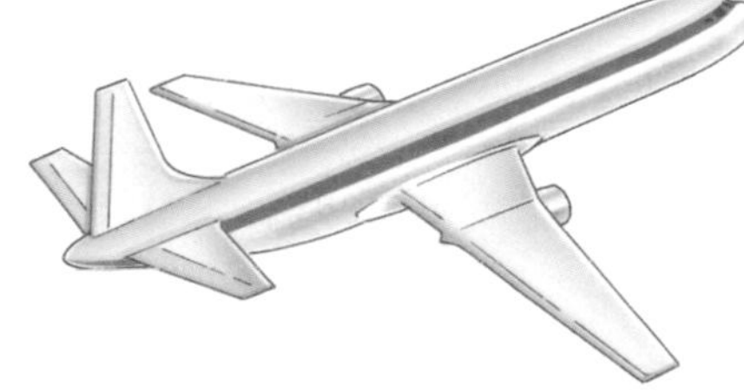

- High up on mountains the air pressure is weak and the air has less oxygen content than air down below.
- Aircraft cabins are artificially pressurized so that the passengers can breathe comfortably even though they are flying high up in the atmosphere.

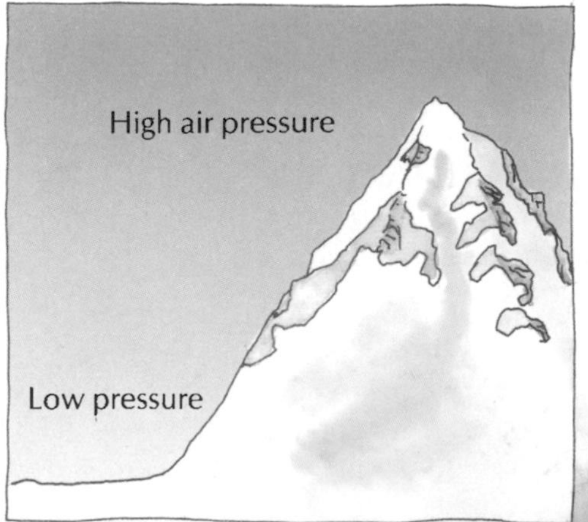

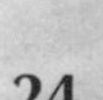

Force 6 – strong breeze
Large tree branches move

Force 9 – strong gale
Chimney pots crash down

Force 12 – hurricane
Whole areas devastated

The wind

Wind is air that is moving. The Sun's rays are reflected upwards from the ground, warming the air above. **Warm air** is light and it rises upwards. **Cold air** is heavier and it sinks into the space left by the rising warm air.

- Some winds blow constantly in regular patterns around the world. They are caused by warm air rising up from the Equator and cold air from polar regions flowing into the space beneath.

- Anemometers are used to measure wind speed. The most common kind has three cups fixed onto a shaft. The stronger the wind, the faster the cups spin around. Their movement controls a dial that indicates speed.

- A current of rising warm air is called a thermal. Some birds like to find thermals. They spread out their wings and let the moving air carry them along. Gliders work in the same way.

Atmosphere layers

The atmosphere is made up of these layers:

- The exosphere – height 500 to 8000 km. Here it is intensely hot, a minimum of 2200°C.

Weather satellites orbit in the exosphere.

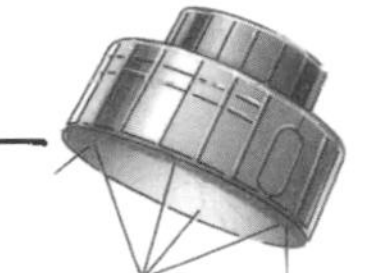

- The thermosphere – height 80 to 500 km. The temperature of this layer increases with height. At the top it is about 2200°C.

When spaceships re-enter orbit, their heat shields burn up in this layer, due to friction.

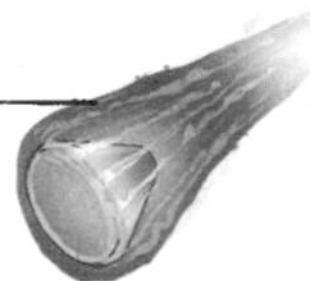

- The mesosphere – height 50 to 80 km. The temperature of this layer gets colder with height. It varies from 10°C to −80°C.

Unmanned balloons have measured the temperature in this layer.

- The stratosphere – height 8 to 50 km (varies from place to place). This layer is cold, but the temperature increases with height. Within this layer is a band of ozone gas, which filters out the Sun's harmful rays.

Aircraft fly in this layer to avoid rough weather.

- The troposphere – height up to 16 km over the Equator, 8 km over the Poles. This layer contains nearly all the water vapour and most of the other gases in the atmosphere. It gets colder with height.

Weather occurs in this layer.

Weather

Here are some unusual weather facts and records:

Rainiest place: Kauai, Hawaii. It rains for 350 days a year.

When water is warmed it **evaporates**, which means that it changes into an invisible gas called **vapour**. When vapour gets cold it changes back into **liquid droplets**. When it gets very cold it becomes solid **ice crystals** that form snowflakes.

Six-sided snowflakes

The water cycle

The **Sun** heats up the world's **oceans** and **rivers**. It makes water evaporate and rise upwards. As the vapour gets higher it gets colder and changes into **water droplets**, which gather around specks of salt and dust in the air. Billions of droplets together form a **cloud**. The droplets grow bigger until they are so heavy that they fall as **rain** back into the oceans and rivers.

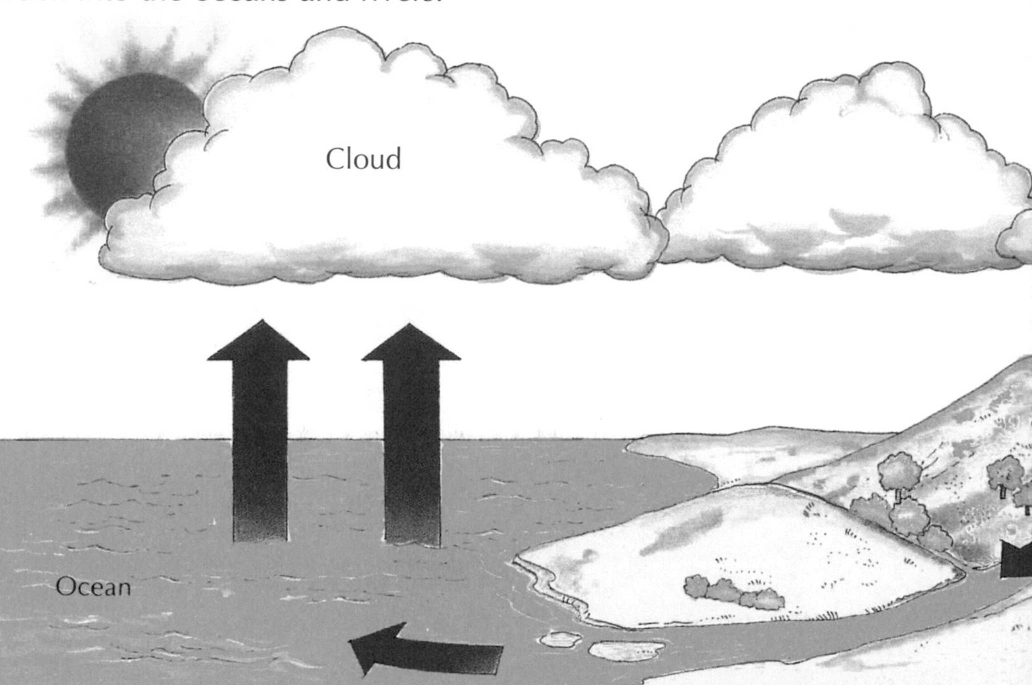

Strange but true

- Some people say they can smell rain. The smell may be gases produced by the damp soil.
- Italian farmers shoot fireworks into clouds to shatter hailstones that damage crops.
- Sea fog was once thought to be the breath of an underwater monster.
- At the North and South Poles the snow never melts.

Types of water

Apart from rain, water vapour in the air causes:

- Snow, which occurs when it is very cold. Water droplets in the air freeze into ice crystals and fall to the ground.
- Fog, which occurs when the ground is cold and the air above it is warmer. The vapour in the air changes into a cloud of water droplets.
- Hailstones, which begin as icy pellets in high storm clouds. They are buffeted about inside the cloud and gradually grow bigger as layers of ice freeze around them. Eventually they grow so heavy that they fall to the ground.

Heaviest hailstone:
Fell in Bangladesh, 1986. It weighed 1.02 kg.

Driest place: Atacama Desert, Chil

Heaviest rainburst:
38.1 mm in 90 seconds, in Guadeloupe, 1970

Air masses

An **air mass** is formed when a vast area of air stays in the same place for some time. It gets warm or cold, depending on the temperature of the land or sea beneath. When an air mass moves, it brings weather changes.

• No new water is ever made in the atmosphere. Instead, the existing water recycles again and again. So any rain you see is likely to have fallen many times before!

• Rainbows, which appear on rainy days when the Sun is shining. You can only see one if you are standing with your back to the Sun. The sunlight shines on the raindrops in the air and is split up into the seven colours of the spectrum (see p24).

• Dew, which occurs when air cools down at night and water vapour condenses into droplets of dew on the ground. The dew evaporates in the morning when the air warms up again.

Clouds

There are ten different kinds of cloud. Each different shape gives a clue to the sort of weather you can expect.

• Cumulus clouds are fluffy, white puffs. They signal fine weather.

• Cirrus clouds are wisps with flicked-back tails. They may signal rain.

• Cirrostratus clouds thinly veil the Sun. They can bring rain or snow.

• Stratocumulus clouds spread out in uneven patches. They can mean dry weather.

• Cirrocumulus clouds look like ripples. They signal weather changes.

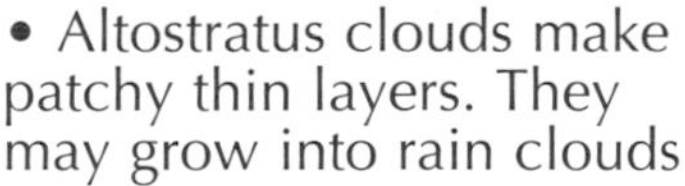

• Altostratus clouds make patchy thin layers. They may grow into rain clouds.

• Stratus clouds spread out in a low grey layer. They mean rain or snow.

• Cumulonimbus are billowing storm clouds that stretch high up into the sky.

• Nimbostratus clouds are dark, low masses signalling rain or snow.

• Altocumulus clouds are fluffy cloud waves. They signal weather changes.

Wild weather

Follow this advice if you get caught in a thunderstorm:

Avoid sheltering under trees.

Sometimes the weather is dramatic and powerful. For instance, 45,000 **thunderstorms** take place every day and most of them are capable of producing as much energy as an atom bomb.

Violent **hurricanes** and **tornadoes** are regular weather features in some parts of the world.

Strange but true

- Cumulonimbus clouds can reach as high as 15 km, twice the height of Mount Everest!
- The ancient Chinese believed that storms were caused by dragons fighting in the sky.
- In 1946 a tornado uncovered buried gold and showered the coins over a Russian town.
- American Roy Sullivan has been struck by lightning a record seven times.

Thunderstorms

Thunderstorms occur when the air is warm and humid and rises upwards very quickly, forming giant towering **cumulonimbus** storm clouds. Inside the clouds, ice crystals and water droplets whirl around, colliding with each other and creating tiny **electrical charges** as they do so. Gradually the charge builds up until giant sparks flash from cloud to cloud or down to the ground and back.

- Lightning finds the quickest path to the Earth, so it usually hits high buildings or trees. Tall buildings are fitted with copper strips called lightning conductors that carry the electric charge safely to the ground.
- You can tell how far away a storm is by counting the seconds between a lightning flash and a thunderclap. The storm is one kilometre away for every three seconds you count.
- Lightning travels down to the ground and then back up again along the same path. The journey is so fast that there only appears to be one flash.
- Lightning heats up the air in its path. The air expands rapidly, making the booming noise of thunder. Lightning and thunder occur at the same time, but you hear the thunder afterwards because sound travels more slowly than light.

- Sheet lightning does not look like a long fork. Instead it looks like a momentary glow in the sky. It is caused by lightning flashing within a cloud.

If you are in a car, stay inside it. You will be safe.

If you get stuck out in the open, crouch down or run for shelter.

Once you are indoors, you will be safe.

Tornadoes

Tornadoes are found mainly on the plains of North America, when small pockets of air rise quickly and create towering fast-spinning funnels of wind that leapfrog across the land. They suck up anything in their path.

• There are about 640 tornadoes a year in North America, mostly in the Plains states of Texas, Oklahoma, Kansas, Nebraska and Iowa. People who live in these areas have storm shelters in their homes to protect them if a tornado passes overhead.

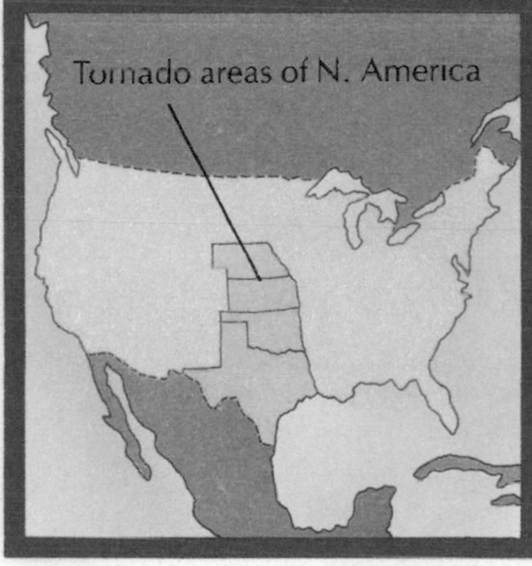

• Tornado winds can spin at up to 640 km/h. They have been known to lift heavy trains into the air.

• A waterspout is a tornado over the sea, a swirling air column that sucks up seawater. If a waterspout moves onto land, it drops its load. This has been known to cause surprise showers of fish and crabs!

Hurricanes

Hurricanes are powerful tropical storms that occur in late summer and early autumn. They begin over warm seas near the Equator, when warm air rises over a wide area and forms huge pillars of cloud full of water vapour.

Cold air rushes in beneath the warm air and a giant spinning wheel of whirling cloud begins to move over the sea surface.

• Hurricanes bring thousands of tonnes of rain and strong winds of up to 320 km/h. They can do a great deal of damage if they reach a coastline.

• A hurricane can stretch over many kilometres, but in the middle there is always a clear, calm patch called the 'eye', usually measuring about 48 km across.

• Hurricanes are given individual names. The first hurricane of the season is given a name beginning with A. The next one gets a name beginning with B, and so on.

• Hurricanes are also referred to as typhoons, tropical cyclones and baguios. In some parts of Australia they are called 'willy willies'.

Climate and Seasons

Here are some places that have unique climates:

Vostok, Antarctica. The coldest place on Earth; colder than a freezer.

The **climate** of a place is the pattern of weather it has from year to year.

Climate varies across the world. For instance, some places are always very cold or very warm, whereas in other areas the temperature changes from season to season.

The **seasons** of spring, summer, autumn and winter come at different times to different places. **Seasonal weather** varies, too. For instance, during summer in Antarctica the temperature is still below freezing, whereas in southern Europe the Sun shines warmly.

Hot and cold spots

The **Sun's rays** hit the Earth in straight lines, but because of the planet's round shape they spread out more at the Poles than they do around the Equator.

When the rays spread out they provide less heat, so the further a place is from the Equator, the colder its climate tends to be.

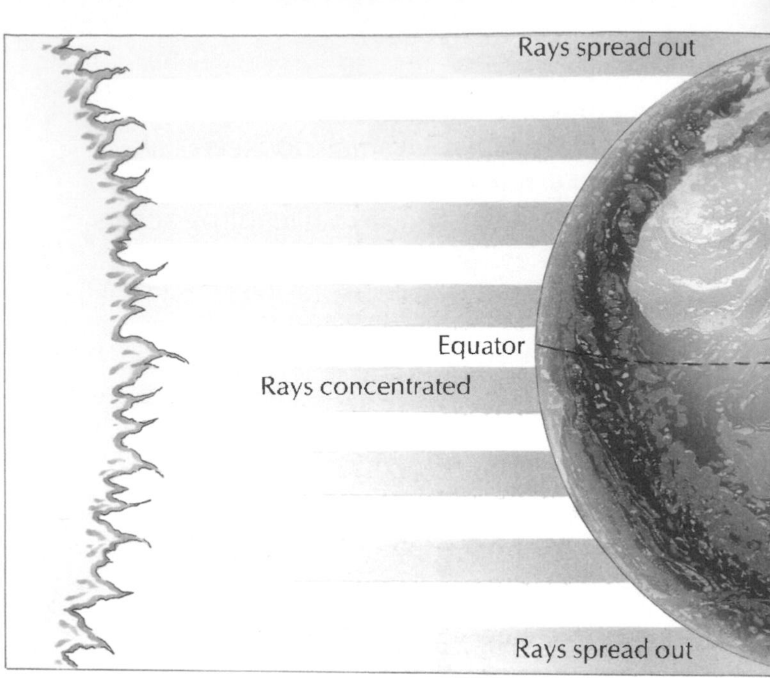

Climate causes

Ocean currents, **distance from the sea**, **wind direction** and **mountains** are all factors capable of having an effect on the climate of a particular place.

- Places near the sea have a 'maritime' climate. The air temperature stays fairly steady all year round because it is influenced by sea temperature, which does not alter much.

- Places that are far from the sea have a 'continental' climate. The land heats up quickly but also cools down quickly, so there is a big temperature difference between summer and winter.

- Big cities often have a climate that is warmer than the surrounding land. Concrete buildings absorb the Sun's heat during the day and radiate it at night, warming the city air.

- The climate can vary within a very small area. For instance, in one garden there might be a cold shadowy corner alongside a warm sunny spot. Small areas like this are called microclimates.

Dallol, Ethiopia. The hottest place on Earth. Average temperature 34.4°C.

Sahara Desert. The sunniest place on Earth.

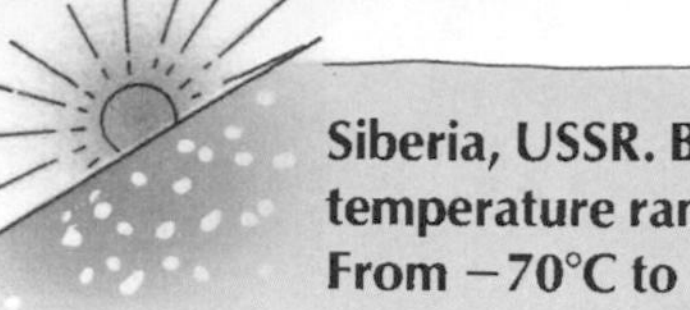

Siberia, USSR. Biggest temperature range. From −70°C to 36.7°C.

World climates

The world is divided into different **types of climate**. They are:

- Polar – Constantly cold; the land and sea are covered by thick ice sheets.
- Temperate – Changeable weather, with warm dry summers and mild winters.
- Subtropical – Warm, with alternate dry and rainy seasons.
- Tropical – Constant hot temperatures and daily rainshowers. Never any seasonal changes.

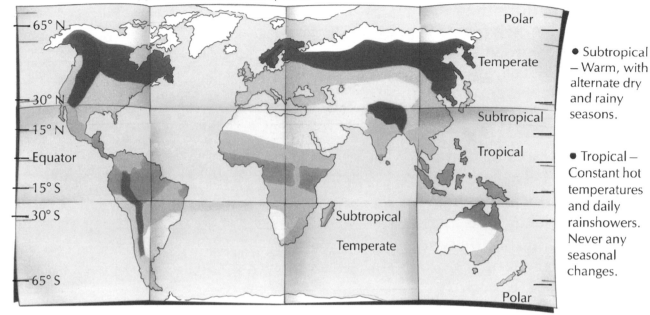

65° N
30° N
15° N
Equator
15° S
30° S
65° S

Polar
Temperate
Subtropical
Tropical
Subtropical
Temperate
Polar

Seasons

The **seasons** are caused by the **Earth's orbit**. For a few months each year half the Earth is tilted towards the Sun and gets strong heat rays, whilst the other half is tilted away and gets weak rays.

The position is gradually reversed through the year. When it is **summer** in one hemisphere it is **winter** in the other. In **autumn** and **spring** the two hemispheres are an equal distance from the rays.

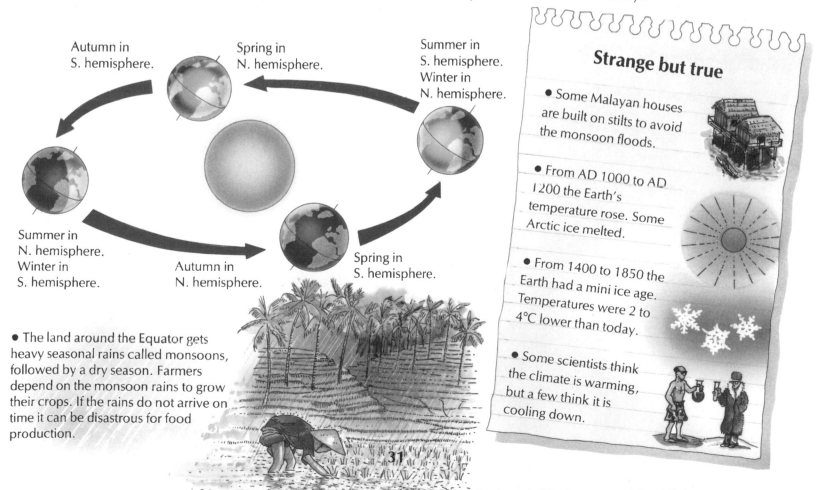

Autumn in S. hemisphere.
Spring in N. hemisphere.
Summer in S. hemisphere. Winter in N. hemisphere.
Summer in N. hemisphere. Winter in S. hemisphere.
Autumn in N. hemisphere.
Spring in S. hemisphere.

- The land around the Equator gets heavy seasonal rains called monsoons, followed by a dry season. Farmers depend on the monsoon rains to grow their crops. If the rains do not arrive on time it can be disastrous for food production.

Strange but true

- Some Malayan houses are built on stilts to avoid the monsoon floods.
- From AD 1000 to AD 1200 the Earth's temperature rose. Some Arctic ice melted.
- From 1400 to 1850 the Earth had a mini ice age. Temperatures were 2 to 4°C lower than today.
- Some scientists think the climate is warming, but a few think it is cooling down.

Plant Life

Here are some plants which are useful to humans:

Rice – the most popular source of food

There are more than 335,000 known **plant species**. They are vital to life on Earth because they produce the oxygen that animals need in order to survive.

Plants grow in most parts of the world. The type of **vegetation** that grows in a particular place depends on the climate and the type of **soil** there is to be found the area.

Food-making

Many plants make their own **food**. In the process they create oxygen and use up **carbon dioxide**.

- Most plants contain a green substance called chlorophyll, which absorbs sunlight. The plants use this energy to make their own food.

- When a plant makes food it mixes carbon dioxide from the air with minerals and water from the soil. The process is called photosynthesis.

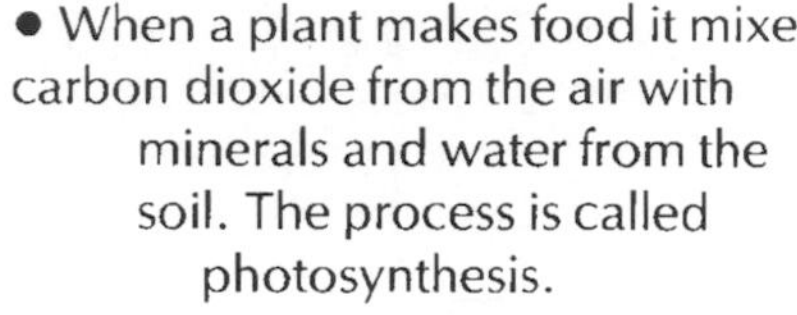

- When animals breathe they give out carbon dioxide. Plants rely on this supply for making their food.

- During photosynthesis plants make oxygen and pass it into the air. Animals rely on this oxygen supply.

Strange but true

- The desert baobab tree can store up to 1000 litres of water in its trunk.
- The oldest living tree is a Californian bristlecone pine named 'Methuselah'. It is about 4600 years old.
- Bamboo can grow up to 91 cm a day.
- There were no grasses in the age of the dinosaurs – only ferns, conifers and cycad plants.

Flowering plants

Many plants grow from **seeds**, and in order for a new plant seed to grow, a tiny **pollen grain** containing a male cell must join with a female cell inside an **ovule**. Some plants produce **flowers** and these contain pollen and ovules.

- Some flowers contain sweet nectar which insects feed on. When an insect visits a flower, tiny pollen grains brush onto its coat. It carries them to the next flower it visits and they join together with the ovules in the new flower.

- Some flowering plants, such as grasses, do not attract insects. Instead they rely on the wind to blow their pollen to other plants.

- After a plant is pollinated, it begins to grow seeds. The seeds eventually drop to the ground. If the weather and the soil conditions are right, they grow into new plants.

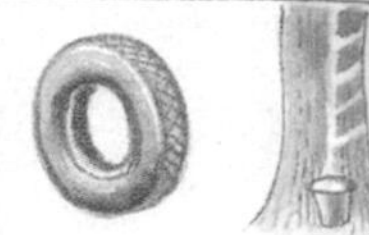

Rubber trees – the sap is used to make rubber

Conifers – the trunks are used to make paper

Cotton plants – the fluffy seeds are used to make cotton

Plants around the world

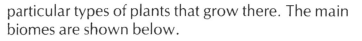

Botanists divide the Earth into six different regions called **biomes**. Each biome is characterized by particular types of plants that grow there. The main biomes are shown below.

• Tropical rainforests cover about 6% of the Earth. They grow in a belt around the Equator. Because there is so much rain in these areas there is a rich variety of plants, more than in any other region in the world. Jungle trees are evergreen, which means they don't shed their leaves.

• North of the jungle areas there are temperate forests of bushy-shaped broad-leaved trees. These are deciduous, which means they shed their leaves in autumn and grow new ones in spring.

• North of the temperate forests there is a huge belt of coniferous forest which covers 1/4 of the Earth. Coniferous trees are good at surviving the cold . They have tough waxy evergreen needles instead of broad leaves.

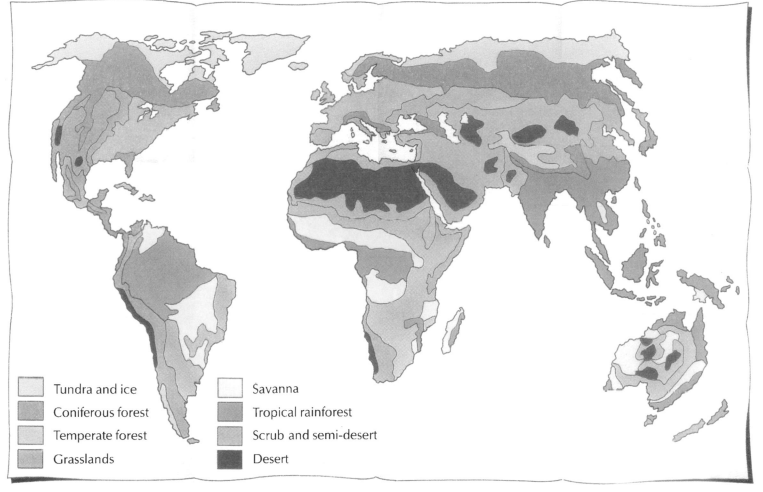

Tundra and ice
Coniferous forest
Temperate forest
Grasslands
Savanna
Tropical rainforest
Scrub and semi-desert
Desert

• North of the coniferous forests lies the tundra, an area where the ground is permanently frozen a few centimetres beneath the surface. There isn't enough soil for large trees to grow here. Instead there are carpets of moss and tiny flowers.

• Grasslands are areas where it is too dry for forests to grow but there is enough rain to stop the land being a desert. Carpets of tough grass grow here, weathering warm summers and cold winters. Grasslands near the Equator are called Savanna.

• A fifth of the Earth's surface is desert, where there is little or no rainfall. Plants which grow here must be able to survive in drought conditions. Many of them have waterproof leaves and thick rubbery flesh for storing moisture.

Rainforests

Here are some common foods first discovered in the world's rainforests:

Bananas

Rainforests are dense jungles that grow in areas of **heavy rainfall** around the **Equator**. They are found in West Africa, Southeast Asia, South America and the islands of the western Pacific.

Rainforests of the world

Rainforests provide a home for the widest variety of animals and plants to be found anywhere in the world. For instance, in just one small area of the **Amazon** rainforest in South America there are likely to be hundreds of different kinds of trees and animals.

A dense rainforest landscape

Rainforest layers

Different types of **animals** and **plants** are found living at different heights in rainforest trees.

- Extra-tall trees called emergents grow above the rest of the jungle at heights between 45 metres and 60 metres. Giant eagles nest in them.
- Lots of animals live in the canopy. This layer grows from about 30 metres to 45 metres high. It is rich in flowers and fruit.
- Rope-like plants called lianas grow up the tree trunks. Animals hang on to them to swing between branches.

- Small saplings and shrubs form the understorey layer, rising to about 10 metres high.
- On the ground there is a thin layer of rotting leaves and vegetation called 'leaf litter'. It provides a home for many insects and fungi.
- The trees spread their roots out near the surface to gather all the food and moisture they can. Some of them grow big flat buttress roots to support their weight.

Rainforest plants

- Rainforest trees flower at different times. Many of them have bright petals and sweet nectar to attract birds and insects to pollinate them (see p32).
- In some rainforests hummingbirds feed on the nectar from flowers. They hover in front of a flower, beating their wings so fast that they make a humming noise. They dip their beaks into each bloom and suck out the nectar with their tongues.

- Many different plants festoon themselves around the forest trees, dangling their roots in the air to pick up moisture.

Cocoa

Cloves

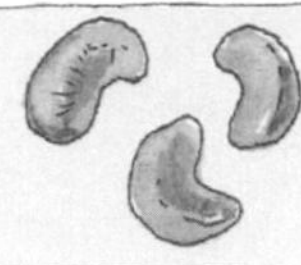

Peppers

Cashews

Rainforest animals

Mammals, **birds**, **fish**, **insects**, **amphibians** and **reptiles** can all be found in the rainforests.

Jaguar

• Rainforest mammals include tree-living cats such as jaguars and margays.

• Jungle reptiles include lizards and snakes of all sorts and sizes.

Anaconda

• Jungle insects include ants, butterflies, termites and beetles of all different kinds.

• Some jungle leaves collect pools of water that attract many kinds of tree frog. Most tree frogs have suckers on their hands and feet to anchor them securely to branches.

Tree frog

• Bright macaws, parrots and toucans are just a few of the birds that nest in the jungle canopy.

Macaw

• Monkeys of all kinds swing from the jungle trees. Most South American monkeys have prehensile tails which they can use as an extra hand to grab onto things.

• Rainforests have rivers teeming with fish. The Amazon river is home to the ferocious piranha.

Piranha

Strange but true

• The goliath beetle is found in African jungles. It grows up to 14 cm long and when it flies it sounds like a small aircraft.

• Amazon army ants sometimes travel in groups up to 20 million strong. They destroy and eat everything in their path.

• Gibbon monkeys look acrobatic, but in fact many of them suffer from broken limbs through falling.

Jungle people

The **people** who live in rainforests are usually grouped in small **tribes**.

• Most rainforest people survive by hunting for meat and gathering plants. They have a great knowledge of the rainforests and know exactly where to find food supplies.

• The traditional livelihoods of the rainforest Indians are increasingly threatened by forest clearing and mining projects. International efforts are being made to help them survive.

Deserts

The wind blows sand dunes into shapes with different names:

Barchan

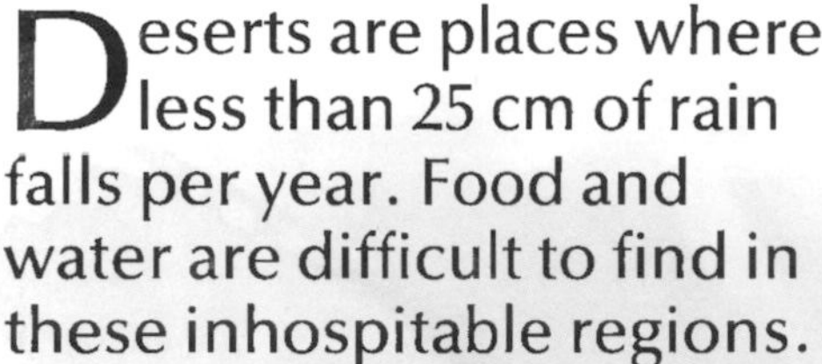

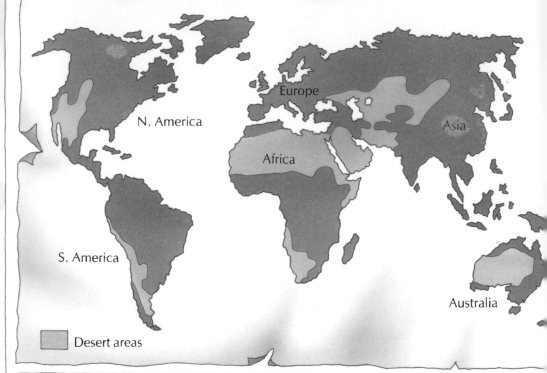

Deserts are places where less than 25 cm of rain falls per year. Food and water are difficult to find in these inhospitable regions.

There are lots of different types of **desert landscape**, ranging from sand dunes to rocky plains and mountains.

Deserts occur for several reasons. Some deserts are so far from the sea that by the time wind reaches them all the moisture in the air has gone.

Some deserts are dry because they are near mountains. All the moisture in the air falls as rain and snow on the mountain tops, before it reaches the desert on the other side.

Deserts of the world

The world's main **desert areas** are shown below:

N. America
Europe
Asia
Africa
S. America
Australia
Desert areas

Desert plants

Desert plants are adapted to drought:

- They gather water through their roots, which either spread out near the surface to soak up dew or grow deep down to moist soil layers.
- Some cacti have pleated skins that stretch so they can store water.

- The biggest cactus is the saguaro, found in the Sonoran Desert in south-west USA. It can grow 15 metres high.

Saguaro cactus

- Many desert plants only flower and seed themselves when rains come. The plant seeds then lie in the ground for years until the next rain shower comes along.

Desert flower

- Desert plants often have bright beautiful flowers that only appear for a short time after rain has fallen. They don't live long, so they must attract pollinating insects quickly. That is why their petals are so colourful.

Seif Star-shaped Parallel Transverse

• North American deserts have rocky plains, deep ravines, salt lakes and canyons. The hottest place is Death Valley, California, where temperatures can reach over 56°C.

• The North African Sahara is the world's biggest desert, covering an area almost the size of the USA. Most of it is rocky. Only about a tenth of it is covered in sand dunes.

• A belt of desert stretches down the west coast of South America. It includes the Atacama Desert in Chile, the driest place in the world. Droughts there last for hundreds of years.

• Most of the centre of Australia is a barren desert plain called the 'Outback', dotted with rocky outcrops such as the famous Ayers Rock.

Ayers Rock

• The Arabian Desert is partly a sea of sand with dunes up to 240 m high. Bedouin tribesmen travel the desert, camping in tents wherever they stop.

• The Gobi Desert in Central Asia has hot summers and severe winters. The people who live there are nomads. They spend their lives travelling the barren, rocky land in search of grazing for their yak herds.

Yak and tribesman

• The Kalahari Desert in Southern Africa is on a huge plateau. In the middle there is a sea of red sand dunes. The Kalahari bushmen hunt and gather food from this wilderness.

Kalahari bushman

Desert animals

Desert animals usually shelter during the heat of the day and come out when the temperature drops in the evening. They get the moisture they need from eating plants or other creatures.

• Most desert spiders do not build webs. Instead they hunt for food. The camel spider is one of the largest desert specimens. It spans up to 15 cm.

• Camels can survive for many days without water. Their nostrils can close up to keep out the dust.

• Desert reptiles include all sorts of snakes and lizards. They stay in the shade when they can.

Strange but true

• Prehistoric paintings show the Sahara as fertile land.

• The first white explorers of the Australian Outback took a boat with them. They were looking for a fabled lake.

• In Saudi Arabia there are solar-powered pay phones in the desert.

• Desert ostriches sometimes eat sand, probably to help their digestion.

Polar Regions

Here are four species of whale that are found off the coast of the Antarctic:

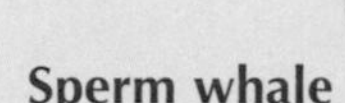

Sperm whale

The Arctic and the **Antarctic** are the coldest regions in the world.

The Arctic is the area within the **Arctic Circle**, an imaginary line going around the North Pole. The **Arctic Ocean** is in the middle, mostly covered by ice. Around the edge there is a belt of **tundra** (see p33).

Antarctica is a small continent surrounding the South Pole and includes the Antarctic Sea. It covers over 9% of the Earth's surface. Most of the Antarctic land is covered by a thick sheet of ice. Wildlife is found only around the coasts and on outlying islands, where the temperature is warmer than it is inland.

The Arctic

For most of the year the Arctic **tundra** is covered in snow. In the brief summer months the snow melts, but it cannot drain away because under the land surface there is a permanently frozen layer of earth called **permafrost**. Instead the water gathers in lakes, pools and bogs.

- Sometimes the wind whips up the Arctic snow and causes 'white outs' which are rather like sandstorms in the desert. White outs can start suddenly and last for days.
- Most Arctic animals are to be found on the tundra. They arrive in summer and migrate south or hibernate underground in winter.
- Tundra plants are small. The grow near the ground to avoid the biting winds and cold temperatures. Some of them have hairy stems that help to keep them warm.

The Antarctic

Antarctica is the **coldest** and **windiest** place on Earth. Its ice sheets hold a large amount of the Earth's permanent ice. In Antarctica:

- The tops of high mountains only just peek above the ice, which is up to 4 km thick in parts.
- The world's biggest icebergs, up to 100 km wide, break off from the coastal ice shelf and drift far out to sea. This process of breaking off is called 'calving'.
- Some areas of coastal land are exposed in summer. Algae and lichen grow here, but there are hardly any other plants.

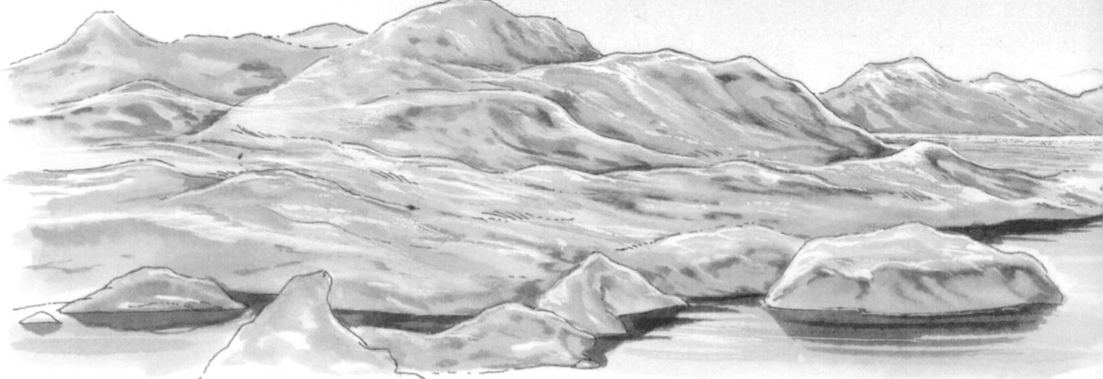

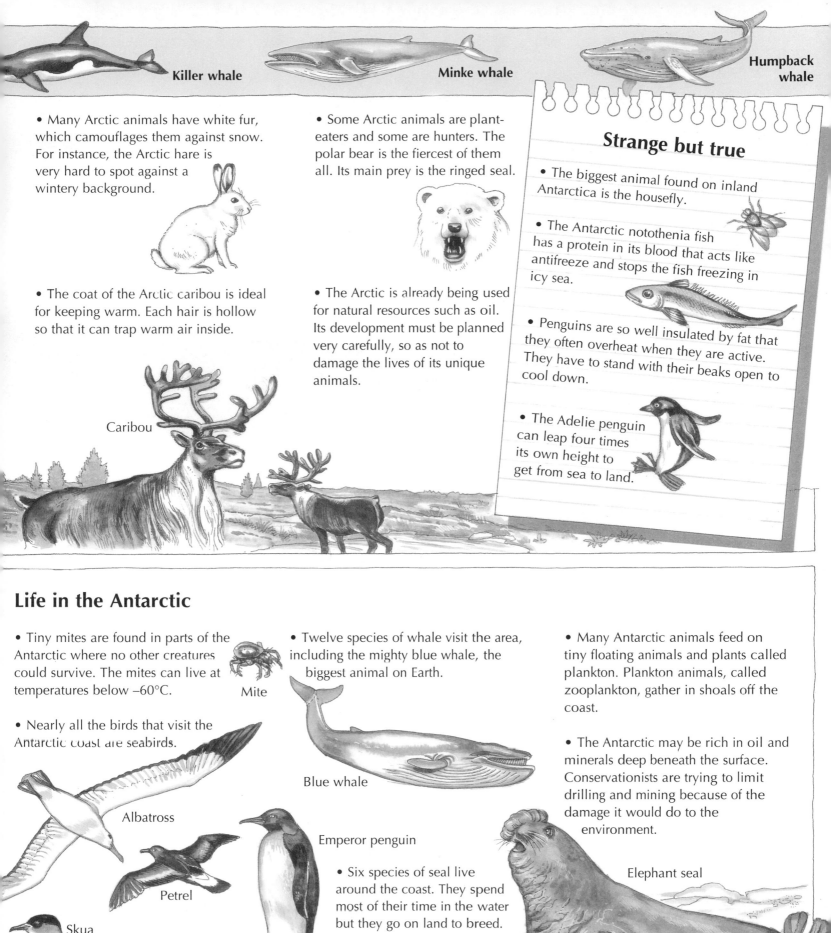

Killer whale

Minke whale

Humpback whale

• Many Arctic animals have white fur, which camouflages them against snow. For instance, the Arctic hare is very hard to spot against a wintery background.

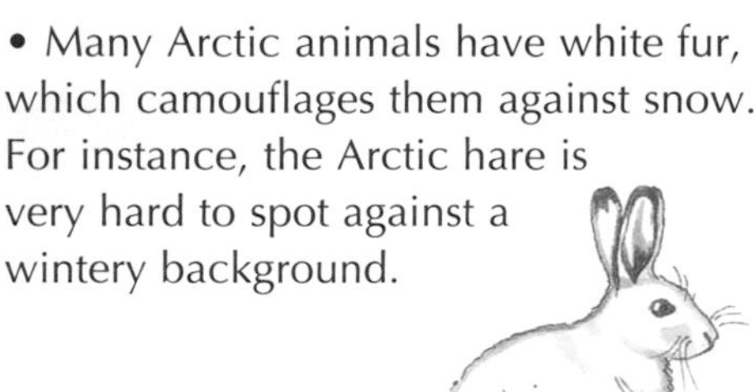

• Some Arctic animals are plant-eaters and some are hunters. The polar bear is the fiercest of them all. Its main prey is the ringed seal.

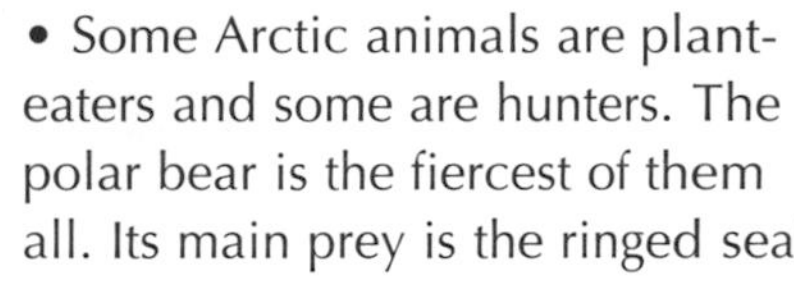

• The coat of the Arctic caribou is ideal for keeping warm. Each hair is hollow so that it can trap warm air inside.

• The Arctic is already being used for natural resources such as oil. Its development must be planned very carefully, so as not to damage the lives of its unique animals.

Caribou

Strange but true

• The biggest animal found on inland Antarctica is the housefly.

• The Antarctic notothenia fish has a protein in its blood that acts like antifreeze and stops the fish freezing in icy sea.

• Penguins are so well insulated by fat that they often overheat when they are active. They have to stand with their beaks open to cool down.

• The Adelie penguin can leap four times its own height to get from sea to land.

Life in the Antarctic

• Tiny mites are found in parts of the Antarctic where no other creatures could survive. The mites can live at temperatures below –60°C.

Mite

• Nearly all the birds that visit the Antarctic coast are seabirds.

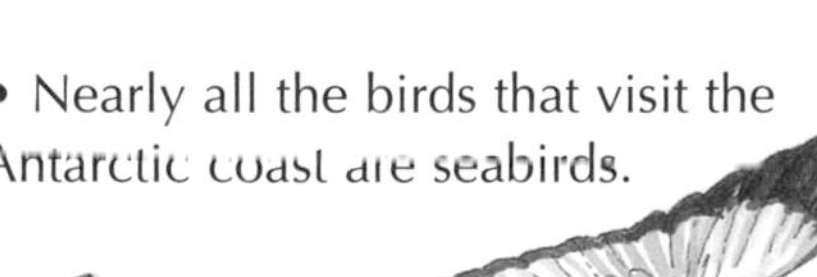

Albatross

Petrel

Skua

• Twelve species of whale visit the area, including the mighty blue whale, the biggest animal on Earth.

Blue whale

Emperor penguin

• Six species of seal live around the coast. They spend most of their time in the water but they go on land to breed.

• Many Antarctic animals feed on tiny floating animals and plants called plankton. Plankton animals, called zooplankton, gather in shoals off the coast.

• The Antarctic may be rich in oil and minerals deep beneath the surface. Conservationists are trying to limit drilling and mining because of the damage it would do to the environment.

Elephant seal

Here are some things that you can do to help cut down on pollution:

Recycle cans, bottles and paper.

The Earth's rivers, seas and soil are threatened by **pollution**.
It even affects the air we breathe. Scientists have realized that pollution is getting worse and that the whole planet will be seriously harmed unless something is done quickly to limit the damage.

Climate alert

Carbon dioxide (CO_2) in the atmosphere traps some of the Sun's heat. The level of carbon dioxide has been rising so much through pollution that the Earth's **climate** may warm up as a result. Global warming is increased by:

- Dirty fumes from car exhausts, factories and power stations
- Burning or cutting down forests. The burning releases fumes and the destruction of plants means that less CO_2 is removed from the atmosphere.
- CFCs, which are chemicals used in some aerosols, fridges and air-conditioning systems. They destroy the ozone layer which protects us from harmful ultra-violet rays (see p25).

Forest alert

It is estimated that 1 sq km of rainforest is destroyed every 2.5 minutes. If this continues, the rainforests will disappear by the year 2050. The destruction of the rainforest is caused by:

- People clearing vast areas to graze their cattle herds.
- Flooding caused by hydro-electric dams being built across rivers.
- Chopping down hardwood trees to make products such as mahogany furniture.

Strange but true

- The USA uses 29% of the world's petrol and 33% of the world's electricity.
- Some Chinese farmers use flocks of ducks instead of pesticides to kill harmful insects.
- The industrial complex of Cubatao in Brazil is known as the Valley of Death because its pollution has destroyed the trees and rivers nearby.

Water alert

The world's rivers and oceans are gradually becoming more polluted. The pollution is caused by:

- Factories discharging polluted waste straight into rivers and seas.
- Oil leaking into the sea from ships and oil terminals.
- Artificial fertilizer and pesticide chemicals washed into the water supply by rainfall.

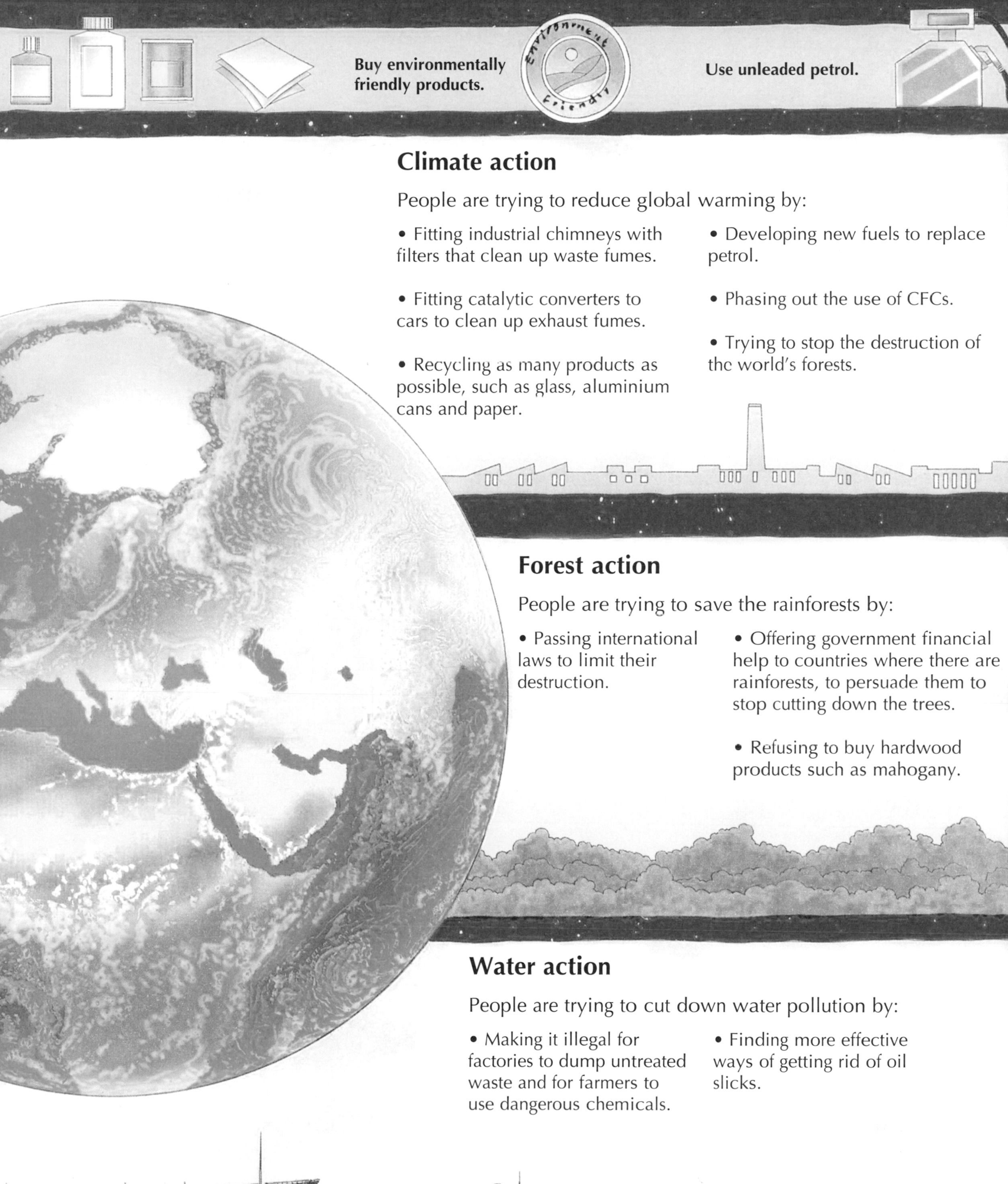

Climate action

People are trying to reduce global warming by:

- Fitting industrial chimneys with filters that clean up waste fumes.
- Fitting catalytic converters to cars to clean up exhaust fumes.
- Recycling as many products as possible, such as glass, aluminium cans and paper.
- Developing new fuels to replace petrol.
- Phasing out the use of CFCs.
- Trying to stop the destruction of the world's forests.

Forest action

People are trying to save the rainforests by:

- Passing international laws to limit their destruction.
- Offering government financial help to countries where there are rainforests, to persuade them to stop cutting down the trees.
- Refusing to buy hardwood products such as mahogany.

Water action

People are trying to cut down water pollution by:

- Making it illegal for factories to dump untreated waste and for farmers to use dangerous chemicals.
- Finding more effective ways of getting rid of oil slicks.

Earth Facts and Lists

The Earth in Space

- The distance between the Earth and the Moon is 384,365 km.
- Light from the Sun takes about 8 minutes to reach the Earth.
- The Earth's nearest star, apart from the Sun, is Proxima Centauri.
- It would take more than four light years to reach Proxima Centauri from Earth.
- The average speed of the Earth in orbit is 29.8 km per second.
- The Earth's density is 5.517 times the density of water.
- The Earth tilts on its axis at an angle of 23°.
- The light we see from the Moon at night does not really come from the Moon itself. What we see is light from the Sun shining onto the Moon's surface.

The Earth from birth

- If history up to AD1 was squashed into a scale of one year, with the Earth's birth on 1 January, the first life on Earth wouldn't begin until the end of March.
- The first dinosaurs would appear in the middle of December.
- The first ape-men would emerge only a few hours before the end of the year.

The Earth's surface

- The Earth's total surface area is 510,100,000 sq.km.
- The total land area of the Earth is 148,800,000 sq.km.
- If you were to jog round the Earth without stopping it would take you about 6 months.

Largest countries

The ten largest countries:

Country	Size
USSR	22,402,200 sq.km
Canada	9,976,139 sq.km
China	9,561,000 sq.km
USA	9,363,123,sq.km
Brazil	8,511,965 sq.km
Australia	7,682,300 sq.km
India	3,287,590 sq.km
Argentina	2,776,889 sq.km
Sudan	2,505,813 sq.km
Algeria	2,381,741 sq.km

Islands

The world's largest islands and their areas:

Island	Area
Greenland	7,618,493 sq.km
New Guinea	2,175,600 sq.km
Borneo	777,000 sq.km
Madagascar	590,000 sq.km
Baffin Island	476,065 sq.km
Sumatra	473,600 sq.km
Honshu	228,000 sq.km
Great Britain	218,041 sq.km
Victoria Island	212,197 sq.km
Ellesmere Island	196,236 sq.km

Peninsulas

A peninsula is a piece of land with water on three sides. These are the world's largest:

Peninsula	Area
Arabia	3,250,000 sq.km
Southern India	2,072,000 sq.km
Alaska	1,500,000 sq.km
Labrador	1,300,000 sq.km
Scandinavia	800,000 sq.km
Iberian Peninsula	584,000 sq.km

Volcanoes

Here are the ten most active volcanoes:

Volcano	Height	Country
Antofalla	6450 m	Argentina
Guallatiri	6060 m	Argentina/Chile
Cotopaxi	5897 m	Ecuador
Sangay	5320 m	Ecuador
Kluchevskaya	4850 m	USSR
Wrangell	4269 m	Alaska
Mauna Loa	4171 m	Hawaii
Galeras	4083 m	Ecuador
Cameroun	4070 m	Cameroon
Acatenango	3959 m	Guatemala

- Toba in north-central Sumatra has the largest volcanic crater, with an area of 1775 sq.km.
- When Laki in Iceland erupted in 1783, its lava flow stretched 65 km, the longest ever recorded.
- There are over 500 active volcanoes in the world.
- About 20 per cent of all volcanoes are underwater.
- Lava from an erupting volcano may be as hot as 1200°C.
- When Mount Tolbachik in the USSR erupted, lava poured out at more than 100 metres per second.
- One eruption from Mauna Loa (in Hawaii) lasted 1½ years.
- The loudest noise ever known was produced by a volcanic eruption at Krakatoa, near Java, in 1883. The sound was heard in Australia, 5000 km away.
- The highest volcano, Cerro Aconcagua (6960 metres), is in the Andes. It is now extinct.
- Lava can take several years to cool down.

Mountains

- About 25 per cent of all land is more than 900 metres above sea level.
- The further up a mountain you go, the colder the air becomes. The temperature drops by 2°C for every 300 metres you climb.
- Tibet is the highest country in the world. Its average height above sea level is 4500 metres.
- Some of the oldest mountains in the world are the Highlands in Scotland. They are estimated to be about 400 million years old.

Highest mountains

Here are the seven continents and their highest mountains:

Continent	Mountain	Height
Africa	Kilimanjaro	5895 m
Antarctica	Vinson Massif	5140 m
Asia	Everest	8848 m
Aust. / NZ	Cook	3764 m
North America	McKinley	6194 m
South America	Aconcagua	6960 m
Europe	Elbrus	5633 m

Longest ranges

Here are some of the longest mountain ranges:

Mountain range	Length	Country
Andes	7240 km	South America
Rockies	6030 km	North America
Himalayas	3860 km	Asia
Great Dividing Range	3620 km	Australia
Trans-Antarctic	3540 km	Antarctica

Glaciers

These are the longest glaciers:

Glacier	Length	Country
Lambert Fischer Ice Passage	515 km	Antarctica
Novaya Zemlya	418 km	USSR
Arctic Institute Ice Passage	362 km	Antarctica
Nimrod/Lennox/ King Ice Passage	289 km	Antarctica
Denman Glacier	241 km	Antarctica
Beardmore Glacier	225 km	Antarctica
Recovery Glacier	225 km	Antarctica
Petermanns Gletscher	200 km	Greenland
Unnamed Glacier	193 km	Antarctica

Rivers and Lakes

- The highest lakes are in the Himalayan mountains, but the highest navigable lake is Lake Titicaca in the Andes, which is 3811 metres above sea level.
- The deepest lake is Lake Baykal in the USSR. At its deepest point it is almost 2 km deep.
- Fresh water from the River Amazon can be found up to 180 km out to sea.
- The muddiest river is the Hwang He, or Yellow River, in China.
- The largest swamp is in the basin of the Pripyat River in the USSR. It covers an area of 46,950 sq.km.

Lakes

Some of the largest lakes in the world:

Lake	Area	Country
Caspian Sea	371,800 sq.km	USSR/Iran
Superior	82,350 sq.km	Canada/ USA
Victoria	69,500 sq.km	Africa
Aral Sea	65,500 sq.km	USSR
Huron	59,600 sq.km	Canada/ USA
Michigan	58,000 sq.km	USA
Tanganyika	32,900 sq.km	Africa
Great Bear	31,800 sq.km	Canada
Ozero Baykal	30,500 sq.km	USSR
Malawi	29,600 sq.km	Africa

Rivers

Here are the ten longest rivers:

River	Length	Location
Nile	6695 km	Africa
Amazon	6570 km	South America
Mississippi/ Missouri	6020 km	North America
Yangtze	5530 km	Asia
Ob/Irtysh	5410 km	Asia
Hwang He	4840 km	Asia
Zaire	4630 km	Africa
Parana	4500 km	South America
Irtysh	4440 km	Asia
Amur	4416 km	Asia

Earthquakes

The strongest earthquakes recorded are:

Date	Country	Strength on Richter Scale
1906	Ecuador	8.6
1952	USSR	8.25
1960	Chile	8.3
1964	Alaska	8.4
2004	Indonesia	9.0

Some of the most disastrous earthquakes:

Date	Country	Number of people killed
1556	China	830,000
1755	Portugal	60,000
1908	Italy	160,000
1976	China	700,000
1978	Iran	25,000
1988	USSR	25,000

Earth Facts and Lists

Waterfalls

These are some of the largest waterfalls and the countries they are in:

Waterfall	Total height	Country
Angel	979 m	Venezuela
Tugela	947 m	South Africa
Utigard	800 m	Norway
Mongefossen	774 m	Norway
Yosemite	739 m	USA
Ostre Mardola Foss	656 m	Norway
Tyssestrengane	646 m	Norway
Cuquenan	610 m	Venezuela
Sutherland	580 m	New Zealand
Kjellfossen	561 m	Norway

Oceans

- The oceans make up 97 per cent of the Earth's water.
- Most of an iceberg is hidden underwater. Only 10 per cent of it floats above the surface.
- The greatest difference in tides is in the Bay of Fundy in Canada. The difference between low tide and high tide is about 16.5 metres.
- The highest underwater mountain is in the ocean between Samoa and New Zealand. Its summit is 8690 metres above the seabed.
- The White Sea, in the USSR, has the lowest temperature, only −2°C.
- The Persian Gulf is the warmest sea. In the summer its temperature reaches 35.6°C.
- The most salty sea in the world is the Dead Sea, in the Middle East.

Coastlines

- The total length of all of Earth's coastlines is more than 500,000 km – the equivalent of over 12 times round the world.
- There are 26 countries that have no coastline at all.
- Hudson's Bay in Canada is the largest bay in the world.

Polar regions

- About 10 per cent of all land on Earth is covered in ice.
- Icebergs can float at about 2.5 km/h, with the help of a strong wind.
- The tallest iceberg ever seen measured 167.6 metres high. It was spotted near Greenland.
- On the tundra only one type of tree grows – the dwarf willow tree. It grows to a maximum height of 10 cm.
- About 75 per cent of all the fresh water on Earth is contained in frozen glaciers.
- People in Greenland live only on the coasts, because most of the country is covered in an ice sheet.

The ice sheet in Greenland:

- is 1.5-3 km thick.
- covers almost 1.5 million sq.km.
- has an average temperature of −20°C.

The Antarctic ice sheet:

- is 3-4 km thick.
- covers 13 million sq.km.
- has temperatures as low as −50°C.

The Arctic Ocean:

- has about 12,000,000 sq.km of floating ice.
- has an average depth of 1500 metres.
- has an average water temperature of −51°C.

- There is no land at all at the North Pole, only ice on top of sea.
- There is six months of light followed by six months of darkness at the Poles.

Deserts

- About 120,000 sq.km of new desert are formed each year.
- Snow has been known to fall in the Sahara Desert.

Here are some of the world's largest deserts:

Desert	Country	Area
Sahara	North Africa	8,400,000 sq.km
Gobi	Mongolia	1,295,000 sq.km
Gibson	Western Australia	647,500 sq.km
Great Victoria	Western/ Southern Australia	647,500 sq.km
Rub al Khali	Southern Arabia	587,500 sq.km
Kalahari	Southern Africa	562,500 sq.km

- Only about 15 per cent of the world's desert areas are sandy.
- Sand dunes can be as high as 400 metres.

Here are some of the worst droughts in history:

Year	Country	Estimated number of people killed
1333-37	China	over 4 million
1769-70	India	3-10 million
1837-38	India	800,000
1865-66	India	10 million
1876-78	India	3.5 million
1876-79	China	9-13 million
1891-92	USSR	400,000
1892-94	China	1 million
1896-97	India	5 million
1899-1900	India	1 million

Weather

Here are some of the worst recent natural disasters:

- 1906 – A typhoon killed 50,000 people in Hong Kong.
- 1955 – In the USA, 200 people were killed by a hurricane.
- 1962 – An avalanche in Peru killed 3000 people.
- 1970 – In Bangladesh a cyclone and tidal waves killed 20,000 people.
- 1975 – Lightning in Zimbabwe killed 21 people.

Here are some of the world's most rainy places:

- Cherrapunji in India has an annual rainfall of 11,430 mm.
- In Debundsehsa in the Cameroon 10,277 mm of rain falls each year.
- Quibdo in Colombia is only slightly drier with 8991 mm.
- Lightning travels at speeds of up to 1500 km per second as it strikes down. It moves even faster as it travels back up again.
- The air in the path of lightning can reach temperatures of 30,000°C.
- A tornado can travel at 50 km/h.
- The winds at the edge of a tornado spin fastest – more than 700 km/h.
- Each year more than 16 million thunderstorms occur.

Plant Life

- The largest tree in the world is a giant sequoia growing in California. It is 84 metres tall and measures 29 metres round the trunk.
- The fastest-growing tree is the eucalyptus. It can grow 10 metres a year.
- The world's oldest trees are the bristlecone pines of California. One of them is about 4600 years old.
- The largest flower comes from the rafflesia plant. The flower can weigh 6 kg and grow to a width of 91 cm.

Here are some of the most heavily forested countries:

Country	% of country's total area covered by forest
Surinam	92
Solomon Islands	91
Papua New Guinea	84
Guyana	83
French Guiana	82
Gabon	78
Finland	76
Cambodia	75
North Korea	74
Bhutan	70

- Rice is the only grass that can grow in water.
- The tallest type of grass is bamboo. It can grow up to about 30 metres high.
- The saguaro is the tallest kind of cactus. It can grow to about 16 metres high.

Here are five different types of cereal:

- Barley
- Maize
- Oats
- Rye
- Wheat

Here are five types of coniferous trees (i.e. they produce cones):

- Cedar
- Douglas fir
- Larch
- Pine
- Spruce

Forests

- Some medicines are made from forest trees. For instance, quinine, which is used to treat malaria, comes originally from a chemical found in the bark of the cinchona tree.
- Only 1 per cent of sunlight reaches the rainforest floor.
- The USA, USSR, China and Malaysia are amongst the top producers of hardwood.

Here are five types of deciduous trees (i.e. they lose their leaves in autumn):

- Ash
- Birch
- Chestnut
- Maple
- Oak

- Lianas are strong rope-like rainforest plants. They can grow to a width of 2 metres and are strong enough to swing on.
- The largest forest in the world covers parts of Scandinavia and northern USSR and has a total area of over 9 million sq.km.

Saving the Earth

- Scientists estimate that the Earth's average temperature could rise by as much as 2-4°C by the year 2030.
- If the Earth's temperature does rise, the ice sheets could melt and flood many coastal regions.
- Over 4 million cars in Brazil are now running on gasohol instead of petrol. Gasohol is a fuel made from sugar cane.

INDEX

Indexes to other sections are on pages 94, 142 and 190.

WILD ANIMALS

Part Two

WILD ANIMALS

Introduction

There are over a million different kinds of animals living on the Earth today. In this Part, you can find out how scientists divide animals into groups like mammals, reptiles, fish and birds.

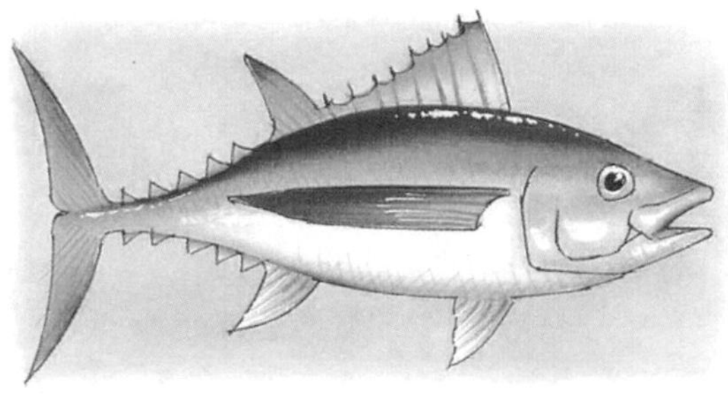

Did you know that the present day is sometimes called the 'Age of the Insects' because they outnumber all the other groups? There are probably many unknown types of insect still to be discovered.

The places where animals live can affect what they look like. For instance, one type of desert mammal called a fennec fox has especially big ears that help to keep it cool in the very hot sun. An unusual shark called a wobbegong has skin that looks like seaweed, so that it can lie unseen on the seabed.

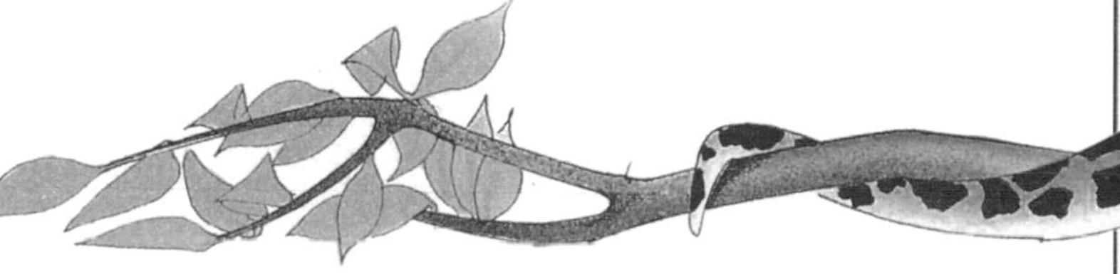

Not all animals live in places like deserts or oceans. Find out how your home could be a good hunting ground and nesting place too.

There are four basic ways that animals reproduce, or make new generations. Tiny bacteria can reproduce every half-hour or so, but large creatures like elephants and whales take over a year.

About 5000 animal species may disappear because of what humans are doing. Discover what can be done to stop this happening.

The Animal Kingdom

Here are some of the smaller animal groups:

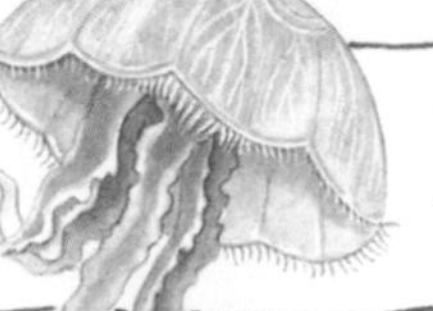

Coelenterates – jellyfish, corals, sea anemones

Animals are creatures that breathe in **oxygen**. They have to **eat** plants or other animals in order to survive.

Animals have been on the Earth in one form or another for about 700 million years. The first animals were tiny single-celled creatures.

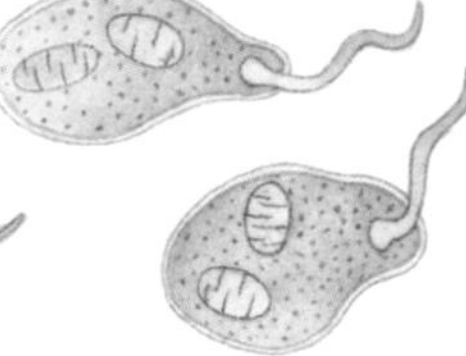

Single-celled creatures

Today many of the living things on Earth are animals. Scientists split them into groups of related creatures.

Animal groups

Here are the main **animal groups:**

• Mammals (see p54) include such different examples as bats, whales, cats, kangaroos and humans. Many large creatures belong to this group.

• Reptiles (see p60) include snakes, lizards, turtles and crocodiles. About 250 million years ago, reptiles dominated the Earth as dinosaurs.

• Amphibians (see p60) have bodies which are adapted to live on land or in water. This group includes frogs, toads, newts and salamanders.

Strange but true

• The present day is sometimes called the 'Age of the Insects'. Insects vastly outnumber all the other insect groups.

• Because grass gives so little nourishment, cows must graze all day to get enough for their needs.

• Some scientists think that apes and humans are descended from a type of rodent, rather like a rat.

Animal food

Animals eat different kinds of **food**, depending on their size, the type of stomach they have and the food available.

• Animals that eat only plants are called herbivores.

Herbivorous zebra

• Animals that eat only meat are called carnivores.

Carnivorous lion

• Animals that eat both meat and plants are called omnivores.

• Predators help to strengthen the animal population. They tend to catch and kill the weakest members of an animal group. The strongest ones are left alive. These are more likely to breed healthy offspring.

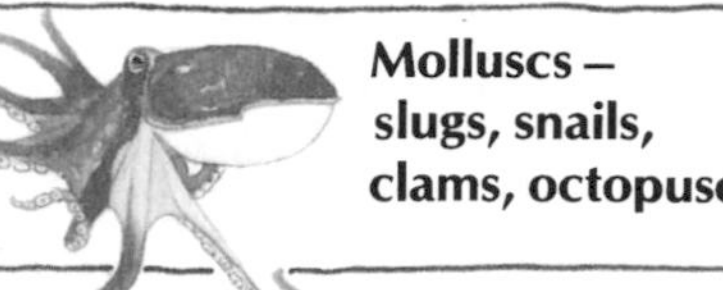

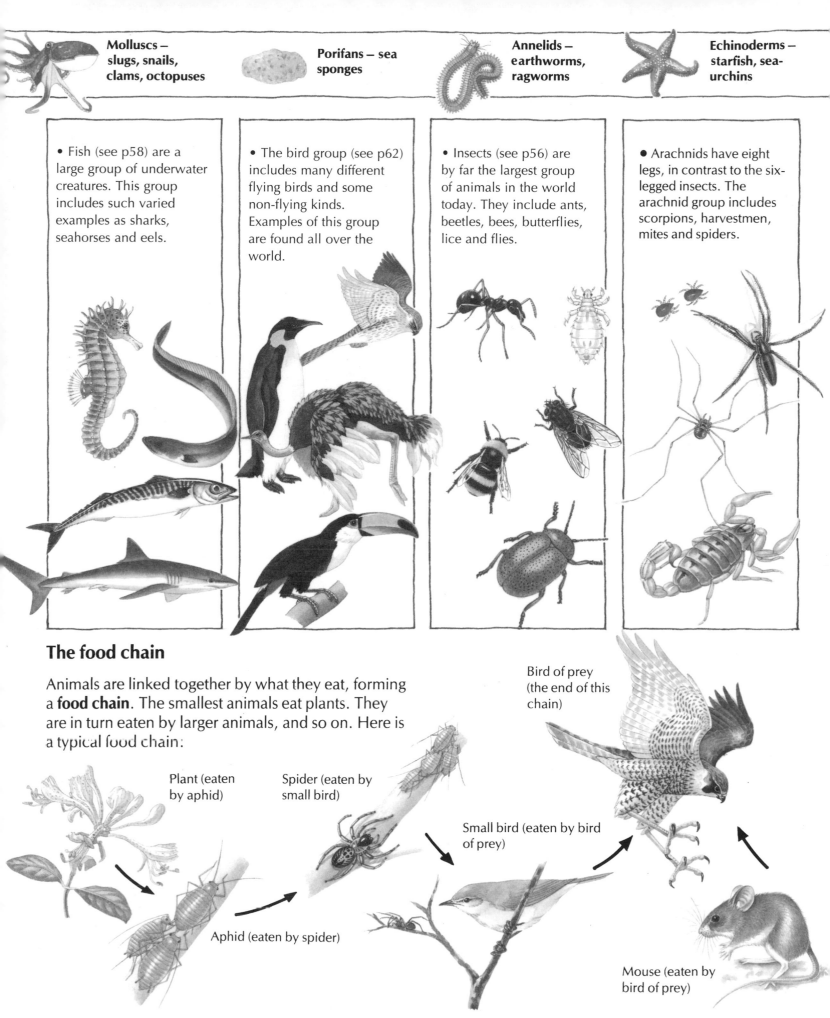

Molluscs – slugs, snails, clams, octopuses

Porifans – sea sponges

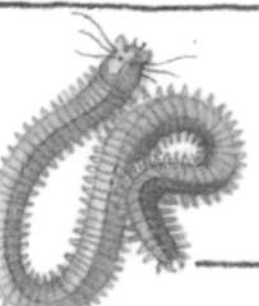

Annelids – earthworms, ragworms

Echinoderms – starfish, sea-urchins

• Fish (see p58) are a large group of underwater creatures. This group includes such varied examples as sharks, seahorses and eels.

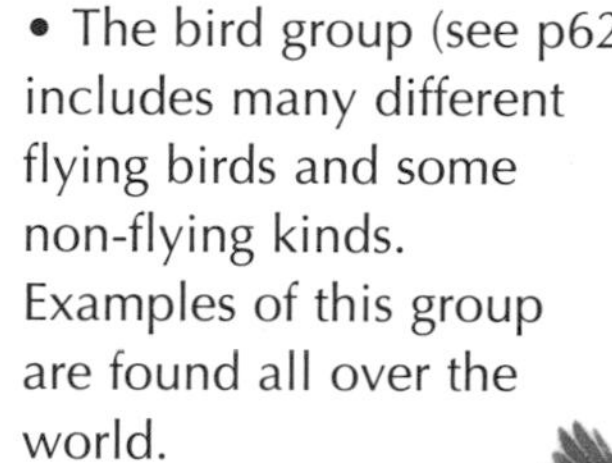

• The bird group (see p62) includes many different flying birds and some non-flying kinds. Examples of this group are found all over the world.

• Insects (see p56) are by far the largest group of animals in the world today. They include ants, beetles, bees, butterflies, lice and flies.

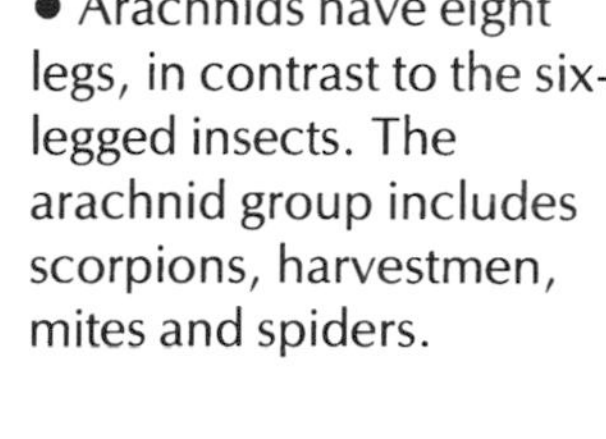

• Arachnids have eight legs, in contrast to the six-legged insects. The arachnid group includes scorpions, harvestmen, mites and spiders.

The food chain

Animals are linked together by what they eat, forming a **food chain**. The smallest animals eat plants. They are in turn eaten by larger animals, and so on. Here is a typical food chain:

Plant (eaten by aphid)

Aphid (eaten by spider)

Spider (eaten by small bird)

Small bird (eaten by bird of prey)

Mouse (eaten by bird of prey)

Bird of prey (the end of this chain)

Mammals

These mammals are very rare, and are in danger of dying out:

Golden lion marmoset (Brazil)

Mammals are a very successful group of animals found all over the world. There are about 4500 species in all.

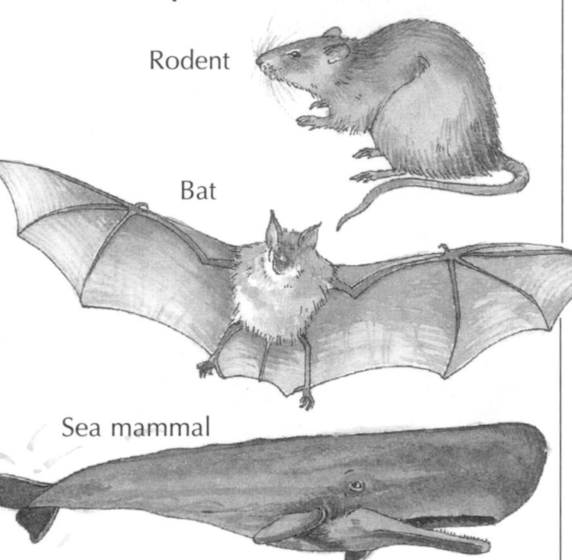

The mammal family includes **bats**, **rodents** (small gnawing creatures such as rats and mice) and some sea animals such as **whales** and **dolphins**. It also includes the **primates**. Human beings are part of the primate group, along with lemurs, monkeys and apes.

Primates

Mammal facts

Mammals have:

- Hairy bodies, to help them keep warm. Some mammals have thick fur; some only have a fine fur.
- A constant body temperature

- Skulls and backbones. Animals with backbones are called vertebrates.
- The ability to suckle their young, which means that they can feed babies with milk from their body.

Different kinds of mammal

Zoologists split mammals into three scientific groups. Each group gives birth to babies in a different way.

- Monotremes lay eggs and hatch their young. There are only two types of monotremes: the duck-billed platypus from Australia and the spiny anteaters or echidnas from Australia and New Guinea.
- Marsupial mammal babies are born very tiny and undeveloped. Most marsupial babies finish growing inside pouches on their mother's body. Kangaroos are marsupials.

Duck-billed platypus

- Placental mammal babies are born alive and well-developed. When a placental baby is growing inside its mother it lives inside a kind of protective sac. Its blood supply is linked to its mother's.

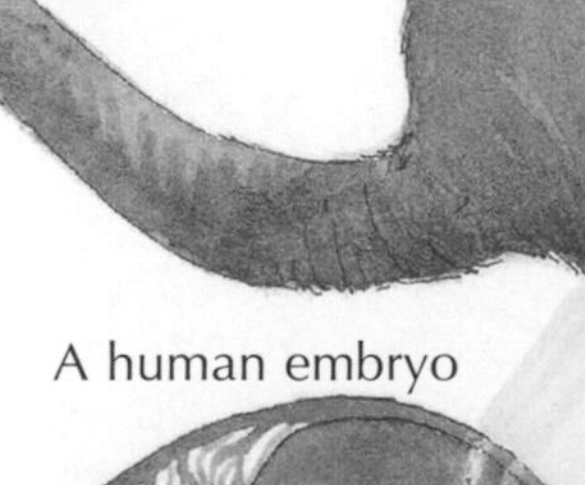

A human embryo

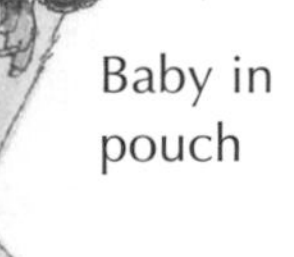

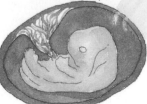

Baby in pouch

Giant panda (China)

Javan rhino (Java)

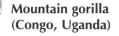

Mountain gorilla (Congo, Uganda)

Amazing mammals

Mammals come in lots of different shapes and sizes. That is partly because they have developed to survive in many different kinds of places. Here are some : **mammal record-breakers:**

- The world's noisiest land animals are South American howler monkeys. When the male monkeys call, their screams can be heard from 16 km away.
- The world's largest land mammal is the African elephant. Adult bull elephants grow over 3 metres tall and weight about 5.7 tonnes.
- Cheetahs are the world's fastest animals on land. They can run up to 70km/h over 400 metres.
- The giraffe is the tallest mammal in the world. It can grow over 5 metres. It has a long neck so that it can reach leaves high up in the trees.

Primates

Primates are the most well-developed mammals. They have:

- Complex brains, which means that they are able to think better than most other creatures in the animal kingdom.
- The ability to stand upright for long periods.
- More highly developed hands than any other animal group. They can use their hands for all kinds of complicated skills.
- Eyes set side by side in the front of the head, which means that they can see more clearly than most other creatures.

Strange but true

- Many mammals sleep for long periods. Lions sleep up to 20 hours a day.
- Gorillas sleep in nests which they build in treetops.

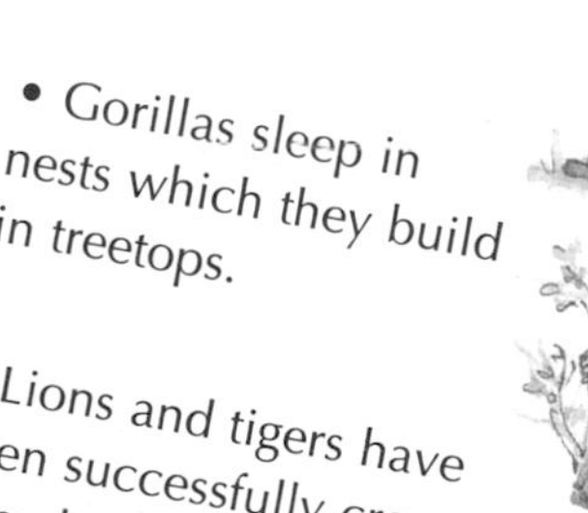

- Lions and tigers have been successfully crossed to make a new animal – the 'tigon'.
- Blue whale babies weigh up to 7 tonnes at birth.

Insects

These insects are dangerous to crops or humans:

Tsetse fly (hot climates) - spreads sleeping sickness

Insects are the biggest animal group. There are vast numbers of them, and there are probably many unknown types of insect still to be discovered.

Insects are found all over the world, even in frozen lands and in scorching deserts where other animals find it hard to survive.

Most insects live on their own for most of their lives, but some insects, such as bees, live in **organized communities** with many companions of the same type.

Insect parts

Insects do not all look the same, but they all have some characteristics in common. **All insects** have:

- A protective outer covering called an 'exoskeleton'. Insects are 'invertebrates', which means that they do not have backbones. They do have internal skeletons.
- A head which carries the eyes, antennae and feeding parts.
- An abdomen, made up of a series of segments. Vital organs such as the heart are inside.
- A thorax, which carries legs and sometimes wings.
- Three pairs of jointed legs.
- Cold blood, which means that they cannot control their own body temperature. They rely on the temperature of their surroundings to keep them alive.

Head

Thorax

Abdomen

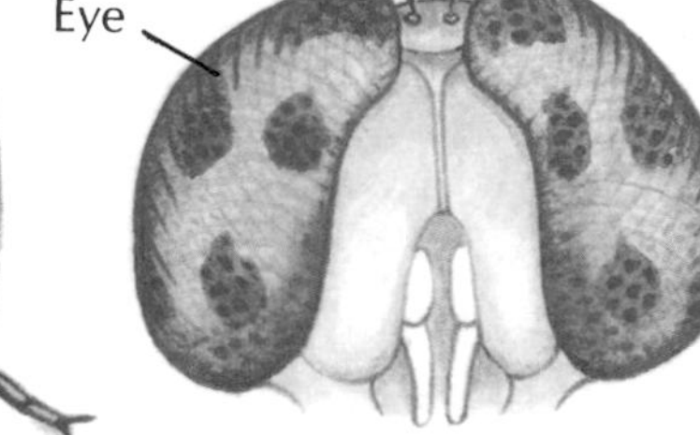

- Many insects have compound eyes, made of hundreds of tiny lenses.

Strange but true

- Some butterflies have scented wings, to attract a mate.
- Some insects produce tiny lights on their bodies to attract mates.
- Crickets have ears positioned on their knees.

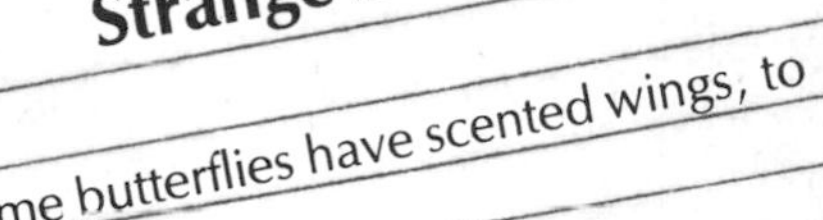

- Prehistoric dragonflies had wingspans up to 76cm across, wider than many modern birds.

Growing up

Some insects go through a complete change of body and appearance called **metamorphosis**. There are four stages:

1. The female insect lays lots of tiny eggs, sometimes on the underside of a leaf.
2. The eggs hatch into larvae. Caterpillars, grubs and maggots are all forms of insect larvae.
3. When the larvae has grown enough it changes into a pupa (or chrysalis), inside a hard cased called a cocoon. The insect's body dissolves and reforms into a new shape.
4. Once the change has occurred, the cocoon splits open and the adult insect comes out. Butterflies, moths, beetles, flies, ants and bees all go through metamorphosis.

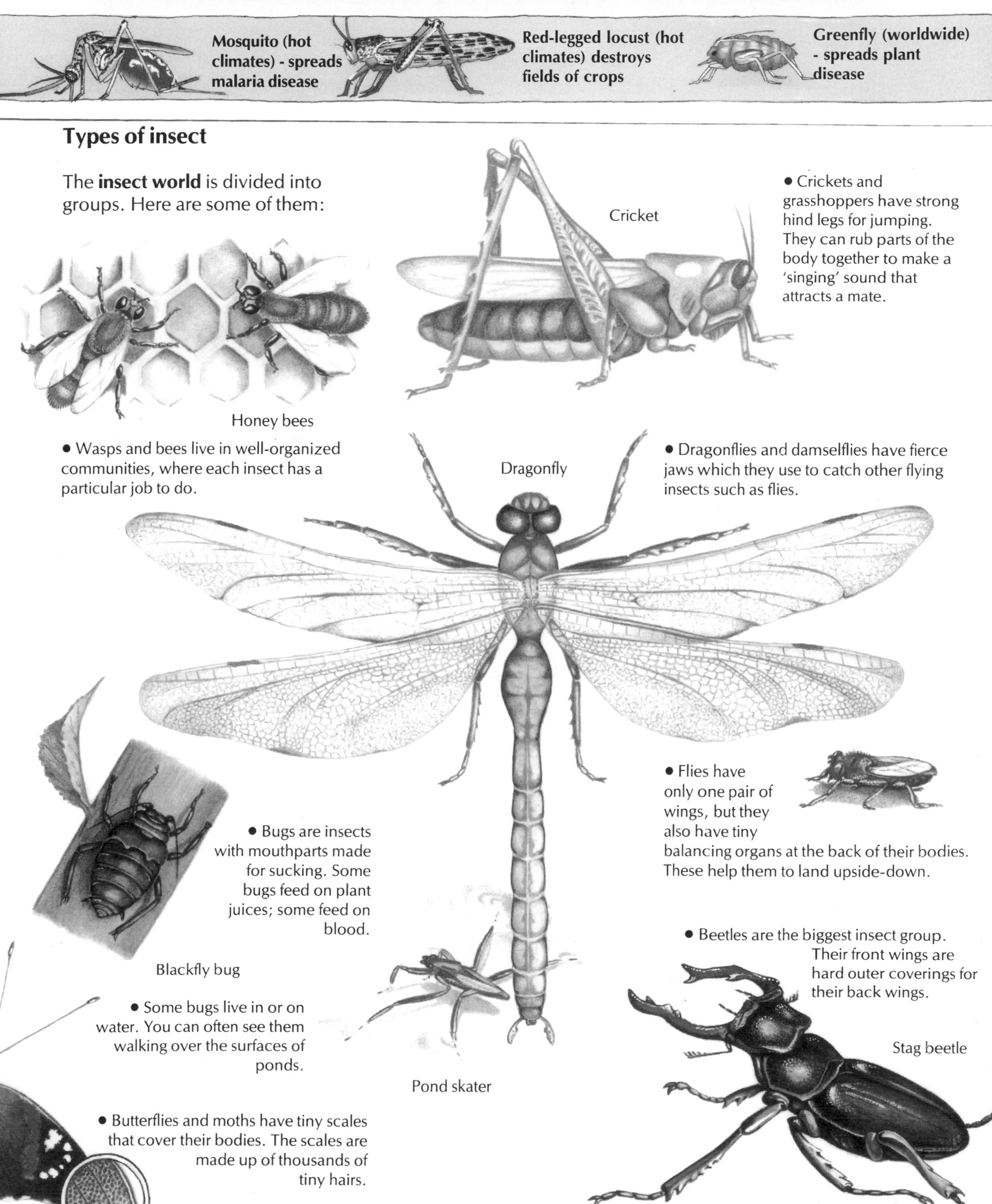

Types of insect

The **insect world** is divided into groups. Here are some of them:

- Crickets and grasshoppers have strong hind legs for jumping. They can rub parts of the body together to make a 'singing' sound that attracts a mate.

- Wasps and bees live in well-organized communities, where each insect has a particular job to do.

- Dragonflies and damselflies have fierce jaws which they use to catch other flying insects such as flies.

- Flies have only one pair of wings, but they also have tiny balancing organs at the back of their bodies. These help them to land upside-down.

- Bugs are insects with mouthparts made for sucking. Some bugs feed on plant juices; some feed on blood.

- Beetles are the biggest insect group. Their front wings are hard outer coverings for their back wings.

- Some bugs live in or on water. You can often see them walking over the surfaces of ponds.

- Butterflies and moths have tiny scales that cover their bodies. The scales are made up of thousands of tiny hairs.

Fish

Fish are used to make these products:

Glue (contains boiled-down fish bones)

Fish live in oceans, rivers, lakes and ponds. They are **cold-blooded**, which means that they cannot change their own body temperature.

There are about 20,000 different **species**, ranging from giant whale sharks about 12 metres long to dwarf gobies no bigger than a thumbnail.

Strange but true

- Pufferfish can puff their bodies up to scare away enemies.
- Salmon live in the sea, but they return to breed in the river where they were born.
- There are probably about a trillion herring in the Atlantic Ocean (a million million million).
- A female cod can lay up to 9 million eggs.

Bony fish

Most fish belong to the **bony fish** group, which means that they have **bone skeletons** inside their bodies. Many of the fish we eat are of this kind.

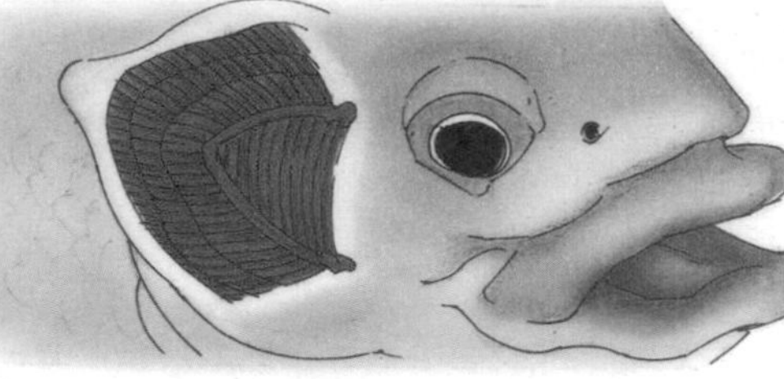

- Bony fish have a gill slit on either side of the body. The slits are covered over with flaps of skin.

- Flat fish, such as plaice and sole, are bony. They lie on one side of their bodies.

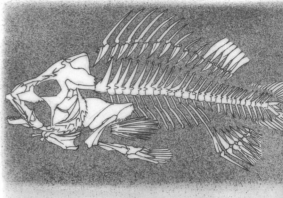

- Most bony fish have a little air-filled sac called a swim bladder inside their bodies. This bladder acts rather like water-wings; it keeps the fish floating in the water.

Fish facts

Most fish have:

- Backbones. All fish are vertebrates.
- A scaly skin, which stays moist and waterproof. Eels and lampreys are the only fish to have smooth skins.

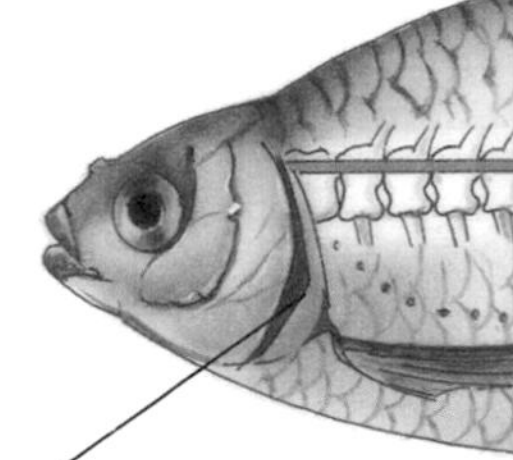

- Gills, which are underneath slits or flaps of skin on either side of the head. When a fish opens its mouth water comes in and washes over the gills. They absorb oxygen from the water and pass it into the fish's body. Waste water goes out through the slits.

Jawless fish

Lampreys and hagfish belong to the **jawless** fish group.

- Jawless fish have round sucking funnels for mouths. They have sharp teeth to hook onto their prey.
- Lampreys suck the blood of prey. Hagfish eat the flesh of their victims.

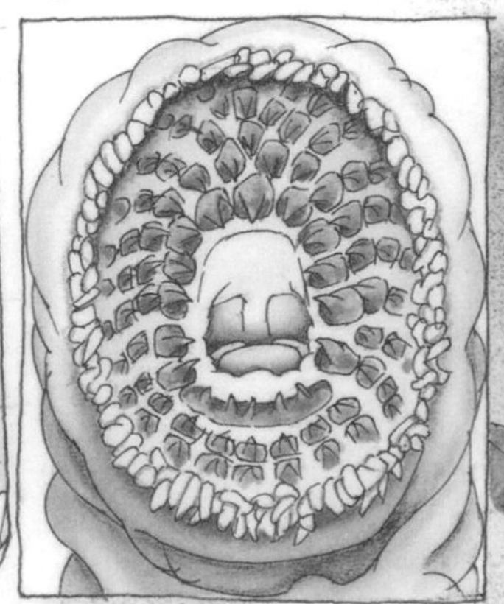

Jawless fish mouth

Lamprey

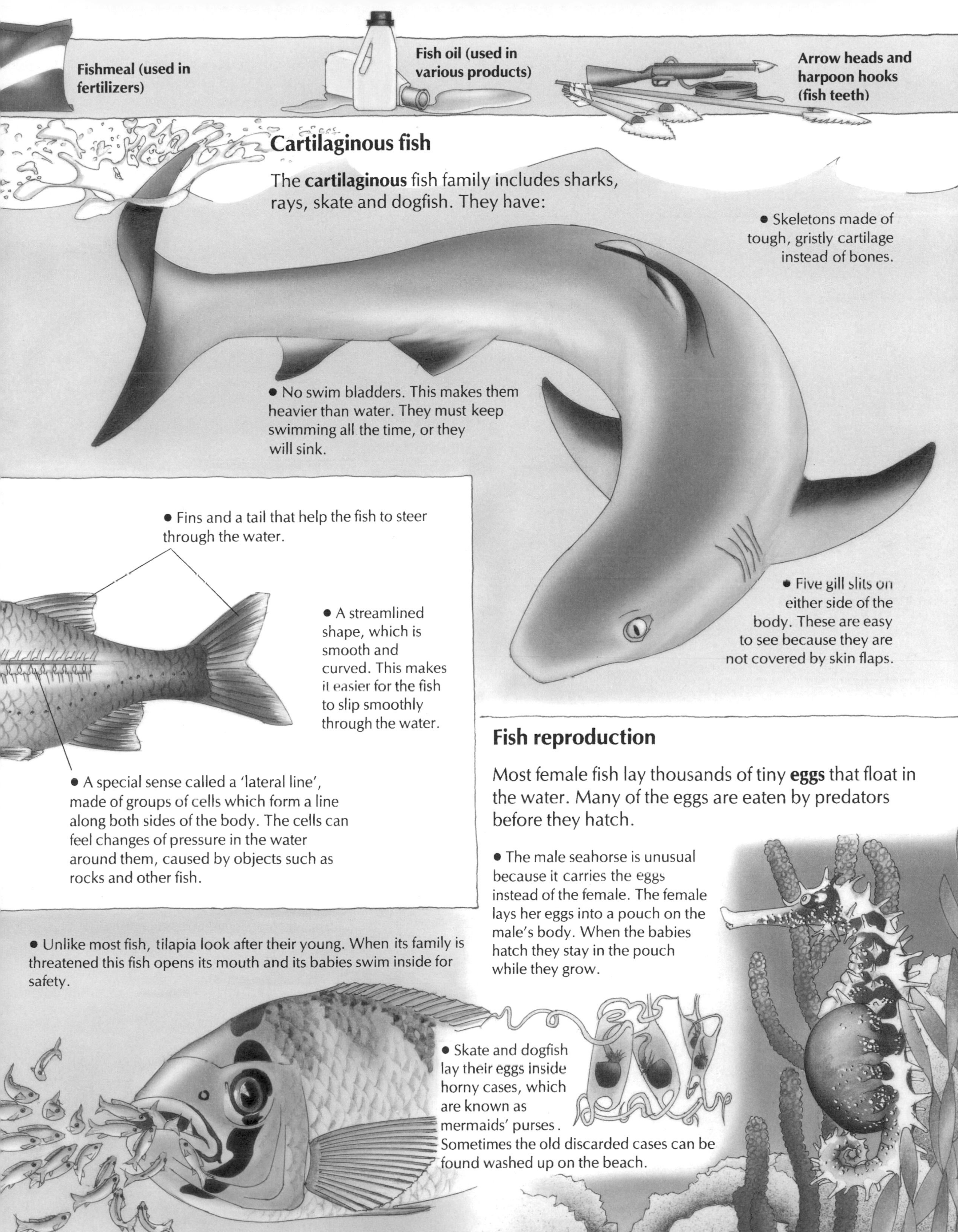

Cartilaginous fish

The **cartilaginous** fish family includes sharks, rays, skate and dogfish. They have:

- Skeletons made of tough, gristly cartilage instead of bones.
- No swim bladders. This makes them heavier than water. They must keep swimming all the time, or they will sink.
- Five gill slits on either side of the body. These are easy to see because they are not covered by skin flaps.

- Fins and a tail that help the fish to steer through the water.
- A streamlined shape, which is smooth and curved. This makes it easier for the fish to slip smoothly through the water.
- A special sense called a 'lateral line', made of groups of cells which form a line along both sides of the body. The cells can feel changes of pressure in the water around them, caused by objects such as rocks and other fish.

Fish reproduction

Most female fish lay thousands of tiny **eggs** that float in the water. Many of the eggs are eaten by predators before they hatch.

- The male seahorse is unusual because it carries the eggs instead of the female. The female lays her eggs into a pouch on the male's body. When the babies hatch they stay in the pouch while they grow.
- Unlike most fish, tilapia look after their young. When its family is threatened this fish opens its mouth and its babies swim inside for safety.
- Skate and dogfish lay their eggs inside horny cases, which are known as mermaids' purses. Sometimes the old discarded cases can be found washed up on the beach.

Reptiles and Amphibians

Here are some unusual-looking amphibians:

Mud pupp
(N. Ameri

Amphibians are a group of animals that spend part of their lives in water and part of their lives on land. **Frogs, toads, newts** and **salamanders** are all examples.

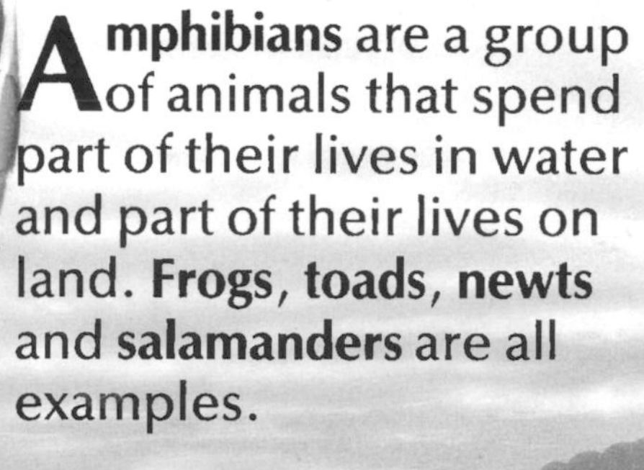

Amphibians

Reptiles live and breed mostly on land, although a few live in water. **Snakes, lizards, crocodiles** and **turtles** are all reptiles.

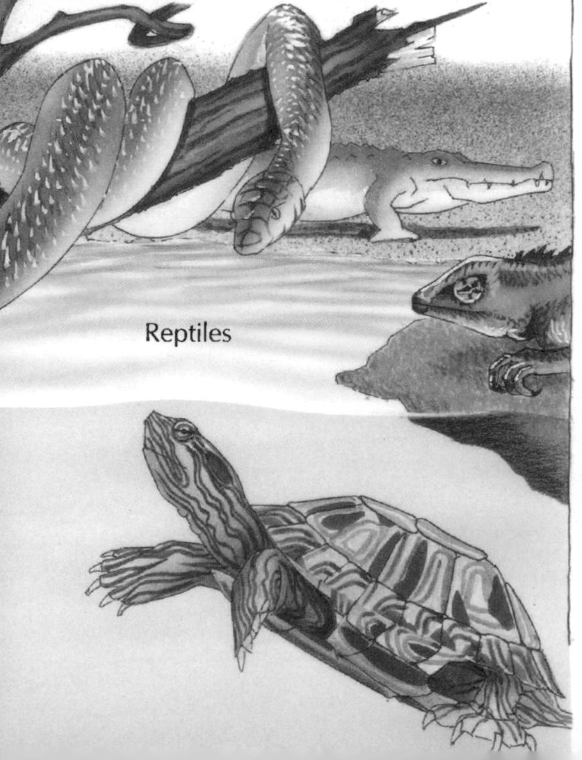
Reptiles

Amphibians

Amphibians have moist **slimy skin**. They always live near **fresh water** because they must return there in order to breed.

- There are swimming frogs, burrowing frogs, climbing frogs and even flying frogs that can glide from tree to tree.

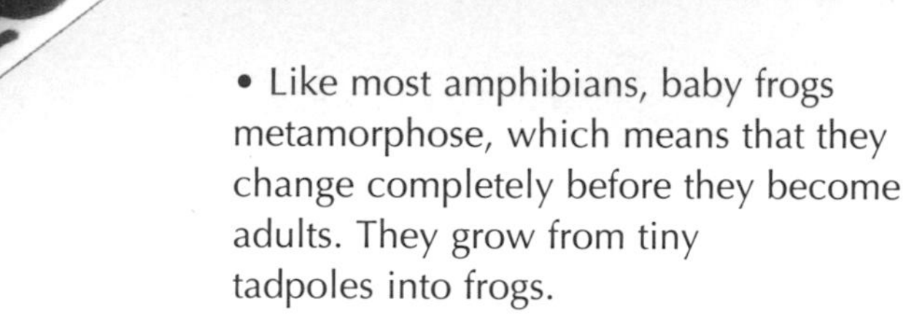

- Like most amphibians, baby frogs metamorphose, which means that they change completely before they become adults. They grow from tiny tadpoles into frogs.

Reptiles

Reptiles are **cold-blooded**, which is why they need to live in warm climates. They have scaly, **waterproof skin** and most of them lay **eggs** with tough protective shells.

Lizards are reptiles with scaly bodies and four limbs:

- Some lizards have collars of skin which they puff out to make themselves look bigger when they are excited or scared.

Frilled lizard

- The largest, heaviest lizard is the komodo dragon from Indonesia. It can grow up to 3 metres long, and is a fierce hunter.

Komodo dragon

Tortoises, **terrapins** and **turtles** are reptiles with protective shells.

- Turtles live in seawater. They only come ashore to lay their eggs.

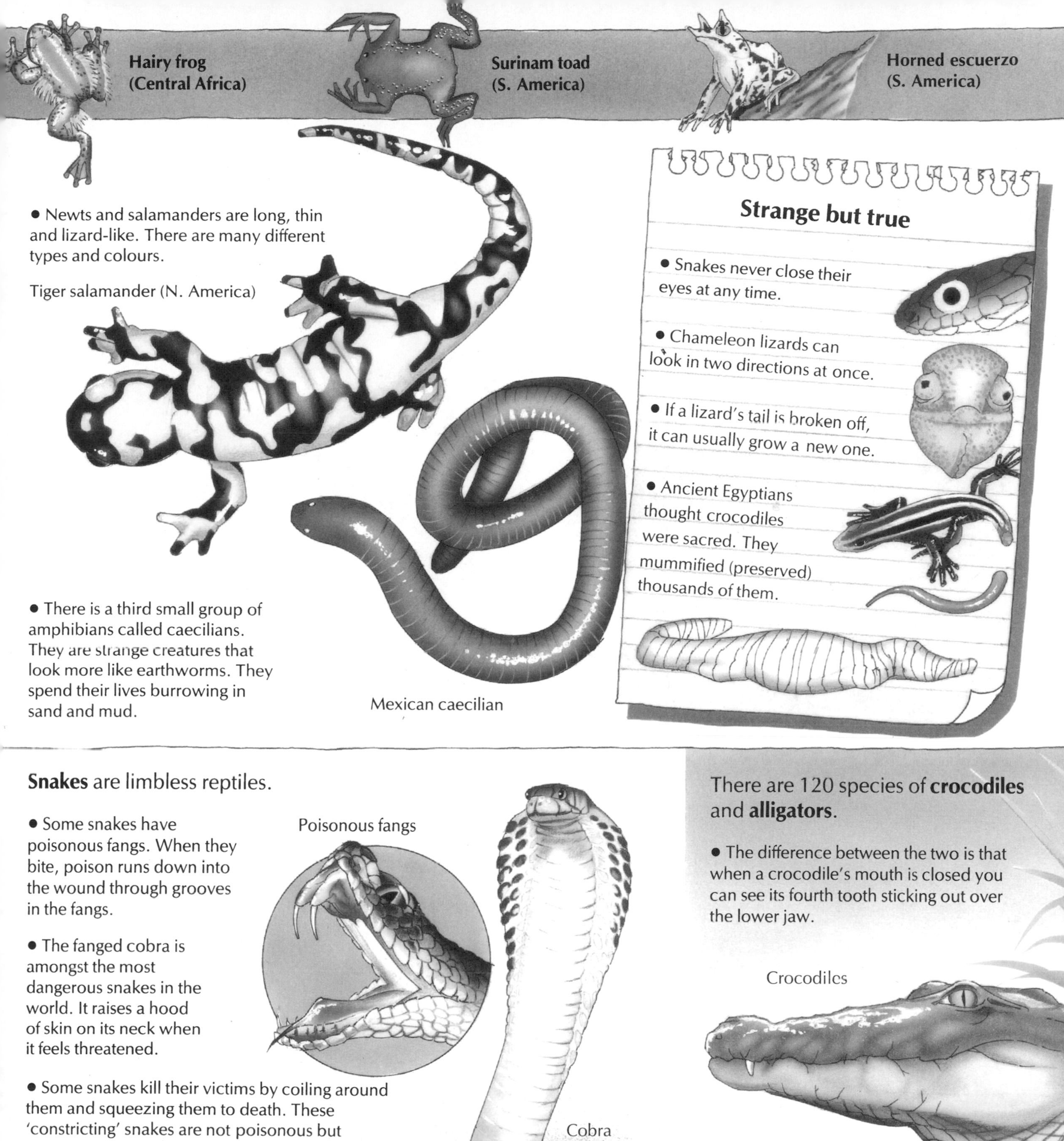

Hairy frog (Central Africa)

Surinam toad (S. America)

Horned escuerzo (S. America)

• Newts and salamanders are long, thin and lizard-like. There are many different types and colours.

Tiger salamander (N. America)

• There is a third small group of amphibians called caecilians. They are strange creatures that look more like earthworms. They spend their lives burrowing in sand and mud.

Mexican caecilian

Strange but true

• Snakes never close their eyes at any time.

• Chameleon lizards can look in two directions at once.

• If a lizard's tail is broken off, it can usually grow a new one.

• Ancient Egyptians thought crocodiles were sacred. They mummified (preserved) thousands of them.

Snakes are limbless reptiles.

• Some snakes have poisonous fangs. When they bite, poison runs down into the wound through grooves in the fangs.

• The fanged cobra is amongst the most dangerous snakes in the world. It raises a hood of skin on its neck when it feels threatened.

• Some snakes kill their victims by coiling around them and squeezing them to death. These 'constricting' snakes are not poisonous but they are often very large. The anaconda and python are examples.

Poisonous fangs

Cobra

There are 120 species of **crocodiles** and **alligators**.

• The difference between the two is that when a crocodile's mouth is closed you can see its fourth tooth sticking out over the lower jaw.

Crocodiles

Birds

These birds have beaks that are shaped to help them catch and eat their food:

Peregrine falcon – sharply curved beak for killing prey

Birds are **warm-blooded** animals with **internal skeletons**. They all have **wings** and **feathers**, although not all birds can fly. There is a wide variety of birds. They live in many different habitats all over the world, from icy polar lands to hot tropical rainforests. Some birds live alone or in small groups. Others live in **colonies** numbering many thousands.

Bird facts

Most birds have bodies designed for flight. All **flying birds** have these physical features:

- A light, waterproof covering of feathers over most of the body. They help birds to fly and also keep body heat in, so the bird stays warm.
- A streamlined body shape. This helps birds to travel smoothly through the air by cutting down air resistance.
- Two wings covered with extra-strong flight feathers. The wings help to raise the bird into the air and the bird keeps itself aloft by flapping them.
- A horny pointed beak for feeding. Different birds have differently shaped beaks.
- Lightweight, partly hollow internal bones.
- Scaly legs and feet with three or four toes and sharp claws.

Strange but true

- The earliest known bird, called Archaeopteryx, lived 150 million years ago. Unlike modern birds it had teeth.
- Swifts spend almost all their lives in the air. They only land to breed.
- Flamingoes are pink because their bodies take on the pink colour of the shrimps they eat.
- The Andean sword-billed hummingbird has a beak longer than its body.

Eggs and nests

Bird species breed at certain times of the year, when the weather is mild and there is a good supply of food.

- Some male birds use complicated dances, special songs, or displays to attract females. For instance, the male peacock shows off its bright tail feathers to interest a mate.

Peacock male

- Eggs vary in colour and shape. For instance, some are speckled so that they are difficult to spot when they are lying in a nest.

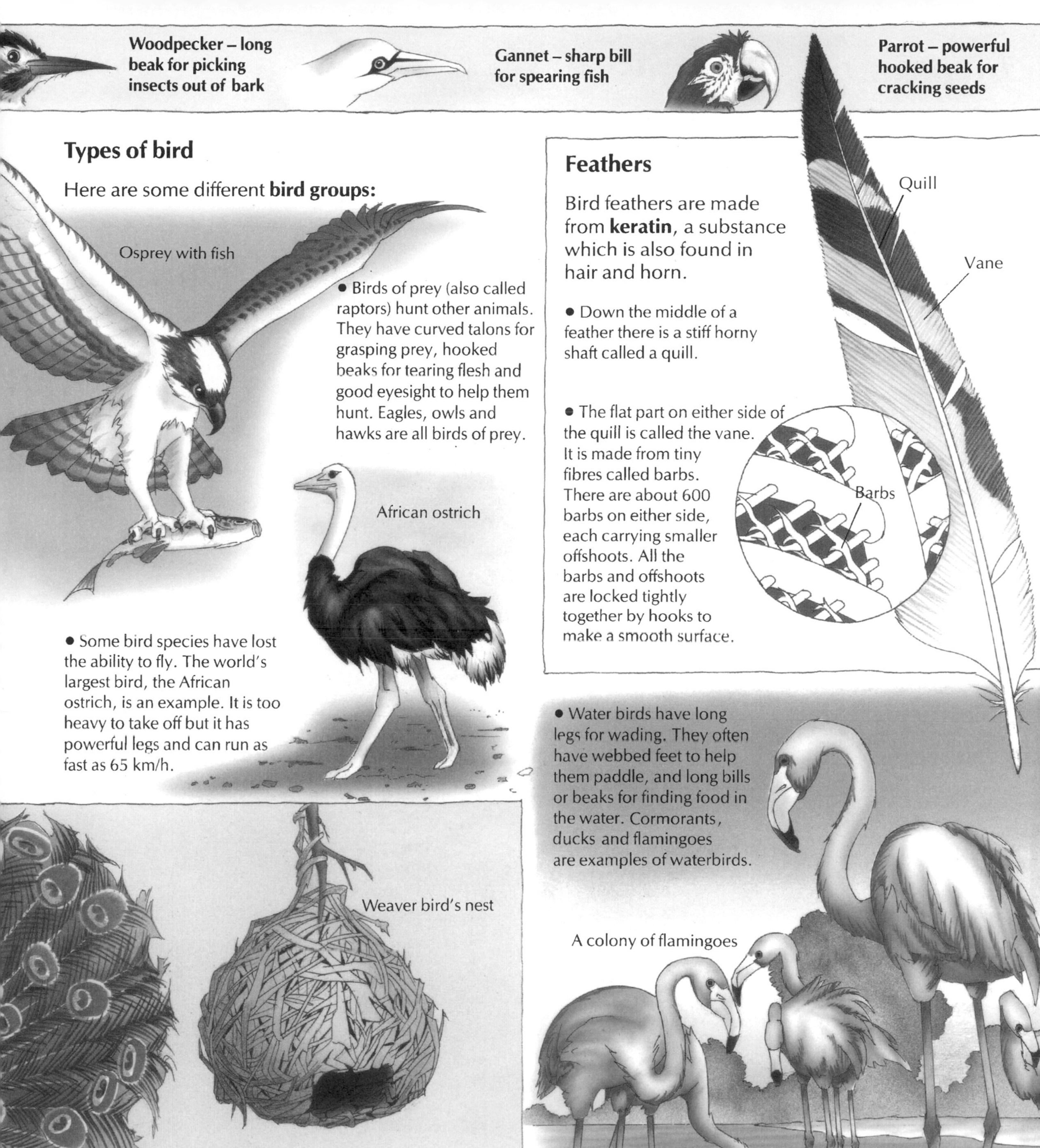

Types of bird

Here are some different **bird groups:**

• Birds of prey (also called raptors) hunt other animals. They have curved talons for grasping prey, hooked beaks for tearing flesh and good eyesight to help them hunt. Eagles, owls and hawks are all birds of prey.

• Some bird species have lost the ability to fly. The world's largest bird, the African ostrich, is an example. It is too heavy to take off but it has powerful legs and can run as fast as 65 km/h.

Feathers

Bird feathers are made from **keratin**, a substance which is also found in hair and horn.

• Down the middle of a feather there is a stiff horny shaft called a quill.

• The flat part on either side of the quill is called the vane. It is made from tiny fibres called barbs. There are about 600 barbs on either side, each carrying smaller offshoots. All the barbs and offshoots are locked tightly together by hooks to make a smooth surface.

• Water birds have long legs for wading. They often have webbed feet to help them paddle, and long bills or beaks for finding food in the water. Cormorants, ducks and flamingoes are examples of waterbirds.

• Most birds build nests where they lay eggs and hatch young. One of the most complicated examples is the carefully woven bell-shaped nest of the weaver bird, found in Africa and Australia.

Grassland Animals

Grasslands can support lots of animals because they eat different foods:

Wildebeest eat short grass

Grasslands are wide, open areas where grasses and shrubs grow.

Temperate grasslands are found in cool parts of the world in the middle of large land masses, where rainfall is low. These areas are often used for cattle.

Tropical grassland is found mainly in Africa and South America. In Africa it is called **savanna**, and in South America it is called **pampas**. Here rain falls only in summer.

Tropical grassland provides a home for many wild animals.

Plant-eating animals

Most grassland animals are **grazers**, eating grass and other plants. Grazers live together in **herds**, for safety. They move about looking for fresh pastures and water pools. Here are some examples of plant-eaters on the **African savanna**:

- Antelope live in most tropical grassland areas. Species include oryx, eland and gazelles. Although they are only 60 cm tall, gazelles can run at 90 km/h to escape danger.

- The African savanna has shrubs and trees as well as grass. These provide food for giraffes, elephants and rhinos.

- Zebras move in large herds, often accompanied by wildebeest. While some zebras graze, others stay on the lookout for lions, their main enemy. Zebras can hear and smell better than most other grazing creatures.

Strange but true

- Elephants spend 23 hours a day eating.
- Some antelope can leap 3 metres in the air from a standing start.
- Vultures sometimes eat so much they can't take off again.
- No two zebras have exactly the same pattern of stripes. Like human fingerprints, each zebra pattern is unique.

Zebras prefer taller grasses

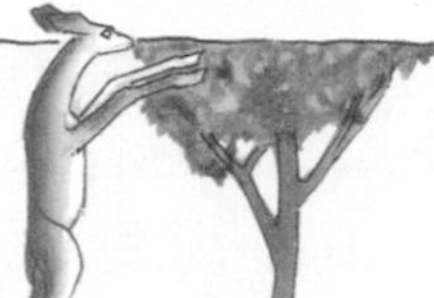

Some antelope stand on their hind legs to reach low tree branches

Giraffes and elephants eat the tops of trees

Meat-eaters

The main threat to the grassland plant-eaters are **meat-eaters** such as lions, leopards and hunting dogs.

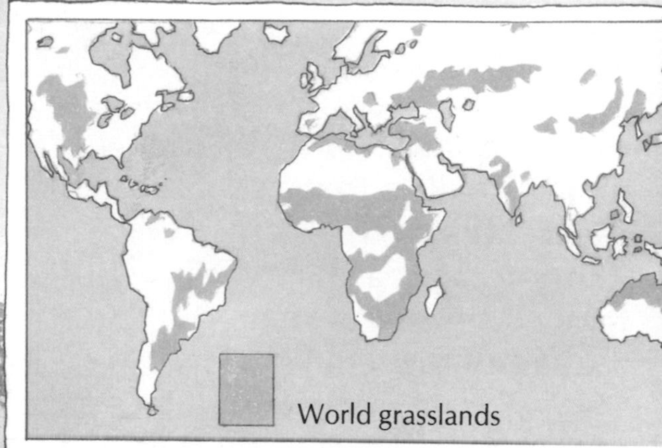

- Lions live in groups called prides. They hunt and kill only when they are hungry. Antelope and zebras are their favourite food.
- African hunting dogs live in large, well-organized packs. They hunt together, separating weak or young animals from herds.

Scavengers

Scavengers are creatures who eat the leftovers from dead animal carcasses. When the grassland hunters have finished with their prey, the scavengers move in to pick the bones clean.

- Vultures are large birds found in many grassland areas of the world. They use their keen eyesight to spot dead animals far below them.
- Hyenas usually eat the remains of another animal's kill, but they will hunt if food is scarce. Their 'chuckling' hunting cry sounds rather like a human laugh.
- Although vultures and hyenas have a bad reputation, they provide a useful 'garbage disposal' service, because if carcasses are left to rot they attract flies and disease.

Rainforest Animals

Here are some of the rarest, most endangered rainforest animals:

Rainforests are hot, steamy jungles that grow in areas on either side of the Equator – an imaginary line that circles the middle of the Earth. Rainforest areas have **high temperatures** and **heavy rainfall** all the year round. They are the richest animal and plant habitats in the world.

Equator

Rainforest area

Strange but true

- The African jungle okapi's tongue is so long, it can be used to lick the creature's eyes.
- The African giant snail grows up to 39 cm long.
- The strongest-known animal poison comes from the arrow-poison frog.
- The Amazon 'Jesus Christ lizard' can run across water.

Rainforest birds

Many **birds** make their home in the rainforest trees.

- Each forest region has its own giant eagle species. These birds build huge twig platforms on top of the highest trees.

Hornbill

Toucan

Macaw

- Brightly-coloured macaws, hornbills and toucans make their nests in holes in tree trunks.
- There are lots of different hummingbird species in the Amazon region. They hover by flowers, drinking the sweet nectar with their long beaks. They beat their wings between 50 and 80 times a minute.

Hummingbird

Rainforest insects

There are many, many thousands of different insect species in the rainforests.

- Ants can be found everywhere in the rainforests. Huge columns of fierce army ants travel through the forest areas of Central America, destroying everything in their path.
- Giant butterflies flit amongst the trees. Many of them are brightly-coloured. This is a signal that they taste horrible.

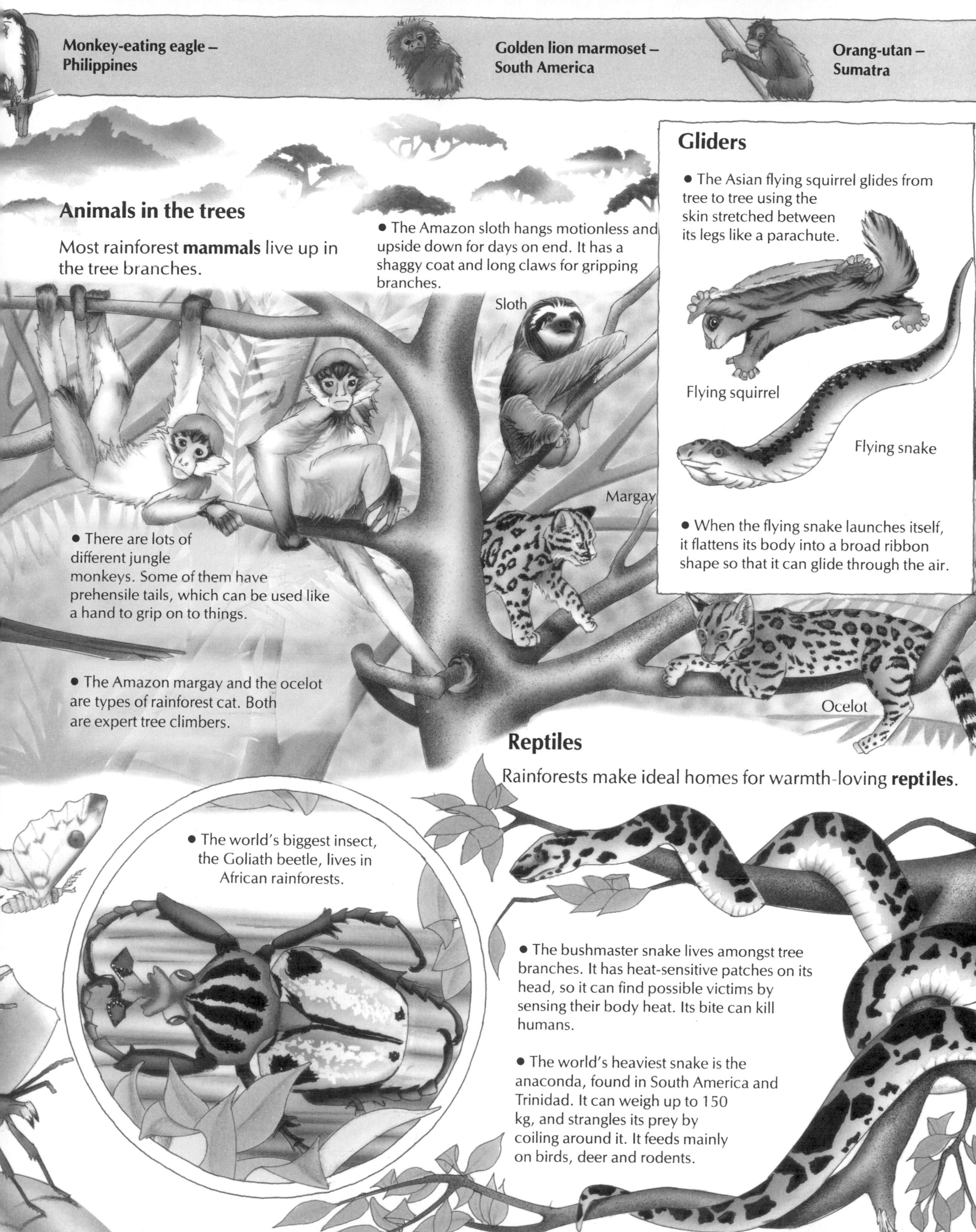

Animals in the trees

Most rainforest **mammals** live up in the tree branches.

- The Amazon sloth hangs motionless and upside down for days on end. It has a shaggy coat and long claws for gripping branches.

- There are lots of different jungle monkeys. Some of them have prehensile tails, which can be used like a hand to grip on to things.

- The Amazon margay and the ocelot are types of rainforest cat. Both are expert tree climbers.

Gliders

- The Asian flying squirrel glides from tree to tree using the skin stretched between its legs like a parachute.

- When the flying snake launches itself, it flattens its body into a broad ribbon shape so that it can glide through the air.

- The world's biggest insect, the Goliath beetle, lives in African rainforests.

Reptiles

Rainforests make ideal homes for warmth-loving **reptiles**.

- The bushmaster snake lives amongst tree branches. It has heat-sensitive patches on its head, so it can find possible victims by sensing their body heat. Its bite can kill humans.

- The world's heaviest snake is the anaconda, found in South America and Trinidad. It can weigh up to 150 kg, and strangles its prey by coiling around it. It feeds mainly on birds, deer and rodents.

Desert Animals

Here are some desert animals with special body adaptations or behaviour:

Ground squirrel (Africa): uses its tail as a sunshade

About one eighth of the Earth's surface is **desert**. A desert is an area where less than 25 cm of rain falls on average each year.

Some deserts are very cold in winter. Others are hot all the year round, with high temperatures during the day and cooler temperatures at night.

Most desert animals tend to come out at night, staying out of the daytime heat by sheltering under rocks or in their underground burrows.

The major problem of desert survival is **lack of water**. Many animals are cleverly adapted to cope with the drought.

Snakes and lizards

Snakes and **Lizards** are cold-blooded and need the Sun's heat in order to survive. Deserts are ideal homes for them.

- There are many different kinds of American rattlesnake, most of them highly poisonous. When a rattlesnake is angry, it makes a warning rattle by shaking scales positioned on the end of its tail.

Rattlesnake

- Sidewinder snakes have developed an efficient way of travelling over soft sand. They use their bodies to lever themselves along, leaving trails of wavy lines behind them on the sand.

Sidewinder snake

Amphibians

- The American spadefoot toad burrows underground during hot weather. It can stay buried for up to 11 months because its waterproof coat keeps moisture in its body. When rain arrives, the toads come out to breed.

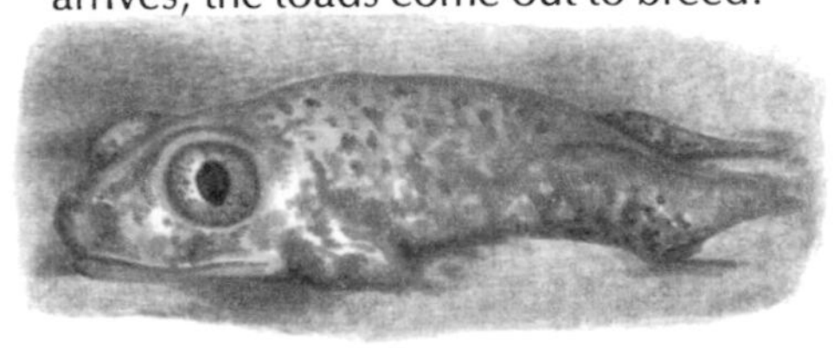

Strange but true

- Crocodile tracks have been found in the middle of the Sahara Desert.

- Prehistoric rock paintings in the Sahara show giraffes, antelope and elephants. None of these animals live in the region today.

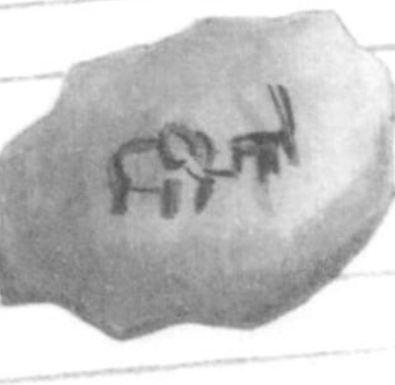

- Australian farmers once called in the army to wage an 'emu war' on Outback desert emus who came on to farms and destroyed crops.

Insects and spiders

There are many different **desert insects** and **spiders**.

- When it rains, the eggs of bugs, beetles and butterflies hatch, after lying dormant for many months.

- A Namib Desert darkling beetle collects water from sea fog that rolls in from the nearby Atlantic. The fog condenses on the beetle's body and runs into its mouth.

- Most desert spiders are hunters. They do not use webs to trap prey. Instead they search for creatures to attack.

Darkling beetle

Red-kneed tarantula (Mexico)

Bighorn sheep (USA): can store water in its stomach

Desert tortoise (USA): keeps cool by licking its head and neck

Moloch lizard (Australia): can condense water from the air onto its skin

Desert mammals

Desert mammals usually stay out of the daytime heat, in order to conserve water. Many of the smaller mammals never drink, getting all the moisture they need from seeds, shoots, or other creatures.

- The Saharan fennec fox has especially big ears that help to keep it cool. Blood vessels run near the skin surface of the ears, giving off heat as air blows across them.

Saharan fennec fox

Kangaroo rat

- The most common desert mammals are rodents. The kangaroo rat is an example. It stores plant seeds deep in its burrow, leaving them to collect moisture from the soil. This way, the rat gets a ready supply of water.

- Camels can survive for many days without regular water or food. They have wide, hairy feet to stop them sinking in the sand, and their nostrils can close up to keep out dust.

One-humped dromedary

Desert birds

Most **desert birds** shelter from the daytime heat beneath rocks or plants.

- The saguaro cactus is found in the Sonoran desert in south-west USA. It can grow up to 15 metres high, and provides a home for several desert birds. Gila woodpeckers peck out nest holes in the rubbery cactus flesh. Tiny elf owls nest in vacant holes and cactus wrens nest in forks.

- The emu is found in Australian desert regions. It is the world's second largest bird (after the ostrich). It grows up to 1.7 metres high, and although it cannot fly it can run up to 64 km/h over short distances.

- Roadrunners are found in Mexico and Arizona. They are famous for their speed. They can run up to 37 km/h to catch snakes and lizards.

Gila woodpecker

Cactus wren

Elf owl

Roadrunner

Northern Forest Animals

Here are some small creatures to be found on the forest floor:

In northern parts of the world there are areas of cool forest which provide a home for all sorts of different creatures.

There are two types of cool forest. In warmer areas the trees are mainly deciduous, which means they shed their leaves in winter. In cold areas the trees are mainly coniferous, which means they have long-lasting needles instead of leaves.

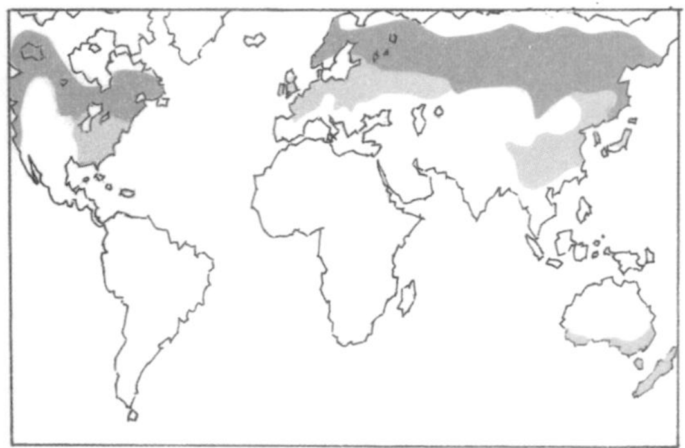

Coniferous forest

Deciduous forest

Many forest creatures are very shy and will hide if they hear strange noises. A good time to spot forest wildlife is at dusk or very early in the morning, when the animals tend to feed.

Deciduous woods

Deciduous trees have widely-spread branches. The gaps between their leaves allow plenty of sunlight through to the forest floor, where lots of plants grow and provide food for animals.

• Foxes live in burrows called 'earths'. They survive well in the forest because they will eat most things and they have very few enemies. During the daytime they lie low. During the night they hunt for birds, rodents and rabbits.

• The wood mouse is one of the most common forest rodents. It has long front teeth for gnawing through wood and nutshells.

Coniferous forests

Trees in coniferous forests are densely packed together. Very little light penetrates to the poor soil beneath, so there are few small plants. There is less animal life than in deciduous forests because there is less to eat.

• Martens have long bodies and short legs. There are several different species, including the pine marten.

Pine marten

• Red deer are common in northern forests. Male deer (stags) have long antlers covered in soft velvet. Each year the antlers drop off and a new pair grows.

• Lots of different insect-eating birds find food amongst the trees.

• Badgers are timid night time creatures. They can see well in the dark and have a strong sense of smell, so it is difficult to watch them without disturbing them.

• Caterpillars and insects feed off the tree leaves, while bark beetles bore into the trunks.

• Wild rabbits live in large groups in complicated tunnel networks called 'warrens'.

• Woodpeckers have strong beaks for drilling nest holes in tree trunks. They can sometimes be heard hammering on wood.

• A squirrel can leap 4 or 5 metres from branch to branch quite effortlessly, using its powerful hind legs to launch itself into the air. It uses its outstretched tail like a rudder, to steer its flight.

Strange but true

• The woodpecker has an extra-strong shock-resistant skull.

• Wood ants squirt powerful formic acid at their enemies.

• Male stags must not be approached when they call during the mating season, as they are liable to attack anyone nearby, mistaking them for a rival.

• Squirrels sometimes wrap their bushy tails around themselves to keep warm.

Mountain Animals

Here are some mountain animals from around the world:

Chinchilla (S. America)

Some animals are adapted to survive the harsh weather conditions often found in **mountains.**

The higher you go, the colder and wetter the climate becomes. Mountain animals tend to have **thick furry coats** or **extra layers of fat** to keep them warm.

Rocky Mountain goat

Mountain animals

• Yaks have long, thick coats to keep them warm in the Himalayan Mountains in Tibet. Sometimes they graze at heights above 4500 metres, making them the highest-living land animals.

Yak

• Llamas and vicuna belong to the camel family. They are farmed for wool and meat by the Quechua Indians high up in the Andean mountains of South America.

Llama

• The spectacled bear lives in the Andes Mountains. It gets its name from round facial markings.

Spectacled bear

• The Apollo butterfly lives high up in mountainous regions across the world. Spiders are found high up, too. However, it is usually too cold for reptiles and amphibians to survive.

Apollo butterfly

• Cougars (also called pumas or panthers) live in the mountain forests of America. They are very strong, powerful animals and can travel hundreds of kilometres a week in search of food.

Cougar

• Rocky Mountain goats are experts at climbing steep rocks. They have hoof pads which give them extra grip and allow them to climb up almost vertical surfaces. Their toes are shaped like pincers to help them get a firm footing.

• The chamois goat can climb very quickly. It has been known to climb over 1000 metres in 15 minutes.

Chamois

Strange but true

• The cougar can jump as high as 5 metres from a standing position.

• High in the mountains the level of oxygen in the air gets less, so some animals have larger hearts and lungs than normal, to compensate.

• A griffon vulture once crashed into an aircraft at the amazing height of 10,800 metres above ground level.

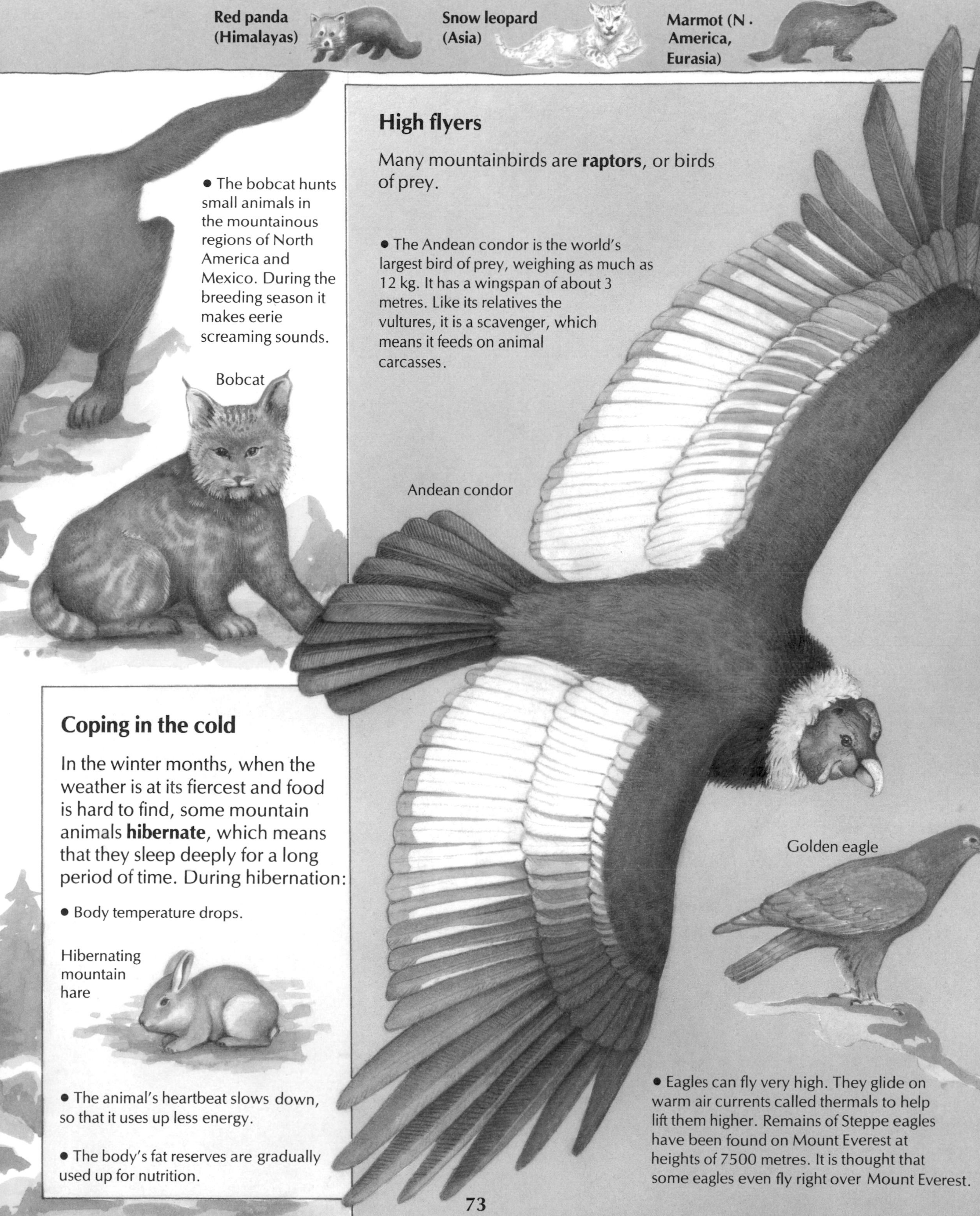

High flyers

Many mountainbirds are **raptors**, or birds of prey.

• The bobcat hunts small animals in the mountainous regions of North America and Mexico. During the breeding season it makes eerie screaming sounds.

• The Andean condor is the world's largest bird of prey, weighing as much as 12 kg. It has a wingspan of about 3 metres. Like its relatives the vultures, it is a scavenger, which means it feeds on animal carcasses.

Coping in the cold

In the winter months, when the weather is at its fiercest and food is hard to find, some mountain animals **hibernate**, which means that they sleep deeply for a long period of time. During hibernation:

• Body temperature drops.

• The animal's heartbeat slows down, so that it uses up less energy.

• The body's fat reserves are gradually used up for nutrition.

• Eagles can fly very high. They glide on warm air currents called thermals to help lift them higher. Remains of Steppe eagles have been found on Mount Everest at heights of 7500 metres. It is thought that some eagles even fly right over Mount Everest.

Polar Animals

Here are some adaptations that polar animals have for living in the cold:

Arctic wolverine – two layers of fur

At the far south of the Earth there is a large area of land called **Antarctica**. It is always frozen over with ice.

Most Antarctic animals are **seabirds** and **ocean creatures** such as seals and fish.

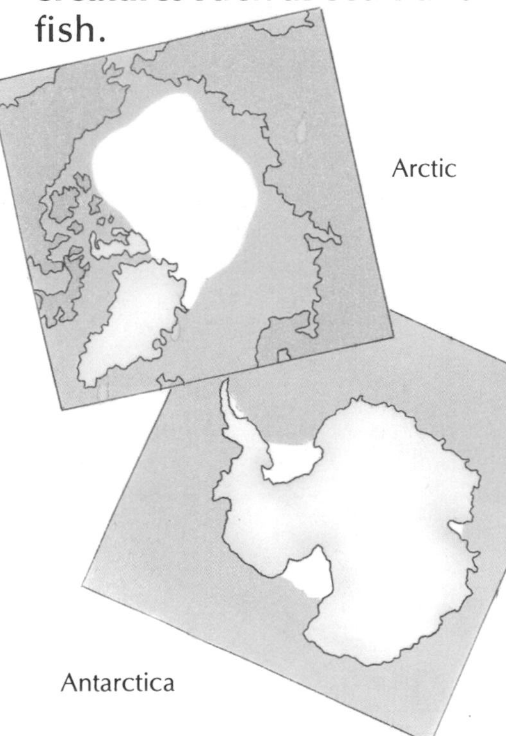

The **Arctic** is the area at the far north of the Earth. The Arctic Ocean is in the middle, covered by a huge floating sheet of ice.

Within the Arctic Circle there is barren land called **tundra**, where most of the Arctic animals live.

Arctic tundra animals

Most animals only come to the Arctic tundra during the short **summer months** and **migrate south** when winter comes. A few species brave the winter blizzards. Some of them burrow underground to wait for warmer temperatures in spring.

- Musk oxen are gentle creatures with warm, shaggy coats. They live in family groups which wander the tundra grazing on grasses. They stay on the tundra in winter.

Musk oxen

- In summer, big herds of caribou (also called reindeer) travel up to the tundra from North America and Scandinavia.

Caribou

- Lemmings are the commonest small tundra animals. They are part of the rodent family. They live in underground burrows during winter and come up to the surface to feed in summer.

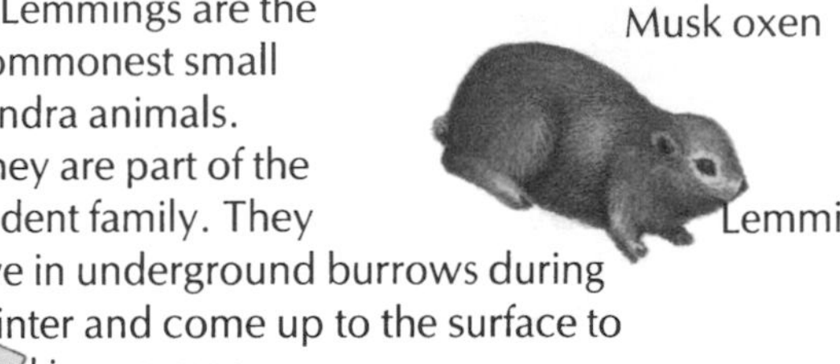

Lemmings

- Polar bears are the fiercest Arctic animals. They stay all year round, hunting for seals. They can swim and dive well and they can sniff the scent of prey from several kilometres away. Male polar bears spend most of the time on their own. Female bears look after their cubs for a year or so.

Polar bears

Arctic whales

- Bowheads are baleen whales. Instead of teeth they have curtains of bony strips. As a whale swims along, the strips sieve the water, collecting tiny shrimp-like krill to eat.

- The beluga is a toothed whale, so it doesn't rely on krill for its food. It feeds on fish at the floe-edge, which is the place where the Arctic pack-ice meets the sea.

Bowhead

Narwhal

- Male narwhals grow long spiralling tusks. They are sometimes nicknamed sea-unicorns.

Beluga

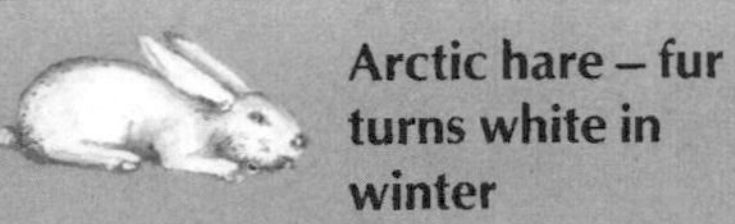

Arctic hare – fur turns white in winter

Seals – lots of fat to keep the cold out

Arctic fox – small body to limit heat loss

Arctic birds

Lots of **seabirds** migrate to the Arctic in summer.

- More than half a million seabird pairs nest in summer on the cliffs of Prince Leopold Island, in the Canadian Arctic.

Seabird

Antarctic animals

Since most of the Antarctic is covered in ice, there are very few land animals. But the oceans are rich in **fish**, **squid** and **krill**, providing plenty of food for other sea creatures. In the Antarctic Ocean region there are:

- Fish that produce a natural kind of anti-freeze to protect themselves from the extremely cold temperatures underwater.

Antarctic fish

- Seven different types of Antarctic seal. They swim under the ice and saw through it with their teeth to make breathing holes that go up to the surface.

Crabeater seal

- Blue whales, the world's biggest, heaviest living creatures. They can grow up to 30 metres long. They feed through baleen plates.

- Very few inland animals. The only ones are flies, mites, lice, fleas and tiny microbes. Mites are the most southerly-living animals on Earth.

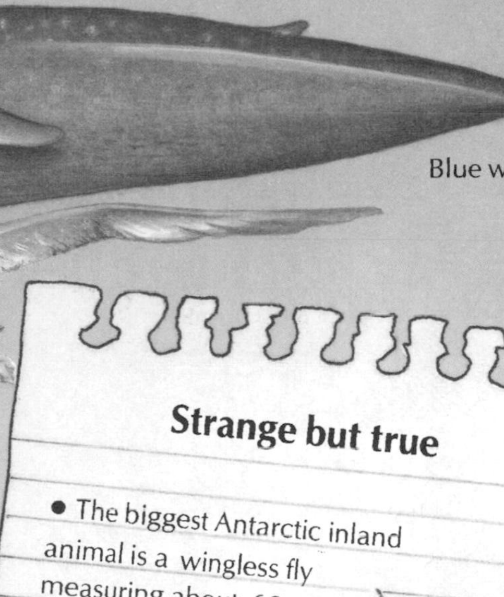

Blue whale

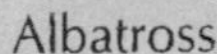

Albatross

- Giant albatross seabirds, which come to the Antarctic coast to breed. They can live for up to 70 or 80 years.

- Several different types of penguin. The biggest one is the emperor penguin, which breeds in large colonies.

Emperor penguin with chick

Strange but true

- The biggest Antarctic inland animal is a wingless fly measuring about 60 mm long.

- Antarctic squid can grow up to 20 metres long. Many of them are cannibals – they attack and eat other squid.

Arctic seals

Seals sit on the Arctic ice-floes or swim in the ocean looking for fish to eat.

Ringed seal

Bearded seal

Undersea Animals

These fish are poisonous:

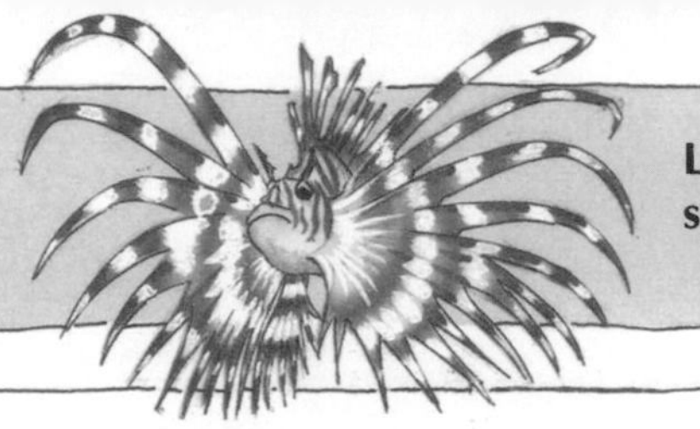

Lionfish: poisonous spines

The **oceans** provide one of the largest wildlife habitats in the world. They cover about 70 per cent of the Earth's surface, and animals live in almost every part.

Ocean wildlife communities vary depending on the temperature and depth of the sea. Animals that live near the water surface are quite different from those that live deeper down.

Coral reefs and seaweed forests provide specialized habitats for particular kinds of creatures.

Ocean food

Ocean creatures have their own **food chain**:

- The food chain begins with tiny floating plants called phytoplankton. They float around in the seawater, near the surface. They are eaten by microscopic floating creatures called zooplankton.

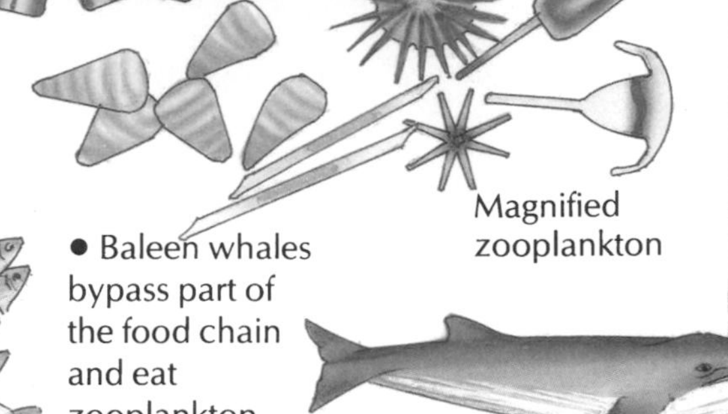

Magnified zooplankton

- The zooplankton are eaten by small fish, which often travel around in groups called shoals.

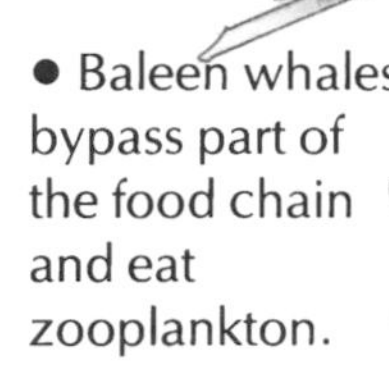

- Baleen whales bypass part of the food chain and eat zooplankton.
- The small fish are eaten in their turn by larger fish, such as tuna.
- Some of the larger fish are eaten by humans.

Coral reefs

Coral reefs are made up of many thousands of individual animals called **polyps**. There are two kinds of corals: **hard** and **soft**.

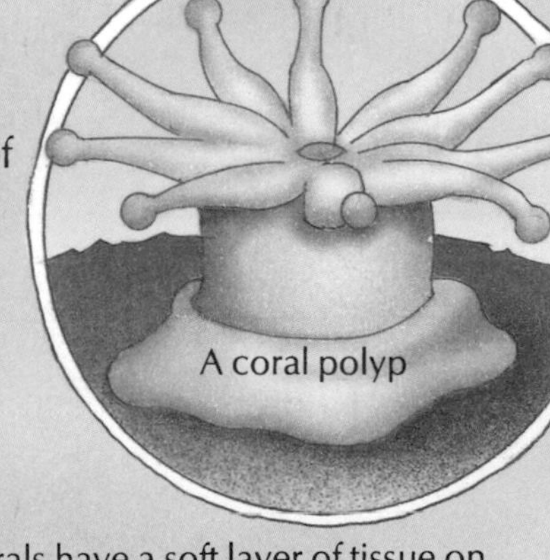

A coral polyp

- A coral polyp is a cylinder-shaped animal with a ring of tentacles. It takes calcium carbonate from the water and makes it into limestone.
- Hard corals build up a hard wall of limestone around themselves. As the polyps grow and increase, a reef grows.
- Soft corals have a soft layer of tissue on the outside of a central rod.

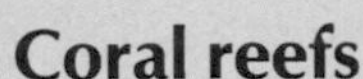

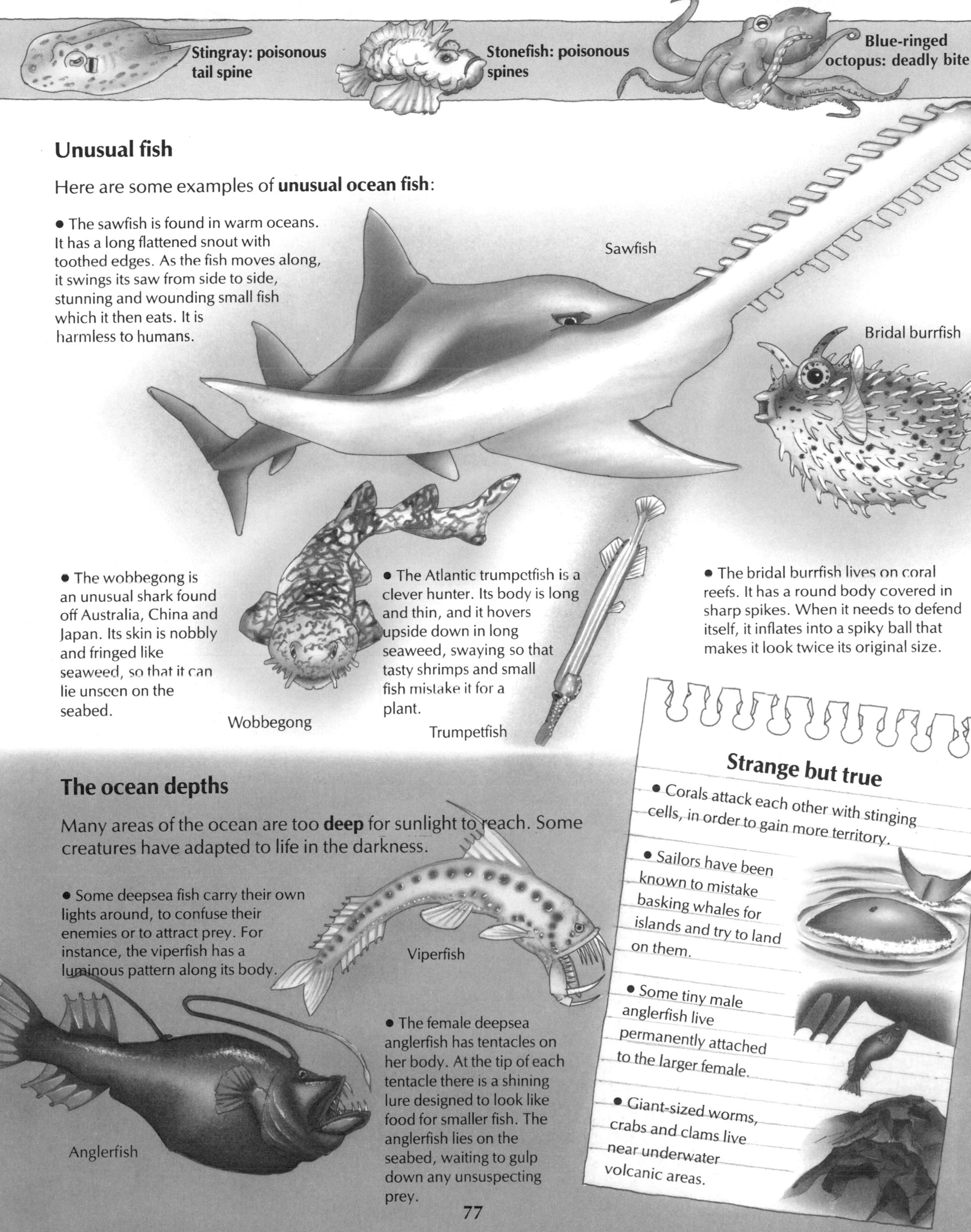

Unusual fish

Here are some examples of **unusual ocean fish**:

- The sawfish is found in warm oceans. It has a long flattened snout with toothed edges. As the fish moves along, it swings its saw from side to side, stunning and wounding small fish which it then eats. It is harmless to humans.

- The wobbegong is an unusual shark found off Australia, China and Japan. Its skin is nobbly and fringed like seaweed, so that it can lie unseen on the seabed.

- The Atlantic trumpetfish is a clever hunter. Its body is long and thin, and it hovers upside down in long seaweed, swaying so that tasty shrimps and small fish mistake it for a plant.

- The bridal burrfish lives on coral reefs. It has a round body covered in sharp spikes. When it needs to defend itself, it inflates into a spiky ball that makes it look twice its original size.

The ocean depths

Many areas of the ocean are too **deep** for sunlight to reach. Some creatures have adapted to life in the darkness.

- Some deepsea fish carry their own lights around, to confuse their enemies or to attract prey. For instance, the viperfish has a luminous pattern along its body.

- The female deepsea anglerfish has tentacles on her body. At the tip of each tentacle there is a shining lure designed to look like food for smaller fish. The anglerfish lies on the seabed, waiting to gulp down any unsuspecting prey.

Strange but true

- Corals attack each other with stinging cells, in order to gain more territory.
- Sailors have been known to mistake basking whales for islands and try to land on them.
- Some tiny male anglerfish live permanently attached to the larger female.
- Giant-sized worms, crabs and clams live near underwater volcanic areas.

Wildlife in the Home

In some parts of the world there are harmful house guests:

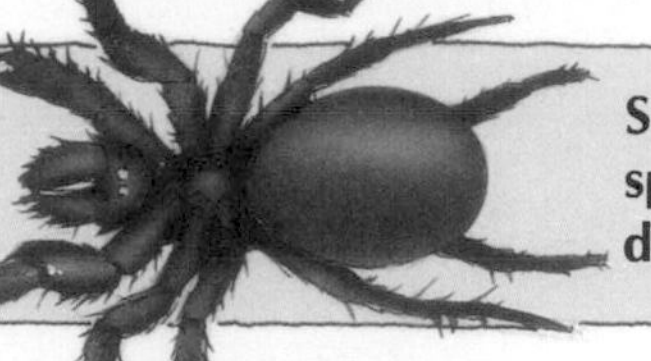

Sydney funnelweb spider (Australia): deadly bite

You may not realize it, but you could be sharing your house with wild animals. Houses are good **hunting grounds** and **nesting places** for a variety of creatures, and they provide food stores, too.

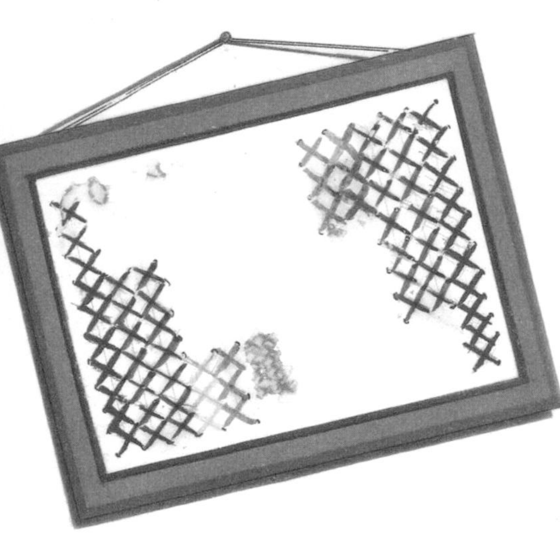

Although modern houses tend to be too clean and dry for some pests, it is not unusual to find the occasional beetle, moth, woodlouse, fly or spider in your home.

Parasites

Parasites are creatures that depend completely on other animals to survive. They often feed on blood.

- Bed bugs grow to about 4 mm long. By day they hide in warm dark places such as mattresses. At night, they come out to feed on their victim, leaving tiny itchy bites.
- Fleas leave itchy swelling bites. Human fleas are not very common, but cat and dog fleas will occasionally bite people.

Bed bug, magnified many times.

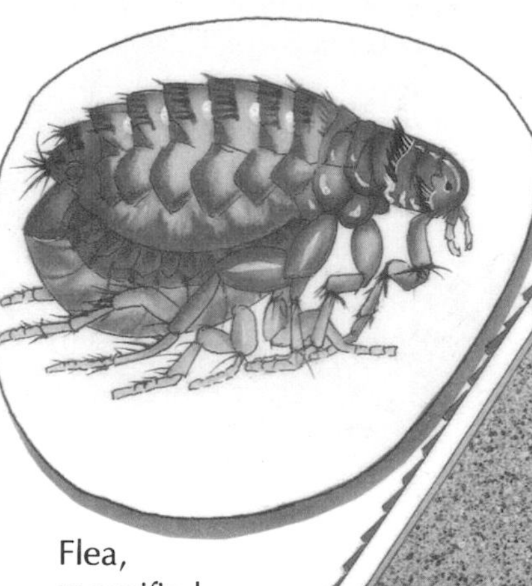

Flea, magnified many times.

- If you vacuum your bed mattress regularly, you won't be visited by bed bugs. However, if you have cats or dogs, you will sometimes get a flea.

Furniture and fabric eaters

Some small house creatures like to eat **wood** and **fabric**. They find a perfect supply of food in furniture, carpets, curtains and clothes.

- Furniture beetles lay their eggs in the crevices of damp wood. When the eggs hatch, the larvae (called woodworm) eat their way to the surface, making tiny tunnels.

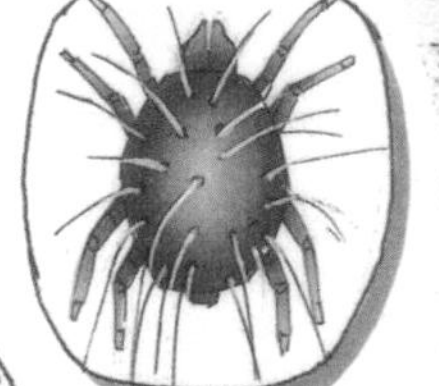

- Clothes moths eat feathers, fur and wool. They live in damp, dark places such as cupboards and old chests and they lay their eggs on clothes or old carpeting.
- Bookworms are beetle larvae that live on paper. They like damp paper best.
- Woodlice like to eat damp paper. They breathe through gills on their legs. The gills must be kept wet, so woodlice live in damp places.
- Carpet beetles lay their eggs amongst carpet fluff. When the larvae hatch they are called 'woolly bears'. They eat feathers, dead insects, fur and wool.

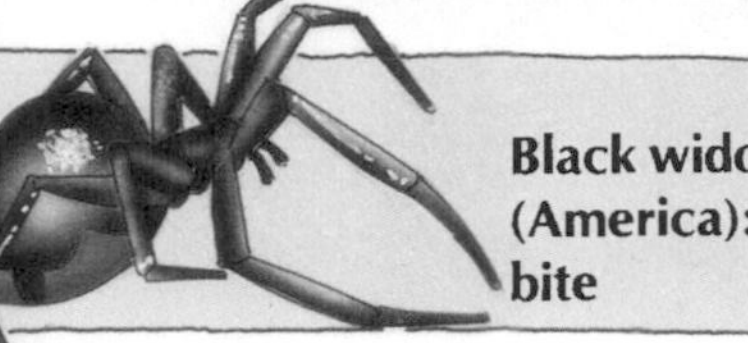

Black widow spider (America): harmful bite

Termites (America): building damage

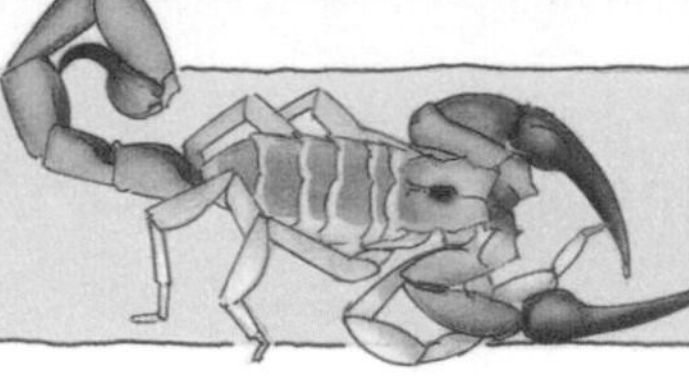

Scorpions (Africa, S. America): harmful sting

Hunters

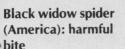

Some house creatures spend their time looking for smaller animals to capture and eat. These **hunters** help to keep the insect population down.

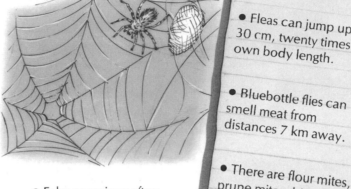

- A house spider's home is usually a sheet of webbing built in a shadowy corner. The spider lives in a silk tube built at the edge of the web. The threads in the web are sticky and trap flying insects, which make the web shake, and the spider then rushes out to kill them.

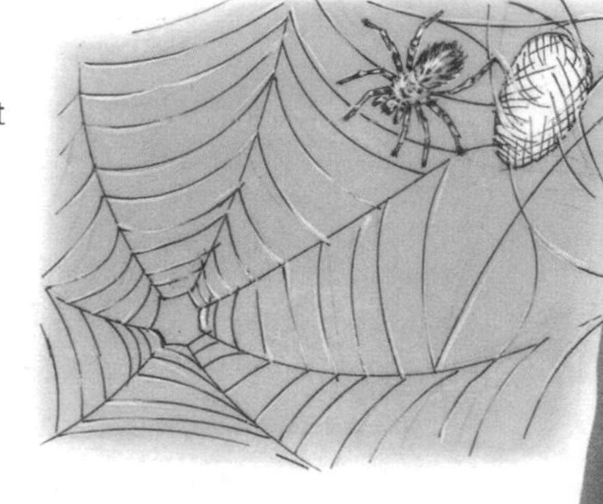

- False scorpions often live in house cellars, amongst piles of damp paper. Although they are small, they are fierce insect hunters.

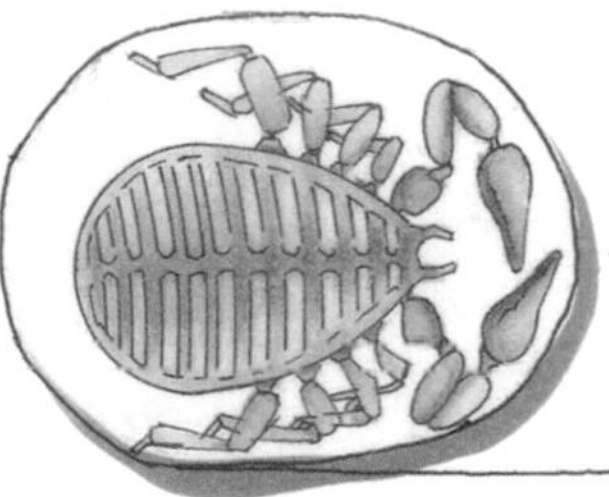

False scorpion, magnified.

Strange but true

- Fleas can jump up to 30 cm, twenty times their own body length.
- Bluebottle flies can smell meat from distances 7 km away.
- There are flour mites, prune mites, biscuit mites, chocolate mites and even cheese mites.
- House mice prefer chocolate, nuts, seeds and cereals to cheese.

Food stealers

Some creatures are out to steal **your food**. An estimated 15 per cent of all stored food ends up inside insects or rodents.

- Food mites are about the size of dust specks. They like to live on stale, damp food that is left at room temperature – inside a larder, for example.

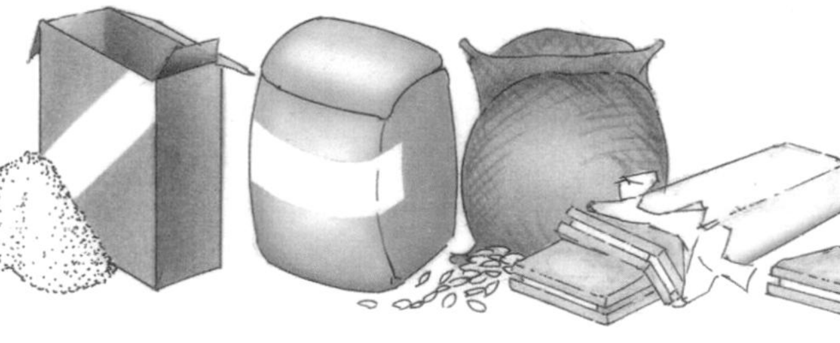

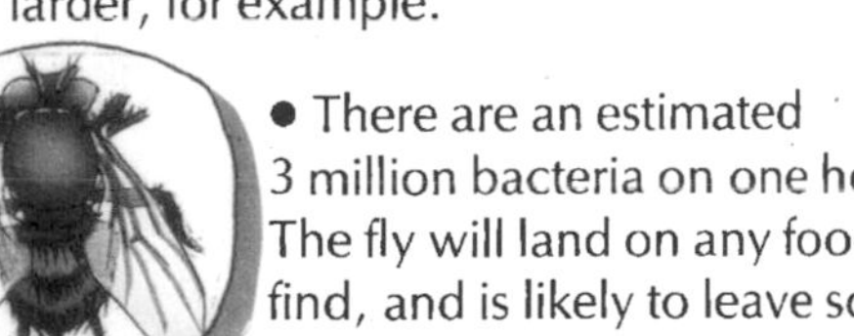

- There are an estimated 3 million bacteria on one housefly. The fly will land on any food it can find, and is likely to leave some bacteria behind when it leaves.

Housefly, magnified.

- House mice live in dark, secret places such as lofts and cellars. They like to eat bread and cereals, but they will occasionally eat more unusual items such as soap and candles!

Bed mite, magnified.

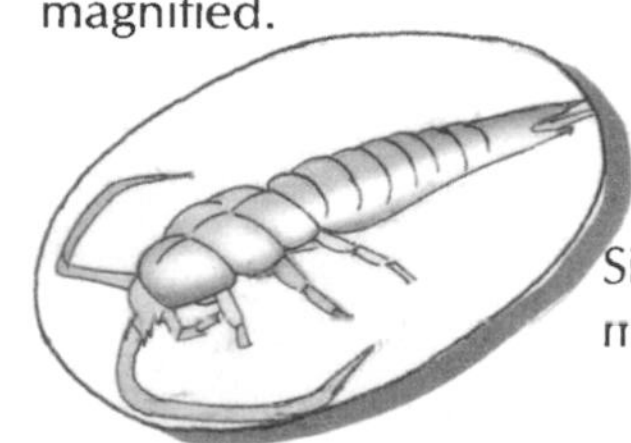

Silverfish, magnified.

- The tiny bed mite eats the scales that constantly fall from human skin. It is widespread but harmless.
- Silverfish are thin, silvery insects about 1 cm long. They live in crevices in bathrooms and kitchens, and come out at night to look for food scraps.

Animal Babies

Pregnancies vary in length. Here are some mammal examples:

Golden hamster: two and a half weeks

All animal species produce **new generations**. Most species reproduce when the climate and food supply is right. For instance, many birds hatch new families in spring, when there is plenty of food to eat.

Within the animal kingdom there are many different kinds of **babies** and methods of **giving birth**.

Babies and parents

Some animals are good **parents**, protecting their babies and teaching them survival skills. However, the majority of creatures give no parental care at all.

- Most fish, amphibians and reptiles lay their eggs and then abandon them. Female fish lay their eggs in the water. Many cannot recognize their own eggs and they often eat them later.

Baby alligator

- The South American discus fish makes sure that its newborn babies stay close to it for protection, by producing a tasty skin secretion which the babies eat.

- Crocodiles and alligators are caring parents. The female digs a pit, lays her eggs and then covers them with vegetation. When the babies hatch they squeal at the mother to dig them out.

Discus fish

- Mammal mothers feed and tend their young. For instance, most monkeys carry their babies with them wherever they go. The babies hold on to the mothers' fur.

Strange but true

- Grey tree frogs build nests of foam hanging over water. The tadpoles drop out of the foam when they hatch.
- The ichneumon fly injects its eggs into a caterpillar. The larvae hatch and eat their way out.
- Bacteria divide themselves once every 30 minutes or so.

Guinea pig: nine weeks

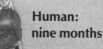

Human: nine months

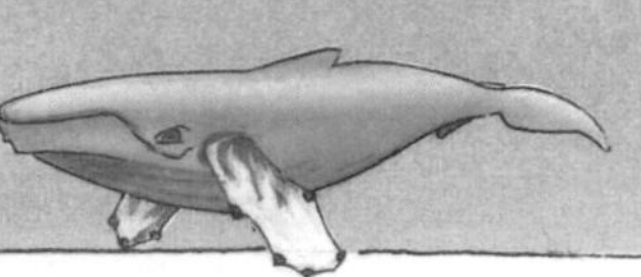

Whale: one year

Elephant: two years

• The female midwife toad lays a string of eggs on land. The male then carries the string wrapped around his back legs. When they are ready to hatch he takes the eggs to the water.

Male midwife toad

• Young domestic fowl chicks must teach themselves to feed. They begin by pecking at everything on the ground, including their own toes! Gradually they learn which things are the best to eat.

• Some cuckoos do not look after their own chicks. Instead they lay a single egg in a smaller bird's nest. The cuckoo hatches and pushes the other chicks out. Then it takes all the food the unwitting parent brings.

Cuckoo chick

Ways of reproducing

Here are the four basic ways that animals **reproduce**:

• The simplest forms of one-celled animals, such as amoebae, reproduce by splitting themselves in half to form two identical creatures. Animals that behave in this way are called asexual.

An amoeba splits in two.

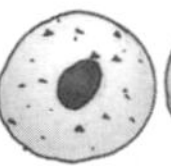

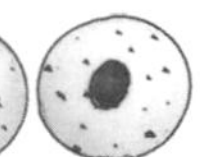

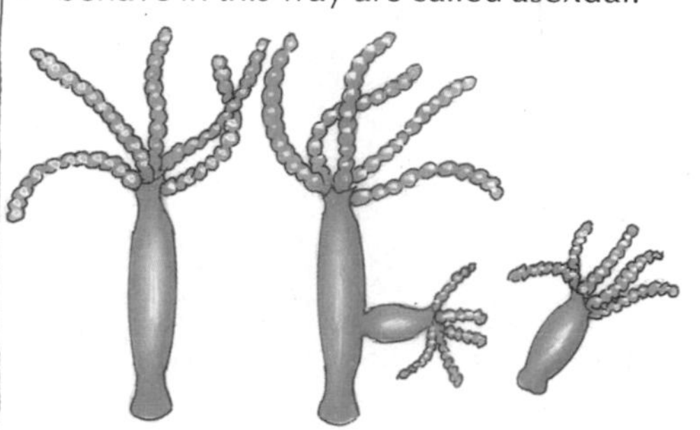
A hydra buds to make a new hydra.

• Some simple animals, such as sea corals and freshwater hydra, produce new creatures by 'budding'. They grow a new branch which is a small version of the parent. Eventually the branch splits off to become a new individual.

• Most animals have different male and female species. The male produces cells called sperm. the female produces egg cells called ova. The male sperm must join with the female egg before a new animal is produced. This method is called sexual reproduction.

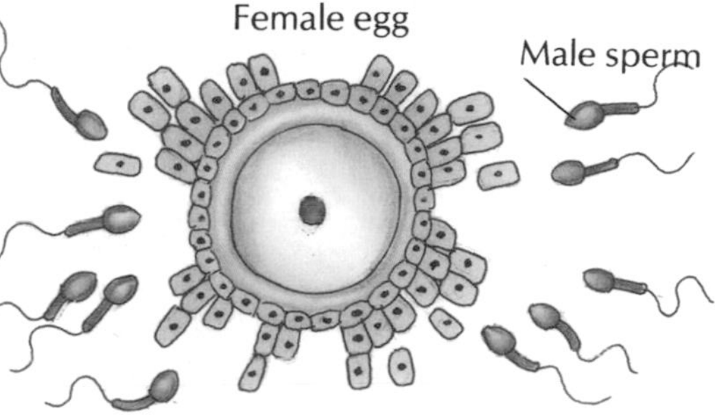

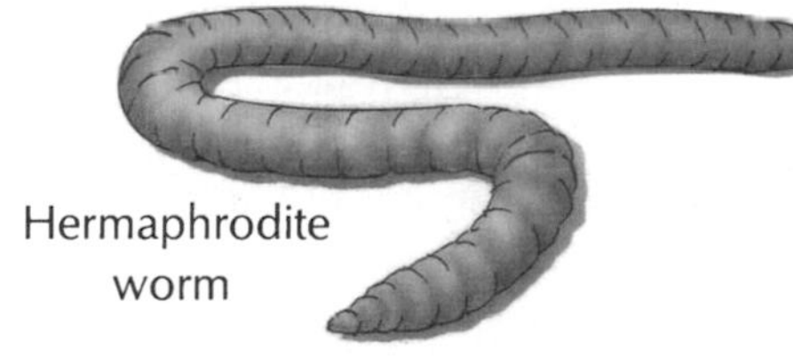
Hermaphrodite worm

• Earthworms and some snails are hermaphrodite. This means that each animal is both male and female, and can produce both sperm and eggs. However, hermaphrodites still have to pair with each other in order to reproduce new creatures.

Eggs and babies

An egg is **fertilized** by a sperm in sexual reproduction. Once this occurs, the egg starts to develop into a new animal.

• Some animals, including most mammals, develop inside their mother's body before they are born. For instance, a newborn foal looks like a miniature version of its parent, and can walk almost immediately.

• Creatures such as birds and many insects lay their eggs once they are fertilized. The babies then develop inside the egg.

Camouflage

Here are some well-camouflaged animals:

A woodcock on its nest

Camouflage is a colouring that **disguises** an animal so that it can hide, or creep up unseen on prey.

Camouflaged animals blend in with their surroundings. For instance, young deer usually have white spot markings that make them harder to see in the dappled light of a forest.

Some animals, such as the zebra, have vivid skin patterns that blur their outlines and make them hard for predators to see.

Changing colour

Some animals can **change colour** to match different backgrounds. Here are some examples:

- The Arctic fox, snowshoe rabbit and ptarmigan live on the Arctic tundra all year round. In winter they turn white to blend in with the snow and in summer they change back to darker colours.

Ptarmigan's winter coat

Ptarmigan's summer coat

- The cuttlefish changes colour as it swims over different plants and rocks. It has sacs of colour pigment in its skin. They expand or contract to produce a wide variety of shades.

Cuttlefish

Master of disguise

The **chameleon** is one of the animal kingdom's masters of disguise. It can change colour very quickly.

- The chameleon has colour cells called chromatophores in its body. Brain signals make the cells smaller or larger to alter the reptile's skin colour.

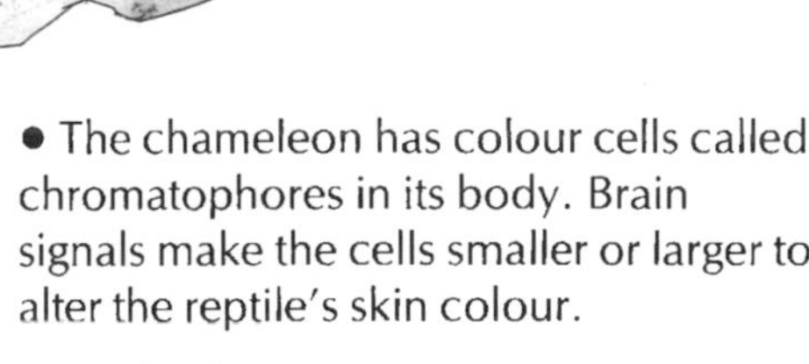

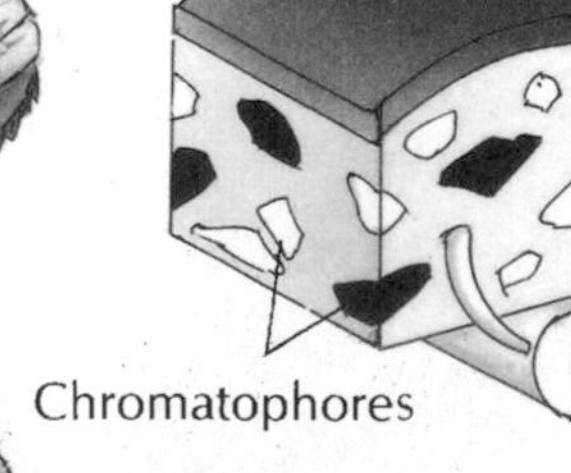

Chromatophores

Nerves in the spine relay brain signals.

An Indian leaf butterfly amongst some leaves

A stick insect on a twig

A flatfish on the seabed

Tricking enemies

These animals fool their enemies by looking like **fiercer creatures**:

- Many butterflies have false eyes on their wings to make them look like a much larger animal.

- The hawkmoth caterpillar is disguised to look like a deadly viper. When it is threatened it puffs itself up to show a false snake's head.

- The king snake is coloured with red, yellow and black rings to make it look like the much deadlier coral snake.

Strange but true

- Sloths let green algae grow on their hair as camouflage.

- A chameleon's colour can alter depending on its mood. In general, the calmer it is the paler it is.

- A nightjar on its ground nest looks just like a branch. Unfortunately, its camouflage is so good that it sometimes gets stepped on.

Sea colour

Creatures that live in the open sea or in cool waters tend to be dull in colour, whilst those that live in warmer waters are often brightly coloured. Many have startling patterns, too.

- The sea dragon is camouflaged to mimic seaweed. It has skin extensions which look like the long strands of weed it swims through.

Sea dragon

Stonefish

- The poisonous stonefish lives in warm waters. It has a speckled, lumpy body that enables it to lurk unseen amongst the stones on the seabed, waiting to grab passing prey.

Insect hide-and-seek

Insects have many enemies, so they are amongst the most effectively camouflaged creatures in the animal kingdom. They use a variety of different tricks to hide from attackers.

- One species of leaf insect has a green, flattened body and wings which look exactly like the leaves it feeds on. The disguise is so successful that the leaf insects sometimes try to eat each other!

- The Italian cricket can throw its voice, just like a ventriloquist, so its enemies never know where it is.

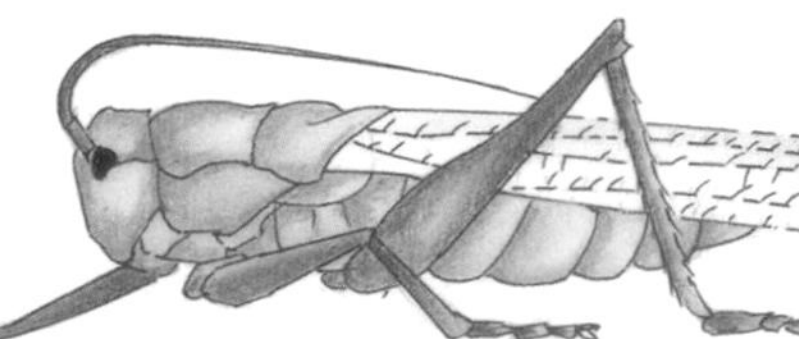

- Peppered moths living in polluted cities have turned dark brown. Members of the same species living in the countryside have stayed a speckled white colour.

Strange Animals

Here are some strange-looking animals:

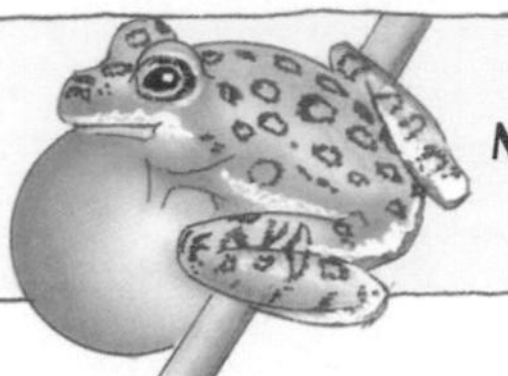

Male tree frog

Some animals have unique **abilities** or **body parts** that no other species possess. These individual features have usually been developed as ways of helping an animal to survive in one way or another. For instance, many creatures have unsual **defence mechanisms** to surprise their enemies.

Some creatures have unique body parts that help them to **feed** or to **survive** in harsh conditions.

Some animals are so extraordinary that scientists are still baffled by the reasons for their behaviour.

Amazing animals

Here are some animals with **unusual skills**:

- The tarsier can turn its head right round to look behind it without moving its body.

Tarsier

- When the three-banded armadillo is threatened by enemies, it rolls itself into a very tight armoured ball.

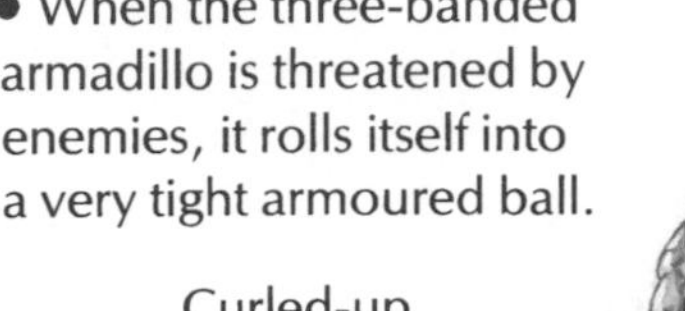

Curled-up armadillo

- A gorilla called Koko was taught by humans to use sign language. She used this skill to signal that she wanted a cat as a pet.

Koko the gorilla

- The Texas horned lizard can squirt blood out of its eyes, possibly as a form of defence against enemies.

Texas horned lizard

Strange but true

- Guillemots can 'fly' underwater.
- Flies take off backwards.
- It takes an elephant calf six months to learn how to use its trunk.
- Crocodiles sometimes climb up trees.

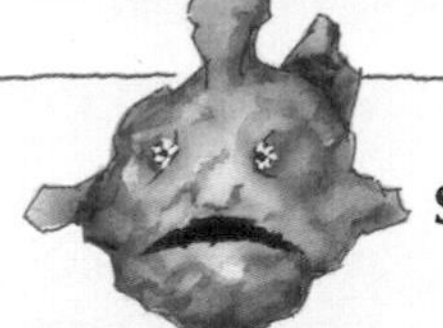

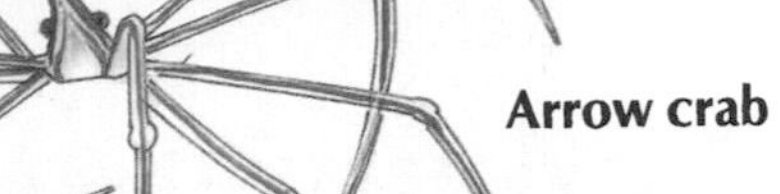

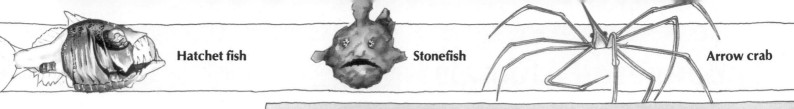

• Most lizards have a tail that can break off if the lizard needs to escape from the grip of a predator. The tail is usually capable of growing again, at least once.

• Giraffes have 45-centimetre long black tongues which they can use to clean their ears.

Curious connections

Here are some strange animal **similarities**:

• The African elephant's closest relative is the hyrax, which is the size of a rabbit.

• The giraffe has seven neckbones, exactly the same number as a human.

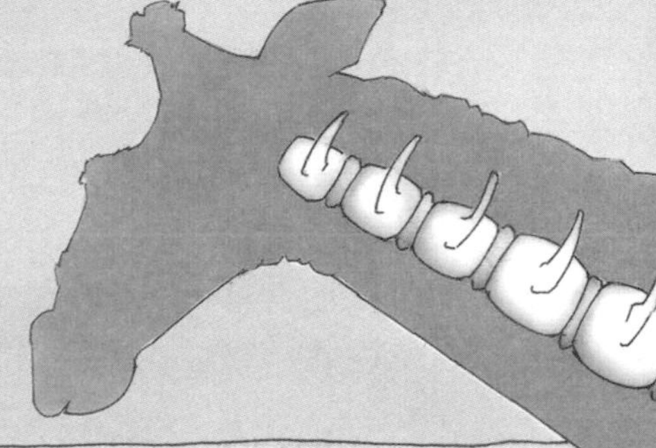

Bizarre birds

Here are some unusual patterns of **bird** behaviour:

• Once the female Emperor penguin has laid an egg, the male keeps it warm by balancing it on his feet under a flap of skin.

• Some birds, such as the reed warbler, can sing two tunes at once.

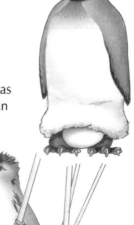

• The hummingbird is the only bird that can fly backwards.

Fascinating fish

The **underwater world** is full of strange surprises:

• The arawana lives in the flooded Amazon rainforest. It can jump up to 2 metres out of the water to feed on small birds or bats in the trees above.

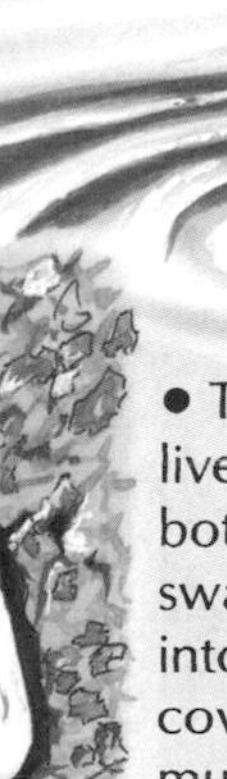

• The African lungfish lives in mud at the bottom of dried-out swamps. It burrows into the ground and covers itself with mucus to keep moist.

• Dolphins, whales and porpoises talk to each other with clicking and whistling noises.

Endangered Animals

These are five of the world's most endangered species:

About 5000 animal species are **endangered**. This means that their numbers are decreasing and that they may die out forever.

An animal species that has disappeared is called **extinct**. The population of some animal species has become so low that they are almost certain to become extinct within the next 20 years.

The endangered panda

Some animals' lives are threatened because their homes and food are being destroyed by **pollution**, **farming** or **building**. Some are **hunted** for their fur and meat. Sadly, there is a huge illegal trade in 'luxury' **animal products** such as rare animal skins and furs.

Land mammals

Although there are organizations to protect endangered wildlife, many animals are still being **poached**, which means that they are killed illegally. Here are some examples:

- The rhinoceros is poached for its horn, which some people believe makes good medicine. Since 1960 the world rhino population has dropped by 85 per cent.
- For many years the African elephant was hunted for its ivory tusks, used for jewellery and ornaments. Now the world ivory trade is banned.
- In Africa, some restaurants serve gorilla steaks. Gorillas are also hunted because they can damage crops. The most endangered species is the mountain gorilla.
- The musk deer is poached for its musk gland, which is used to make perfumes and is said to help treat snake bites.

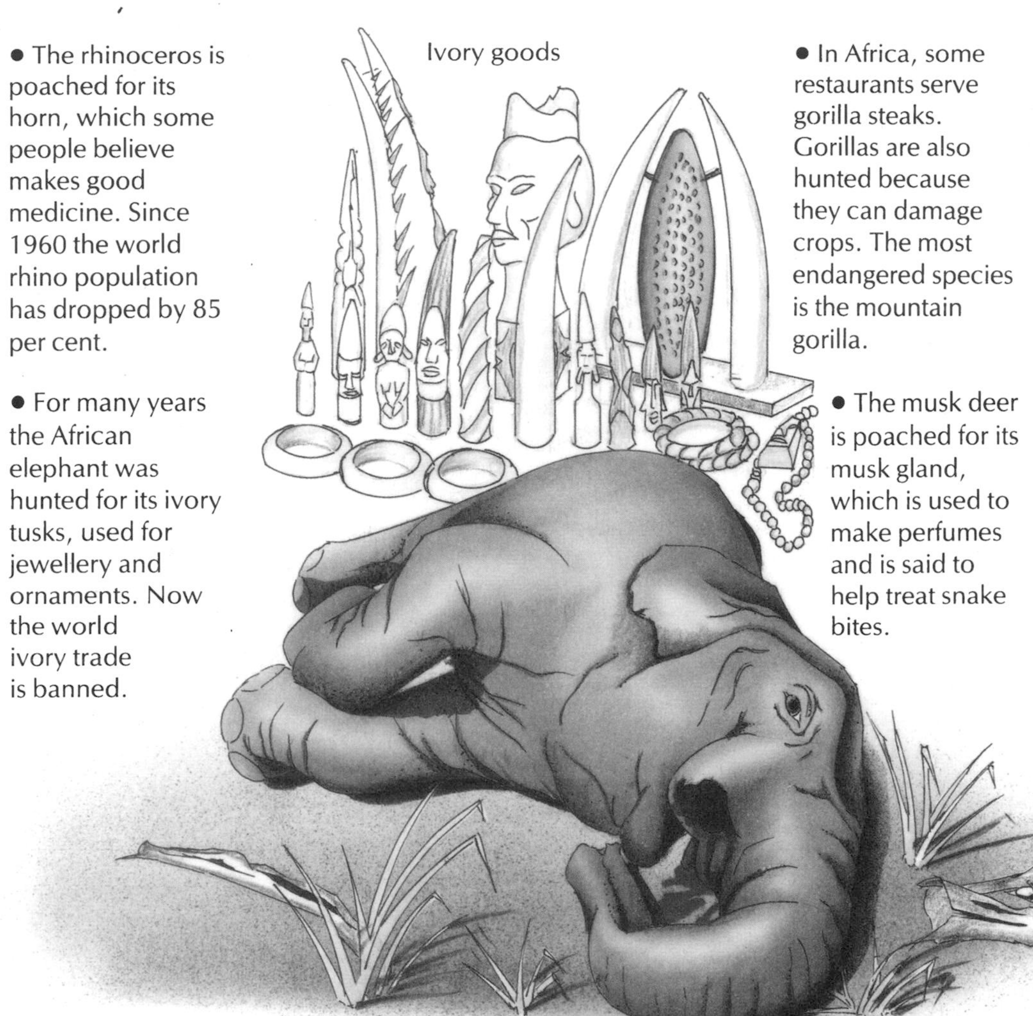

Marine threat

Harmful chemicals and **oil** find their way into the oceans, making them hazardous for ocean life. Some creatures may escape the pollution, only to become victims of other life-threatening dangers:

- Some countries hunt whales for scientific reasons, but sometimes the carcasses are used illegally for food, despite strict hunting laws.
- Many dolphins and other sea creatures die when they are trapped in huge fishing nets.

Birds in danger

About one fifth of all the world's endangered species are **birds**. **Oil pollution** causes a large number of bird deaths, but many are **trapped** or **shot** by humans. Protection laws are hard to enforce.

Rare hyacinthine macaws

- Exotic birds are often captured illegally and sold worldwide as caged pets. Amongst the rarest species is the large hyacinthine macaw of the Brazilian rainforest.

A cormorant clogged with oil

- An estimated 300,000 seabirds died when oil was spilt from a tanker off Alaska in 1989.

- Several well-known species of fish may eventually disappear because of overfishing. If shoals are caught more quickly than the fish can reproduce, the numbers decline.

- Many turtles have been forced away from the beaches where they breed, as hotels and tourism take over. Sometimes turtles have been deliberately killed.

Loggerhead turtle

Herring shoal

Strange but true

- In Japan you can buy a pair of real turtleshell glasses for about £1000.
- Rare African gorillas are sometimes shot so that their hands can be used to make ashtrays.
- When a mother river dugong is killed, the tears of her young are bottled and sold as good luck potion.

Saving Animals

Conservation efforts have saved these species from extinction:

All over the world, groups of people are working to **protect** endangered animals and to limit fur, skin and ivory hunting.

Areas of land called **reserves** have been set aside to provide safe homes for rare animals. There are also underwater nature reserves, where scuba diving and fishing are limited.

Sometimes rare species are kept in **zoos**, where they can safely breed new generations. Occasionally some of these animals are released back into the wild to build up the species once more.

Project tiger

Until recently, the **tiger** was one of the most threatened animal species in the world. In 1972 the Indian government and the Worldwide Fund for Nature launched **Operation Tiger**:

- Tiger reserves were set up across India and Asia to provide safe areas where hunting is banned. Here the animals can breed without disturbance.
- Thanks to the Operation Tiger project, the number of tigers in India alone has more than doubled to over 4000 since the opening of the reserve areas. The tiger is no longer top of the endangered species list, and numbers are continuing to grow.

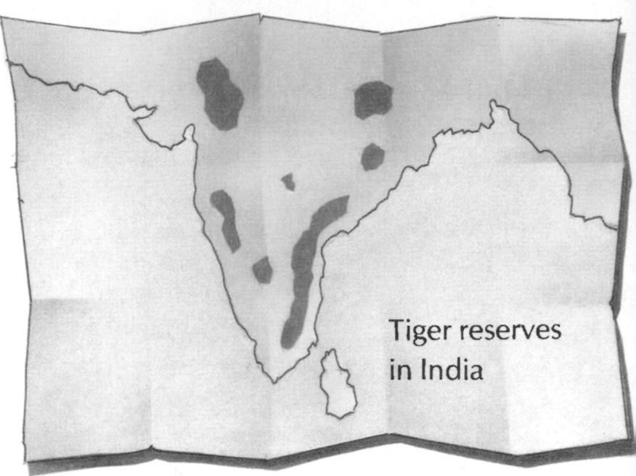

- Thousands of people pay to visit the reserves every year. The money helps to maintain the land on the reserves and goes towards funding important research.

Bengal tiger

Strange but true

- The rare kakapo parrot lays one egg every four years.
- The coelacanth fish was thought to be extinct for 70 million years, until one was found alive in 1938.
- Insecticide pollution has been traced in the bodies of Antarctic penguins, thousands of kilometres from civilization.

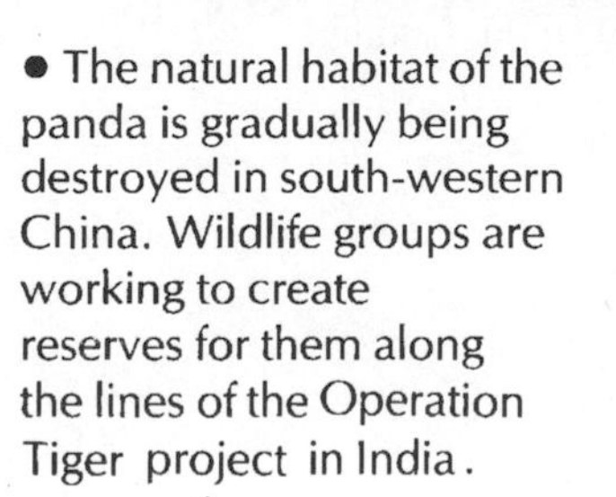

- The natural habitat of the panda is gradually being destroyed in south-western China. Wildlife groups are working to create reserves for them along the lines of the Operation Tiger project in India.

Buffalo

Mountain pygmy possum

Mauritius kestrel

Zoo work

- The Arabian oryx became extinct in the wild 20 years ago. Surviving oryx were reared in Arizona, USA, and the species is now back in the wild.

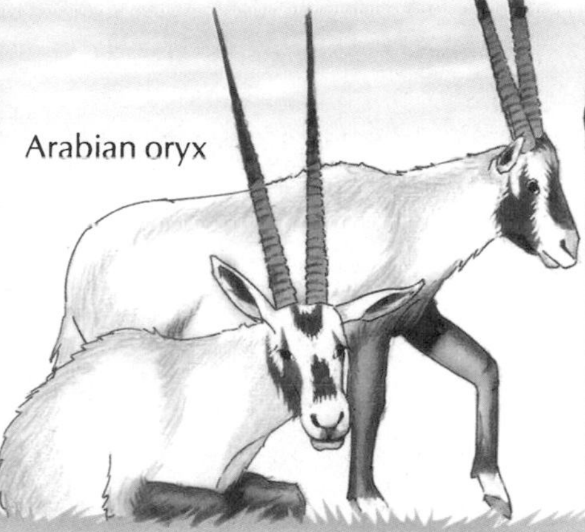
Arabian oryx

- Several endangered monkey species have been bred in zoos. However, it is not always safe to release them back into the wild because their jungle homes are still being destroyed.

- The rare Chatham Island black robin was saved from extinction by New Zealand wildlife experts, who used tom tits to foster the robin chicks.

Chatham Island robin

Extinct animals

An animal is officially **extinct** if it has not been seen for over 50 years. Here are some animals forced into extinction by humans.

- The dodo bird once lived on Mauritius. It was killed off in the seventeenth century when humans arrived on the island.

Dodo bird

- The great auk was hunted to extinction in the North Atlantic. It disappeared in the 1500s.

Great auk

- The South African quagga looked like a zebra. It was hunted for food until it died out.

What you can do

Here are some things **you** can do to help protect wildlife:

- Do not buy endangered animal skins or ivory products.

- Never steal birds' eggs from nests.

- Join your local conservation group, to help conserve the wildlife that lives near you.

Worldwide Fund for Nature badge

Wild Animals Facts and Lists

Wild cats

Wild cats are found in all the continents of the world. This table shows where some wild cats live:

	Asia	Africa	India	China	South America	North America	Europe
Cheetah	•						
Hyena	•	•	•	•			
Jaguar					•		
Leopard	•	•	•	•			
Lion		•	•				
Lynx	•	•	•			•	•
Ocelot					•		
Puma						•	
Tiger	•		•	•			

Endangered and extinct animals

- Scientists believe that up to a third of all known plant and animal species may be extinct by the year 2500.
- Dinosaurs became extinct about 65 million years ago.
- The passenger pigeon from America was killed for food and became extinct in 1899.
- Here are some more endangered animals:

Arabian oryx
Cranes
Crocodiles
Giant tortoises
Golden cats
Indian lions
Lynx
Rhinoceroses
Sand lizards
Spiny anteaters
Tasmanian wolves
Platypus
Tigers
Tragopan pheasants
Wallabies
Whales

The last dodo died in 1681

Pets and wild animals

Some wild animals are now often kept as pets:

The common European tortoise
The Australasian cockatiel
The Australian budgerigar
African and Asian waxbills
African and Asian gerbils
South American cavies, or guinea pigs
Asian and North European hamsters
(All present-day golden hamsters in capitivity are descended from a litter found in Syria in 1930.)

Flightless birds

Here are some examples of birds that cannot fly, even though they have wings:

Emus
Cassowaries
Penguins
Wattlebirds
Ostriches
Kakapo parrots

Burrowing animals

These animals live in burrows:

Mongooses
Aardwolves
Hyenas
Burrowing clams
Fiddler crabs
Congo eels
Moles
Rabbits
Wombats

The foods animals eat

Here are some examples of animals that eat meat only (carnivores):

Anacondas
Crocodiles
Eagles
Komodo dragons
Polar bears
Praying mantis
Tigers
Lions

Here are some animals that eat plants and meat (omnivores):

Baboons
Badgers
Bush babies
Bustards
Cockroaches
Common snapper
Earwigs
Harvestmen spiders

These animals eat carrion (the remains of dead animals):

Carrion beetles
Golden eagles
Hyenas
Vultures

Pests

- Pests are creatures that destroy crops or other plants.
- Aphids are insects that carry plant diseases and damage plants by eating them.
- Quelea birds may damage whole fields of grain, partly because of the huge numbers that feed together.
- Locusts fly in huge swarms and will eat the leaves and fruit of any plant they land on.

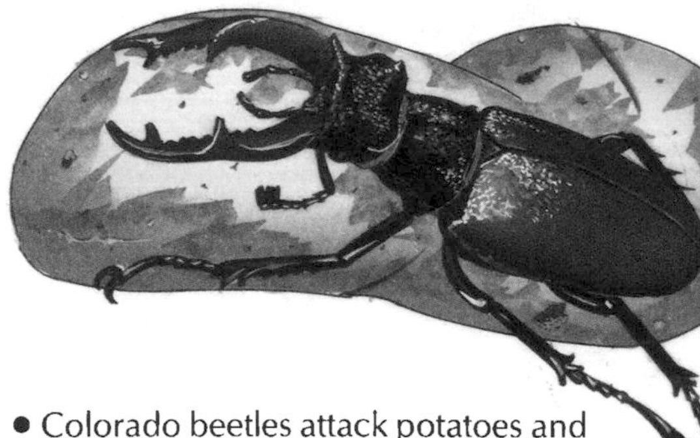

- Colorado beetles attack potatoes and ruin them.

Plant eaters

Here are some examples of animals that eat only plants:

Bears (except polar bears)
Green turtles
Iguanas
Emus
Gorillas
Rhinoceroses
Zebras
Antelopes
Elephants

Animal communication

Animals communicate with each other so that they can find food, or to attract a mate. This is how some animals communicate:

- Silk moths use their scent to attract a partner.
- Glow-worms have a green light that attracts other glow-worms.

- Mayflies swarm together and 'dance' over the water.
- Honey bees do an elaborate dance that directs the other bees to food.
- Ants leave trails to mark the route from their nest so they can return.
- Blue whales make sounds that can be heard by other whales up to 850 kilometres away.
- Squirrelfishes make noises that can be heard even out of the water.
- Sticklebacks swim in a zig-zag pattern to attract females.

Changing shape

Here are some examples of animals that go through metamorphosis (change of shape) at different stages in their life:

Earwigs
Grasshoppers
Dragonflies
Butterflies
Moths
Flies

Migration

Some animals migrate (travel from one place to another) at certain times of the year to breed or find food. These are some examples:

- The North American monarch butterfly travels as far as Australia for the winter months.
- Salmon hatch in rivers and migrate to the sea, returning to their birthplace to breed.
- Eels migrate up to 5600 kilometres to reach their breeding grounds.
- Tuna fish travel long distances to reach the Mediterranean where they breed.
- Many birds migrate, but the Arctic tern travels furthest. It flies from the Arctic to the Antarctic, and back again, a trip of 32,000 kilometres.

Camouflage

Here are some examples of animals that can change colour quickly as a way of hiding from their enemies or prey:

Chameleons
Grouper fish
Flatfish
Octopuses
Tree frogs
Blossom spiders

Night-time animals

Nocturnal animals come out at night to feed or hunt, and rest during the day. These animals are nocturnal:

Many frogs and toads
Coral snakes
The Kakapo parrot
Owls
Nightjars
Opossums

Regrowing limbs

Here are some animals that can regrow parts of their bodies if damaged:

- Starfish can grow new 'arms'.
- Slow-worms can regrow broken-off tails.
- Lizards can grow new tails.

Whales

There are 90 species of whales, dolphins and porpoises. Here are some whales and their sizes:

Blue whale	30 metres
Gray whale	15 metres
Sperm whale	13 metres
Killer whale	6 metres
Pygmy sperm whale	4 metres
Narwhal	4 metres

Hibernation

- To hibernate means to go into a deep sleep through the winter.
- Newts, hedgehogs, bats and dormice hibernate over the winter.
- Only two kinds of birds hibernate, and they are both nightjars.

Desert creatures

This is how some desert animals survive:

- Camels store fat in their humps and water in their stomachs.
- The addax antelope does not need to drink very often.
- Jerboas burrow deep underground to keep away from the heat.
- Rhinoceroses bath in muddy water which then dries on them, protecting them from the Sun.

Biggest sea creatures

These are some of the largest creatures to be found in the sea, apart from whales:

Ribbon worm	54 metres
Whale shark	18 metres
Giant squid	17 metres
White shark	12 metres
Giant spider crab	3.65 metres
Starfish	1.37 metres
American lobster	1 metre

Dangerous animals

- One golden poison-dart frog could kill up to 1500 people with its poison.
- The mosquito carries diseases such as malaria, elephantiasis and yellow fever. Malaria kills over a million people a year.
- The great white shark is the most feared man-eating shark.

Wild Animals Facts and Lists

Reptiles

This table shows the average sizes of some reptiles:

Anaconda	9 metres
Reticulated python	9 metres
Saltwater crocodile	8 metres
King cobra	5.48 metres
Boa constrictor	4.26 metres
Mamba	2.13 metres
Leatherback turtle	2 metres
Grass snake	1 metre
Thread snake	114 mm
Gecko lizard	17 mm

This is how long it takes some reptile eggs to hatch:

Grass lizard	42 days
Marine turtle	55 days
Alligator	61 days
Python	61 days
Tortoise	105 days

Amazing eyes

- The giant squid has the largest eyes of any animal. They can be 39 cm across, which is 16 times wider than a human eye.

- A peregrine falcon can spot its prey from more than 8 km away.

- The golden eagle can spot its prey from over 3 km away.

Giant invertebrates

- The bird-eating spider from South America has a body as big as a child's hand.

- The African giant snail measures over 390 mm when fully grown.

- The Borneo dragonfly has a wingspan of 190 mm.

Birds

- There are about 100 billion birds in the world.

- There are 9000 species of birds.

- The North American ostrich is the tallest bird, at 2.74 metres.

Fast fliers

Spine-tailed swift	170 km/h
Pigeon	96 km/h
Hawk moth	53 km/h
Monarch butterfly	32 km/h
Honeybee	17 km/h

Beaks

The shape of birds' beaks gives a clue to the food they eat and how they eat it:

Hooked bills	eating flesh
Baggy beaks	scooping fish
Spear beaks	spearing fish spearing worms
Parrotbills	cracking seeds
Pointed beaks	spearing insects eating seeds
Crossbills	removing seeds from fir cone scales
Chisel beaks	boring nest holes and feeding
Tiny beaks	catching insects in the open mouth while flying

Wing shapes

Hovering birds	small, broad wings
Gliding birds	long, thin wings
Diving birds	wings fold back
Circling birds	long, wide wings
Dodging, diving birds	short, wide wings

Animal nests

Nests are made by many animals in lots of different ways:

- Swans make floating nests of reeds and sticks.

- Sticklebacks make nests using sand and weed.

- Swallows make nests using grasses woven or stuck together with mud and spit.

- Queen bumblebees often use old underground voles' nests in which they make a wax egg chamber.

- Siamese fighting fish make nests out of bubbles, which they hold together like shampoo froth.

- Bald eagles make the biggest nests. They can measure 2.9 metres across by 6 metres deep.

Treetop colonies

These birds make treetop nests in groups:

Crows
Herons
Storks
Pelicans
Weaver birds

Eggs

Here are the biggest and smallest bird egg sizes:

Ostrich	177 mm
Helena's hummingbird	12.7 mm

- After an egg has been laid, the time it takes to hatch is called its 'incubation time'.

Egg incubation times:

Finch	12 days
Thrush	14 days
Wren	16 days
Falcon	28 days
Ostrich	42 days
Hawk	44 days
Emperor penguin	63 days
Royal albatross	79 days

Animal sizes

These are the heights of some animals:

Giraffe	5.79 metres
African elephant	3.02 metres
Ostrich	2.74 metres
Brown bear	2.43 metres

Weights

Animal weights, from smallest to largest:

Bee hummingbird	1.4 grams
Mouse	22.4 grams
Goliath beetle	85 grams
Rat	455 grams
Marmoset	0.68 kg
Ringtail monkey	2.72 kg
Otter	5.89 kg
Armadillo	6.12 kg
Ocelot	19.27 kg
Porpoise	46.72 kg
Cheetah	57.83 kg
Alligator	57.83 kg
Llama	170 kg
Polar bear	324 kg
Moose	362 kg
Pilot whale	680 kg
Walrus	1625 kg
African elephant	7112 kg
Sperm whale	37,593 kg
Blue whale	155,963 kg

Animal pregnancies

This is how long some babies take to grow inside their mothers before they are born:

Opossum	13 days
House mouse	19 days
Chimpanzee	237 days
Camel	406 days
Giraffe	410 days
Rhinoceros	560 days
Indian elephant	624 days

Animal speeds

- The slowest land mammal is the three-toed sloth of tropical South America. Its average speed is 2.13 metres a minute.

- The sleepiest mammals are armadillos, sloths and opposums. They spend 80 per cent of their lives sleeping or dozing.

Animal lifespans

This is how long some animals live:

Mayfly	1 day
Mouse	2-3 yrs
Rattlesnake	18 yrs
Lion	25 yrs
Hippopotamus	40 yrs
Ostrich	50 yrs
African elephant	60 yrs
Dolphin	65 yrs
Rhinoceros	70 yrs
Tortoise	100 yrs

Animal skins

- Snakes and lizards have scaly skins. The rough scales underneath help a snake to move along. The skin is watertight, enabling snakes and lizards to live in or out of the water.

- Tortoises have developed their scaly skin into an armoured shell.

- Furry or feathered skins keep some animals warm in winter.

- Birds lose some of their feathers in the summer to keep cool.

- Birds such as penguins oil their feathers from an oil gland in their skin to waterproof themselves.

Animal feet

- Swans and ducks have webbed feet which they use as paddles when swimming.

- The blue-footed booby uses its webbed feet to incubate its eggs during breeding.

- Lizards, newts, gorillas and lemurs are examples of animals that have five toes on each foot. Toes are used for climbing and gripping.

- The elephant's foot is also five-toed, but is round and massive to support its weight.

History of how life began

The development of animals and plants has taken millions of years. The facts below shows this evolution as if it had happened in a year.

- January 1: the Earth forms.

- March 29: bacteria and other simple life forms appear.

- November 27: the first fish develop in the sea.

- December 15: the first dinosaurs appear.

- December 28: various mammals develop.

- December 31: the first ape-men appear. Modern humans develop just hours before the end of the year.

INDEX

Indexes to other sections are on pages 46, 142 and 190.

PEOPLE

Part Three

PEOPLE

Introduction

In this Part, you can discover how your body works, how people live around the world, and some important things that people have done in the past.

Humans are remarkable, and the human body is an amazing collection of parts, including thousands of kilometres of internal tubing. Did you know that, on average, one person eats 50 tonnes of food and drinks 50,000 litres of liquid in a lifetime?

Life on Earth has changed more during the last hundred years than at any other time in history.

Human beings are the only creatures that wear clothes, because people's bodies don't have any fur or feathers to protect them.

Did you know that some nomadic people live in tents, so that they can move around looking for work or pasture for their animals?

People believe in many different gods and religions, and have done for thousands of years. Early humans believed their gods created geographical events such as thunderstorms.

Find out about people who have become famous in history for their daring deeds, or for helping others, or for things that they have created.

The First People

These are some of the kinds of tools and weapons used by early people:

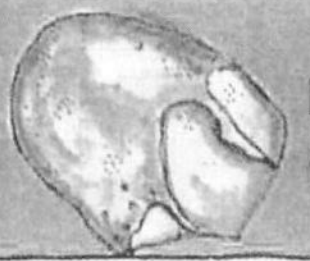

Pebble tools: Homo habilis (2.5 million years ago)

The first recognizable **human beings** probably appeared about 2 million years ago, although groups of human-like creatures existed before then. People looking similar to ourselves have lived on Earth for only about 100,000 years – which is just a fraction of time in the history of the Earth.

The first humans

Scientists studying **fossils** of bones and other remains have managed to piece together some idea of what the **first humans** were like.

Australopithecines

• Around 3.5 million years ago, Australopithecines lived in Africa. They had ape-like faces but walked upright and probably used sticks and pieces of bone as tools.

Neanderthal skull

Modern skull

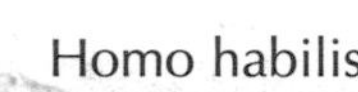

Homo habilis

• Two million years ago, creatures called Homo habilis (handy man) lived in Africa. They had larger brains than Australopithecines. They sharpened stones to make tools, built shelters and worked together to hunt animals.

Strange but true

• The axes in use today are very similar to some of the earliest hunting weapons.

• About 30,000 years ago, some humans in Central Europe built huts from mammoth bones covered over with animal skins.

• Early humans may have learned to cook meat by accidentally dropping it onto a fire.

• The human being's nearest animal relatives are thought to be chimpanzees, gorillas and orang-utans.

Homo erectus

• Homo erectus (upright man) appeared 1.6 million years ago, first in Africa then also spreading to Asia. These people were taller than Homo habilis, with larger brains. They used many different stone tools and discovered how to use fire for cooking and keeping warm.

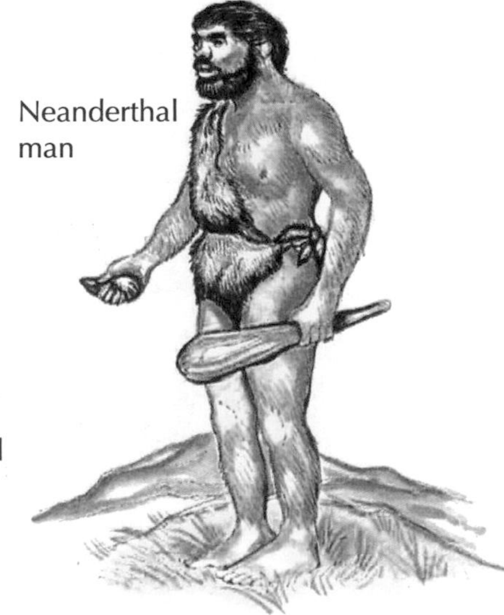

Neanderthal man

• About 200,000 to 100,000 years ago, Homo sapiens (thinking man) appeared. People today belong to this group. The Neanderthal people were an early kind of Homo sapiens. They lived in caves in Europe until 40,000 years ago, wore animal skins and made carvings of animals.

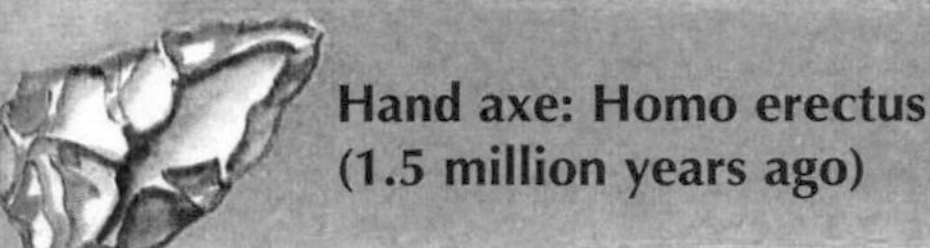
Hand axe: Homo erectus (1.5 million years ago)

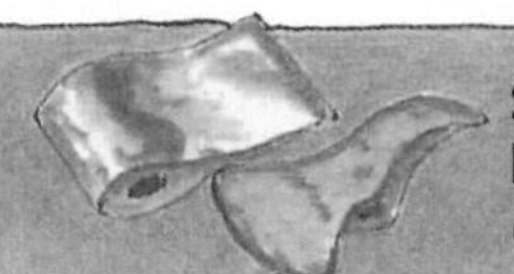
Stone spears on wooden handles: Neanderthal people (42,000 years ago)

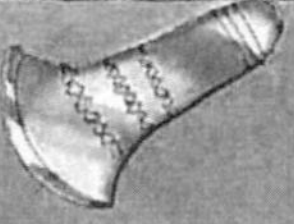
Bronze tools: Modern people (5000 years ago)

The first modern people

The Neanderthal people gradually died out, but by this time other types of **Homo sapiens** had developed and spread around the world. These are some of the things the **first modern humans** did:

- Decorated tools with pictures of animals and painted hunting scenes on the walls of their cave homes.
- Made jewellery from shells and animal teeth, and clothes from skins sewn together with needles made of bone.

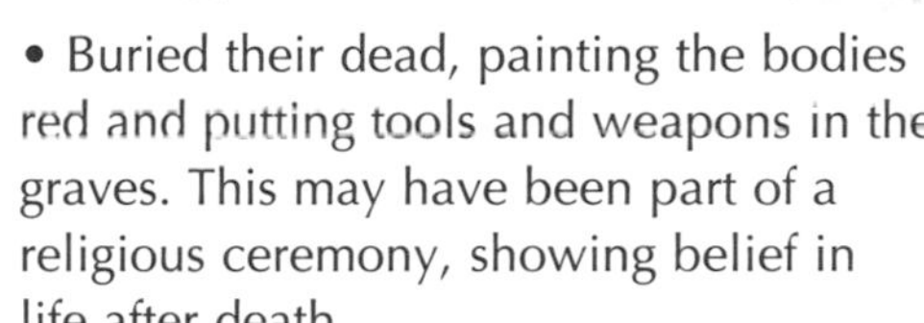

- Buried their dead, painting the bodies red and putting tools and weapons in the graves. This may have been part of a religious ceremony, showing belief in life after death.

The first farmers

At first, people lived as **nomads**, which means they wandered around in small groups or tribes searching for good hunting grounds. About 10,000 years ago an important change took place. People living in the Middle East began to settle down and farm. These **first farmers** learned how to:

- Sow seeds and grow crops.
- Capture wild goats and sheep and breed them to provide people with milk, meat and skins.
- Build houses of mud and straw that dried hard in the sun.
- Bake bread in ovens. Early bread was flat and hard.

Towns and trading

When people settled in groups or communities, they sometimes produced more goods than they needed for themselves. So they began to **trade** their extra goods for other things made by people nearby. Gradually, towns grew in size and became busy trading centres.

- People living in settled farming communities had more time to develop skills such as pottery, weaving and tool-making.
- Eventually, some people became craftworkers, specializing in making certain goods to sell.
- Before money was invented, people swapped goods. People with spare wheat, for example, might swap it for pottery.

People of the World

Here is the average length of life in some countries today:

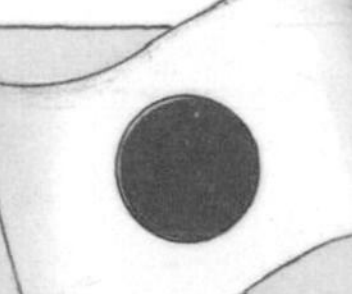

Japan: 79 years

For thousands of years the **number of people** living on Earth increased very slowly. Early peoples lived **shorter lives** than most people do today. Very little was known about **medicine**, so many people died from illness or injury before they reached old age.

Today, in many countries people are better housed and fed and there are **medical services** to take care of illness, so people live longer. As a result, the number of people in the world has grown rapidly.

B.C. and A.D.

The letters B.C. after a number mean the years before the birth of Christ. A.D. stands for the Latin words *anno domini* (year of Our Lord) and means a date after the birth of Christ.

- B.C. numbers count backward, so (for example) 1000 B.C. is further back in time than 500 B.C.

How cities have grown

These are the populations of some of the world's largest **cities**, now and in the past:

The population explosion

About 155 people are born every minute of every day. This recent rise in population is often called the **population explosion**. If this rate of growth continues, the world population will have trebled by the end of the next century.

- World population grew much more slowly in the past. It took about 11,500 years for it to grow from 10 million to 500 million. Since 1800 it has grown very quickly.

This diagram shows how the population has increased over the last thousand years.

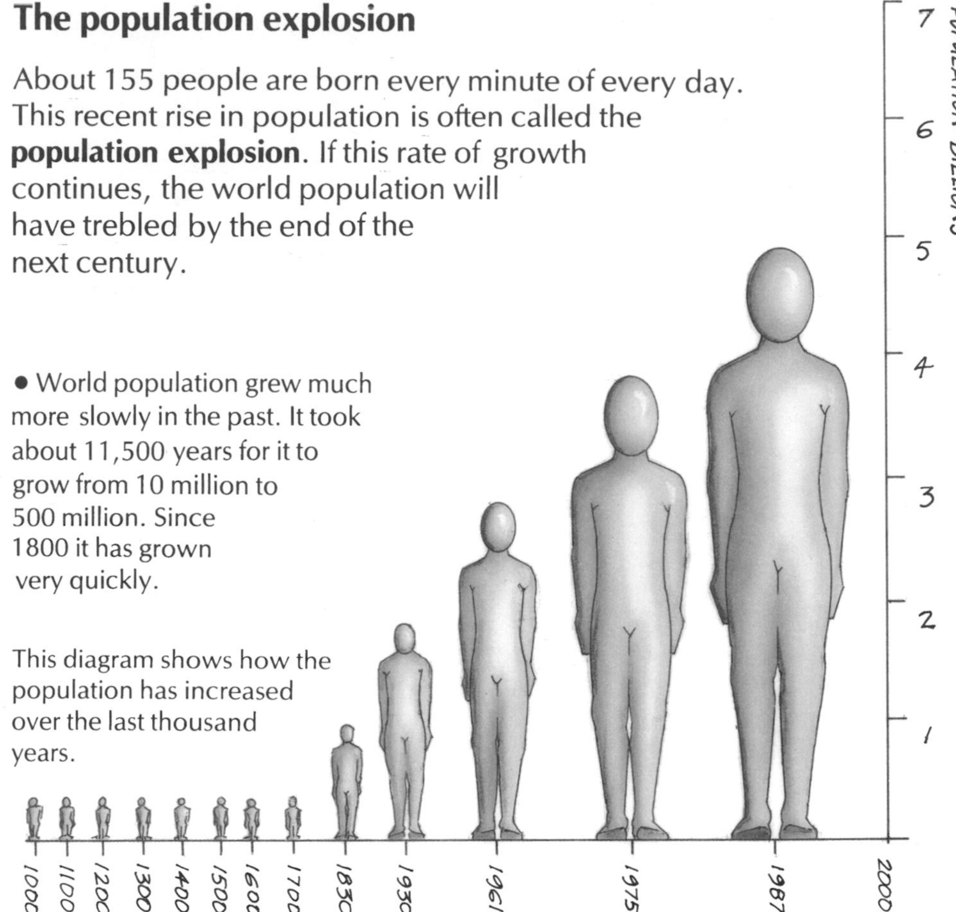

These are some **population figures** from the past:

- In 8000 B.C. there were probably only about 6 million people in the world. Most lived in Asia and Africa.
- By A.D. 1, people had spread to most parts of the world. The population had grown to about 255 million.
- By 1600 the world population had doubled to about 500 million.
- In 1987 the world population rose to 5 billion, ten times as many people as in 1600. About three-fourths of the world's people today live in Asia and Europe.
- At its present rate of growth, the world population doubles about every 40 years.

- 27,000 B.C.: The city of Dolní Vestonice (in modern-day Czech Republic) contained about 100 people

- 7800 B.C.: Jericho (now in occupied Jordan) contained about 27,000 people

- As early as 133 B.C., Rome was a huge city with a million inhabitants

Great Britain:
75 years

U.S.A.:
76 years

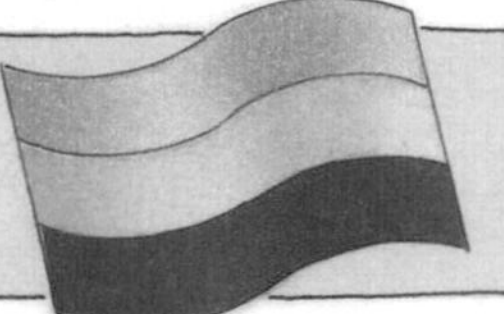

Ethiopia:
52 years

Strange but true

- The Chinese population is increasing at 35,000 a day — over 12 million a year!

- At present, one person in three is under 15 years of age. Fewer than one person in ten is over 64 years of age.

- It is estimated that the average length of life in A.D. 400 was about 33 years for a man and 27 for a woman.

Population problems

The rapid rise in population has created many **problems**:

- Shortage of food. To feed everyone, we will have to produce more food and share it out more fairly.
- Pollution due to the increased use of fuels. Supplies of oil, coal, and gas are also running low and cannot be replaced.

- Destruction of wildlife habitats for housing, industry, and farming.
- Widespread poverty and hunger, especially in Africa and Asia.
- Shortage of housing.
- Unemployment.

Countries

At present, the world is divided into about 170 **independent countries**. This number keeps changing, as countries join together or become separate.

- An independent country is one that has its own government, makes its own laws and has its own flag.

- The smallest independent country is the Vatican City in Rome. It is an area of 109 acres (0.4 sq-km) governed by the Roman Catholic Church.
- The country with the highest population is China, with over 1 billion people living there.

- In these countries most people live in towns or cities: UK 91%, Australia 85%, U.S.A. and Japan 76%. In these countries, most people live and working in farming communities: India 72%, Kenya 80%, and Burkina Faso (Africa) 91%.

- London did not have one million inhabitants until 1800; now it has some 8 million

- Some modern cities:
2006: Tokyo, Japan, 12 million
2005: Mexico City, 8.8 million
2005: New York City, 8 million
2006: Shanghai, China, 9.8 million

The **human body** is made up of many different parts, including billions of **cells**, thousands of miles of **tubing**, and hundreds of **muscles and bones**. Each of the many different parts of the body has its own special job, but all the parts have to work together to keep the body alive.

Cells

Everything in the body is made up of tiny living units called **cells**. A fully grown body has about **50 billion cells**.

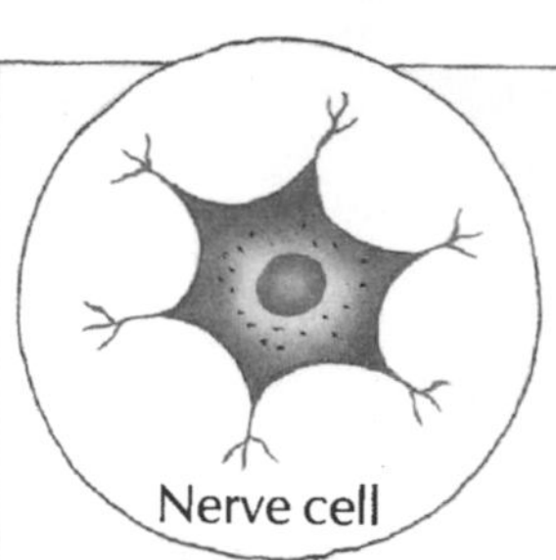

Nerve cell

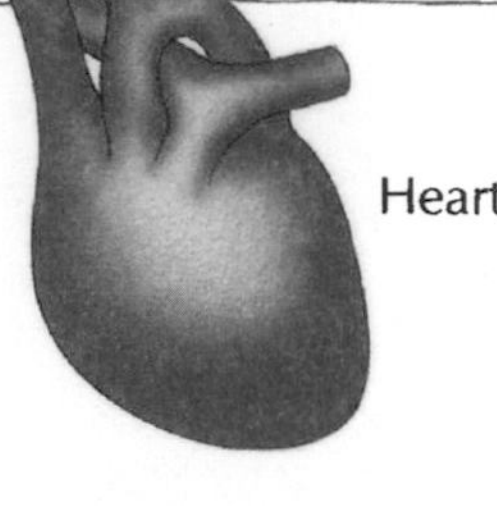

Heart

Heart position

- A group of similar cells doing the same job is called tissue. Muscles and nerves are tissues.
- Different types of tissue working together form organs, such as the heart and the lungs.

The skeleton

The **skeleton** is a framework, made of about **206 bones**, that supports the body, gives it shape, and protects it from damage.

- The skull protects the brain and the ribs protect the heart.
- Joints are where two bones meet. Some are fixed but others can bend.

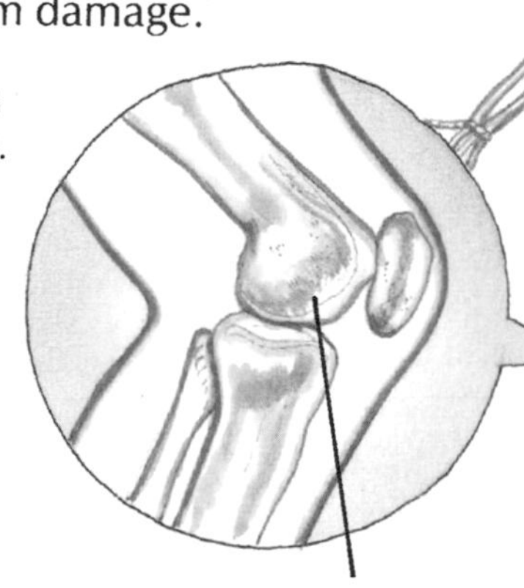

Movable knee joint

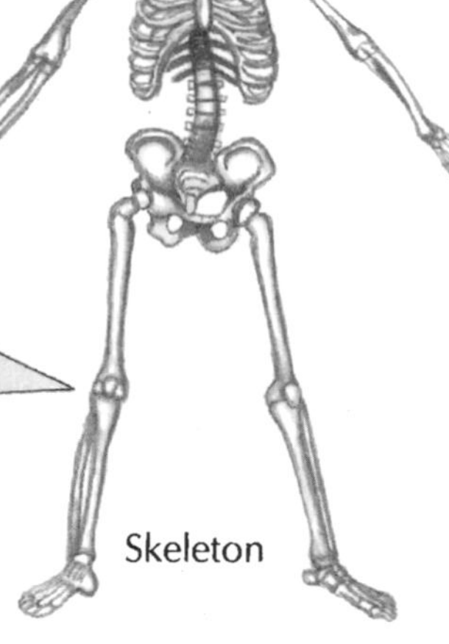

Skeleton

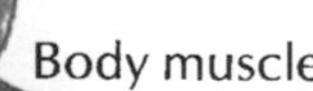

Muscles

The human body has about **650 muscles**. They enable the skeleton to **move**.

- Muscles move by contracting (tensing) or relaxing (loosening). They are joined to bones by fibres. When muscles contract, the fibres pull the bones and make them move. Most muscles work in pairs, pulling opposite ways.

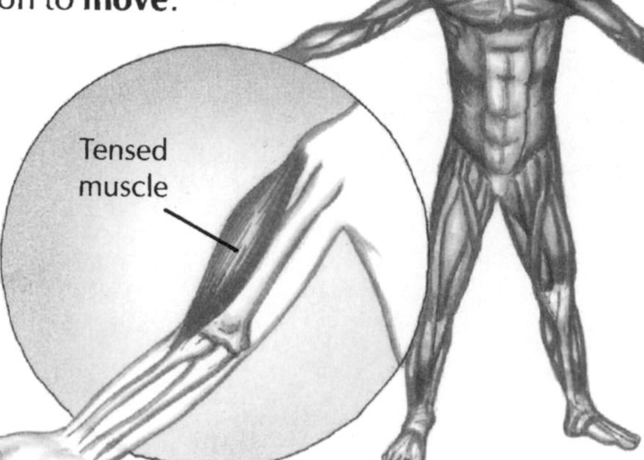

Body muscles

Strange but true

- The hair on your head usually lives for 2 to 6 years before dropping out. Eyelash hairs last for only about 10 weeks.
- Most people have 12 pairs of rib bones, but some have 13.
- On average, a human being eats 50 tons of food and drinks 13,000 gallons (50,000 litres) of liquid in a lifetime.
- Each person walks about 15,000 miles (25,000 km) during a lifetime.

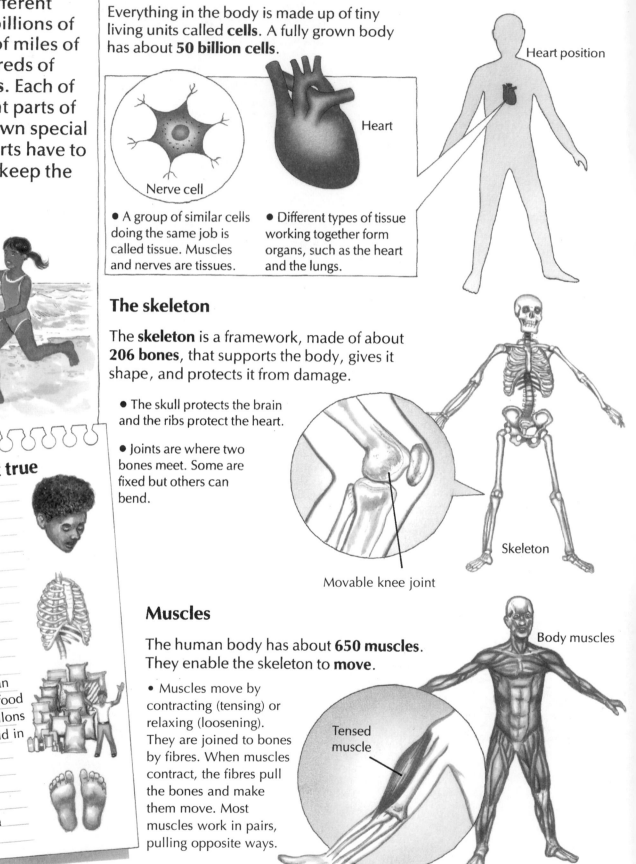

Normal body temperature averages 98°F (37°C)

If your temperature rises to 100°F (38°C) you feel hot and feverish

Most body heat is lost through the top of your head

The blood system

Blood carries **oxygen gas** and dissolved food particles called **nutrients** to all the cells in the body, so that they can make **energy**.

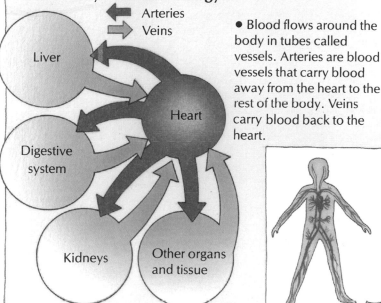

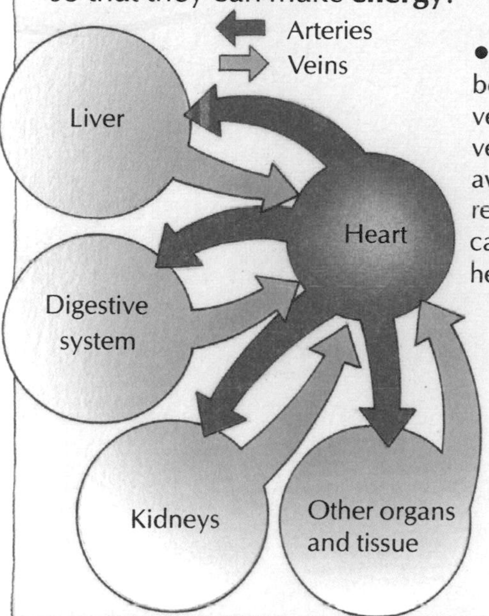

- Blood flows around the body in tubes called vessels. Arteries are blood vessels that carry blood away from the heart to the rest of the body. Veins carry blood back to the heart.

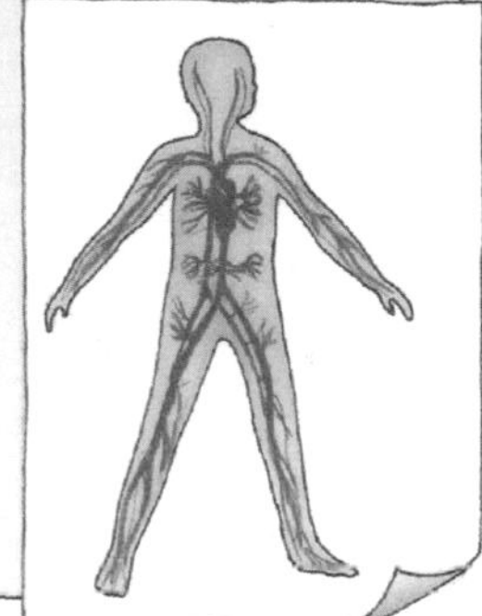

The lungs

Oxygen passes into the blood through the lung walls when we breathe in. Waste **carbon dioxide** gas is passed back into the lungs from the blood.

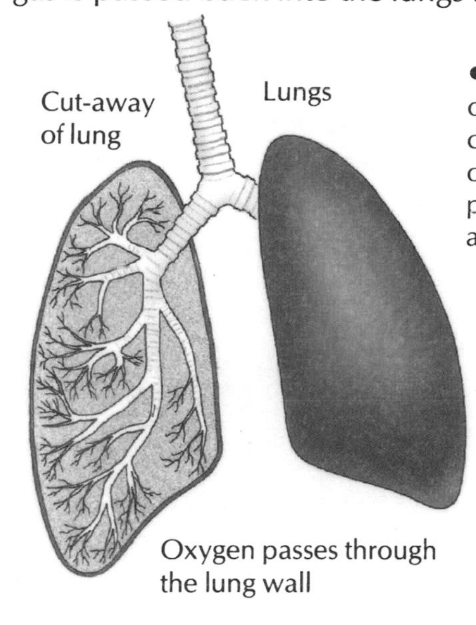

- There are two lungs, one in each side of the chest. They are spongy organs made of tightly packed tissue, nerves, and blood vessels.

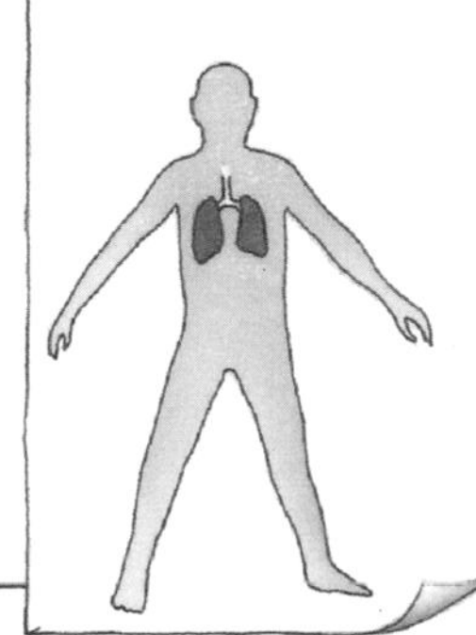

The digestive system

Everything a human being eats has to be broken down by the body before **nutrients** from the food can be taken into the blood and turned into energy.

This process takes place in the **digestive system**, a series of connected parts that make up a passage beginning at the mouth and ending at the anus.

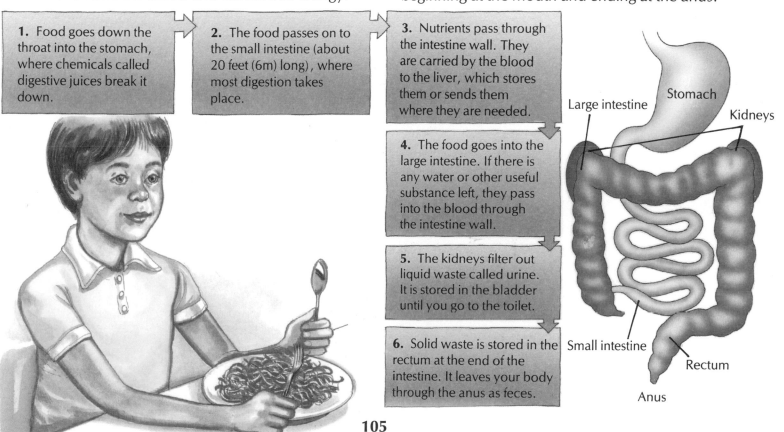

1. Food goes down the throat into the stomach, where chemicals called digestive juices break it down.
2. The food passes on to the small intestine (about 20 feet (6m) long), where most digestion takes place.
3. Nutrients pass through the intestine wall. They are carried by the blood to the liver, which stores them or sends them where they are needed.
4. The food goes into the large intestine. If there is any water or other useful substance left, they pass into the blood through the intestine wall.
5. The kidneys filter out liquid waste called urine. It is stored in the bladder until you go to the toilet.
6. Solid waste is stored in the rectum at the end of the intestine. It leaves your body through the anus as feces.

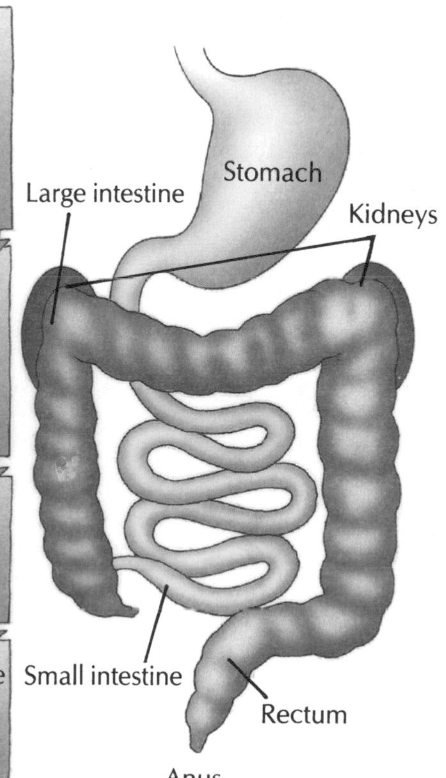

Body Controls

Different areas of the brain control different functions:

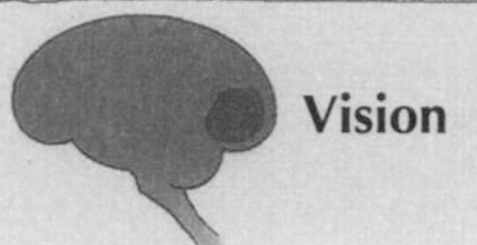

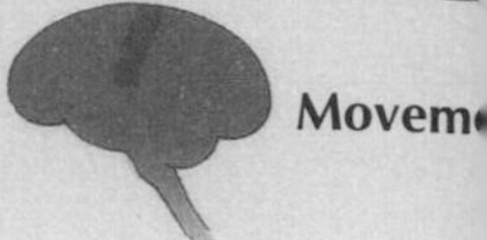

The human body has a very efficient system for **sensing** the world around it. It can feel, see, hear, smell and taste things and deal with all this information better than any computer. It has to do this to survive.

All the information the body receives is processed by the **brain**, which is thought to be more highly developed in humans than in any other animal species.

Brain power

The brain is the body's control centre. It keeps the body running smoothly, thinks and makes decisions, stores memories and produces feelings such as happiness, anger and sorrow.

• The body is continually sending messages to the brain, telling it what is happening. The brain sends messages back, telling the body parts what to do. The messages pass along nerves that run throughout the body.

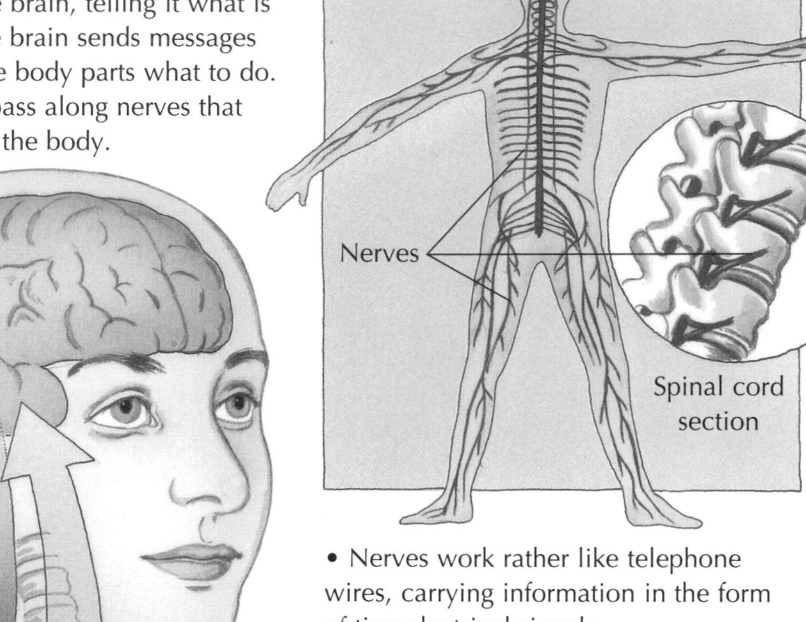

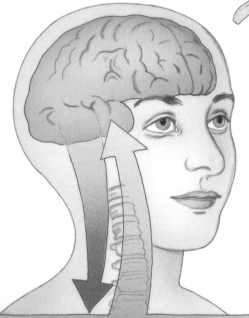

• Nerves work rather like telephone wires, carrying information in the form of tiny electrical signals.

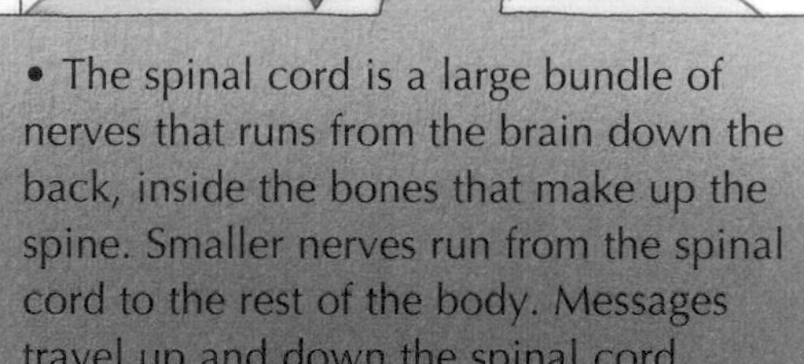

• The spinal cord is a large bundle of nerves that runs from the brain down the back, inside the bones that make up the spine. Smaller nerves run from the spinal cord to the rest of the body. Messages travel up and down the spinal cord.

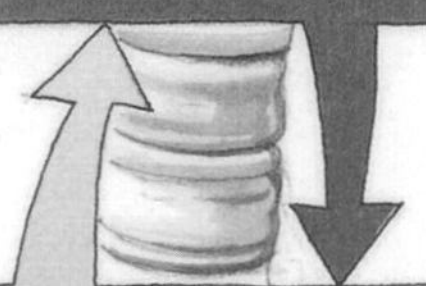

• The brain gets messages about the world outside the body from the senses. People have five main senses – sight, hearing, smell, taste and touch. The sense organs are the body parts that sense things. They are the eyes, ears, nose, tongue and skin.

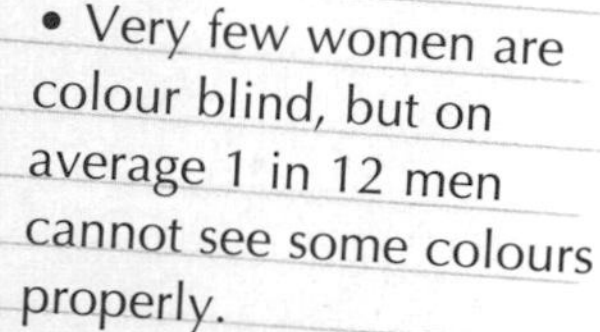

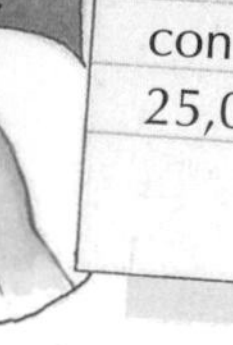

Strange but true

• An adult's brain weighs about 1.4 kg. It is roughly the size and shape of a cauliflower.

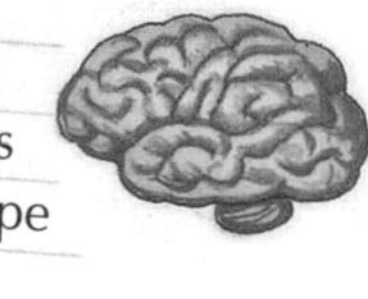

• The body's fastest messages pass along the nerves at 400 km/h.

• Very few women are colour blind, but on average 1 in 12 men cannot see some colours properly.

• One brain cell may be connected to as many as 25,000 other brain cells.

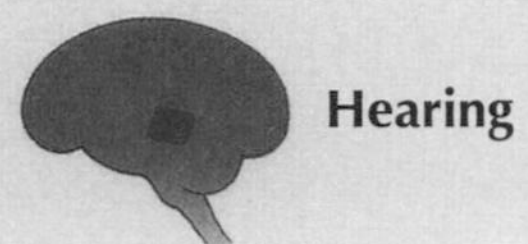

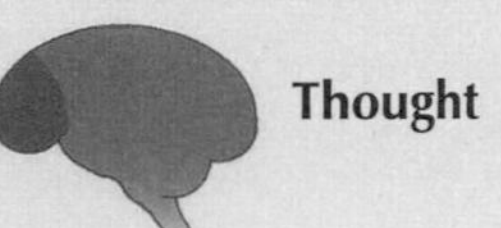

Seeing

The **eye** has a special lining called the **retina**. This contains cells that are sensitive to light. Messages from these cells pass along **nerves** to the **brain**, which works out what the eyes are looking at.

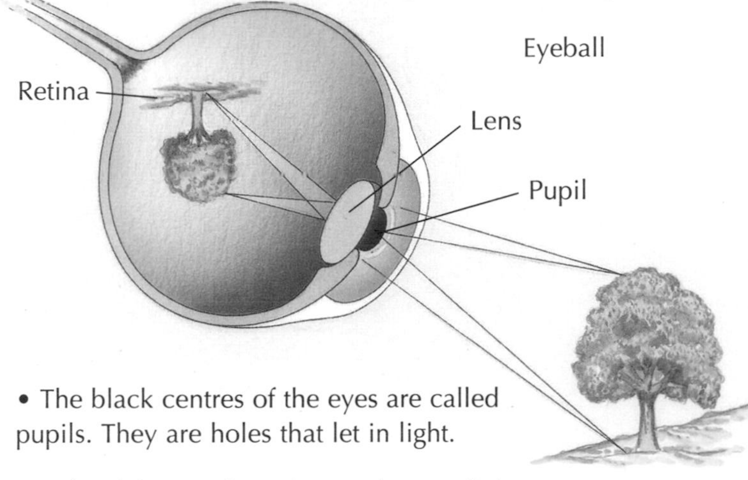

• The black centres of the eyes are called pupils. They are holes that let in light.

• Behind the pupil is a lens. It focuses light rays into an upside-down picture on the retina inside the back of the eyeball. The brain turns the image the right way up.

Hearing

The part of the ear you can see is called the **outer ear**. The collects and funnels sounds into the **inner ear**. Inside the inner ear:

• The sounds make the eardrum vibrate, or shake. The vibrations pass on through two small bones called the hammer and the anvil, and then through a group of three tiny bones called the stirrup.

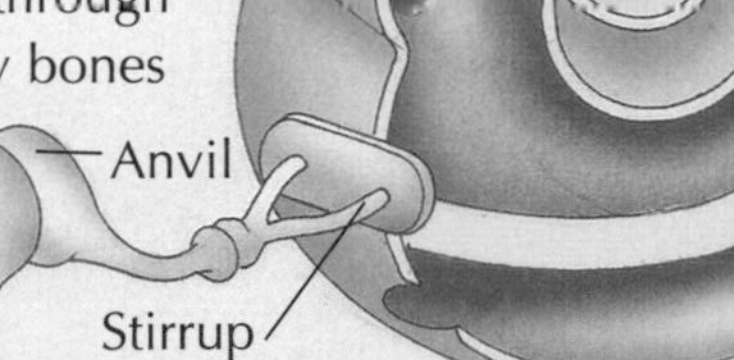

• Finally the vibrations reach a coiled tube called the cochlea. This is filled with liquid and line with tiny hairs connected to nerve endings. These pass messages about the vibrations to the brain.

Smelling and tasting

Inside the back of the **nose** there are nerve endings that pick up **smells** and send messages about them to the brain. On the **tongue**, special groups of cells called **tastebuds** pick up and send messages about **taste**.

• Tiny smell molecules travel though the air and enter the nasal cavity behind your nose.

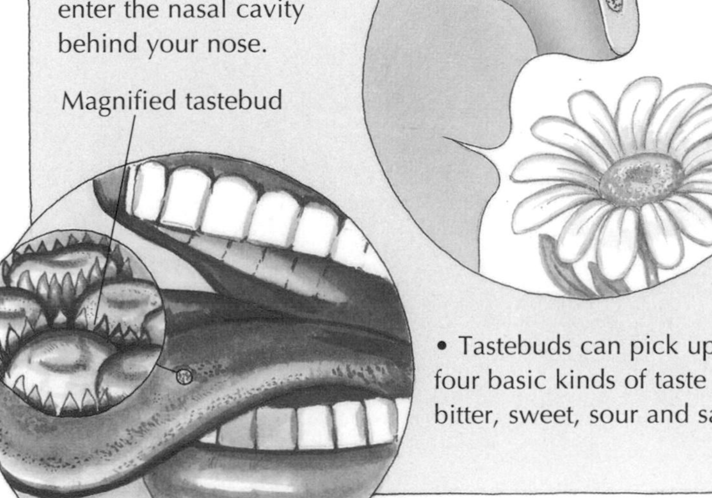

• Tastebuds can pick up four basic kinds of taste – bitter, sweet, sour and salty.

Touching

Your **skin** is full of nerve endings that supply the brain with information about **touch**. There are lots of different nerve endings to pick up information about different kinds of touch sensation.

• A piece of skin the size of a small coin has at least 35 nerve endings in it, as well as over 3 million cells, 1 metre of blood vessels and many tiny bundles of cells called glands, which produce sweat and oil.

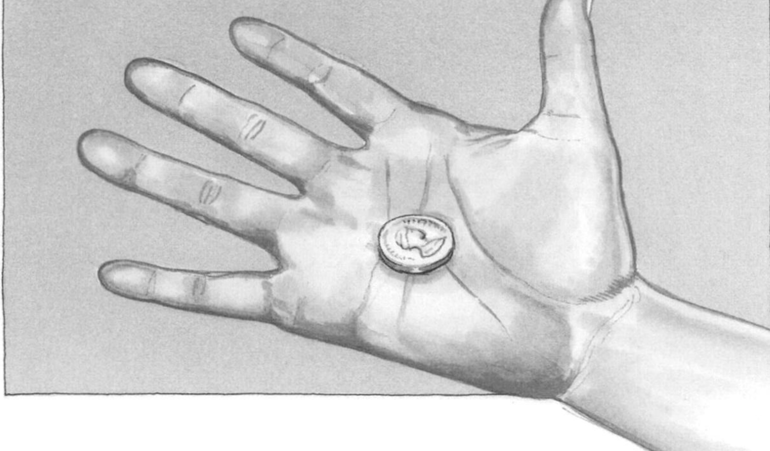

New Life

These are some of the things a human body is made of:

Fat: as much as in 7 bars of soap

All new life begins with just one **cell**. To make this first cell, a male **sperm** must enter a female **egg** called an **ovum**. The cell then starts growing and dividing to make new cells. These divide in turn to make the millions of cells found in the human body. The creation of new life is called **reproduction**.

People grow and change throughout their lives, from birth to old age. No two human beings are exactly the same in looks or in personality, but everyone goes through the same stages of development.

How babies are born

The moment when a sperm enters an egg is called **conception** or **fertilization**.

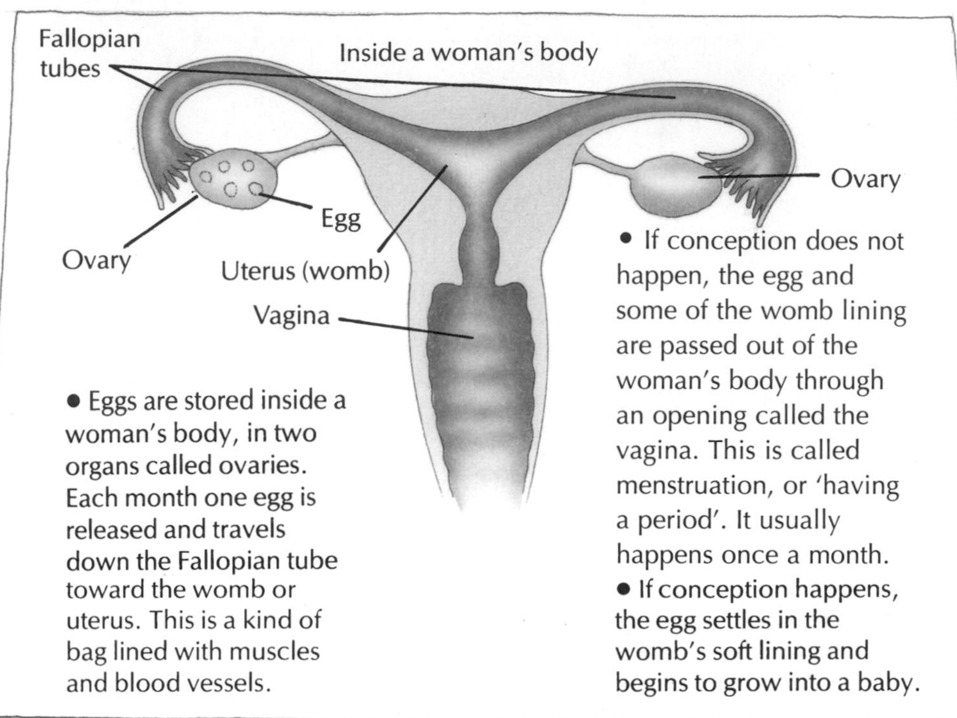

Inside a woman's body
Fallopian tubes
Ovary
Egg
Ovary
Uterus (womb)
Vagina
• Eggs are stored inside a woman's body, in two organs called ovaries. Each month one egg is released and travels down the Fallopian tube toward the womb or uterus. This is a kind of bag lined with muscles and blood vessels.
• If conception does not happen, the egg and some of the womb lining are passed out of the woman's body through an opening called the vagina. This is called menstruation, or 'having a period'. It usually happens once a month.
• If conception happens, the egg settles in the womb's soft lining and begins to grow into a baby.

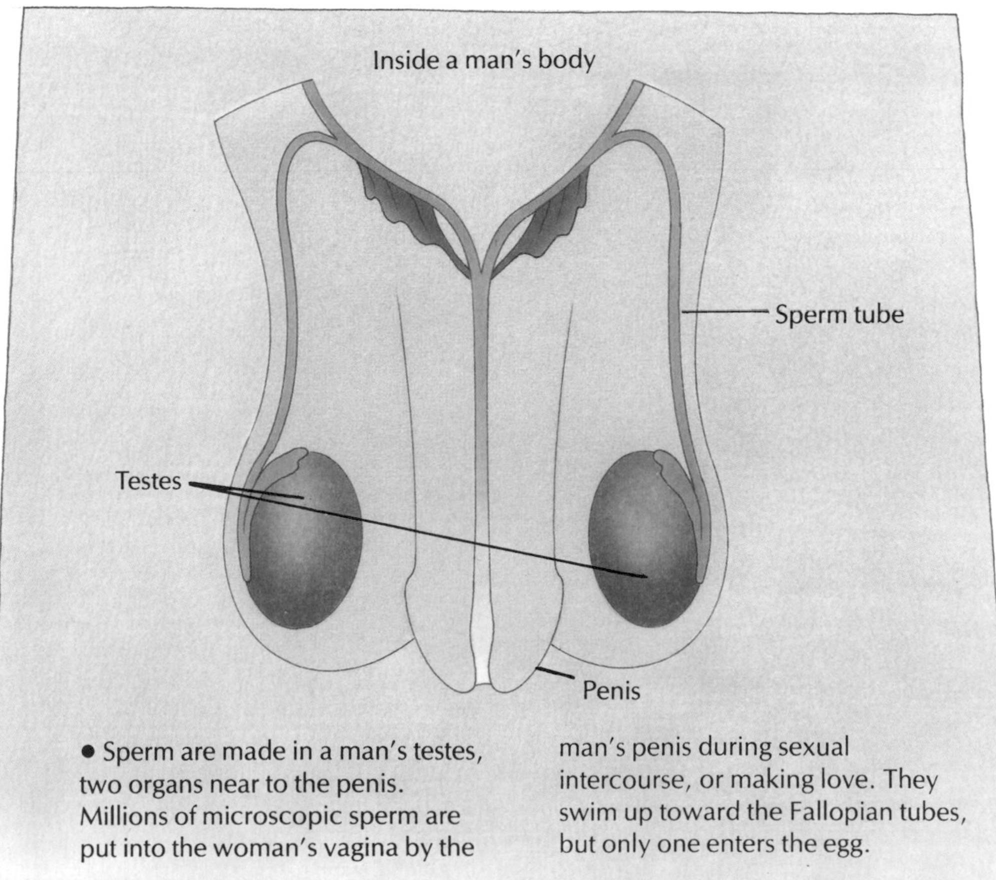

Inside a man's body
Sperm tube
Testes
Penis
• Sperm are made in a man's testes, two organs near to the penis. Millions of microscopic sperm are put into the woman's vagina by the man's penis during sexual intercourse, or making love. They swim up toward the Fallopian tubes, but only one enters the egg.

Strange but true
• Children tend to grow faster in spring and summer.
• On average, women tend to live longer than men.
• If you carried on growing as fast as a baby does in the womb, you would be 50 feet (15m) by the time your were 10 years old!
• The most babies born to a mother at one birth is 10.

Iron: as much as in a 1 inch (2.5 cm-long) nail

Carbon: as much as in 9000 pencils

Water: two-thirds of the body is water. Adults contain about 12 gallons (45l).

How babies grow

From **conception** to **birth** takes about 38 weeks. Here are some of the stages along the way:

- Six weeks: the baby is very small, about an inch (2.4 cm) long. It has begun to develop a nervous system, a heart, a digestive tract, and sense organs. It has buds that will develop into arms and legs.
- Twelve weeks: the baby is between 2½ and 3 inches (6.25 cm and 7.5 cm) long. It is inside a fluid-filled bag called the amniotic sac, connected to its mother by an umbilical cord.
- Twenty-eight weeks: the baby is between 12 and 14 inches (30 and 36 cm) long and weighs about 30 ounces (900 grams.) A creamy-colored wax has now developed over its body.
- Around 38 weeks: the baby is ready to be born. It is 20 inches (50 cm) long and weighs 6 to 11 pounds (3 to 5 kg).

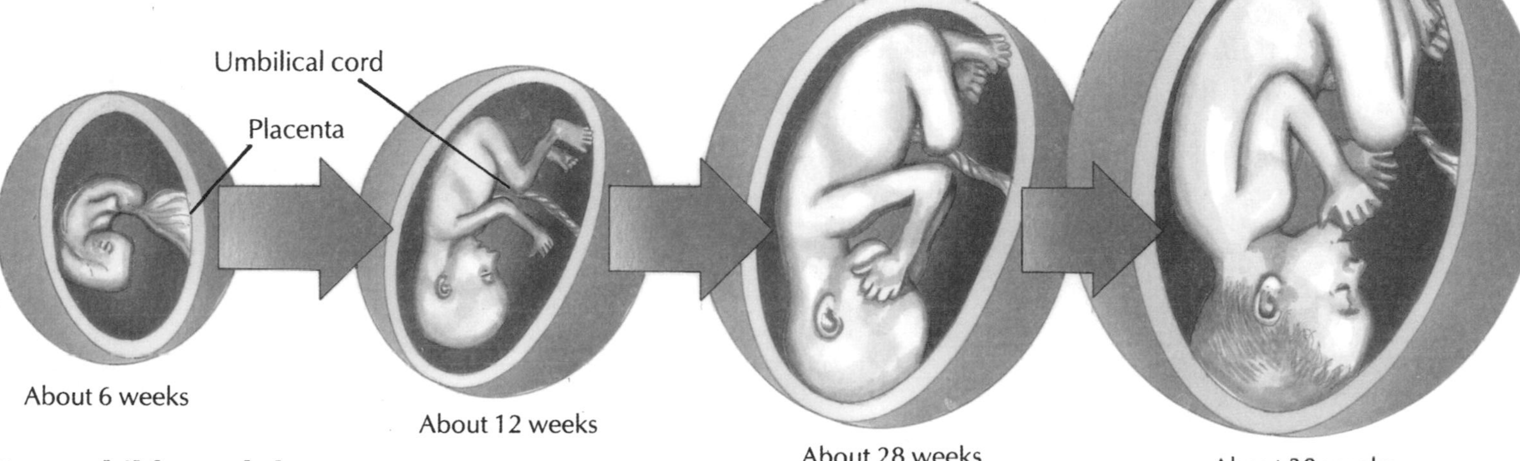

About 6 weeks

About 12 weeks

About 28 weeks

About 38 weeks

From child to adult

The period of time when children are growing into adults is called **adolescence**. The early part of adolescence, when bodies change, is called **puberty**. The changes take place at any time between the ages of 10 and 15. Here are some of them:

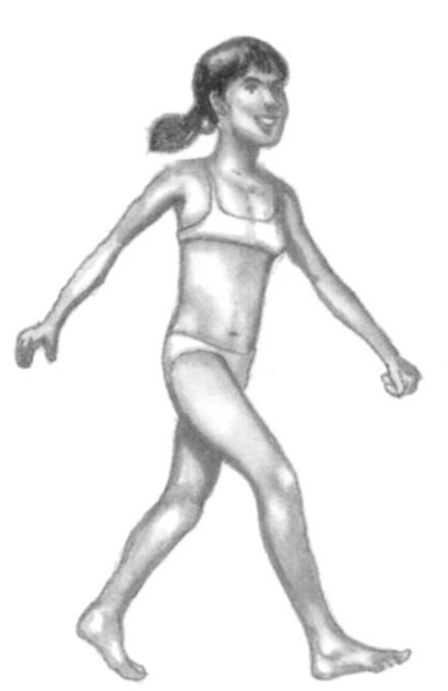

- Girls start to menstruate (have periods). Their breasts start to grow bigger, their hips get broader and they grow more body hair.

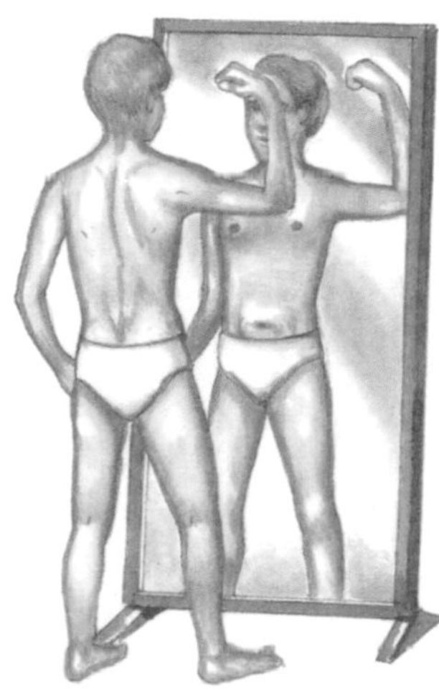

- Boys start making sperm in their testes. They grow facial hair and their voices 'break' or deepen. Their shoulders and chests become broader.

Growing older

Once people are fully grown their bodies very slowly start to **wear out** and **slow down**.

- When women get older, eggs stop being released from their ovaries. They cannot have babies any more because menstruation stops. This time is called the menopause. For most women it happens some time during their late 40s or early 50s.

- In old age, bones become more fragile, skin stretches and wrinkles, and hair often goes white and gets thinner. Muscles become weaker and some people cannot hear or see as well as they once could.

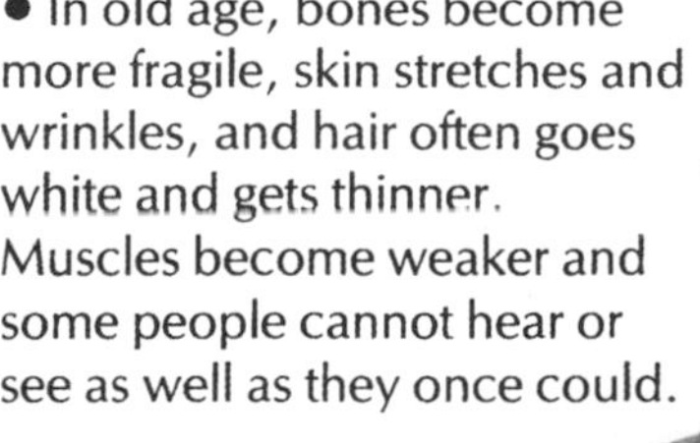

Living Together

Here are some wedding customs from around the world:

India: Hindu brides draw red patterns on their hands and feet

Most people live in small groups called **families** that contain **parents**, **children**, and (sometimes) other **relatives**. One important purpose of the family is to look after its members. The aged and sick can be looked after by younger members of the family, and babies and young children can be cared for until they are old enough to look after themselves.

Not all families are the same. Here you can find out about some of the ways people live around the world.

Families

There are different **kinds of families**. Nuclear families are the most common kind, but there are many other family patterns.

• Nuclear family: a mother, father, and a child or children living together.

• Extended family: a large group of grandparents, parents, children, and other relatives all living together.

• Single-parent family: a child or children living with one parent only.

• Commune: a large group of people living together as a family, but not necessarily related.

• Clan or tribe: a large group made up of families that are related to each other.

Strange but true

- The custom of giving wedding rings dates back to ancient Roman times.
- An American man called Glynn Wolfe has been married a total of 27 times!
- Viking families always sent their children away to live with other people.
- 6516 couples were married in the same mass ceremony in South Korea in 1988.

Greece: guests pin money on the bride and groom's clothes

Africa: gifts of cattle are given to the bride's family

Britain: horseshoes are given to the bride as a symbol of good luck

Marriage

Marriage is an agreement to live together made by a man and a woman. The **wedding** or **marriage ceremony** is important in many religions. It is usually a time for **celebration**.

• In societies such as Australia, Canada, Europe, and the United States, most people are free to choose who they want to marry.

• In most societies, people have one marriage partner at a time. This is called monogamy.

• In a few societies, men can have more than one wife at a time. This is called polygamy.

• A common-law marriage is when a couple live together as husband and wife but do not go through a legal or religious marriage ceremony.

• Some married couples decide that they are not happy living together. In many societies they can end the marriage by getting divorced.

• In some places, such as India and the Middle East, parents choose marriage partners for their children.

Having babies

Different societies around the world have special **customs** for the birth of a baby:

• The Mbuti pygmies of the African rain forests tie a piece of jungle vine around a new baby's waist. They attach a small piece of wood to the vine to pass on the strength of the forest to the baby.

• The Ainu hunters of northern Japan make a tiny cut in a new baby's thigh. They dress the cut with fungi to pass on the magical power of sacred trees.

• The Nootka tribe, from the northwest coast of North America, believe that twins are magical. If a family has twins, the parents and children are kept apart from the rest of the tribe for four years, so their magical properties will develop.

• In many societies births are followed by a religious festival. In Christian countries babies are christened. They have the sign of the cross made on their foreheads with holy water.

Talking To Each Other

Here are some language facts:

Most widely spoken language: Mandarin Chinese, 715 million people

Although many creatures communicate with each other using sounds, only humans have developed spoken language to tell each other about their ideas and feelings.

There are about 5000 languages in the world today, but many of them are spoken only by small groups of people. Most languages have variations or dialects – different forms of a language that are spoken only in particular areas.

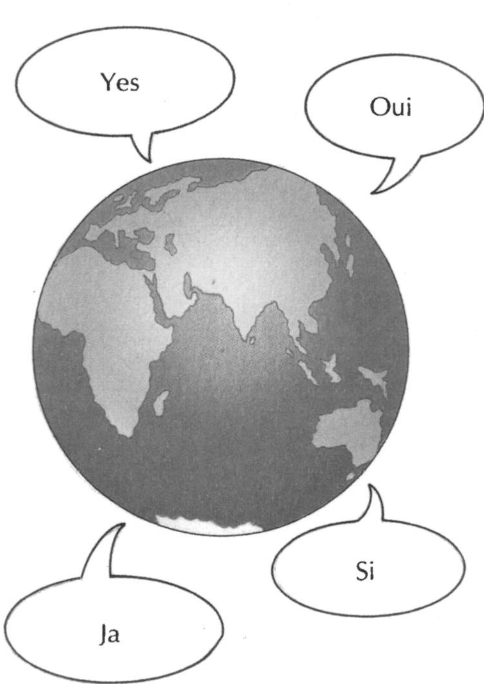

People have tried to invent a new language that everyone in the world could share. The most successful so far is **Esperanto**, which more than 100 million people have learned since its invention in 1887.

Learning a language

Most young children learn the **language** spoken by their **family** very easily, almost without knowing they are doing so.

- Babies learn by listening to the voices they hear around them and by copying sounds and words.
- By the time they are two years old, most children can use several hundred words.
- Children who are brought up hearing two languages all the time soon learn to speak both. Someone who speaks two languages is called bilingual.

Languages

Languages are divided into groups, called **families**. All the languages in a family developed from one earlier language.

- About 48% (almost half the world's people) speak a language from the Indo-European family. This includes all the major languages of Europe as well as some from Iran and India.
- About 23% (nearly a quarter of the world's people) speak one of the Chinese family of languages.

mat (Russian)
meter (Greek)
madre (Spanish)
mutter (Germany)
mère (French)
mother (English)

- Here are some words for "mother" in Indo-European languages. They all come from the word *mata*, which is "mother" in the ancient Sanskrit language.

Changing languages

Languages change all the time. Words may be **borrowed** from other languages, or **invented** to name a new idea or object.

- Many English words have been invented. For example, the word *television* was invented using *tele* (a Greek word meaning "far") and *vision* (from the Latin word for "to see").
- These English words were borrowed: *Mosquito* (Spanish), *Tea* (Chinese), *Sugar* (Arabic), *Shampoo* (Hindi), *Ski* (Norwegian), *Robot* (Czech), *Ketchup* (Malay), *Parka* (Russian).

Language spoken in more countries than any other: English

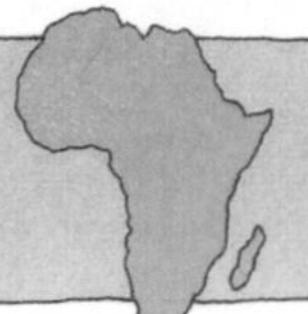

Number of languages spoken in Africa: about 1000

Alphabet with the most letters: Cambodian, 72 letters

Writing things down

Writing developed much later than spoken language. Here are some facts about **written languages**:

Hieroglyph examples

Greek alphabet

**αβϐγδεζηθικλμνξοπρσςτυφϕχψω
ΑΒΓΔΕΖΗΘΙΚΛΜΝΞΟΠΡΣΤΥΦ
ΧΨΩ 1234567890 .,:;**

Arabic alphabet

ابتثجحخدذرزسشصضطظعغفقكلمنهويلا
١٢٣٤٥٦٧٨٩٠

Chinese symbols

生 拿
火.個
。
你 燈

- The first written languages used picture symbols to represent whole words.
- The earliest-known picture symbols were used in the Iranian region in about 3500 B.C. The Ancient Egyptians began using picture symbols called hieroglyphics in about 3000 B.C.
- Most modern languages are written in alphabets. The words are spelled out with letters. Each letter represents a sound.
- The Phoenicians, who lived along the Mediterranean, developed the first alphabet in about 1000 B.C.
- Chinese is the only major modern language that has no alphabet. Instead it has around 50,000 picture symbols.
- Some Chinese words are made from one symbol. Others are made up of various symbols mixed together.

Speaking without words

Movements made by the face, head, arms, hands, and body can signal thoughts and feelings almost as clearly as spoken words. These signals are called **body language**.

- When people are nervous they often fidget with their hands.
- The distance between people who are talking to each other is important. If one person stands too close, the other one may feel threatened and move away.
- Body language varies from place to place. For example, in some countries looking a person straight in the eye means that you are honest and truthful. In other countries it is regarded as bad manners.

Strange but true

O

- O is the oldest letter in our alphabet. It has not changed since 1300 B.C.
- The small country of Papua New Guinea has about 500 separate languages – about 10% of the world's total.

- The greatest number of languages spoken by one person is 28.
- The most complicated written character in Chinese is made up of 64 brushstrokes and means 'talkative'!

Food

Here are some unusual foods from around the world:

Africa: locusts, grubs, and ants

Without food, people cannot survive. Food gives the body **energy** to make it work.

To stay healthy, you need a **balanced diet**: a good mixture of the different kinds of food available. Sadly, many people in the world today do not have enough food to eat.

Meal with animal products

Vegetarian meal

All food comes from plants or animals. Humans are **omnivorous**, which means they are able to eat both meat and plants. However, some people choose to be **vegetarian**, which means they do not eat meat.

Plant food

Plants that grow well in a particular part of the world provide the **staple diet**, or main food, of that area. Here are some staple foods and the places where they are eaten:

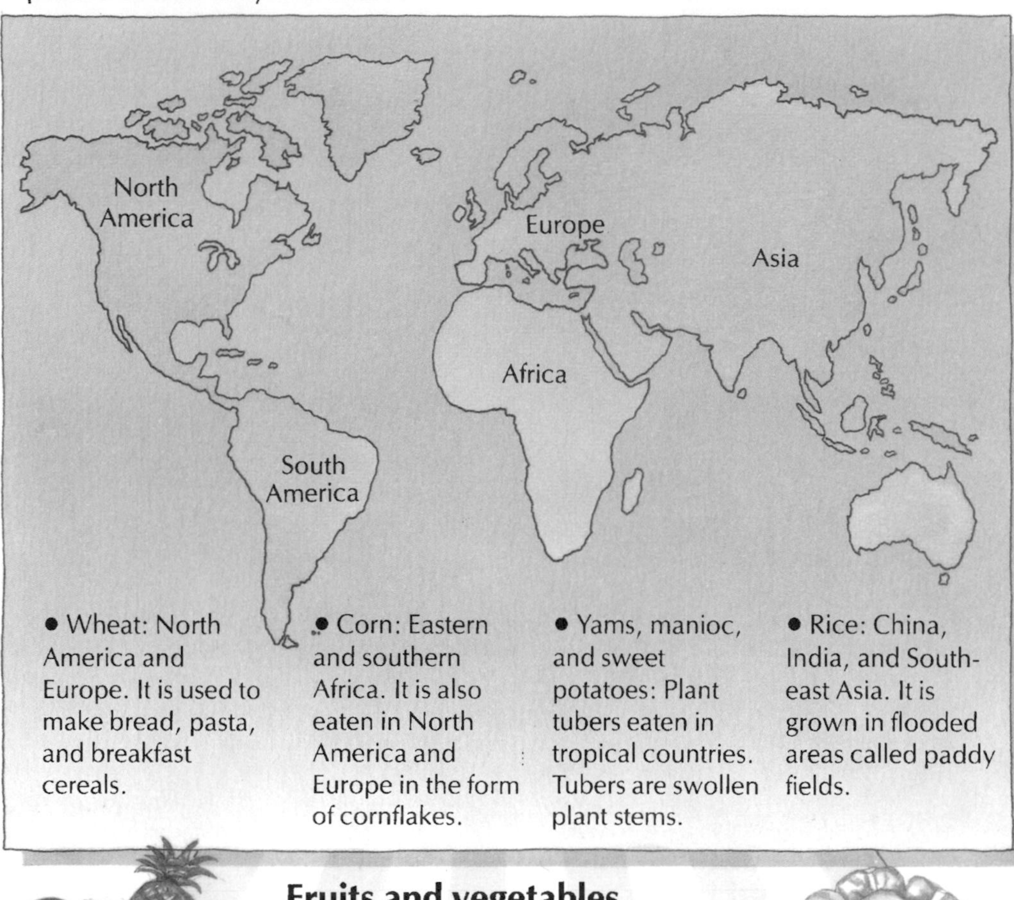

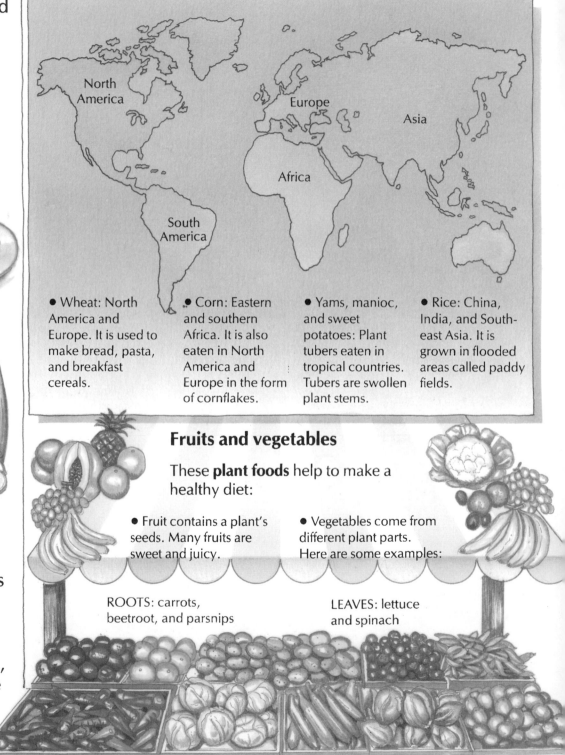

- Wheat: North America and Europe. It is used to make bread, pasta, and breakfast cereals.
- Corn: Eastern and southern Africa. It is also eaten in North America and Europe in the form of cornflakes.
- Yams, manioc, and sweet potatoes: Plant tubers eaten in tropical countries. Tubers are swollen plant stems.
- Rice: China, India, and South-east Asia. It is grown in flooded areas called paddy fields.

Fruits and vegetables

These **plant foods** help to make a healthy diet:

- Fruit contains a plant's seeds. Many fruits are sweet and juicy.
- Vegetables come from different plant parts. Here are some examples:

ROOTS: carrots, beetroot, and parsnips

LEAVES: lettuce and spinach

STALKS: celery and asparagus

BUDS: cabbage and brussels sprouts

SEEDS: peas, beans, and sweet corn

FLOWERS: cauliflower

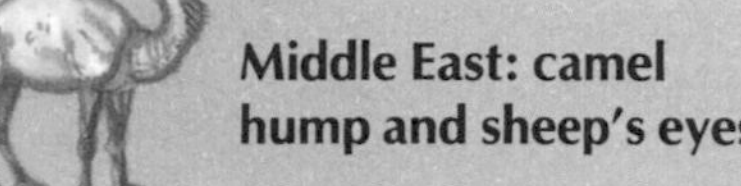

Central and South America: alligator

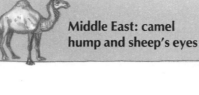

What food contains

Food contains **nutrients**, which the body needs to keep it healthy. Here are the main nutrients, what they do, and a list of some of the foods in which they are found:

Nutrients	What They Do	Where Found
Proteins	Help the body cells to grow and repair injuries	Meat, fish, cheese, eggs, beans
Carbohydrates	Provide energy	Bread, potatoes, pasta, rice, flour, sugar
Fats	Build body cells and provide energy	Milk, cheese, oils, butter, oily fish, nuts
Vitamins	Keep the body healthy	There are about 20 vitamins, found in many different foods. Vitamin C, for example, is found in fruit and vegetables
Minerals	Many minerals are found in food, including calcium (builds teeth and bone) and iron (keeps blood healthy)	Cheese, milk (calcium) Liver, brown bread (iron)

Cooking food

The first humans ate their food raw. Then, about 500,000 years ago, people learned how to use fire for **cooking**. This is what cooking does:

- Breaks down tough food so that you can eat and digest it more easily. Cooking different foods together creates new tastes.
- Helps to preserve food from going rotten. It also destroys some nutrients, so vegetables and fruit are sometimes better for you if eaten raw.

Strange but true

- The longest sausage ever made was 13 miles (21 km) long – enough to reach to the top of the world's tallest building 44 times.
- Kebabs (meat cooked on skewers) were invented by Turkish soldiers who spiked meat onto their swords to roast in a fire.
- The first plates were simply large pieces of bread that you ate along with the meal.

Clothes

Here are some traditional clothes from around the world:

Brazil: Mardi Gras carnival dress

Human beings are the only creatures that wear **clothes**. People need clothes because, unlike most other animals, they have no **fur or feathers** to protect them.

The earliest people wore simple clothes made of **animal skins** to protect their bodies. Over the years people began to use clothes for decoration as well as for comfort.

Clothes can tell you something about a person — for instance, which part of the world they come from, or what work they do.

Making clothes

Over thousands of years, humans have developed **tools** for making clothes and have learned how to make and use lots of different **fabrics** (materials).

- The first needles were made of bone. They were used about 40,000 years ago.
- The first sewing thread was made from narrow strips of leather.

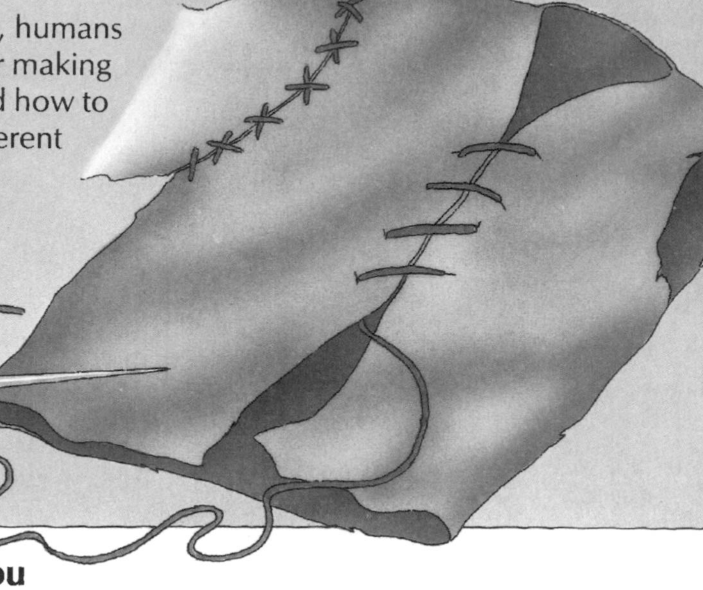

What clothes tell you

Clothes can sometimes tell you what **work** people do or what **group** they belong to. Here are some examples of this:

- To show wealth and power: rulers such as kings and queens sometimes wear robes and crowns to show their power.
- For protection at work: astronauts, firefighters, and surgeons all wear special clothing to protect their bodies.

- To show membership of a group; sports teams wear uniforms; fans wear the team's colours.

- To show authority: police, soldiers, pilots, ships' officers, and many others wear uniforms that people can identify.

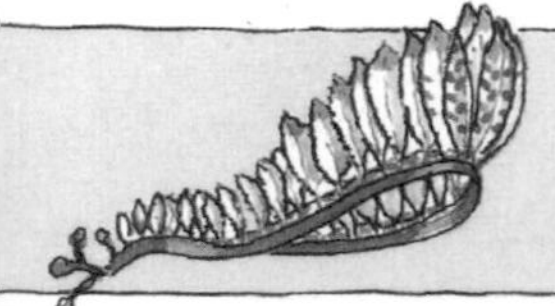

North America: Native American headdress

Hawaii: grass skirt and flowers

Africa: tribal celebration dress

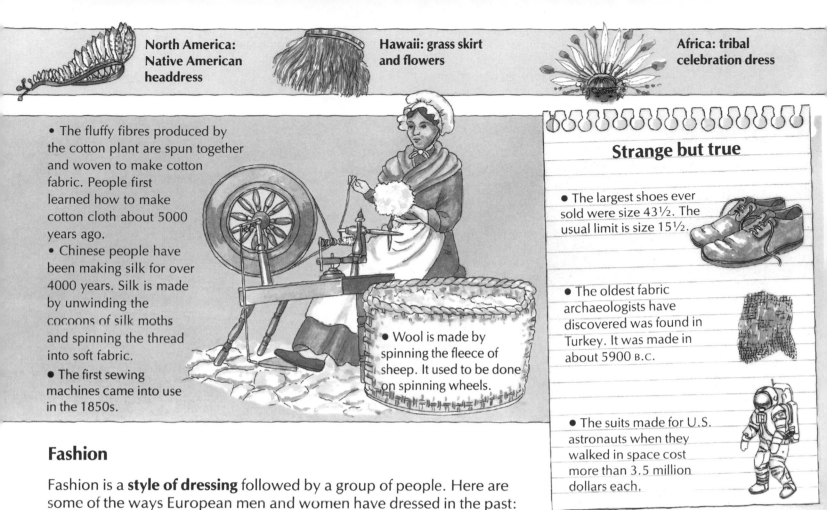

• The fluffy fibres produced by the cotton plant are spun together and woven to make cotton fabric. People first learned how to make cotton cloth about 5000 years ago.

• Chinese people have been making silk for over 4000 years. Silk is made by unwinding the cocoons of silk moths and spinning the thread into soft fabric.

• The first sewing machines came into use in the 1850s.

• Wool is made by spinning the fleece of sheep. It used to be done on spinning wheels.

Strange but true

• The largest shoes ever sold were size 43½. The usual limit is size 15½.

• The oldest fabric archaeologists have discovered was found in Turkey. It was made in about 5900 B.C.

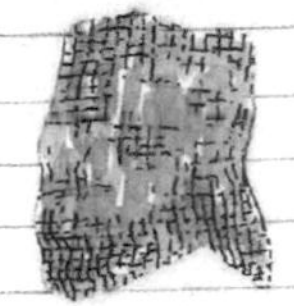

• The suits made for U.S. astronauts when they walked in space cost more than 3.5 million dollars each.

Fashion

Fashion is a **style of dressing** followed by a group of people. Here are some of the ways European men and women have dressed in the past:

• About 700 years ago, men and women wore long robes.

• About 500 years ago, many men wore doublets (jackets with a padded chest) and hose (leggings).

• Long pants for men did not appear until about 1830. Women did not wear pants regularly until about 1940.

• Today, many boys and girls wear the same kinds of clothes. Jeans and t-shirts are popular in many countries.

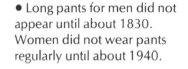

Climate

Clothes are designed to keep people warm or keep them cool, according to the **climate**.

• In the freezing Arctic areas of Canada, Greenland, and Russia, people wear layers of thick padded clothing to keep warm.

• In many hot countries, people wear long cool robes to protect them from the Sun.

Homes

Here are some unusual houses from around the world:

Syria: beehive-shaped mud houses

People need homes where they can eat, sleep and shelter from the weather. Most houses are made of materials that are easy to find in the place where they are built. They are usually designed to suit the climate of their area.

In some countries people build their own homes. In other countries, architects design houses and builders construct them.

Strange but true

• The world's largest palace has 1788 rooms. It was built for the Sultan of Brunei.

• Lavatories were not installed in most houses until the mid 1800s.

• The world's tallest apartment block is the Metropolitan Tower in New York. People live in the top 48 storeys, with 30 office floors below.

Shapes and sizes

Here are some traditional house styles from around the world, built to suit the **climate** and local **materials**.

• Iceland: turf roofs are used to keep the heat in.

• Arctic: Inuit people build temporary houses made of blocks of snow, called igloos.

Homes on the move

Nomads are people who have no fixed home. They move around looking for work or pastures for their animals.

Middle East: cave dwellings

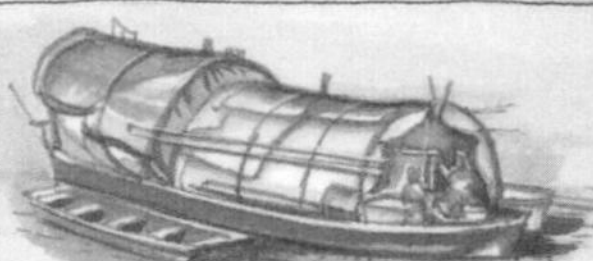
Hong Kong: houseboat on the harbour

California: experimental house run on solar power

• South America: the Quechua Indians build homes of mud bricks with thick pampas grass on the roof.

• Around the Mediterranean: many houses are painted white to reflect sunshine. Some have window shutters to keep the inside cool.

• Switzerland: houses have long-sloping roofs so that snow can slide off them in winter.

• Asia: in marshy areas, people live in houses built on stilts to protect them from floods and wild animals.

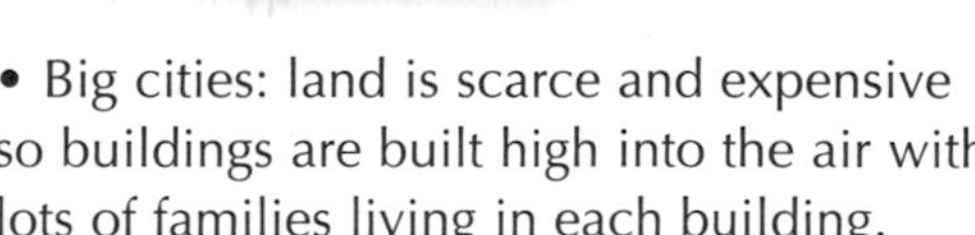
• Big cities: land is scarce and expensive so buildings are built high into the air with lots of families living in each building.

• In the 19th century, North American settlers lived in covered wagons as they travelled across the country to the West.

• In the Sahara Desert nomadic people live in tents made from cloth of woven goat hair. The sides can be rolled up to let cool breezes in.

• In Iran the Turkoman people live in circular tents made of wood and felt.

• In Siberia some nomadic people live in tents made of walrus skin.

Houses in the past

Here are some **ancient** house styles:

• Prehistoric dugout hut (Europe: about 3000 B.C.).

Roman villa

• Roman villa built around a courtyard (Europe: about 2000 years ago).

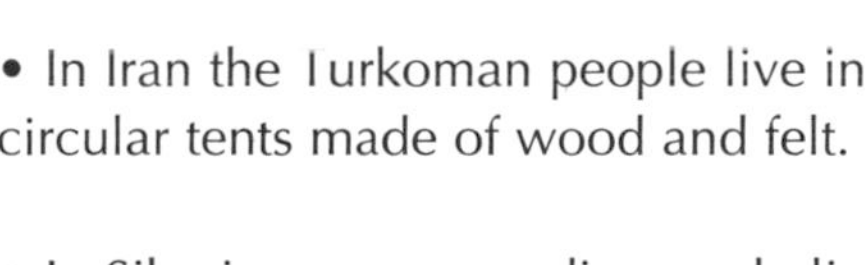

• Half-timbered houses (parts of Northern Europe: 500 years ago).

Half-timbered houses

Religion

These are some religious buildings in which people worship:

Christians: church

Religions are beliefs that are found all over the world. They have **rules of behaviour** that their followers obey, and a **god** or **gods** that they worship. There are usually special **religious ceremonies** and **places of worship**.

Religion began thousands of years ago. Early humans explained natural events such as thunderstorms by saying that gods made them happen. People also made gods of the Sun, Moon, and Earth. They prayed to them for good hunting or crops. Today, millions of people follow one or other of the major world religions.

World religions

These are the major **world religions**:

- Christianity: found by Jesus Christ, whose birth over 2000 years ago marks the beginning of the Christian calendar. Christians believe there is one God, and that Jesus Christ was God on Earth in human form. Their holy book is the Bible.
- Hinduism: developed in India at least 2500 years ago. There are many gods, with Brahma as the most important. Hindus believe in reincarnation, which means that people are reborn many times. In each new life they are rewarded or punished for their deeds in an earlier life.
- Shinto: a Japanese religion whose followers believe that spirits are present in all living things. They worship at holy places called shrines.

An Anglican (Christian) bishop

Strange but true

- Archaeologists think that some caves in Europe were used as places of worship more than 14,000 years ago.
- The world's largest temple is Angkor Wat in Cambodia. It is over 1000 years old.
- The largest recorded gathering of people was at a Hindu religious festival in India in 1989. It was attended by about 15 million people.

Holy objects

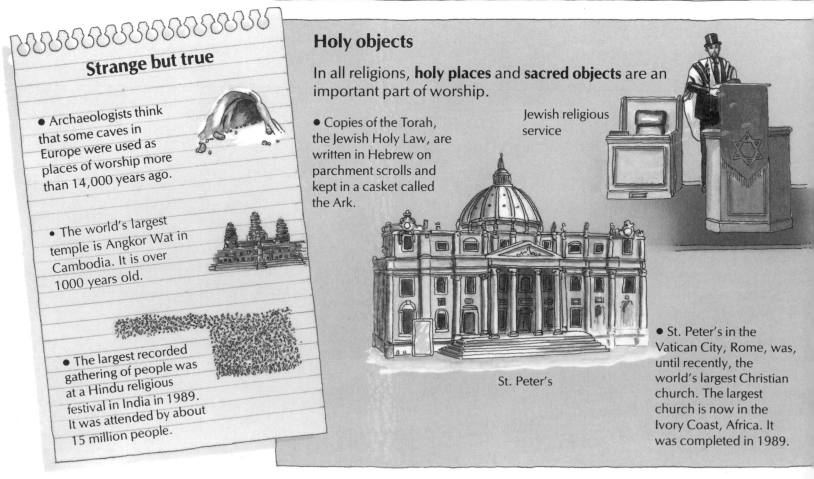

In all religions, **holy places** and **sacred objects** are an important part of worship.

- Copies of the Torah, the Jewish Holy Law, are written in Hebrew on parchment scrolls and kept in a casket called the Ark.

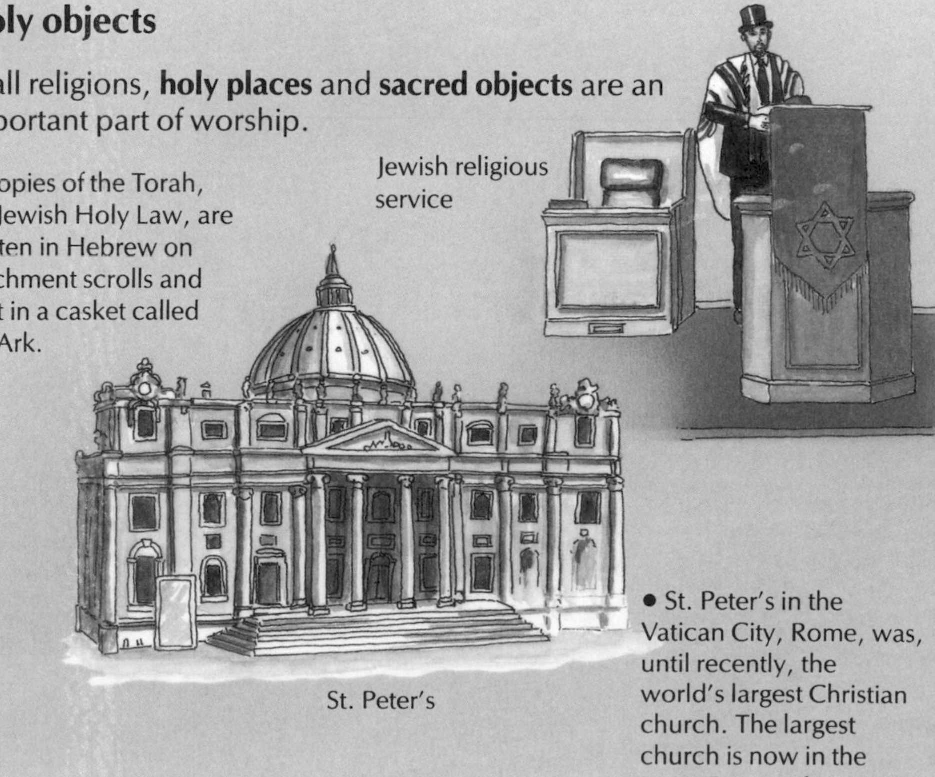

Jewish religious service

St. Peter's

- St. Peter's in the Vatican City, Rome, was, until recently, the world's largest Christian church. The largest church is now in the Ivory Coast, Africa. It was completed in 1989.

Muslims: mosque

Jews: synagogue

Hindus and Buddhists: temple

A Buddhist priest

• Buddhism: founded in India about 2500 years ago by Siddhartha Gautama, who was given the title 'Buddha'. He said that people could escape suffering and find perfect peace ('nirvana') by following his teachings.

• Islam: the religion of Muslims – people who follow the teaching of Muhammad. It was founded some 1400 years ago in the Middle East when the prophet Muhammad received messages from Allah (God). They were written down to form the Koran, the Islam sacred book.

• Judaism: the religion of Jewish people, founded more than 4000 years ago. Jews believe in one God who has chosen them to pass on his Commandments (laws) to the world. They believe a Messiah (saviour) will come from God to bring peace to the world.

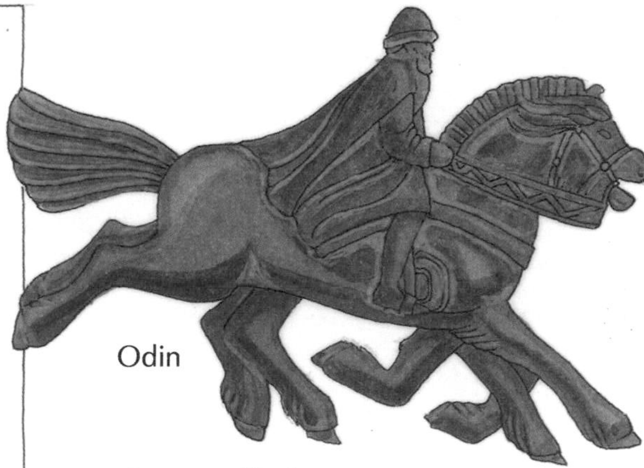

Odin

Ancient religions

• The Viking people of Scandinavia had many gods. The most important, Odin, rode an eight-legged horse. The gods lived in a paradise called Valhalla.

• Aztec people, who lived in Mexico about 800 years ago, worshiped many gods. They made human sacrifices by killing people and tearing out their hearts.

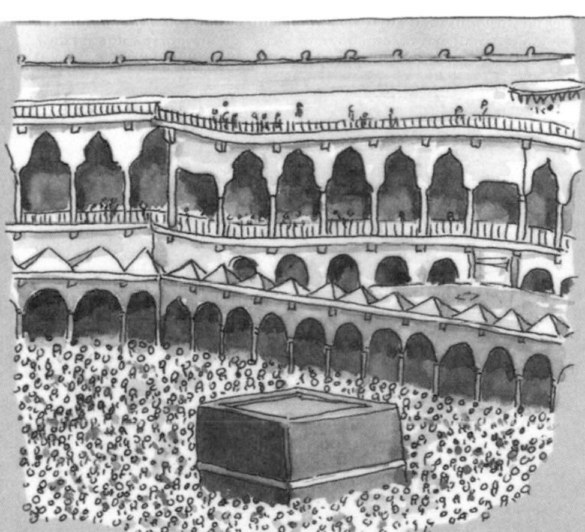

The Ka'bah in Mecca

• The Ka'bah in Mecca, Saudi Arabia, contains a sacred black stone. It is the most holy shrine of Islam. Many thousands of Muslims visit it each year.

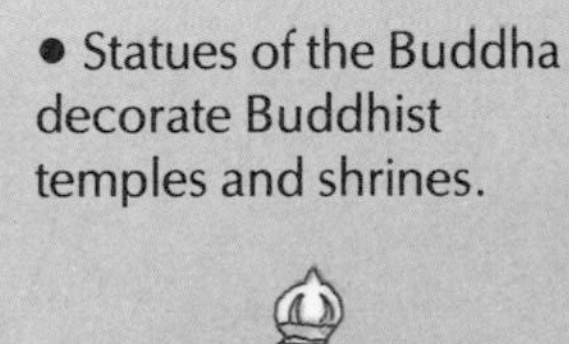

• Statues of the Buddha decorate Buddhist temples and shrines.

Statue of Zeus

• The Ancient Greeks believed in many gods and goddesses, who lived on Mount Olympus. Zeus was the chief god.

• Ancestor worship still survives in parts of Africa and China. People believe the dead look after the living, so they perform ceremonies to their ancestors in the hope they will bring good luck.

Government

These revolutions overthrew governments:

1642: the English Civil war; King Charles I was executed

To live together in peace, people need to agree on certain rules or **laws**. Each country of the world has a **government** that makes decisions about how a country should be run, and makes the laws for its people. The kind of government varies from one country to another.

Governments collect **taxes**, which is money taken from the wages that people earn. These taxes are used to pay for such things as schools, hospitals and roads.

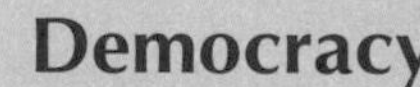

Democracy

Most Western countries are **democracies**. Democracy means:

- 'Rule by the people'. People vote to choose representatives who take part in the government of the country.
- There is a choice of political parties to elect (vote for).
- There are basic human rights, such as the freedom to criticize the government.

Communism

There have been **communist** governments in what was the USSR, and in China, Cuba and parts of Africa. Under communism:

- People can vote, but only for officials of the Communist Party.
- All factories, farms and shops are owned by the State.
- There is no freedom of speech; no-one is allowed to criticize the government or its leaders.

Dictatorship

In a **dictatorship**, one person holds all the power. The people are not allowed to take any part in government or to criticize the leader.

- The Ancient Romans sometimes passed all power to one man – a dictator – in times of war. This ensured that they had a strong leader in a time of trouble. After the war, his power was supposed to end.
- Modern dictators include Hitler (Germany), Stalin (USSR), Mao Tse-tung (China), Ceausescu (Romania) and Saddam Hussein (Iraq).

Strange but true

- English medieval monks practised a form of communal government. They owned all their possessions jointly.
- New Zealand was the first country to allow women to vote. This happened in 1893.
- The world's largest election was held in India in 1989. Over 304 million people voted and 3.5 million staff were needed to collect the votes.

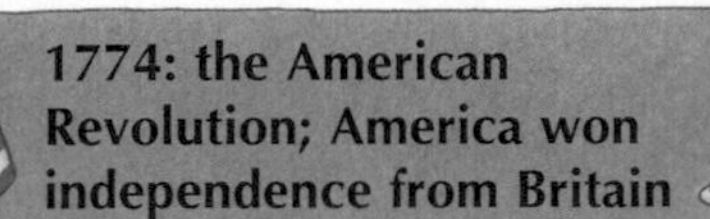

1774: the American Revolution; America won independence from Britain

1789: the French Revolution; the king was overthrown and a republic set up

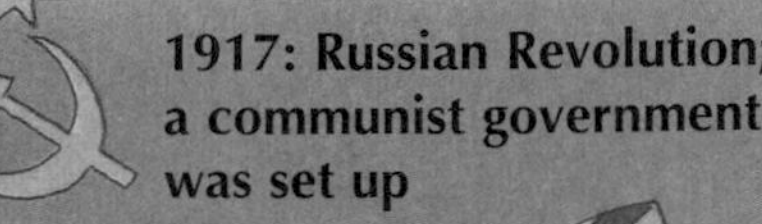

1917: Russian Revolution; a communist government was set up

Government by parliament

The **parliament** comes from an old French word meaning 'to talk'. Parliament is where politicians elected by the people meet to discuss problems and govern the country. The **British parliamentary system** is the oldest in the world:

• The British parliament is divided into the House of Commons and the House of Lords. Members of the House of Lords are not elected.

• Many other countries have parliaments based on the British system.

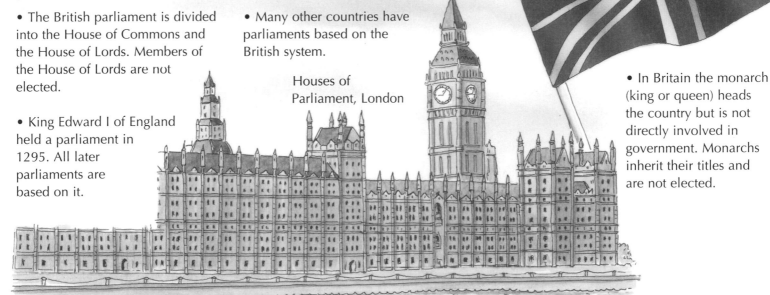

Houses of Parliament, London

• King Edward I of England held a parliament in 1295. All later parliaments are based on it.

• In Britain the monarch (king or queen) heads the country but is not directly involved in government. Monarchs inherit their titles and are not elected.

Government of the USA

The United States of America is a **republic** (a country without a king or queen). It is led by an elected **president**.

• Each state of the USA has its own local government. The national government in Washington controls all the state governments.

The White House, Washington, home of the US President

• People vote in elections for the political party they want to govern the country. The leader of the winning party becomes the president.

• There are three branches of government: the Executive, Congress and the Supreme Court. In this way, power is divided and each branch is able to check the actions of the other two.

• Congress is divided into an upper and lower house – the Senate and the House of Representatives.

The Arts

Here are some landmarks in the history of photography, film and TV:

1820s France: the first photographs taken by Joseph Nicéphore Niepce

Human beings express their thoughts and feelings through art, by writing stories and plays, drawing, playing music, painting pictures and making sculptures.

Cave painting

Some arts are ancient. Prehistoric cave paintings and carvings, Ancient Greek poetry, sculptures and buildings still survive. They show the creativity of people long ago. Today there are also **modern art forms** such as cinema, television and photography.

Literature

Literature is written art. It includes **poetry**, **plays** and **novels**.

- The oldest poems and stories were told out loud, not written down. They were passed down by memory from one storyteller to another.
- When more people learned to read and write, stories were written down. Most books were written and illustrated by hand until printing became widespread in the 15th century.
- The first story books for children were written in the 19th century. *Swiss Family Robinson* and *Alice in Wonderland* were among the first children's stories every published.

From left to right: quill pen, fountain pen, typewriter and word processor

Strange but true

- Decorated bones dug up in Germany may be the most ancient pieces of art ever found. They are about 35,000 years old.
- In 1517, Francis I, King of France, bought the 'Mona Lisa' to hang in his bathroom.
- The original Globe Theatre in London had no roof. If it rained, performances were cancelled.
- Audiences at the Globe were noisy and rowdy. Fights often broke out in front of the stage.

Visual Arts

Visual arts include painting, drawing and sculpture.

- Prehistoric people painted pictures of animals and hunters on cave walls. Some have been found that were painted about 25,000 years ago.
- One of the world's best-known paintings is the 'Mona Lisa', painted by Leonardo da Vinci between 1503 and 1507. Now it is too valuable to be given a price.

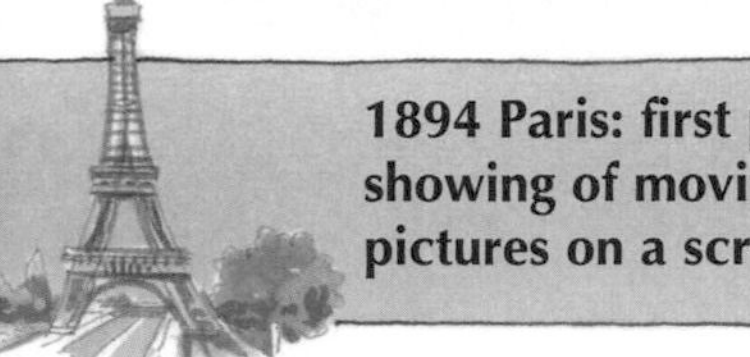

1894 Paris: first public showing of moving pictures on a screen

1922 Berlin: first public showing of a film with sound added

1929 London: first TV sets for sale and first TV programmes broadcast

Drama

Plays are stories written for actors to perform. Today they are usually acted in purpose-built **theatres**.

• Ancient Greek plays were performed in open-air theatres. Actors wore masks and took part in plays that told stories about Greek gods and heroes.

• In Europe, about 500 years ago, people watched plays about Bible stories. Actors performed on open carts that could be moved from place to place.

• The world-famous playwright William Shakespeare lived in England in the 16th century. Many of his plays were performed at the Globe Theatre in London.

• The Globe was circular in shape. Rich members of the audience sat on or around the stage. Poor people stood in front of the stage. Women were not allowed to act, so boys played women's parts.

Music

Here are some of the most common groups of **musical instruments**:

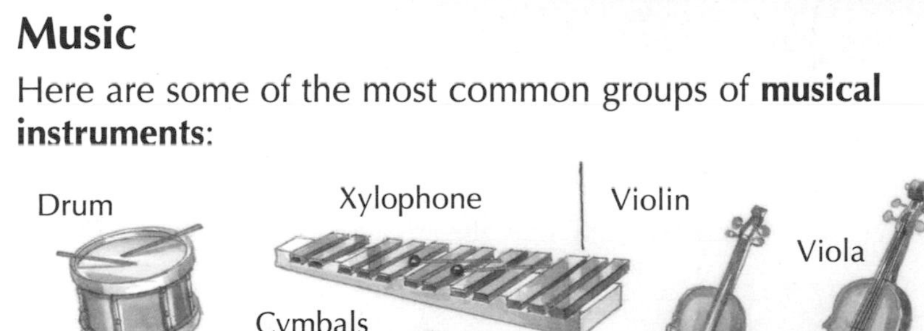

• Percussion instruments make a noise when they are tapped or hit.

• Percussion instruments make a noise when they are tapped or hit.

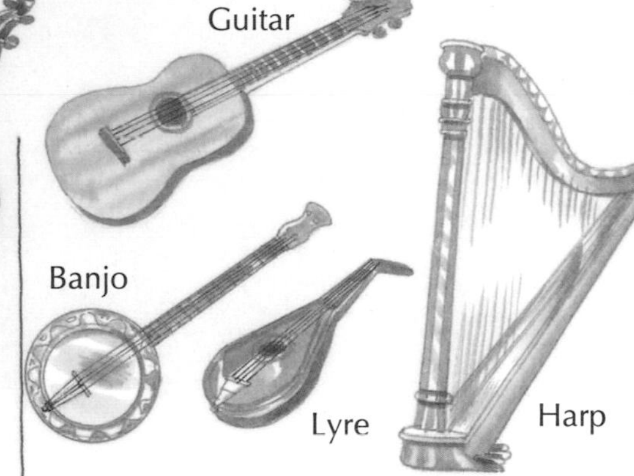

• Some stringed instruments are plucked with the fingers.

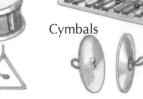

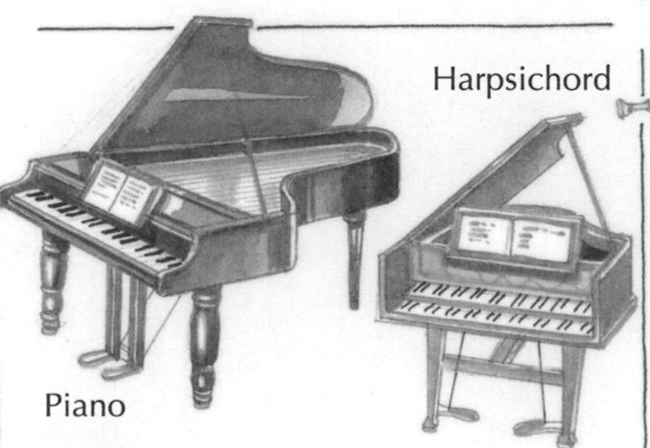

• Keyboard instruments have keys that you press with your fingers. Each key makes a different sound.

• These wind instruments are made of brass.

• These wind instruments have reeds that you blow across to make a sound.

Famous People

These are some other famous people from the past:

Columbus (1451-1506): explorer who sailed to the West Indies and Central America

Only a small number of people from the past have become so **famous** that their names are still remembered long after their death. Some of these people became famous for their **daring deeds** and **leadership**. Others are famous for helping to improve other people's lives. Many are remembered because the stories of their lives are so **dramatic**.

Tutankhamun

Tutankhamun was a **pharaoh**, or ruler, of ancient Egypt. He died in 1352 B.C. He has become famous because, more than 3000 years after his death, his tomb was discovered containing gold, jewels and many other beautiful objects.

- Tutankhamun became pharaoh when he was 11 years old. He married an Egyptian princess.
- He died when he was about 18.
- In 1922, archaeologists discovered his tomb in Egypt in the Valley of the Kings.
- The pharaoh's body was mummified (preserved and wrapped in bandages) inside a coffin made of solid gold.

Queen Elizabeth I

Queen Elizabeth I lived from 1533 to 1603. She was one of the most famous **rulers of England**. Her court was well known for its poets, painters, musicians and playwrights.

- Elizabeth was born in 1533, the daughter of King Henry VIII and Anne Boleyn. When Elizabeth was a baby, her father had her mother beheaded.
- When she was a young girl she was locked up for a while in the Tower of London by her half-sister Mary. Mary thought Elizabeth was plotting against her.
- After Mary's death, Elizabeth came to the throne of England. She was 25 and reigned for another 45 years.

Today, television, cinema and newspapers can quickly make people famous all over the world. In the past it was difficult to become well known. Here you can find out about some famous people from the past.

Mozart (1756-1791): musical genius who began composing at the age of five

Queen Victoria (1819-1901): popular and longest-reigning British monarch

Picasso (1881-1973): Spanish painter who influenced modern art

Napoleon Bonaparte

Napoleon, who lived from 1769 to 1821, was a famous French **leader** and **ruler**. He conquered large parts of Europe and made himself emperor over them.

- He was born on the island of Corsica and went to a military school in Paris.
- He became head of the French army and won many victories throughout Europe.
- He reorganized France by improving the law, banks, trade and education. He also encouraged the sciences and the arts.
- In 1804 he crowned himself emperor of France. His wife, Josephine, was made Empress.
- When his enemies in Europe invaded France, Napoleon was sent into exile on Elba, an island off the coast of Italy.
- He escape from Elba and returned to France, gathering an army. However, he was finally beaten at the Battle of Waterloo.

Abraham Lincoln

Abraham Lincoln lived from 1809 to 1865. He was a famous American politician. From a humble background he rose to become the sixteenth **president of the United States**, leading the country at a dramatic point in its history.

- Lincoln grew up as a farmer's son, living in a log cabin in Kentucky. He studied law and began to take an active part in politics.
- In 1860 he was elected President of the United States. The American Civil War broke out soon after. Lincoln led the Union generals during the war.
- He worked to change laws and to improve life for all Americans. In particular he brought about the end of slavery in the United States.
- Towards the end of the Civil War, Lincoln was shot dead by a political enemy while at the theatre.

Strange but true

- The Ancient Egyptians used to mummify animals such as cats, baboons, dogs and crocodiles as well as kings.
- Potatoes and tobacco were unknown in Europe until sailors brought them back from the Americas in the 16th century.
- Abraham Lincoln went to school for less than a year. He taught himself to read and write.

Gandhi

Gandhi was an important **Indian leader**. He lived from 1869 to 1948. During his life he worked to bring peace and justice to the world. People admired him for his ideas and courage.

- He was born in India and went to study law in London when he was 19.
- As a lawyer in South Africa and in India he worked to help the poor and suffering, trying to change laws that were unfair.
- Many Indian people called him 'Mahatma', which means 'great soul'.
- He led the Indian people in their struggle for independence from Britain.
- Gandhi believed there was no need to be violent to solve the world's problems. To draw attention to his beliefs he sometimes went on hunger strikes that endangered his life.
- Shortly after India became independent, Gandhi was shot dead by an enemy at an open air prayer meeting.

Inventions

These are some ways of telling the time:

2000 B.C.: Egyptian shadow clock

Early humans learned to use simple stone tools over 2 million years ago. Since then people have gradually gathered **knowledge** and **skills**. Now there are many **inventions** that have changed the way people live.

The number of inventions has increased enormously in the 20th century. People who lived only a hundred years ago would be amazed to see how we can now send messages around the world in seconds, cure diseases, and even send people to the Moon!

Transportation

Until about 200 years ago, **transportation** was slow, difficult, and uncomfortable. Since that time there have been many changes:

• Late 1700s: Road-building improved, so more people began to travel in horse-drawn coaches.

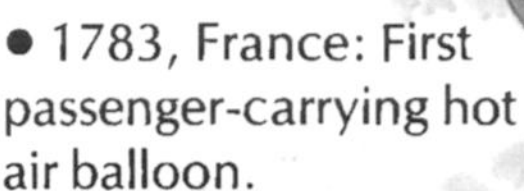

• 1783, France: First passenger-carrying hot air balloon.

• 1803, Great Britain: Richard Trevithick built the first steam locomotive to pull wagons.

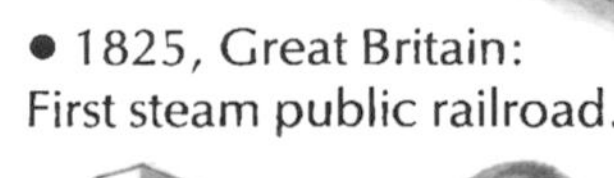

• 1825, Great Britain: First steam public railroad.

• 1885, Germany: First gasoline-driven car.

• 1903, U.S.A.: First powered flight by Orville and Wilbur Wright's aeroplane, Flyer 1.

• 1950s, worldwide: First jet-engined airliners introduced, able to carry many passengers at high speed.

1300: Mechanical clock

1929: Clock powered by quartz crystal

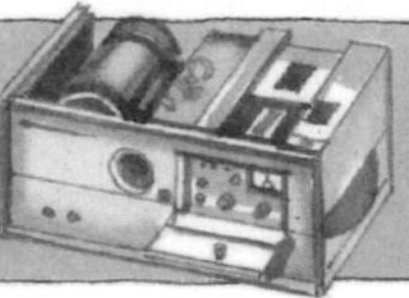

1969: Atomic clock accurate to one second in 1,700,000 years

Communications

Ideas spread quickly when they can be easily passed on to other people. These are some important stages in the development of **communications**:

• Paper: In about 3500 B.C. the Egyptians invented paper called papyrus. It was made from reeds. The Chinese invented the modern kind of paper almost 2000 years ago.

• Printing: In 1450 Johannes Gutenberg of Germany invented a press that could print books easily. Books before this time were copied by hand.

• Telephone: In 1867, the inventor Alexander Graham Bell developed the telephone. For the first time people could speak to each other over long distances.

A modern telephone

• Radio: In 1894 Guglielmo Marconi experimented with radio waves and used them to send messages without any wires being needed.

• Satellites: In 1957 the first satellite was sent into space by the USSR. Satellites now send telephone and TV signals around the world.

Bell's telephone

Strange but true

• The abacus, a counting frame with beads, was first used about 5000 years ago. It is still used in parts of Asia.

• In 1909 the fastest any human being had flown was 34 mph (54.7 km/h). By 1976 this had risen to 1363 mph (2193 km/h)–a 4000 percent increase!

• The longest recorded freight train had 500 cars, 6 engines and was 4 miles (6.4 km) long.

Medicine

Here are some important developments in **medicine**:

• 1796: Edward Jenner made the first *vaccine*(a tiny amount of a disease). When injected with vaccine, the body is protected from catching that disease.

• 1846: Ether, the first successful *anesthetic*, was used. Anesthetics deaden pain and make surgery safer.

• 1867: Joseph Lister performed the first operation using *antiseptics*. They kill the germs that cause illness. Before their use, many patients died from infections.

• 1895: *X rays* were discovered by Wilhelm Röntgen. X rays are invisible waves of energy that pass through flesh but are absorbed by bone. This allows pictures to be taken of the inside of the body.

• 1939: Penicillin, the first *antibiotic*, was developed. Antibiotics are drugs that kill the bacteria that cause illness.

• 1967: The first heart *transplant* was performed. Transplant operations enable unhealthy organs such as hearts, lungs, or kidneys to be replaced with healthy ones.

Sports and Games

These are some popular games and when and where they were invented:

Checkers: Egypt, about 2000 B.C.

In prehistoric times, as people hunted for food, they learned to run and to throw. The **oldest sports** — running, throwing, archery, and wrestling — grew out of hunting skills. As people began to settle into farming communities, they turned these skills into sports for **exercise** and **amusement**.

Soccer, the world's most popular team game.

Today there are thousands of different sports and games, each with their own **rules**. Some involve just one person testing out his or her skill against another. Some involve teams of people competing against each other. Taking part in games and sports is not only healthy exercise; it is fun, too. Even just being a spectator can be exciting.

The Olympic Games

The first **Olympic Games** were held about 2000 years ago at the Temple of Zeus, in Olympia, Greece.

- Soldiers in ancient Greece were trained to run, jump, and throw. They competed against each other in the Olympic athletic events.
- Winners of the ancient Games were given an olive branch and treated as national heroes.
- In Ancient Greece the Games were a festival of mind and body, and included poetry and music as well as athletics.

Team games

Many of the world's most **popular sports** involve two **teams** competing against each other. Here are some examples:

- Soccer – Number in team: 11
Ball: round, leather
How ball is moved: kicked
Object: to score goals by kicking the ball into a netted goalmouth

- Football – Number in team: 11
Ball: oval, leather
How ball is moved: carried/thrown
Object: to gain points by carrying ball into endzone or kicking ball over H-shaped posts

- Baseball – Number in team: 9
Ball: small, horse-hide
How ball is moved: hit with long cylindrical wooden bat
Object: to score runs around a diamond-shaped field.

Baseball

- Cricket – Number in team: 11
Ball: small, leather-covered
How ball is moved: hit with flat side of long wooden bat
Object: to score runs between two sets of wooden wickets

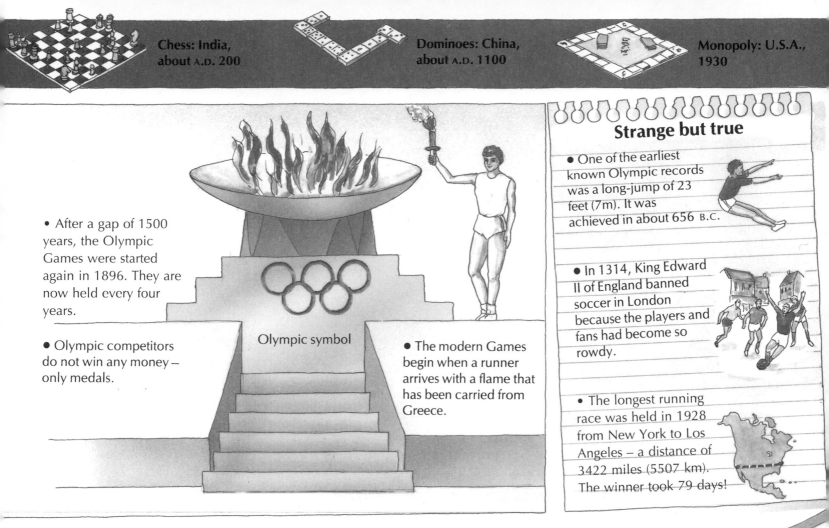

Chess: India, about A.D. 200

Dominoes: China, about A.D. 1100

Monopoly: U.S.A., 1930

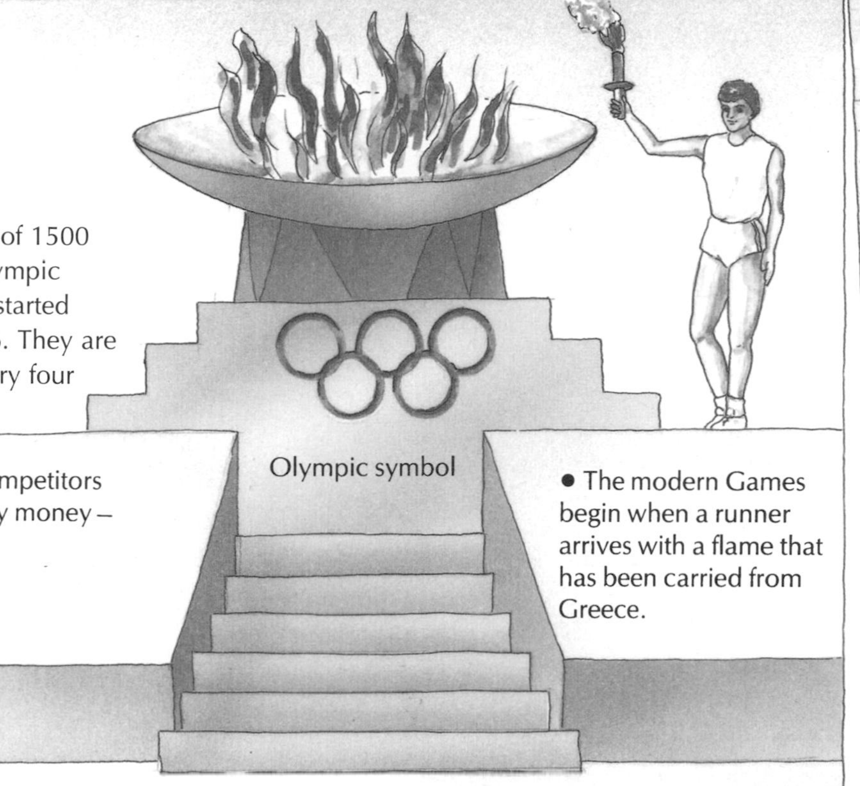

• After a gap of 1500 years, the Olympic Games were started again in 1896. They are now held every four years.

• Olympic competitors do not win any money – only medals.

• The modern Games begin when a runner arrives with a flame that has been carried from Greece.

Strange but true

• One of the earliest known Olympic records was a long-jump of 23 feet (7m). It was achieved in about 656 B.C.

• In 1314, King Edward II of England banned soccer in London because the players and fans had become so rowdy.

• The longest running race was held in 1928 from New York to Los Angeles – a distance of 3422 miles (5507 km). The winner took 79 days!

Indoor games

Not all games involve physical strength. Many call for **mental skills**, or rely on **luck**. Here are some of the world's best-known **indoor games**:

• Chess: an ancient strategy game played on a board of 64 black and white squares. Each player has black or white pieces: 1 king, 1 queen, 2 bishops, 2 castles, 2 knights, and 8 pawns.

• Checkers: related to chess but older and simpler. It is played with round counters.

• Ludo, Snakes and Ladders: games of chance relying on luck. Moves of counters are controlled by throwing dice.

• Backgammon: a mixture of chance and skill. Players use a coloured board and have 15 counters each. They throw two dice and try to be first to move all their counters round and off the board.

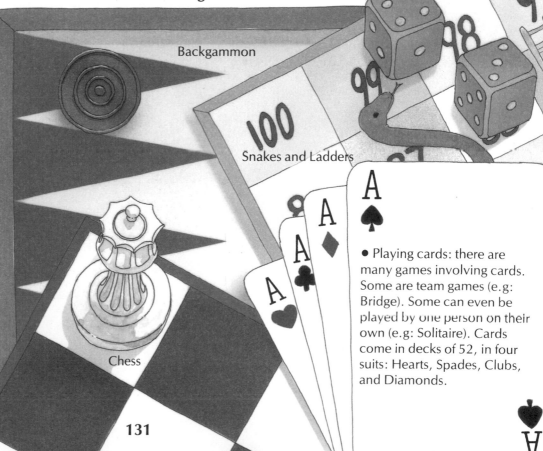

• Playing cards: there are many games involving cards. Some are team games (e.g: Bridge). Some can even be played by one person on their own (e.g: Solitaire). Cards come in decks of 52, in four suits: Hearts, Spades, Clubs, and Diamonds.

Limits and Records

These are some important "firsts" in world exploration:

About AD 1000: Vikings may have reached North America from Europe

There are many **feats of daring** that people have achieved over the centuries. They range from **explorations** of the world's most isolated places to **breaking records** by pushing human skills to the limit.

New records are being set all the time as humans strive to break barriers of endurance and achievement.

Human heights

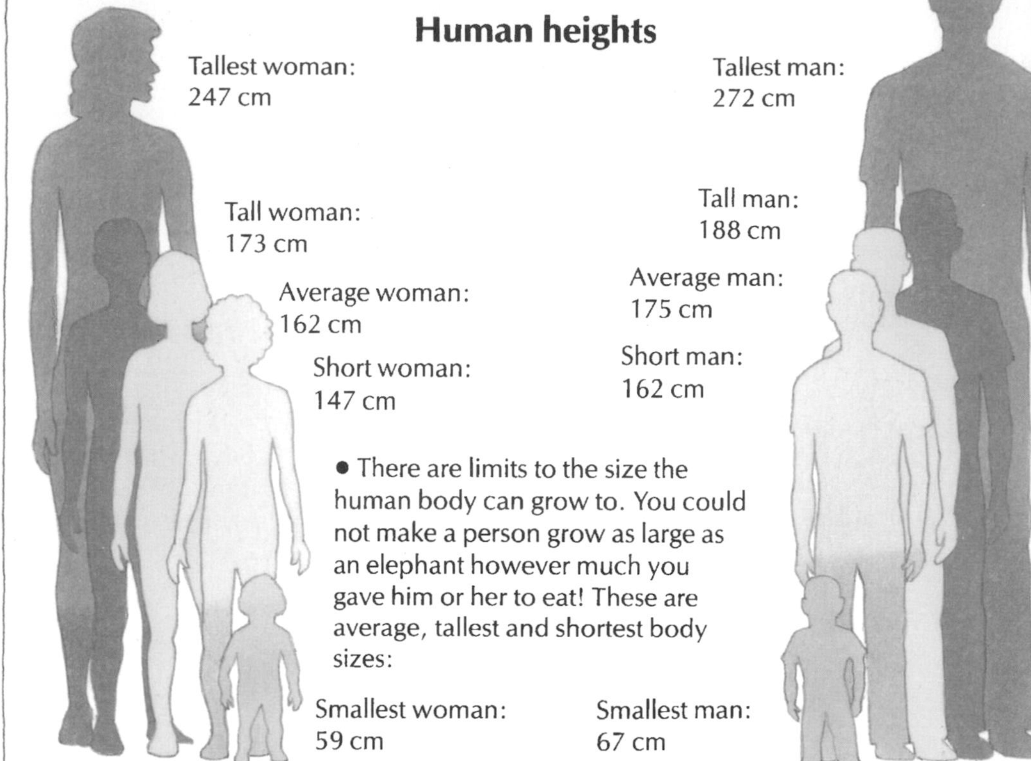

Tallest woman: 247 cm

Tall woman: 173 cm

Average woman: 162 cm

Short woman: 147 cm

Tallest man: 272 cm

Tall man: 188 cm

Average man: 175 cm

Short man: 162 cm

- There are limits to the size the human body can grow to. You could not make a person grow as large as an elephant however much you gave him or her to eat! These are average, tallest and shortest body sizes:

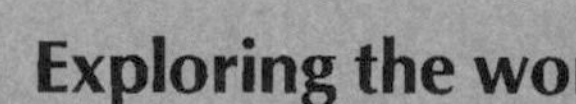

Smallest woman: 59 cm

Smallest man: 67 cm

Exploring the world

Some people have been prepared to risk their lives and suffer great discomfort to be the first **explorers**. Here are some famous achievements of exploration:

- A Norwegian team first reached the South Pole in 1911 after a 53-day march.
- The first polar round-the-world trip began in 1979 in London. The explorers travelled to the South Pole, the North Pole, and back to London (a distance of 56,325 km). They reached home in 1982.
- On 21 July 1969, US astronaut Neil Armstrong became the first person to walk on the Moon.
- The longest recorded swim was 2938 km down the Mississippi River in 1930. The swimmer spent 742 hours in the water.
- The first people to climb Mount Everest, the highest mountain in the world, were Edmund Hilary and Tenzing Norgay, in 1953.

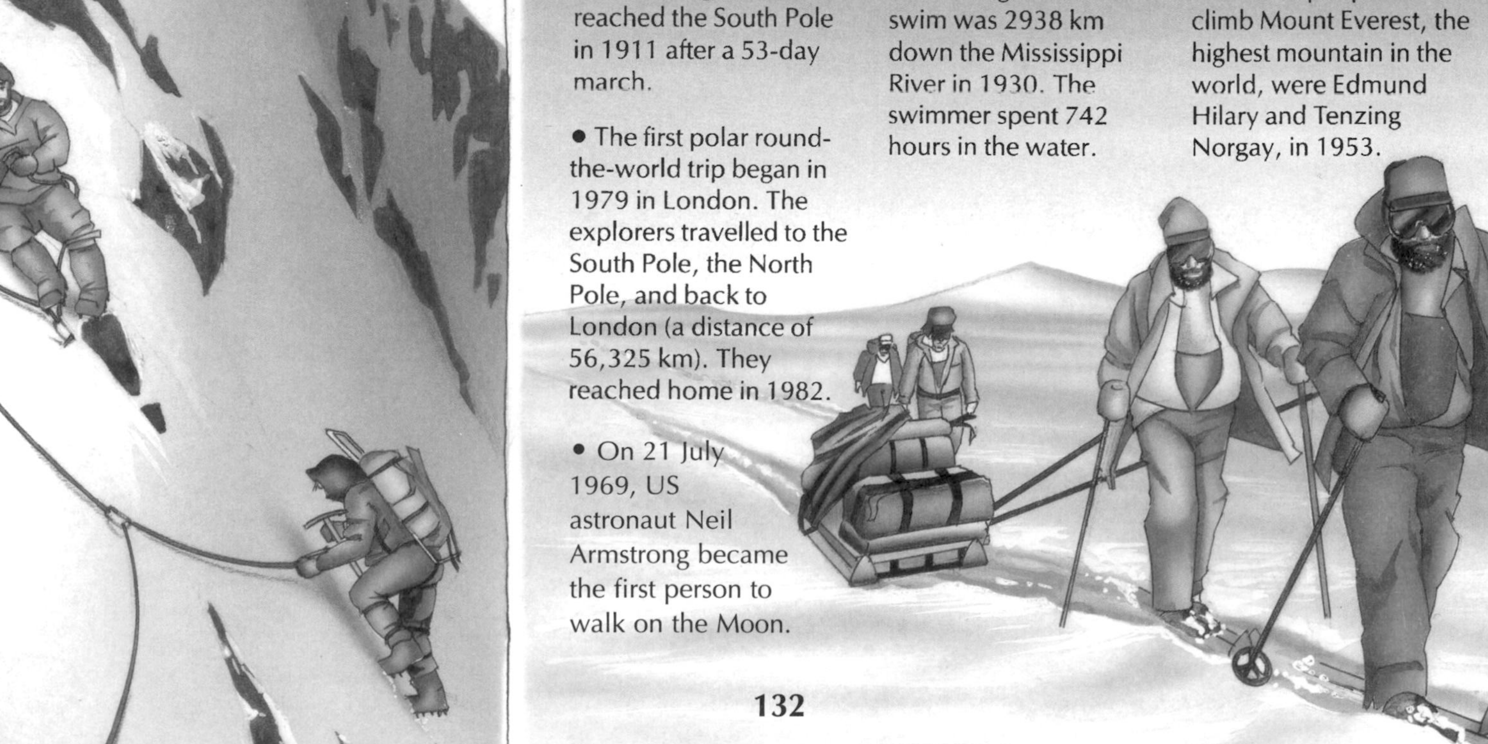

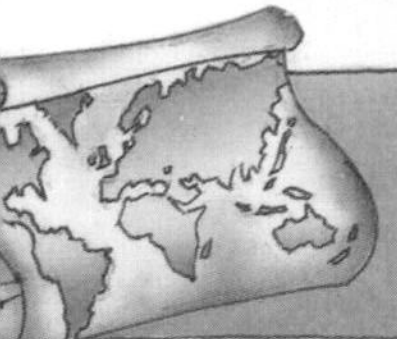

1519-22: Ferdinand Magellan sailed right around the world

1642-44: Abel Tasman reached Australia and sailed around it

1804-06: Lewis and Clark crossed the U.S.A. overland

Heights and depths

Modern technology has enabled people to reach the depths of the **ocean** and the heights of **Space**.

• Apollo 13 astronauts reached a height of 400,187 km above the Earth.

• The highest a hot-air balloon has flown is 34,668 metres over the Gulf of Mexico in 1961.

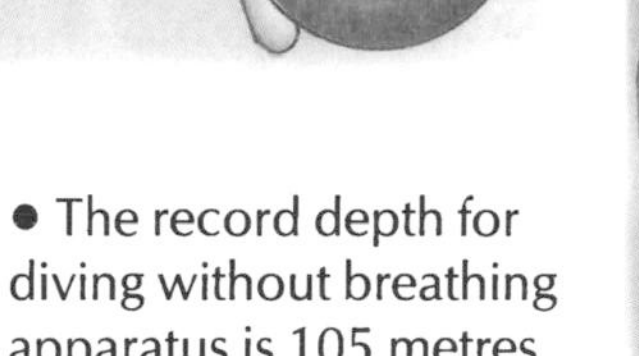

• The record depth for diving without breathing apparatus is 105 metres.

• The furthest anyone has reached into the sea depths is 10,916 metres, inside a submersible craft exploring the Pacific Ocean.

Strange but true

• The human brain is five times smaller than an adult elephant's brain.

• The record for balancing on one foot with no support is 34 hours.

• A baby's head is about a quarter of its total body length. An adult's head is only about one eighth of its total height.

Human limits

There are many things humans cannot do as well as some animals can:

• They are not as fast as cheetahs, which can run at 100 km/h.

• They are not as strong as a rhinoceros beetle, which can carry 850 times its own weight on its back.

• They cannot smell as well as the Emperor moth, which can detect smells 11 km away.

• They cannot hear as well as dolphins and bats, which can hear sounds too high-pitched for humans to hear.

• They cannot eat as much as the Polyphemus moth, which eats 86,000 times its own birth weight in 48 hours.

• They cannot make as much noise as South American howler monkeys, whose cries can be heard 16 km away.

Conflict and Crime

These organizations work for world peace and the relief of suffering: OXFAM Oxfam: famine relief

Through the ages, people have waged **wars** and committed **crimes**. This negative side of human nature is often caused by greed for money, property or power. Sometimes, though, people have been driven by poverty and injustice to be violent or break the law.

Strange but true

- The longest jail sentence passed was in the U.S.A. – 10,000 years for a triple murder.
- The shortest war on record lasted for just 38 minutes on 27 August 1896. It was fought between the U.K. and Zanzibar (now Tanzania).
- China has the largest army in the world, with over 2 million soldiers.

Weapons

Warfare has changed over the centuries. Here are some of the weapons people have invented to defend themselves and attack others:

- Hand weapons are used for stabbing or hitting. They are the oldest group of weapons, and include clubs, swords and spears.
- Catapults are early examples of shooting weapons. Guns and cannons came later. Modern versions include machine-guns, torpedoes and guided missiles.
- Catapults are early examples of shooting weapons. Guns and cannons came later. Modern versions include machine guns, torpedoes and missiles.
- Booby-trap weapons probably originated from animal-trapping methods. Modern booby-traps include landmines that explode when touched.
- Modern bombs include the devastating nuclear bomb, which can poison the atmosphere with radiation.

Wars

Wars have been waged throughout history. Here are some facts about **warfare**:

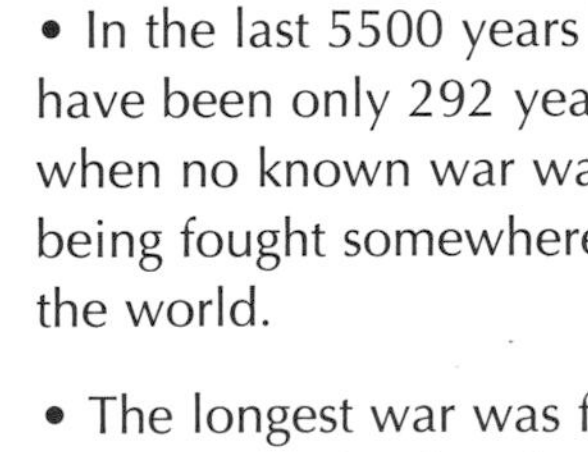

- In the last 5500 years there have been only 292 years when no known war was being fought somewhere in the world.
- The longest war was fought between England and France. It lasted 115 years, from 1338 to 1453.
- World War II (1939-1945) cost approximately £1050 billion. That is more than all the world's previous wars put together.
- World War II also saw the greatest loss of life of any war. About 54 million people died.
- It is estimated that in 1988 the amount spent on weapons throughout the world was £460 billion. That is equal to £72 for every person

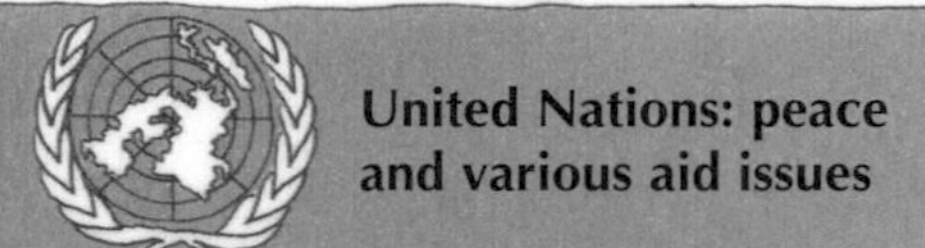
United Nations: peace and various aid issues

Red Cross and Red Crescent: medical aid

Amnesty International: helping political prisoners

Crime

All societies have laws. **Crimes** are acts that are forbidden and are punished by law. Here are some major crimes:

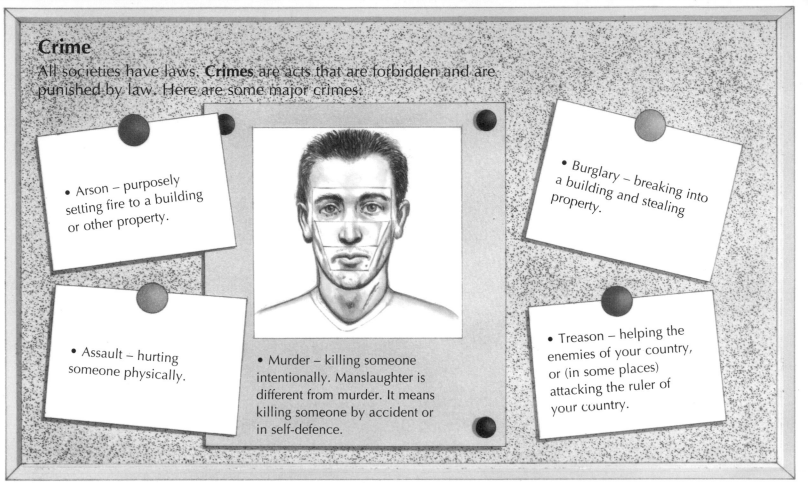

- Arson – purposely setting fire to a building or other property.
- Assault – hurting someone physically.

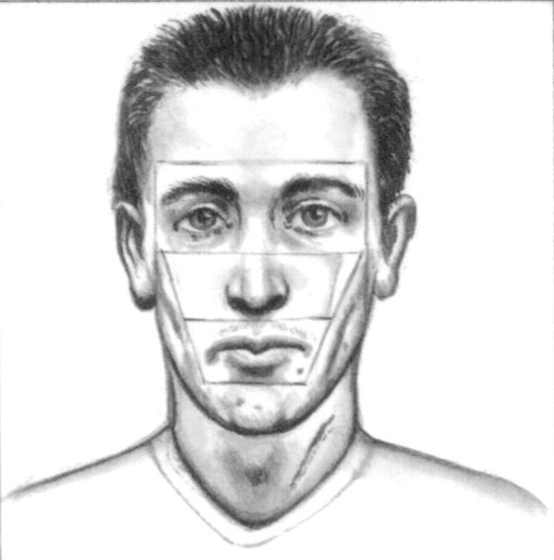

- Murder – killing someone intentionally. Manslaughter is different from murder. It means killing someone by accident or in self-defence.
- Burglary – breaking into a building and stealing property.
- Treason – helping the enemies of your country, or (in some places) attacking the ruler of your country.

Punishment

A person found guilty of a crime is punished. This is intended to **stop them offending** again, and to **discourage other people** from committing crimes. Here are some methods of **punishment**:

- Imprisonment: Criminals are locked in jail, away from society.
- Community service: Offenders are not imprisoned, but they are made to work for the community.
- Fines: Offenders pay for their crimes by handing over a sum of money.
- Probation: Offenders are not imprisoned but their behaviour is regularly checked by officials called probation officers.
- Death penalty: in China, South Africa, Turkey, Iran, Saudi Arabia, Malaysia and 38 states of the U.S.A., murderers are put to death.
- In Australia and Britain the death penalty has been kept for those who commit treason.

The Future

These are some things people can do to help protect the atmosphere:

Use waste heat from factories to heat homes

Life on Earth has changed more during the last hundred years than at any other time since people lived on the planet. It is impossible to know what further changes will happen in the future, but it is clear there will be great **challenges** to meet.

One of the greatest challenges will be to preserve life on the planet from **pollution**. Ways will have to be found, too, of sharing out the **world's resources** more fairly.

Pollution

Pollution of the **environment** is threatening the world's water and air. International laws, together with conservation efforts by everyone, can help to limit the damage.

- The build-up of carbon dioxide gas in the Earth's atmosphere has resulted in global warming — the slow warming up of the air temperature.
- Acid rain contains poisonous substances leaked from factories and cars. It can quickly destroy plantlife.
- CFC gases (used in spray aerosols and refrigerators) seem to be damaging the Earth's ozone layer, a blanket of gas about 15 miles (25 km) above the ground.
- Oceans and rivers are sometimes polluted by poisonous industrial waste that can kill fish and affect drinking water. Many countries now have laws to limit this pollution.
- Carbon dioxide is released by burning fossil fuels such as coal, gas, and oil. It also increases when forests are destroyed, because trees use up the carbon dioxide.

Saving animals and plants

The actions of people have put many **animals** and **plants** in danger of **extinction**, which means that they may die out altogether. World organizations and governments are working to stop this continuing.

- Some of the world's rarest plant species are known by only one specimen.
- Each year an area of rain forest about the size of Switzerland disappears. The trees are cut for wood or cleared for mining or farming.
- An animal is declared extinct if it has not been seen for 50 years.

Extinct dodo

Insulate houses so they need less heating

Plant more trees

Use more buses and trains so the number of cars can be reduced

Strange but true

- A solar power station in California will soon be using the Sun's power to produce enough electricity to supply a million people.
- Throughout the world, almost 750 million people suffer from lack of food. This is twice the population of Europe.
- The Arabian oryx antelope became extinct in the wild but has been saved by zoos.

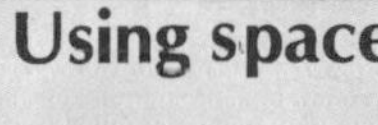

New sources of power

The world's supplies of coal, gas, and oil are being used up rapidly as cities and industries develop. In the future, people may learn how to use **new sources of power** that do not run out:

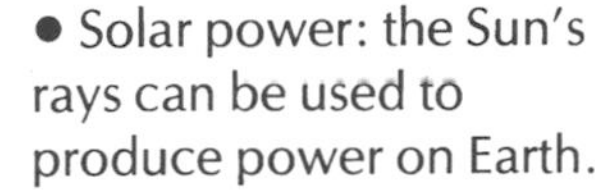

- Wind power: electricity can be generated by using windmills that turn simply by the power of the wind.
- Water power: experiments are taking place to find out how to use the power of the world's oceans and rivers to produce electricity.

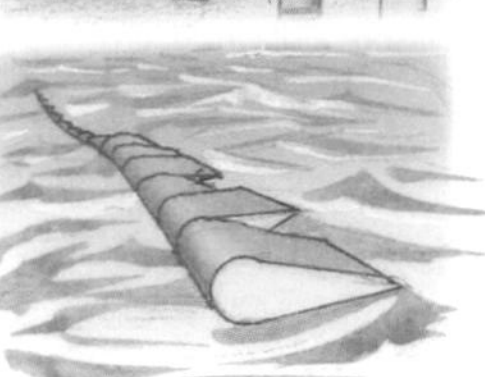

- New fuels: these can be made from tiny algae plants, from alcohol, and even from animal dung.

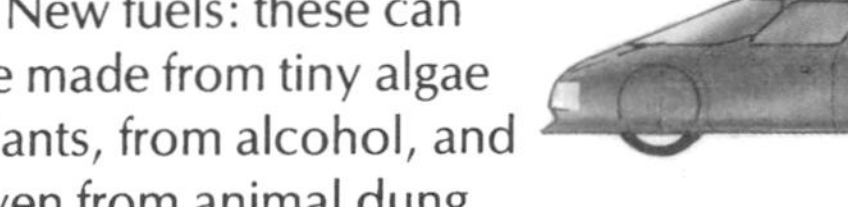

- Solar power: the Sun's rays can be used to produce power on Earth.
- Nuclear fusion: by joining atoms together, enormous amounts of power could be generated. This would be safer than the atomic power in use now.

Using space

Space could be a very useful **resource**. Here are some possible future developments:

- Raw materials such as iron ore could be mined on the Moon.
- Giant solar power stations could orbit the Earth, sending down power gathered from the Sun.
- People may be able to live in space, on space stations orbiting the Earth.

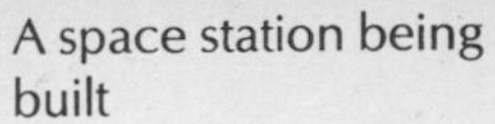

A space station being built

People Facts and Lists

Early people

These are the approximate dates when scientists believe our human ancestors lived:

Australopithecus: 1-8 million years ago
Homo habilis: 1.4-2.6 million years ago
Homo erectus: 250,000-1.6 million years ago
Homo sapiens: first appeared about 280,000 years ago
Neanderthal people: 35,000-140,000 years ago
Modern people: first appeared 30,000-50,000 years

Prehistoric remains of early people

Here are some of the most important prehistoric finds made by anthropologists:

Year found	Find	Where found	Dating from (years ago)
1856	Neanderthal skull and bones	Germany	120,000
1868	Cromagnon skeleton (Homo sapiens)	France	35,000
1924	Australopithecus skull	Botswana	1 million
1974	Australopithecus skeleton (Lucy)	Ethiopia	3-4 million
1975	Homo erectus skull	Kenya	1.5 million
1980	Homo sapiens	Tanzania	120,000

• Anthropologists who discovered the oldest Australopithecine skeleton called her 'Lucy' after the Beatles song 'Lucy in the Sky with Diamonds'.

• Lucy died around 3 million years ago. She was about 20 years old when she died and only 106 cm tall.

Population

These are some of the most crowded countries in the world:

Country	People per square km in 1990
Monaco	14,681
Singapore	4369
Vatican City	2500
Malta	1117
Bangladesh	784
Bahrain	726
Maldives	718
Barbados	598
Taiwan	561
Mauritius	529

Some of the least crowded countries in the world are:

Country	People per square km in 1990
Greenland	0.1
Western Sahara	0.5
Mongolia	1.4
Mauritania	1.9
Australia	2.2
Botswana	2.2
Libya	2.4
Surinam	2.5
Canada	2.9
Iceland	3.2

• There are 235 people per sq km in Britain and 26 per sq km in the U.S.A.

The human body

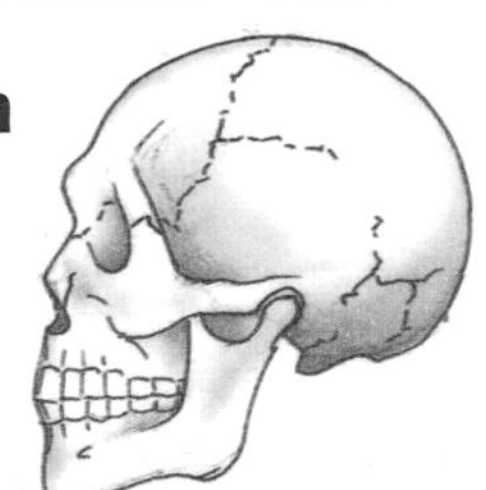

• Most people spend about a third of their lives asleep.

• The heart beats about 70 times a minute. That is nearly 37 million times a year!

• The longest and strongest bone in the body is the femur, or thigh bone.

• There are about 650 muscles in the human body.

• There are four basic blood groups found throughout the world. They are called A, AB, B and O. Group O is the most common.

• Some people have such good colour vision that they can tell the difference between as many as 300,000 different shades of colour.

• The human ear can pick out more than 1500 different musical tones.

• It is impossible to sneeze with your eyes open!

People of the world

• Scientists who study the way the world's peoples are related to each other study the following, which can vary from group to group:

Skin	Blood group
Hair	Colour blindness
Language	Type of ear wax
Skeleton	Inherited diseases

Languages

Ciao!
Zdrastvyi!
Bonjour!
Hello!

Language	Number of speakers
Mandarin Chinese	788 million
English	420 million
Hindustani	300 million
Spanish	296 million
Russian	285 million

• Other widely spoken languages include Arabic, Portuguese, Bengali, German and Japanese. They each have about 100-200 million speakers.

• The English and American languages are similar but not exactly the same. Here are some differences:

English	American English
Sweets	Candy
Cheque	Check
Draughts	Checkers
Bread roll or scone	Biscuit
Biscuit	Cookie
Nappy	Diaper
Chemist's shop	Drugstore
Lift	Elevator
Autumn	Fall
Tap	Faucet
Ground floor	First floor
Petrol	Gas
Handbag	Purse
Terrace house	Row house
Pavement	Sidewalk
Frying pan	Skillet
Braces	Suspenders
Drawing pin	Thumb tack

Food

The energy content of food is measured in calories. This is how many calories some foods contain:

Food	Number of calories in 100 grams
Butter	740
White sugar	394
Wholewheat bread	318
White bread	233
Rice (boiled)	123
Potatoes (boiled)	80
Peas	41
Cabbage (boiled)	9

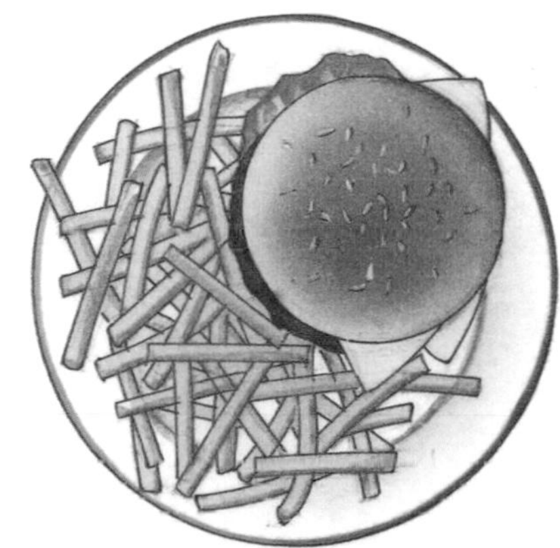

• An adult man needs an average of 3000 calories a day. A woman needs about 2200.

This is how many calories per day most people get, on average, in some countries of the world:

Country	Number of calories/day
U.S.A.	3600
Australia	3300
Brazil	2600
China	2600
India	2200
Chad (Africa)	1700

This is how many calories some activities use up:

Activity	Calories used per hour
Resting in bed	60
Driving a car	168
Washing up	230
Walking at 6 km/h	492
Cycling at 21 km/h	660
Running at 8 km/h	850

Clothes

These are some traditional clothes from around the world:

Clothing	Worn by Men/Women	Country
Aba – long robe	M	Nigeria
Dhoti – white cotton loin-cloth	M	India
Fustanella – pleated kilt	M	Greece, Turkey
Kaftan – long loose robe	M	Middle East and North Africa
Kilt – pleated skirt in the special colours of a family, or clan	M/W	Scotland
Kimono – long loose robe with wide sleeves and a sash	W	Japan
Parka – fur-lined padded coat	M/W	Arctic, Alaska
Sari – long, wide strip of decorated cloth worn wrapped around the body and often also over the head	W	India

• In China, in the past, only wealthy people were allowed to wear yellow. Most people wore blue, because the blue dye was cheap.

• Traditionally, Chinese brides wore red. White was the colour of funerals.

• Levi Strauss made the first pair of blue jeans in 1850. They were intended as work trousers for American miners.

• In Ancient Rome only the wealthy wore purple clothes as the dye came from an expensive shellfish.

People Facts and Lists

Religion

These are the world's most popular religions:

Religion	Number of followers
Christianity	1,758 million
Islam	935 million
Hinduism	705 million
Buddhism	303 million
Sikhism	18 million
Judaism	17 million

• 233 million people throughout the world describe themselves as atheists (who do not accept any god) and a further 866 million people describe themselves as non-religious.

Government

British Kings and Queens

These are the most recent British monarchs:

George I	1714-1727
George II	1727-1760
George III	1760-1820
George IV	1820-1830
William IV	1830-1837
Victoria	1837-1901
Edward VII	1901-1910
George V	1910-1936
Edward VIII	1936 (abdicated)
George VI	1937-1952
Elizabeth II	1952-

U.S. Presidents

These are the first five Presidents of the United States of America:

President	Years in office
George Washington	1789-1797
John Adams	1797-1801
Thomas Jefferson	1801-1809
James Madison	1809-1817
James Monroe	1817-1825

Other more recent Presidents:

President	Years in office
Richard Nixon	1969-1974
Gerald Ford	1974-1977
Jimmy Carter	1977-1981
Ronald Reagan	1981-1989
George Bush	1989-1993
Bill Clinton	1993-2001
George W. Bush	2001-2009

Ten famous children's books

Hans Christian Andersen	Fairy Tales (including *The Emperor's New Clothes)*
J M Barrie	*Peter Pan*
Lewis Carroll	*Alice's Adventures in Wonderland*
Clive King	*Stig of the Dump*
Rudyard Kipling	*The Jungle Book*
C S Lewis	*The Lion, the Witch and the Wardrobe*
A A Milne	*Winnie-the-Pooh*
R L Stevenson	*Treasure Island*
Mark Twain	*The Adventures of Huckleberry Finn*
Roald Dahl	*The BFG*

Ten great writers

Here is a list of ten great writers and one of their best-known works:

Jane Austen	*Pride and Prejudice*
Charlotte Bronte	*Jane Eyre*
Emily Bronte	*Wuthering Heights*
Miguel de Cervantes	*Don Quixote*
Geoffrey Chaucer	*Canterbury Tales*
Dante	*Divine Comedy*
Charles Dickens	*Great Expectations*
Dostoevsky	*Crime and Punishment*
Herman Melville	*Moby Dick*
Tolstoy	*War and Peace*

Painters

These are some of the world's famous painters:

Artist	Dates	Nationality	Major subjects
Sandro Botticelli	1444-1510	Italian	Religious pictures
Pieter Brueghel	1520-1569	Flemish	Pictures of village life
John Constable	1776-1837	English	English landscapes
Leonardo da Vinci	1452-1519	Italian	Mona Lisa
Paul Gauguin	1848-1903	French	People and landscapes of Tahiti, South Pacific
Michelangelo	1475-1564	Italian	Religious pictures on the Sistine chapel ceiling, Vatican City
Claude Monet	1840-1926	French	Impressionist pictures
Pablo Picasso	1881-1973	Spanish	Many styles, including Cubism that changed modern art completely
Rembrandt	1606-1669	Dutch	Portraits
Joseph Turner	1775-1851	English	Landscapes
Vincent Van Gogh	1853-1890	Dutch	Landscapes, people, and everyday objects

Ten famous composers

Composer	Dates	Nationality
Bach	1685-1750	German
Beethoven	1770-1827	German
Brahms	1833-1897	German
Britten	1913-1976	English
Chopin	1810-1849	Polish
Gershwin	1898-1937	American
Haydn	1732-1809	Austrian
Mozart	1756-1791	Austrian
Stravinsky	1882-1971	Russian
Tchaikovsky	1840-1893	Russian

Cinema

• The first film with sound, called a 'talking picture', was *The Jazz Singer*, made in 1927.

• The world's largest motion-picture theatre complex is in Brussels, Belgium. It has 24 screens and seats 7000 people.

• The world's largest motion-picture theatre is Radio City Music Hall, in New York City. It has 5874 seats.

Inventions

These are the approximate dates when some important discoveries were made:

Invention	When	Where
Pottery	7000 B.C.	Iran
Bricks	6000 B.C.	Jericho
Writing	4000 B.C.	Mesopotamia
The wheel	3200 B.C.	Mesopotamia
Glass	3000 B.C.	Egypt
Printing	770 B.C.	Japan
Gunpowder	A.D. 950	China

These modern objects were invented a surprisingly long time ago:

Knitting machine	1589
Microscope	1590
Thermometer	1592
Submarine	1620
Adding machine	1623
Pressure cooker	1679
Machine gun	1718
Lightning rod	1752
Parachute	1783
Battery	1800
Burglar alarm	1858

Around the world

These are the times it took various craft to go round the world:

1500s Sailing ship 2 years

1929 Airship 21 days 7 hr

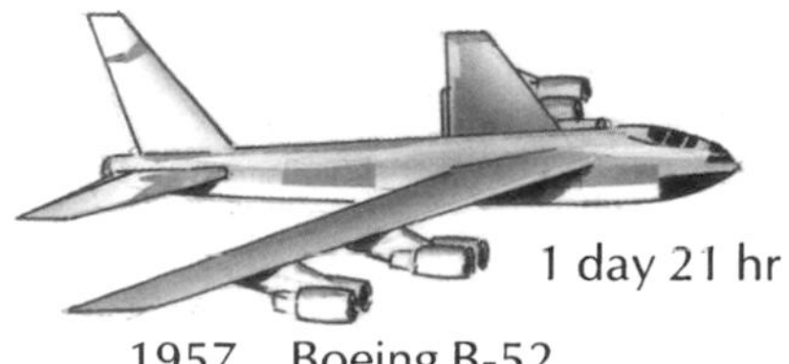

1957 Boeing B-52 1 day 21 hr

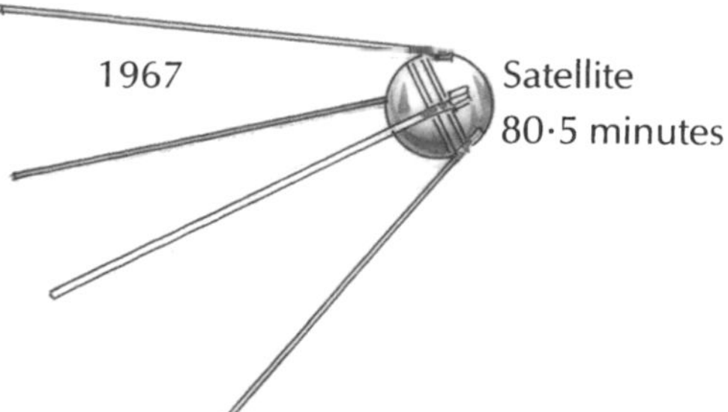

1967 Satellite 80·5 minutes

Conflict and crime

• The number of prisoners in the United States at the end of 1990 reached a record high of 77,243.

• A survey in 1986 showed that more than 8 people per 100,000 in the U.S.A. were murdered that year. That was twice as many as in the next highest countries in the survey — Hungary, Israel, and Australia. Norway had the fewest murders.

• During World War I, more than a million soldiers were killed or wounded at the first Battle of the Somme in 1916.

• About 2.5 million people died at the Battle of Stalingrad in 1942-43, fought between the Germans and the Russians during World War II.

• In all, about 55 million people were killed during World War II. Almost half of these people were from the USSR.

These countries fought each other in the two World Wars:

War	Dates	Won by	Against
World War 1	1914-18	Belgium, Britain and the Empire, France, Italy, Japan, Russia, Serbia, U.S.A.	Austria-Hungary, Bulgaria, Germany, Ottoman Empire
World War II	1939-45	Australia, Belgium, Britain, Canada, China, Denmark, France, Greece, Netherlands, New Zealand, Norway, Poland, South Africa, U.S.A., USSR, Yugoslavia	Bulgaria, Finland, Germany, Hungary, Italy, Japan, Romania

Olympic Games

• The first recorded Olympic Games were held in 776 B.C., although they were probably held for many years before this.

• The ancient Games included running, jumping, wrestling, discus throwing, boxing, and chariot racing.

• The first modern Games, held in 1896, had only 311 competitors, of whom 230 were from Greece.

These were the top medal-winning countries in the 1988 Olympic Games:

Country	Gold	Silver	Bronze
USSR	55	31	46
E. Germany	37	35	30
U.S.A.	36	31	27
W. Germany	11	14	15
Bulgaria	10	12	13
S. Korea	12	10	11

Miscellany

• A scientist has calculated that about 60 billion people died between the years 40,000 B.C. and 1990. This means that about 9 percent of all people who have ever lived are alive today!

• If the age of the Earth (4.6 billion years) is likened to a single year, the following events take place on 31 December, the last day of the year:

4.15 pm: Appearance of humanlike beings

11.10 pm: Arrival of earliest inhabitants in Europe

14 seconds before midnight: Birth of Christ

• Using this same comparison, the life span of someone who lived to be 120 years old would be just three-fourths of a second.

INDEX

Indexes to other sections are on pages 46, 94 and 190.

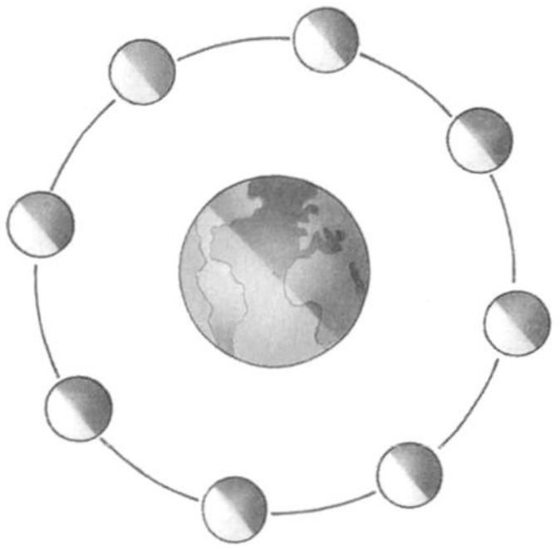

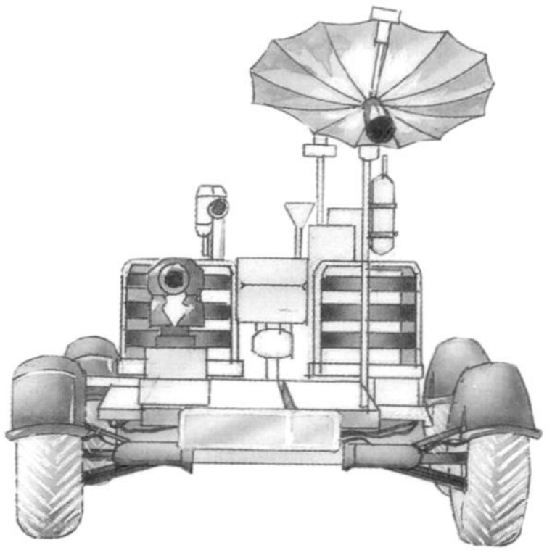

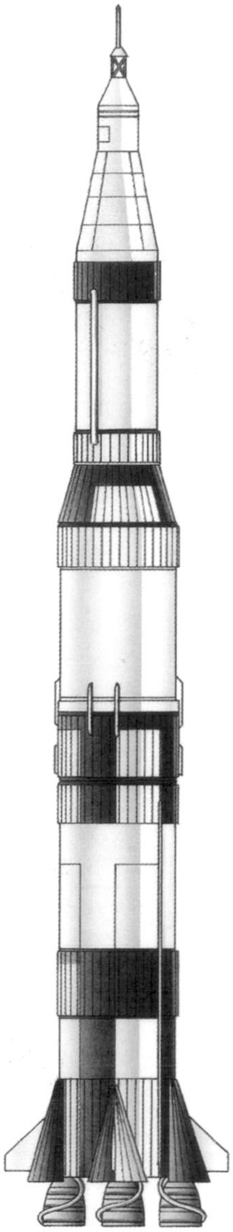

SPACE

Part Four

SPACE

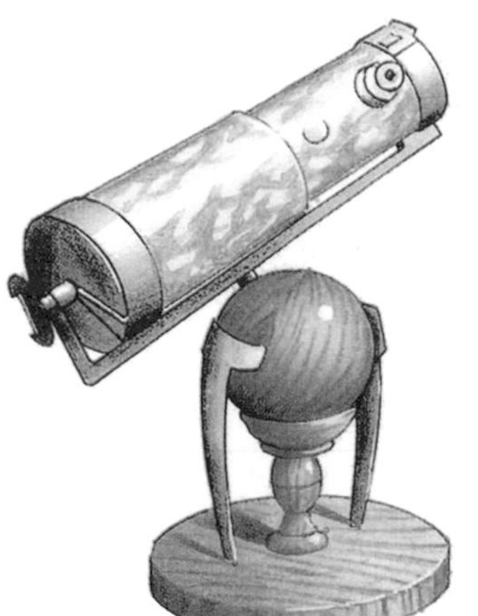

The term 'billion' in this Part means one thousand million.

Introduction

Space contains our own planet, Earth, and our own star, the Sun. Both belong to a galaxy called The Milky Way, which contains about 100 billion stars. In this Part, you can find out about other planets, stars and galaxies, and discover what scientists know about Space.

Earth is one of nine planets that go round the Sun. Jupiter, the biggest, is so huge that all the other planets in the Solar System could fit inside it.

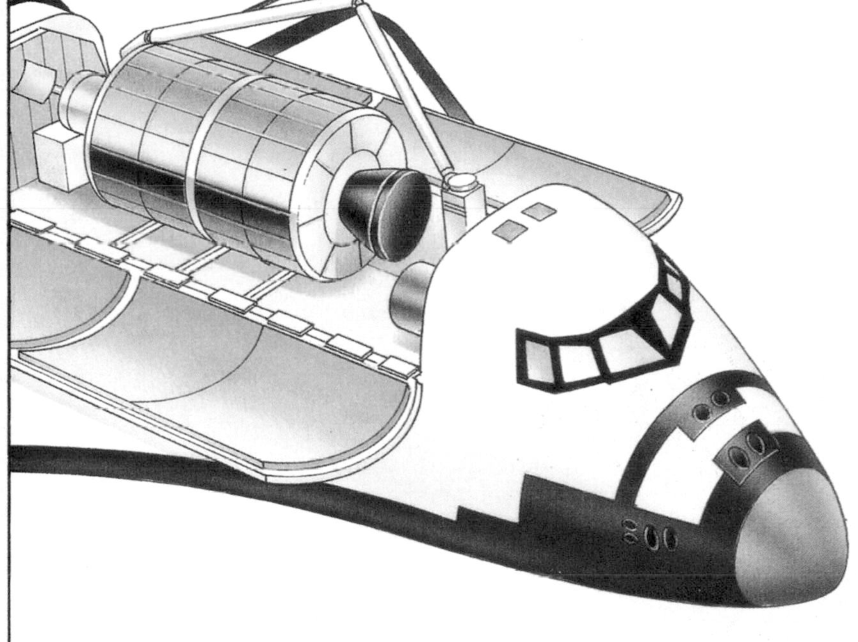

Scientists call the Sun a yellow dwarf star. You can read about other types of stars too, including some that seem to turn into mysterious black holes.

Not everything in Space is huge. Meteoroids are tiny fragments of rock that usually burn up near the Earth in flashes of light called meteors or shooting stars. More than 20 million meteoroids are thought to enter Earth's atmosphere every day!

People have been interested in the stars and planets early times, but the Space Age didn't begin until the 1950s. Since then, space flights have helped astronomers to learn much more.

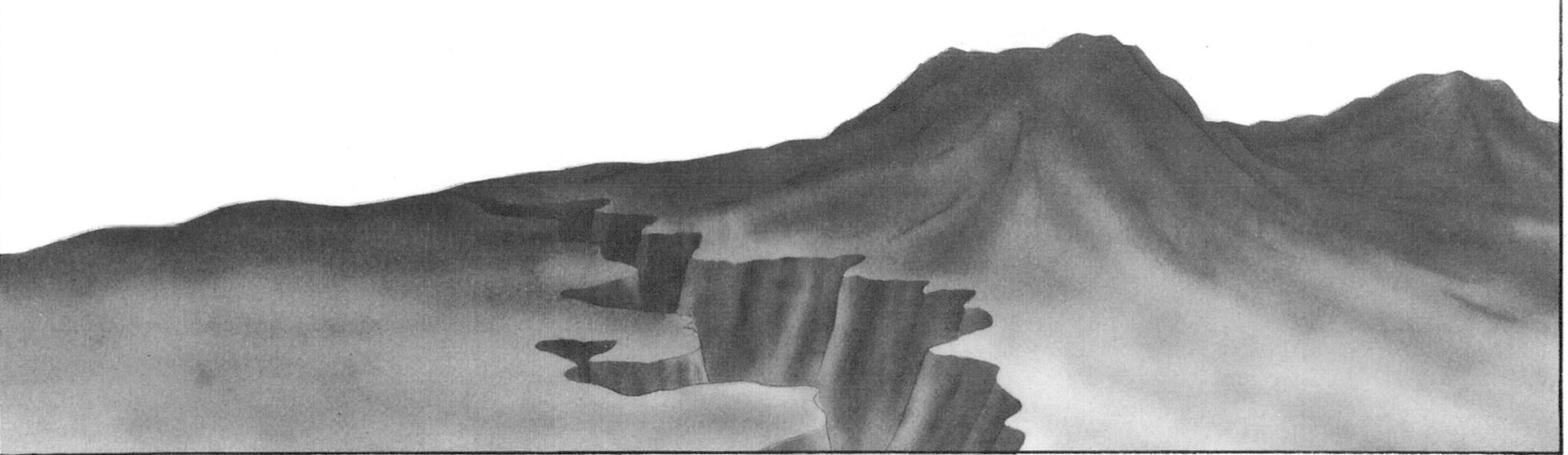

The Universe

Our galaxy seems enormous, but it is really only a smudge in Space:

Earth's diameter is about a million times the height of a 13 metre-high tree

The Universe goes on for ever. Most of it is **empty space**, with huge swarms of stars called **galaxies** shining out into the blackness. Our Sun belongs to a galaxy called the **Milky Way** containing about 100 billion stars. There are billions of galaxies in the Universe.

Our Sun is a star. Other stars may also have planets, comets and other space bodies circling round them. There are probably other planets like the Earth in the Universe.

The Solar System

The **Solar System** is the name given to our Sun and all the space bodies that revolve around it, including the Earth.

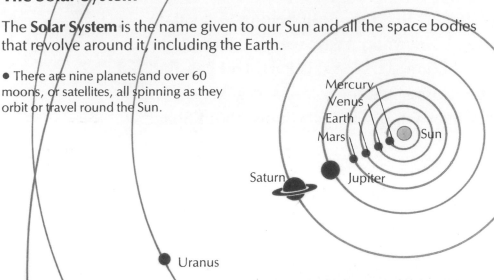

- There are nine planets and over 60 moons, or satellites, all spinning as they orbit or travel round the Sun.

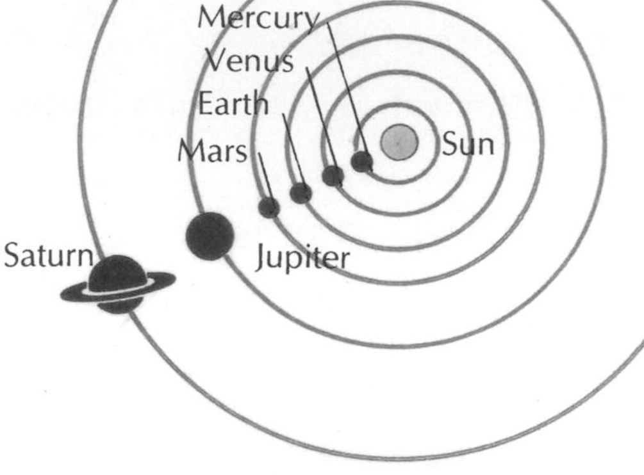

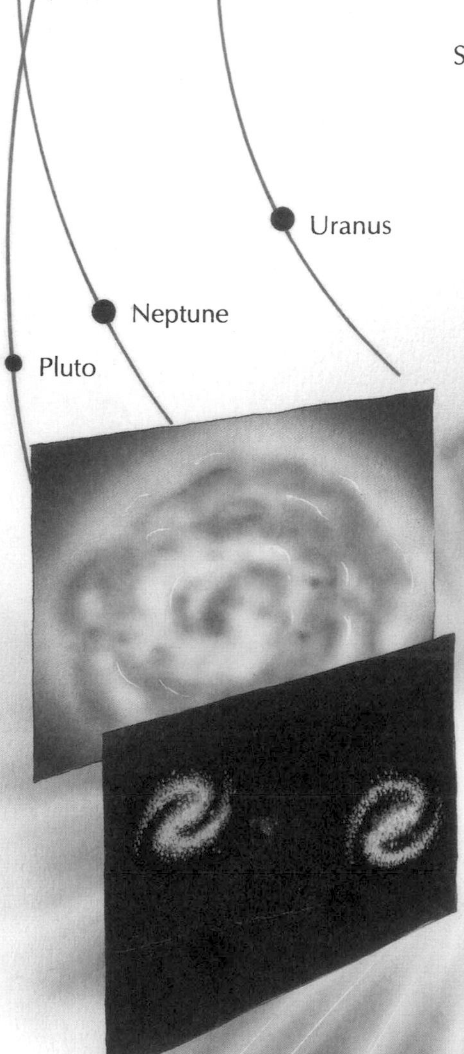

- The Solar System was probably formed about 5 billion years ago.

The Big Bang theory

Most scientists believe the Universe began about 14 billion years ago with a gigantic explosion they call the **Big Bang**.

- The bang blasted hot material out in all directions. It was far hotter than a nuclear explosion, or even the centre of the Sun.
- As this material cooled, it turned into hydrogen and helium. These are the two most common 'elements', or substances, found in the Universe.
- Galaxies and stars began to form out of hydrogen and helium about one billion years after the Big Bang.

Clues to the Big Bang

There are some **clues** to show that the Big Bang happened. Two of the most important clues are:

- The galaxies are flying further apart, as if from the force of an explosion.
- Space is still slightly 'warm' from the last traces of the explosion.

The Solar System is about a million times wider than the diameter of Earth

Our galaxy is about 100 million times wider than the Solar System

The distance to the furthest visible object in the Universe is about 100,000 times our galaxy's width

Theories about the future

There are **two main theories** about what will happen to the Universe in the future. They are:

- The Open Theory, which says that the Universe started with the Big Bang and the galaxies will carry on expanding for ever.
- The Closed Theory, which says that the Universe will stop expanding. The pulling force of gravity will slowly drag the galaxies back towards each other again until there is a Big Crunch!
- The latest observations made by astronomers show that the Open Theory is more likely to be the correct one.

Gravity

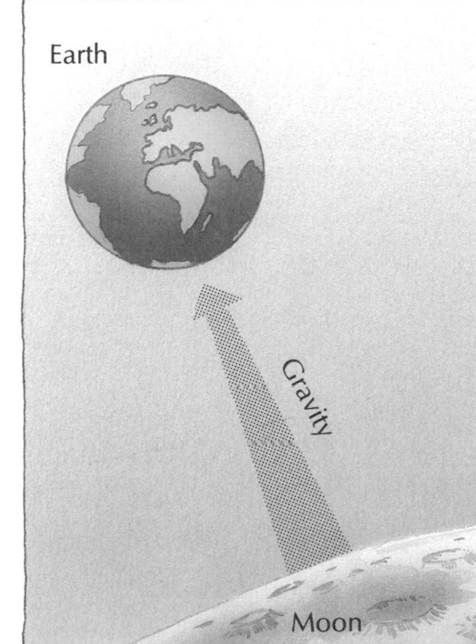

Gravity is the **pulling force** that exists between things. It is the force that keeps the Moon orbiting round the Earth.

- The Sun's gravity keeps the planets in orbit, and stops them from flying off into Space as they spin round.
- The Sun has a much greater pull of gravity than the Earth, because it has 333,000 times as much mass (amount of material) as Earth.
- Your weight is the force of the Earth's gravity pulling you down on to its surface.

Strange but true

- The temperature when the Big Bang happened was about 1 billion billion billion °C.
- A hundredth of a second later (the time needed to take a snapshot), it had cooled to 1 billion °C.
- Most of the material in the Universe is invisible. Some of it may exist as dark particles between galaxies.

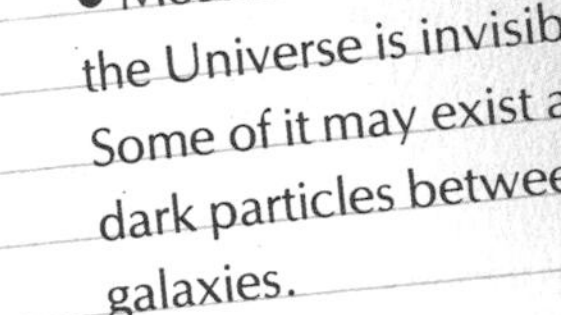

Measuring Space

Distances in Space are too vast to be measured in kilometres, so scientists measure in **light-years**. A light-year is 9460 billion km – the distance travelled by light in one year.

- The nearest star to the Sun is called Proxima Centauri. It is 4.3 light-years away, which means it takes 4.3 years for its light to reach Earth.

Radio telescope

Hubble space telescope

How far can we see?

- Radio telescopes on Earth have helped astronomers to detect very distant objects. The most distant galaxy so far observed by astronomers is at least 6 billion light-years away.
- Some telescopes have been put into Space. They can 'see' more clearly than telescopes on Earth and can detect invisible energy waves. One day they may discover new planets.

The Stars

Stars are different colours depending on how hot they are:

Bluish stars – surface temp. 20,000-50,000 °C

The stars in the sky look small because they are so far away. In fact they are huge. Each star is a glowing **ball of gases** held together by gravity. Most of this gas is **hydrogen**. In the hot fury of a star's 'core', or centre, hydrogen reaches a temperature of at least 10 million °C.

The heat inside a star changes hydrogen atoms into the atoms of another gas called **helium**.

When this happens there is an '**atomic reaction**' and a flash of energy is given out. Billions of these flashes of energy keep the star hot and make it shine.

The **Sun** is the nearest star to Earth. It is only a middle-sized star but it looks big to us because it is so close – only 150 million km away!

The birth and death of a star

Stars are born in clusters. A **cloud of gas and dust** called a **nebula** breaks up over millions of years into smaller clouds which are then pulled tighter and smaller by their own gravity. Eventually they heat up and start to shine.

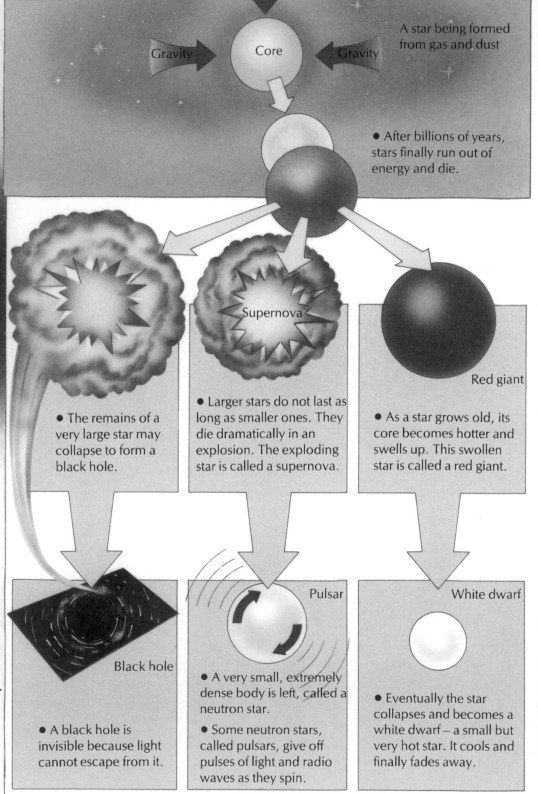

A star being formed from gas and dust

• After billions of years, stars finally run out of energy and die.

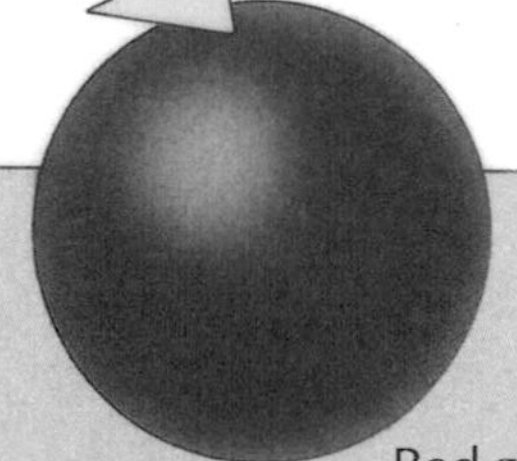

Red giant

• The remains of a very large star may collapse to form a black hole.

• Larger stars do not last as long as smaller ones. They die dramatically in an explosion. The exploding star is called a supernova.

• As a star grows old, its core becomes hotter and swells up. This swollen star is called a red giant.

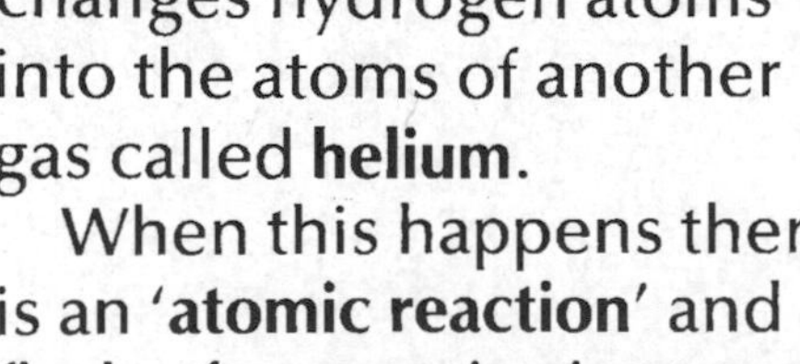

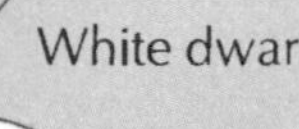

Black hole

Pulsar

White dwarf

• A black hole is invisible because light cannot escape from it.

• A very small, extremely dense body is left, called a neutron star.

• Some neutron stars, called pulsars, give off pulses of light and radio waves as they spin.

• Eventually the star collapses and becomes a white dwarf – a small but very hot star. It cools and finally fades away.

Blue-white stars – surface temp. 10,000-20,000 °C

White stars – surface temp. 8000-10,000 °C

Yellow stars – surface temp. 5500-8000 °C

Orange stars – surface temp. about 5000 °C

Red stars – surface temp. 4000 °C or below

The electro-magnetic spectrum

Stars give off different kinds of **energy waves**, or **radiation**. Each kind has a different wavelength. Together they are called the **electro-magnetic spectrum**.

- We can see one kind of energy wave – visible light. The others are invisible.
- Special instruments are used to detect radiation. Dangerous X-rays and gamma rays are blocked by the Earth's atmosphere and are studied from Space.

Radio waves (longest wavelength)

Microwaves

Infra-red waves

Visible light

Ultra-violet light

X-rays

Gamma rays (shortest wavelength)

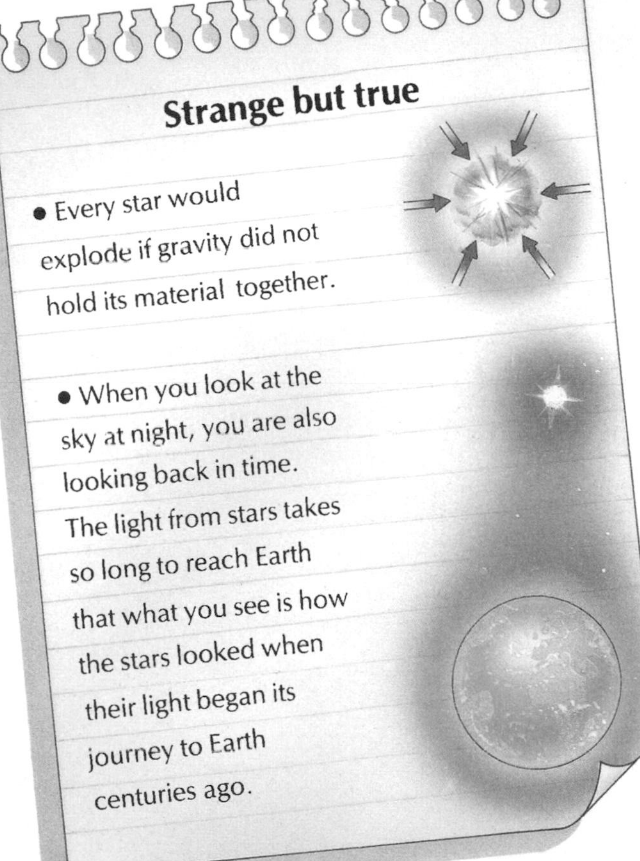

Strange but true

- Every star would explode if gravity did not hold its material together.
- When you look at the sky at night, you are also looking back in time. The light from stars takes so long to reach Earth that what you see is how the stars looked when their light began its journey to Earth centuries ago.

The Sun as a star

Sun

The Sun was formed from a **nebula** about 5 billion years ago, and will burn for about another 5 billion years.

- The Sun is the source of life on Earth. Without its light and heat, Earth would be dead and icy.

Different kinds of stars

Some stars, like the Sun, shine with a **steady light**. Other kinds of stars don't shine steadily. They are called **variable stars**.

- Variable stars fade and brighten over and over again.

- Some stars have a regular cycle of fading and getting brighter. For example, the star called Delta Cephei reaches full brightness every 5 days 9 hours.
- Some variable stars are really binary systems – two steadily shining stars orbiting each other. They seem to fade when one blocks light from the other and brighten when they are both visible at the same time.
- Sometimes a binary system star blazes very brightly for just a few nights. This is called a nova. It probably happens when a cloud of gas from one star explodes as it reaches the other star.

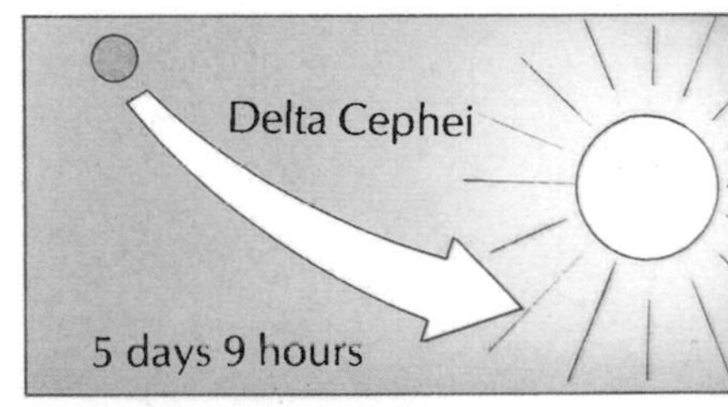

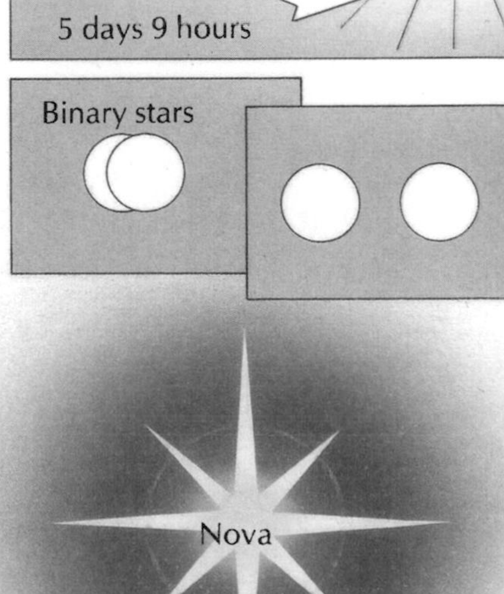

The Constellations

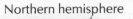

These are the five brightest stars that can be seen from Earth:

Sirius
magnitude minus 1.5
8.7 light-years away

Constellations are **patterns of stars** in the night sky. The shapes they seem to make were given names in ancient times, and many of these names are still used today.

The stars that make up constellations are not really close to each other. Sometimes the stars that look closest are really far apart – they just happen to be in line with each other and so look like a group when viewed from Earth.

Hemispheres

On maps, Earth is divided in half by an imaginary line called the **Equator**. One half is known as the **northern hemisphere**. The other is called the **southern hemisphere**.

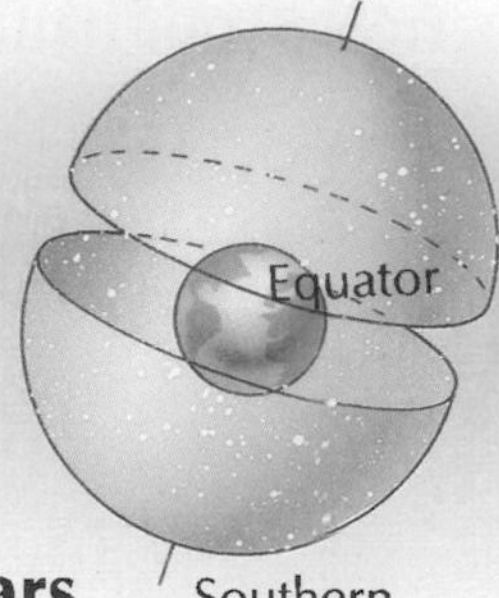

- Viewed from the Earth, stars appear to form patterns on the inside of a huge imaginary sphere. Like the Earth, this 'star sphere' is also divided into northern and southern hemispheres.

Some northern hemisphere stars

- The constellation Taurus (the Bull) contains a group of stars called the Pleiades, or the Seven Sisters (although there are actually far more than seven stars). They are 400 light-years away.

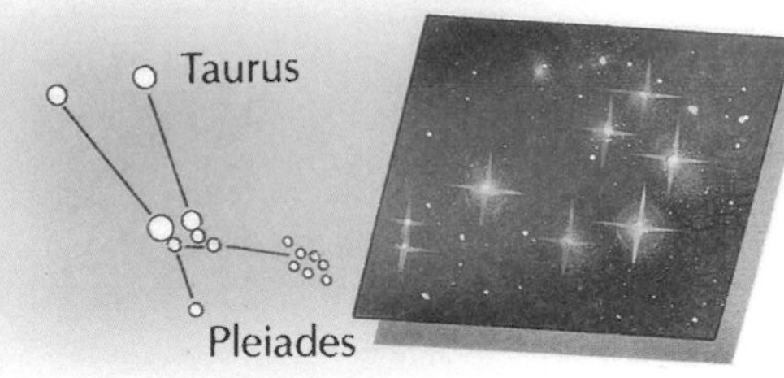

- The constellation Ursa Major (the Great Bear) is often called the Plough. It contains a group of seven bright stars.

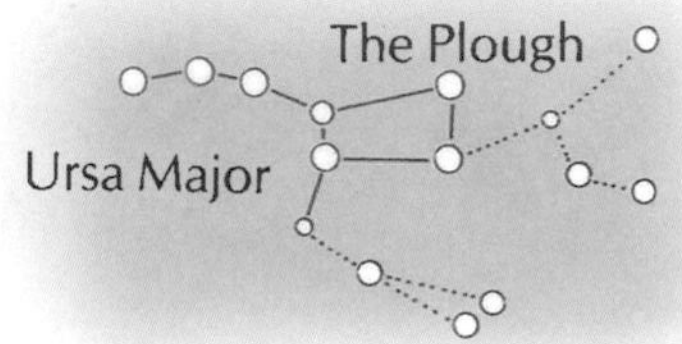

- The Andromeda galaxy is a dim smudge in the Andromeda constellation. It is 2 million light-years away.

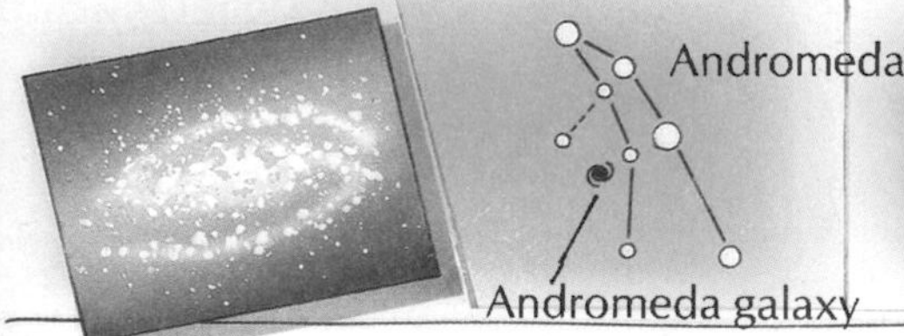

- Polaris, the North Star, is in the constellation Ursa Minor (the Little Bear). It appears to be fixed in the sky, and so for centuries has helped travellers find north.

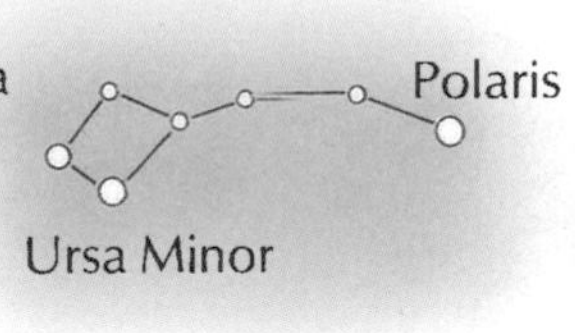

Star drift

During the night, stars seem to **rise**, **move** across the sky and then **sink** out of sight. They do not really move, however. It is the **turning Earth** that makes the stars appear to move across the sky.

- Stars seen from the North and South Poles appear to move around the sky in level paths, without ever rising or setting at all.
- If photographic film is exposed to a starry sky for some hours, the stars leave trails on the film as they appear to move across the sky.

Star trails on photographic film

Canopus
magnitude minus 0.7
230 light-years away

Alpha Centauri
magnitude minus 0.3
4.3 light-years away

Arcturus
magnitude 0.06
38 light-years away

Vega
magnitude 0.04
27 light-years away

Some southern hemisphere stars

• Proxima Centauri, our nearest star apart from the Sun, is part of the Centaurus constellation. It is 4.3 light-years away.

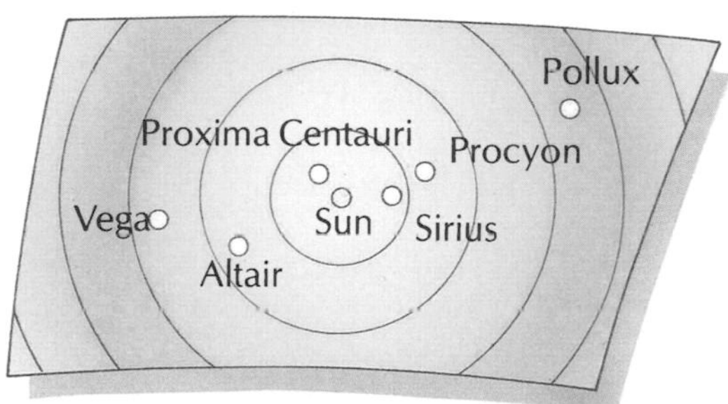

• The constellation called Canis Major (the Great Dog) contains Sirius, the brightest star in the sky. It is also called the Dog Star.

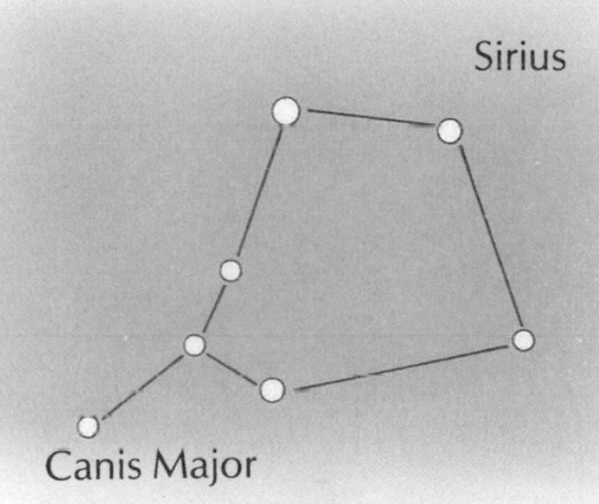

• The Southern Cross is the smallest constellation. Two of its stars can be lined up to point due south, which is useful for navigation.

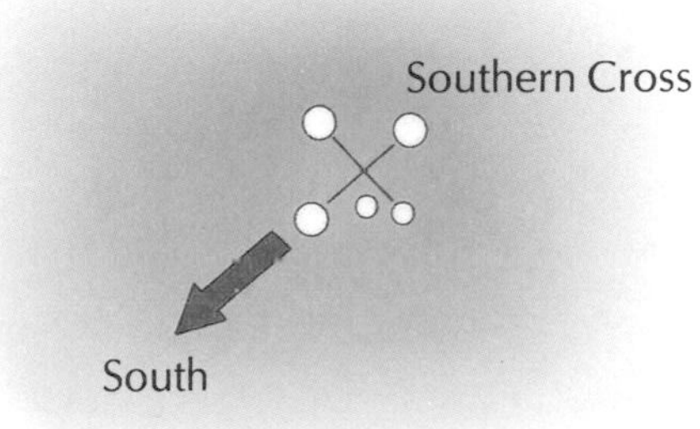

• The Magellanic Clouds, two small irregular galaxies, are the Milky Way's closest companions in Space. They are about 200,000 light-years away.

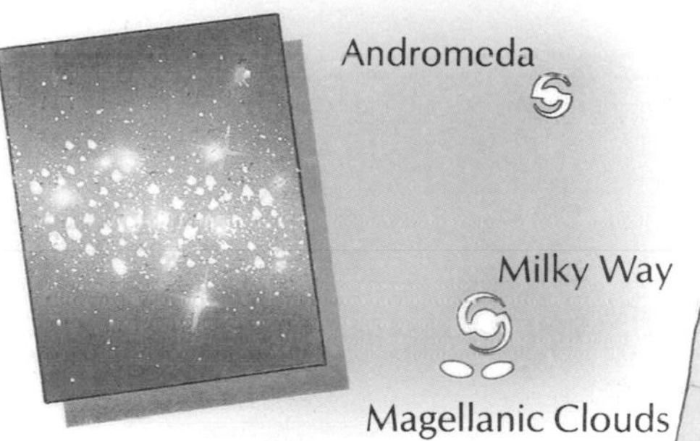

Orion the hunter

Some constellations, such as **Orion**, belong to both the **northern** and the **southern hemispheres**.

• Orion was named after a famous hunter in ancient Greek mythology.

• Betelgeuse is a variable red giant star, in Orion.

Orion

• Three stars make up Orion's belt.

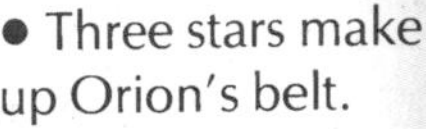

• The Horsehead Nebula, south of Orion, is a dark cloud of cold gas and dust shaped like a horse's head.

Strange but true

• The African Dogon tribe say their ancestors knew about the invisible star Sirius B thousands of years before scientists discovered it in 1862.

Sirius B
Sirius

• In the constellation Corona Borealis there is a star that sometimes dims when tiny black particles hide it from view.

• North American Indians tested warriors' eyesight by seeing how many stars of the Pleiades they could spot!

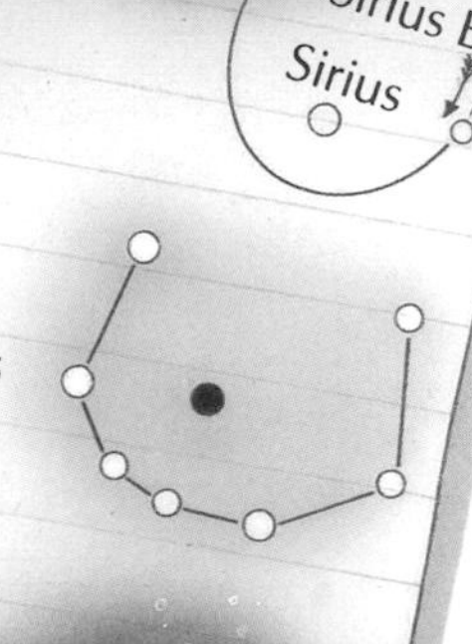

Star brightness

The brightness of a star is called its **magnitude**. Astronomers have given each star a **magnitude rating**.

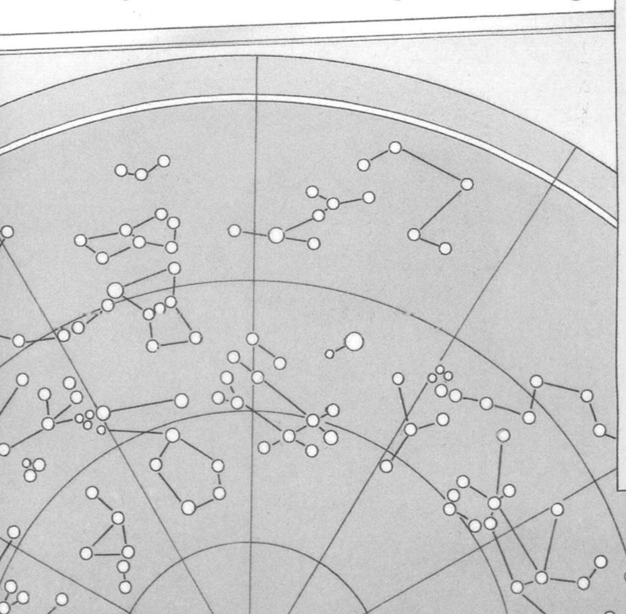

• The higher the number, the dimmer the star. The dimmest stars visible without a telescope have a magnitude of about 6. A magnitude 0 star is very bright. The brightest stars have minus numbers.

• Sirius, the brightest star in the sky, has a magnitude of minus 1.5.

Galaxies

Here are some galaxies that are close enough to Earth to be studied:

M81: a spiral galaxy

Galaxies are **huge groups** containing hundreds of millions of **stars**. They were probably formed about a billion years after the Big Bang when the Universe was quite young.

No-one knows how many galaxies there are in all, but there are probably billions.

Galaxies often move together in groups, called **clusters**. Our galaxy is in a cluster of about twenty galaxies, but there are much bigger groups containing thousands of galaxies.

The Milky Way

Our galaxy is called the **Milky Way**. It contains about 100 billion stars. The **Sun** and the **Solar System** are more than halfway out from the centre to the edge of the galaxy.

- It takes light about 100,000 years to travel from one side of the Milky Way to the other. (Light takes only 8½ minutes to travel to Earth from the Sun.)
- The whole Milky Way rotates in Space. It takes the Sun 225 million years to revolve once around the centre of the galaxy. This is called a galactic year.
- The centre of our galaxy cannot be seen from Earth because it is hidden by dust and gas.

- The central bulge of the Milky Way contains almost half of all the stars in the galaxy. They are much closer together than the Sun and its neighbouring stars.
- Although they are so close together in Space terms, stars collide with each other in the centre of the galaxy only rarely – perhaps one collision every 1000 years.

M51: the Whirlpool, about 14 million light-years away

M77: a spiral galaxy

M87: a strong source of radio waves

M104: a spiral nicknamed the Sombrero

Galaxy shapes

These are the four main **galaxy shapes**:

Spiral

Barred spiral

• Spirals turn like a lit Catherine wheel, or cream swirling in a cup of coffee. Our galaxy is a spiral.

• Barred spirals look like two tadpoles joined at the head. They have a bar shape in the centre and two long arms.

Elliptical

Irregular

• Elliptical (oval) galaxies look like squashed circles. It is thought they contain older stars.

• Irregular galaxies contain a lot of dust and form no definite shape.

Strange but true

• There may be a huge black hole at the centre of our galaxy that is gradually sucking in the surrounding light and gas.

• The ancient Greeks called our galaxy the Milky Way because they thought it was made from drops of milk from the breasts of the Greek goddess Hera.

• Giant elliptical (oval) galaxies, found at the centre of large clusters, may be 'eating up' smaller galaxies.

Neighbouring galaxies

The **biggest galaxy** in our group is the **Andromeda Spiral**. It is about 2 million light-years away from Earth and contains about 400 billion stars.

• Andromeda can be seen from Earth with the naked eye.

• Our nearest galaxy neighbours are the Magellanic Clouds. These are two small irregular galaxies. The larger galaxy contains about 10 billion stars and is 180,000 light-years away. The other galaxy is much smaller and further away.

• The Magellanic Clouds were first sighted in 1521 by the explorer Ferdinand Magellan.

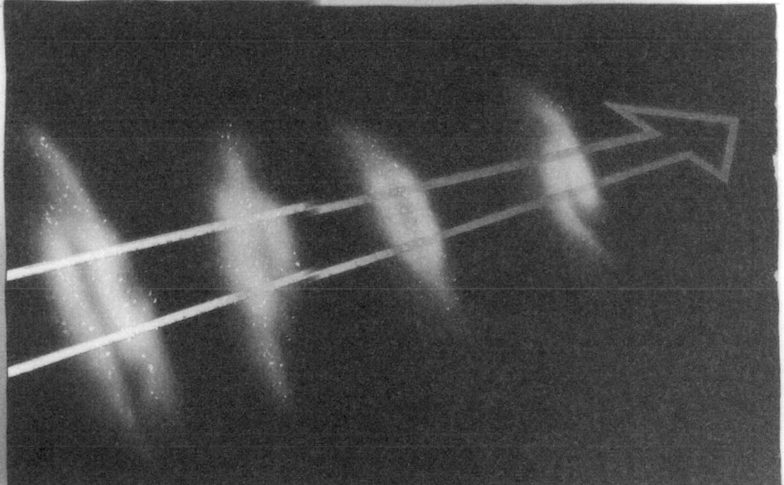

Red shift

As galaxies speed away from Earth, the light from them gets distorted so that it appears red. This is known as **red shift**. The faster a galaxy is moving away, the more red it will seem to be. The red colour cannot be seen by the eye. Astronomers study it using special instruments.

Space Oddities

These satellites study Space oddities outside Earth's atmosphere:

Although scientists know much about the Universe, there are still many strange things in Space that have not been fully explained. **Black holes** are the most mysterious. It seems that they exist, but they can never be seen!

Black holes

Some **very rare stars** contain as much material as fifty or more Suns. They are the brightest stars in the Universe yet they turn into **black holes** – the blackest objects in Space.

1 When these stars die they keep on shrinking, because the pull of gravity is so strong.

2 They shrink down to a tiny speck, called a singularity or black hole.

3 Although tiny, the black hole contains all the material from the huge star.

4 A black hole's gravity is so strong that no light can escape from it.

5 Astronomers have not seen a black hole, but they have found stars they think may have a black hole nearby.

Anything that falls into a black hole can never come out again because gravity will crush it to nothing.

Quasars and **cosmic rays** are other space objects that still baffle scientists. If you think of the Universe as a giant jigsaw, only a few pieces have so far been fitted together.

Quasars

Quasars are very distant objects that send out far more **light** than ordinary galaxies. They may also send out strong **radio waves**.

- Quasars seem to be sending out tremendous energy from a small space inside them. This could come from gas whirling around a giant black hole at the centre of the galaxy.

- The name 'quasar' is short for quasi-stellar (star-like) object.

- Quasars may have been a stage that some galaxies went through early in their lives. Because they are billions of light-years away, we are seeing them today as they were billions of years ago.

Space Telescope

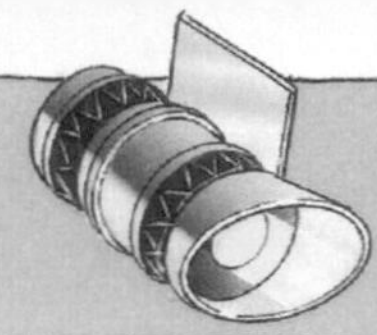
IRAS (Infra-red Astronomical Satellite)

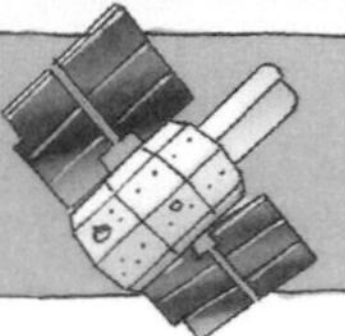
OAO (Orbiting Astronomical Observatory)

Detecting black holes

Some **binary star systems** may contain a star that has turned into a black hole. Gas from the other star would swirl around the black hole before being pulled into it, giving off high-energy radiation, including X-rays.

Earth

- X-rays cannot travel through Earth's atmosphere, so they are studied by satellites that send information back to Earth.

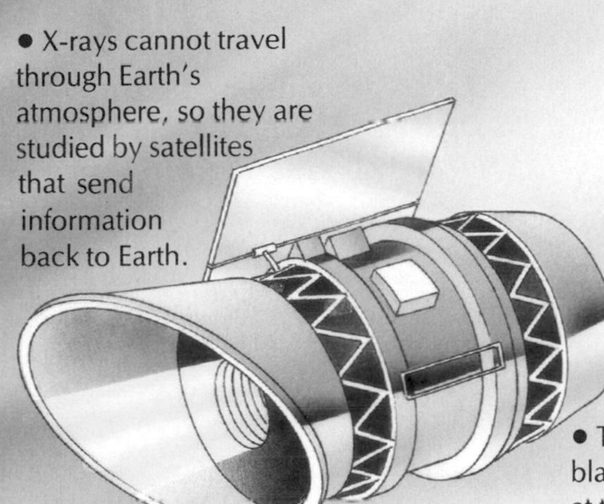

- A hot supergiant star in the Cygnus constellation has an invisible companion called Cygnus X-1. It is probably a black hole.

- There are many other suspected black holes, including a giant one at the centre of our galaxy .

Strange but true

- If the Sun became a black hole, it would be only a few kilometres across – but it could swallow the Earth!

- A quasar turns out heat and light a billion billion times more efficiently than the Sun does.

- Cosmic rays can affect tree growth. Some astronomers have studied tree rings to find out how the number of cosmic rays reaching the Earth has changed over the centuries.

Cosmic rays and neutrinos

Cosmic rays are tiny **particles** that travel in Space at high speed and constantly shower Earth. They may come from exploding **stars**. Most of them do not penetrate Earth's atmosphere.

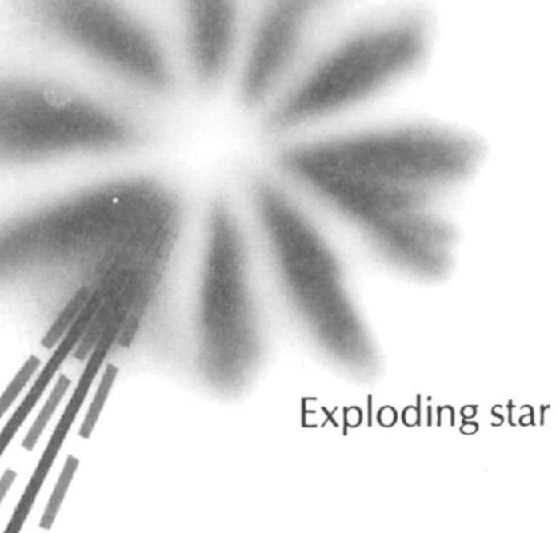
Exploding star

Cosmic rays

- Some cosmic rays bounce off into Space.

Earth's atmosphere

- Some cosmic rays reach the Earth's surface.

- Some cosmic ray particles are called neutrinos. These can pass right through the Earth itself as if it were not there!

- Several million neutrinos will pass through you as you read this page!

Neutrinos pass right through the Earth.

New planets?

There are nine planets in our Solar System. Scientists are trying to find **other planets** circling other stars.

- Throughout the Universe, there are probably millions of other stars with Solar Systems. Each could have its own planets.

- So far, no other planets have been found. Astronomers who thought they had found a planet outside the Solar System in 1991 later announced that they had made a computer error.

The Sun

The Sun has three main surface layers:

Photosphere – The shining surface we see from Earth

The Sun, like all stars, is a ball of fiercely **hot gas.** Hydrogen gas deep inside it is constantly being turned into helium. This releases energy in the form of **light** and **heat**.

The Sun is the nearest star to Earth. In Space terms it is relatively close – only about 150 million km away! The Sun has shone steadily for thousands of millions of years. If it went dim for only a few days, most life-forms on Earth would perish.

Features of the Sun

These are some of the Sun's more **spectacular features:**

- Enormous eruptions of gas, called prominences, rise continually from the surface of the Sun. Some reach out into Space as far as 2 million km.

Arched prominences

Sunspots

- Sunspots are darker, cooler areas that appear on the Sun's surface from time to time. Some are much larger than the Earth and can last for months. Smaller ones last for only a few days or weeks.

- Every 11 years or so, sunspots become more common and then fade away. This is called the sunspot cycle.

Solar flares

- Solar flares are violent explosions of energy from the Sun's surface. They shoot particles at high speed out into Space. On Earth they can produce strange effects, such as the glowing lights, called aurorae, that sometimes appear in the night sky.

Sun facts

- The diameter or distance through the centre of the Sun is 1,392,000 km.

- The temperature at the core is believed to be about 14 million °C. At the surface it is 6000°C.

- A million bodies the size of the Earth could be squashed inside the Sun.

- The Sun is 92 per cent hydrogen. At the centre is a core of helium. Around this core 4 million tonnes of the Sun's material is turned into energy every second.

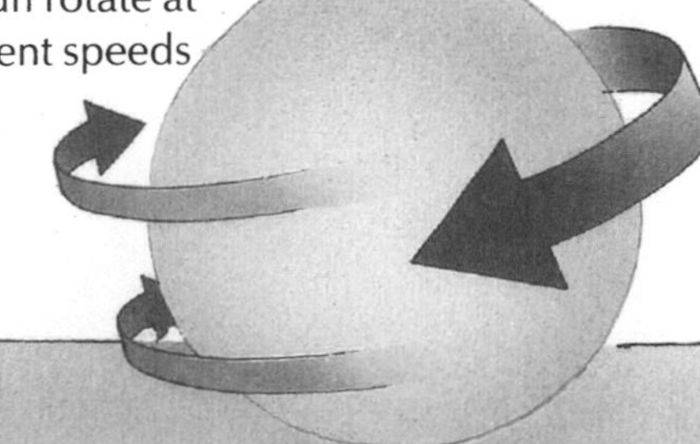

Different parts of the Sun rotate at different speeds

Different speeds

- Because the Sun is made of gases, different parts of it can rotate at different speeds. The centre part, or Equator area, rotates faster than the Poles.

- Energy from the core takes a million years to reach the Sun's surface, but only 8½ minutes to travel from the Sun's surface to the Earth.

Chromosphere – A layer a few thousand km deep that shines pink during an eclipse

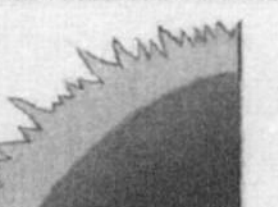

Corona – The outer atmosphere that stretches millions of km into Space

WARNING Never look directly at the Sun. It can damage your eyes and blind you.

Solar eclipses

Occasionally the **Moon** passes in front of the Sun so that it **blocks out sunlight** from part of the Earth. This is called a **total solar eclipse**.

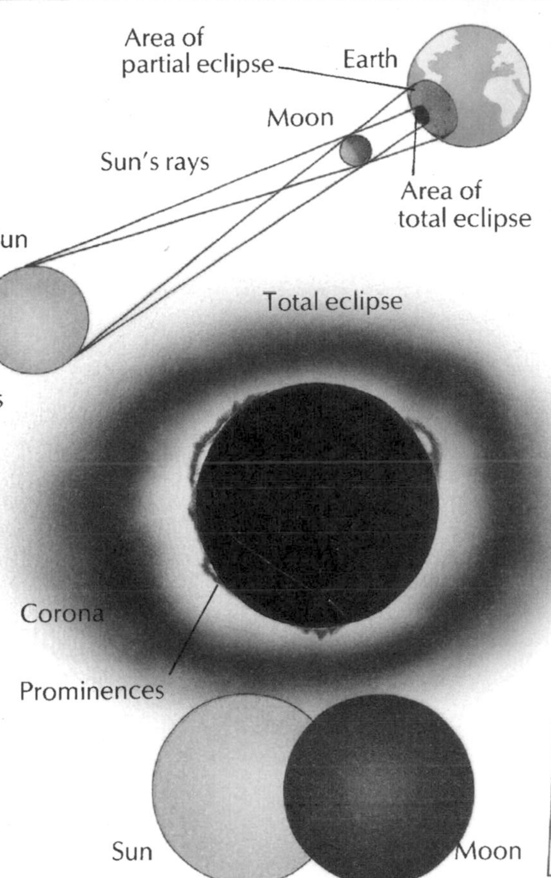

- If the eclipse is total, the Sun's faint atmosphere or corona shines out in the darkened sky. This is the only time it can be seen from Earth.
- During a total eclipse, prominences can sometimes be seen flaring out around the darkened outline of the Sun. Eclipses provide scientists with good opportunities for studying such things as prominences and the corona.
- When the Moon blocks out only part of the Sun's light, this is called a partial eclipse.

Strange but true

- The Sun is described by scientists as a yellow dwarf star.
- There may be a connection between the appearance of sunspots and changes in the weather on Earth.
- Sound waves produced inside the Sun make it swell and shrink by a kilometre or so every few minutes.

What will happen to the Sun?

Like all stars, the Sun is **changing**. This is what scientists believe will happen to it:

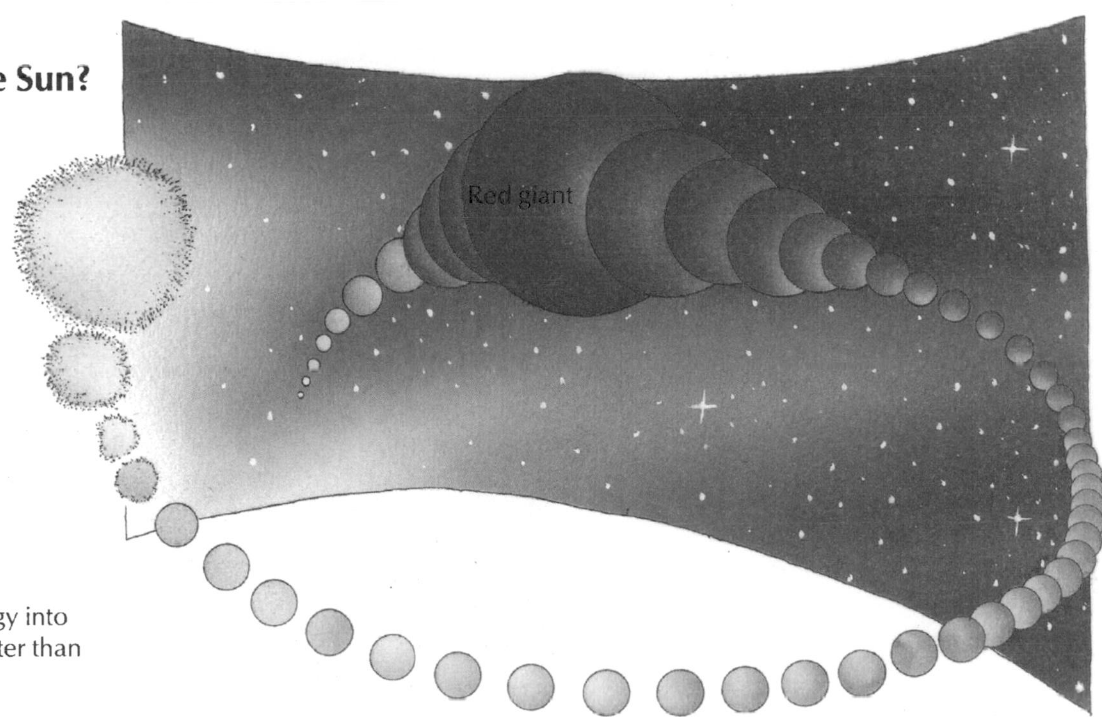

1 Several billion years from now, the Sun will have a crisis. The hydrogen supply around its core will start to run out, and our star will begin to collapse.

2 This collapse will put new energy into the core so the Sun will blaze hotter than ever.

3 The blast of energy will force the higher gas layers outwards. The Sun will become a red giant, 100 times its present diameter and 500 times brighter.

4 The red giant will fill Earth's sky. The great heat will melt the surface of the Earth into seas of lava.

5 Eventually the Sun will cool and shrink, becoming a white dwarf star about the size of Earth.

The Moon

Here are some Moon facts:

Average distance from Earth 382,400 km

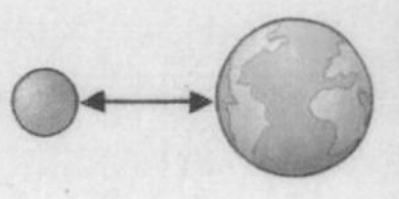

The Moon is an airless ball of **rock** about a quarter the diameter of the Earth. It circles round the Earth once every 27.3 days. It has no **light** of its own, but reflects light from the Sun.

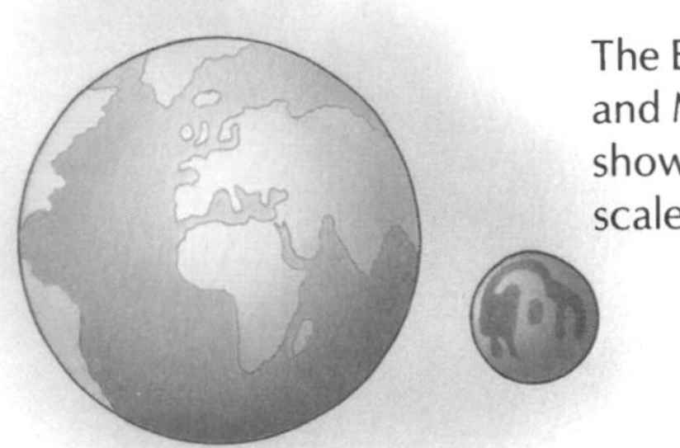

The Earth and Moon shown to scale

The Moon has probably always been lifeless, but it has had a violent, turbulent history. Most of the **craters** on its surface were caused by solid space bodies called meteoroids crashing into it between 3 and 4 billion years ago. The darker areas are called **maria** (seas). They are made of lava that flowed out from inside the Moon about 3 billion years ago.

Gravity

The Moon is much smaller than Earth and so has much weaker **gravity**. Astronauts had to be weighted down to help them walk properly on the Moon's surface.

Astronauts on the Moon

- It is gravity that causes ocean tides on Earth to rise and fall. The gravity of the Sun and Moon pulls the Earth's oceans into bulges. The Earth rotates beneath these bulges, producing two high tides a day.

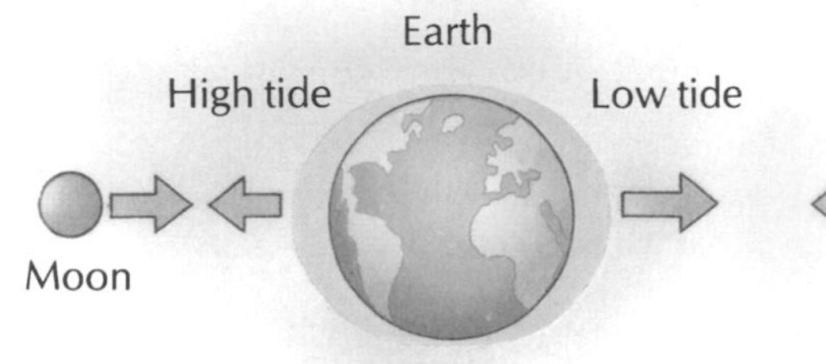

Phases of the Moon

The Moon keeps the same **side** facing Earth all the time, so we only see this one side of it. As the Moon travels around the Earth, we see a varying amount of this side each day. These different amounts, or stages, are called the **phases of the Moon**.

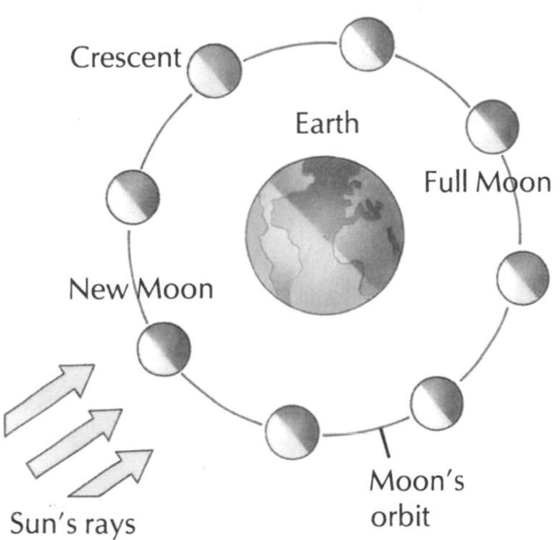

- When the Moon is seen as a crescent, only a sliver of the side facing Earth is sunlit.
- As the Moon moves round the Earth, it appears half-lit and then finally fully lit (the Full Moon). At this stage the whole of the side facing Earth is sunlit.
- After Full Moon, the shape changes back to half and finally to a thin crescent. It then disappears for a few nights (New Moon) and the process begins again.
- It takes 29.5 days for the Moon to move through all its phases from New, through Full, and back to New again.

Crescent Half Moon Half Moon Crescent

Waxing Moon Full Moon Waning Moon

- As the Moon grows from crescent to Full, it is called the waxing moon.
- As it shrinks back to a crescent, it is called the waning moon.

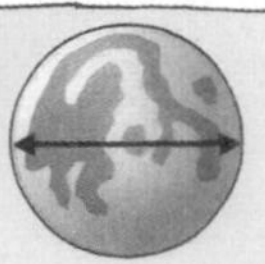

Diameter
3476 km

Temperature
on sunlit side 100°C
on dark side −170°C

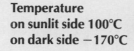

Gravity
One-sixth as strong as Earth's gravity

The Moon's surface

The Moon's **surface** is covered with craters, ridges, mountains and valleys. The dark maria are the smoothest parts because the lava that created them flowed over and covered old craters. These are some facts about the Moon's surface:

- The biggest Moon crater that can be seen from Earth is called Bailly. It is about 290 km across.
- The largest Moon crater is on the far side of the Moon and so cannot be seen from Earth.
- Because the Moon has no air or water to wear rocks away, the Moon's surface has remained unchanged for thousands of millions of years.

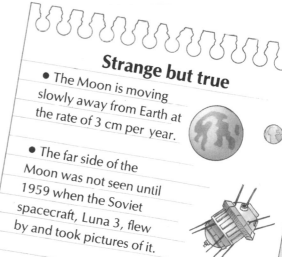

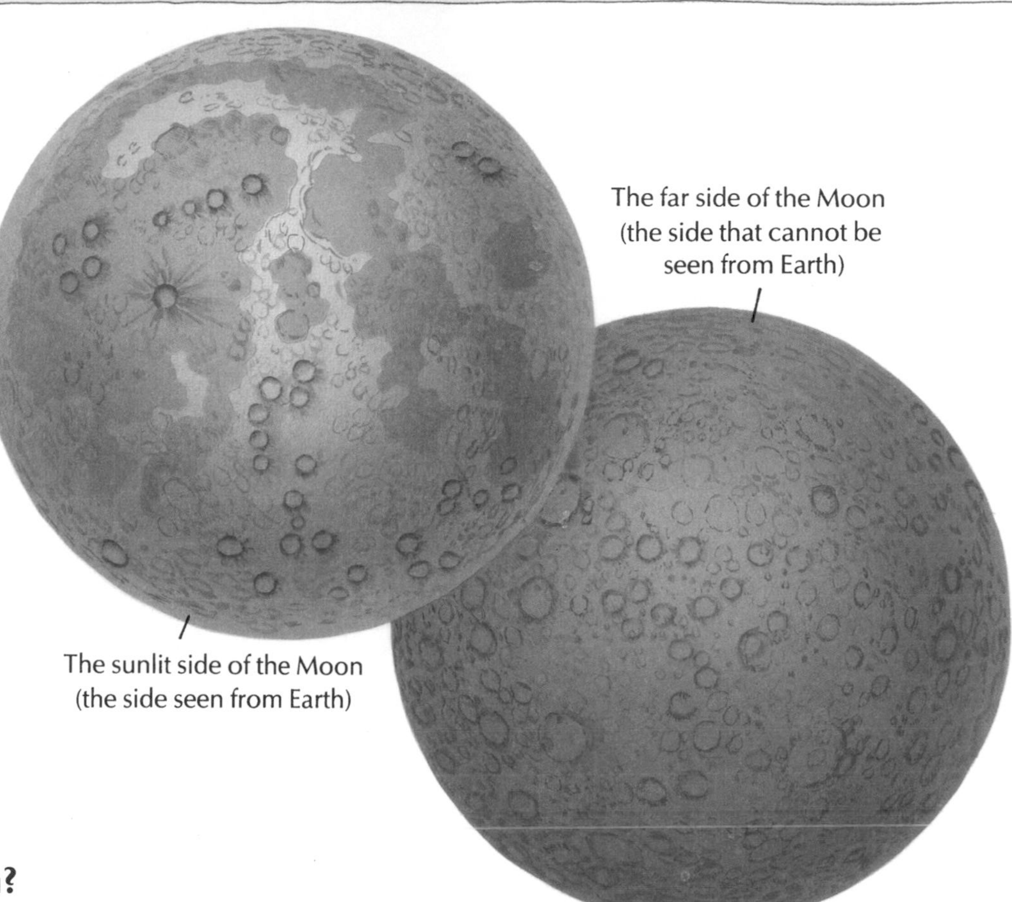

Where did the Moon come from?

The Moon and Earth are roughly the same age. Scientists are unsure where the Moon came from. Here are four theories:

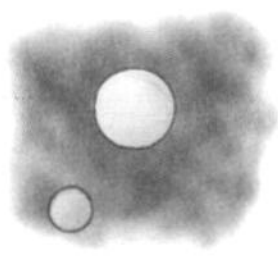
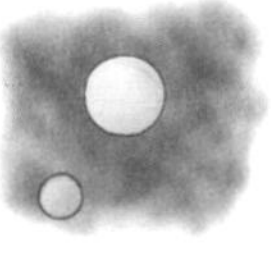

1 The Moon and Earth formed together from the same dust and gas cloud.

2 The Moon was a wandering space body that came close to Earth and became trapped in Earth's orbit.

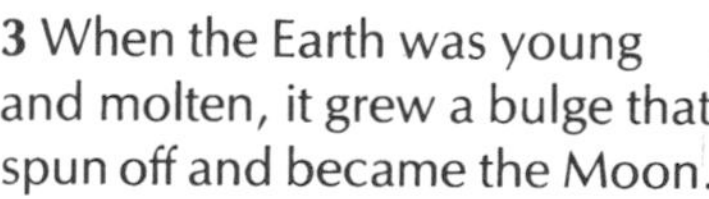

3 When the Earth was young and molten, it grew a bulge that spun off and became the Moon.

4 A small planet hit the young molten Earth and threw material into orbit, which got drawn together to form the Moon.

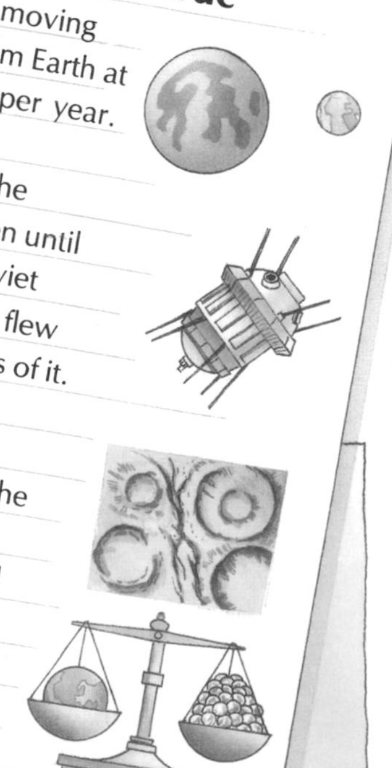

Strange but true

- The Moon is moving slowly away from Earth at the rate of 3 cm per year.
- The far side of the Moon was not seen until 1959 when the Soviet spacecraft, Luna 3, flew by and took pictures of it.
- Earth's gravity has pulled on the side of the Moon that faces Earth, causing a bulge several kilometres high.
- It would take 81 Moons to weigh the same as Earth.

Lunar eclipses

The Earth casts a long **shadow** in Space on the side away from the Sun. A **Lunar eclipse** happens when the Moon passes into the darkest part of this shadow. During a total Lunar eclipse, the Moon looks dark brown colour.

Sun
Earth
Moon
Earth's shadow

Earth and the Solar System

Here are some facts about the Earth:

Temperature of the core about 5000° C

Earth is a smallish, rocky planet. It is in just the right place in the Solar System to allow **life** to be supported. If Earth were nearer to the Sun, it would be too hot for life as we know it to survive. If it were further away, it would be too cold.

Seen from Space, Earth is a beautiful **bluish disc** with swirling white clouds. It looks blue because so much of its surface is ocean.

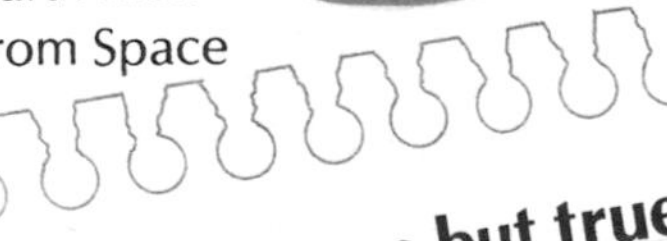

Earth seen from Space

Strange but true

- The Icelandic island of Surtsey was formed between 1963 and 1966. It began when an underwater volcano suddenly erupted, shooting columns of lava high into the air.
- Some underwater volcanoes are higher than Mount Everest.
- The Himalayan mountains were formed when India (then an island) collided with the rest of Asia.

Earth's position in the Solar System

Earth is the third planet from the Sun. Its closest neighbours are Venus and Mars.

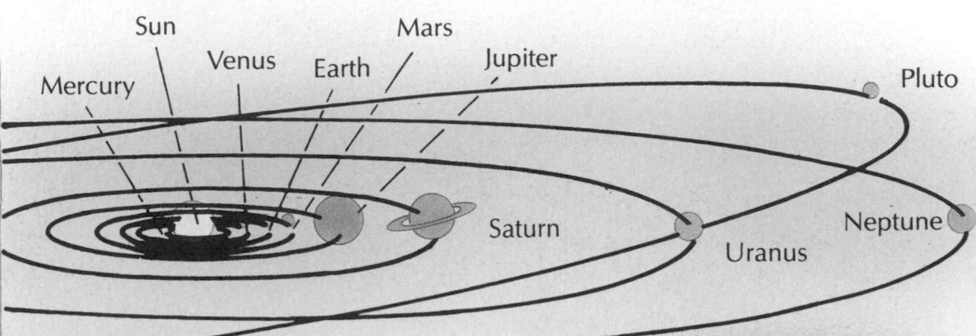

How Earth began

Earth was formed about 4.6 billion years ago, from **small rocky bodies** that collided with each other as they whirled around the Sun.

- These collisions gave out so much energy that the Earth glowed red-hot as further rocky bodies crashed into it.
- After several hundred million years, Earth reached its present size. The collisions died down and the Earth started to cool.
- The metal in the Earth sank to the centre, forming the core, with the lighter rocks forming the mantle and crust.

Crust, mantle and core

This is what the Earth might look like inside. At the centre is the **core**, surrounded by the **mantle**. The **crust** is a thin outer layer.

- The Earth's core is about 7000 km across and is probably made of iron and nickel. The outer part is liquid and the inner part solid.
- The mantle is made of rock. It contains most of the Earth's material.
- The crust is made of lighter rocks that floated to the top when Earth was molten. It varies from 6 to 40 km thick.

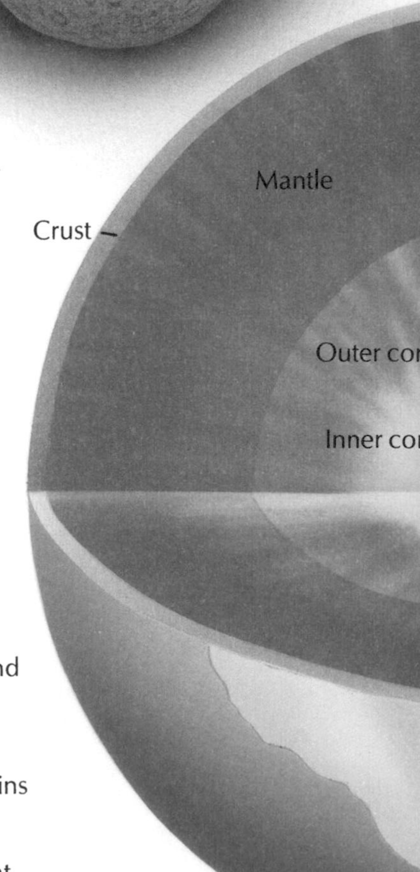

Diameter across the centre: 12,756 km

Weight: about 5,974,000,000,000 billion tonnes

Surface: two-thirds is covered with water

Earth's atmosphere

Earth is surrounded by an **atmosphere**, which enables life to survive on the planet. This is what the atmosphere does:

- Provides the air we breathe.
- Protects Earth from harmful rays from Space.
- Protects Earth from space debris, such as meteors.
- Stops Earth getting too cold at night or too hot in the day.

Layers of the atmosphere

The atmosphere can be divided into these **different layers**:

- Exosphere
(500-8000 km above the Earth)
Weather satellites orbit in this layer.
- Ionosphere
(80-500 km above the Earth)
This layer protects the Earth from harmful rays.
- Mesosphere
(48-80 km above the Earth)
Unmanned balloons have measured the temperature of this layer.
- The ozone layer is part of the stratosphere, at about 40 km high.
- Stratosphere
(10-48 km above the Earth)
Jet aircraft fly in this layer.
- Troposphere
(From the ground to 10 km high)
We live in this layer and all Earth's weather happens in it.

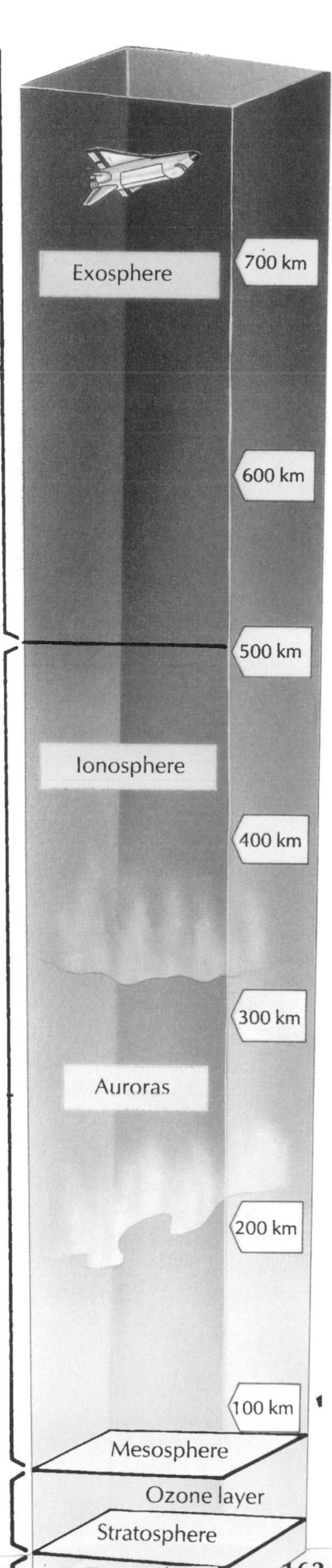

Volcanoes

Volcanoes are openings in the Earth's crust where molten (melted) rock from inside bursts through the surface. Some molten rock (called **lava**) spills out. It can build up round the opening to form a **mountain**.

- Earth has more than 1300 active volcanoes, many of them under the sea.
- The islands of Hawaii and Iceland are made of rock that erupted out of the sea from underwater volcanoes.
- Most volcanoes are found near where the plates of the Earth's crust (see below) collide with each other.

Plates

The Earth's **crust** is not an unbroken shell. It is a jigsaw of about 15 huge **rocky pieces** called **plates** that continually push and slide against each other.

- When two plates collide, the rocks they are made of can get squashed and pushed up into the air. Some mountains were formed that way.

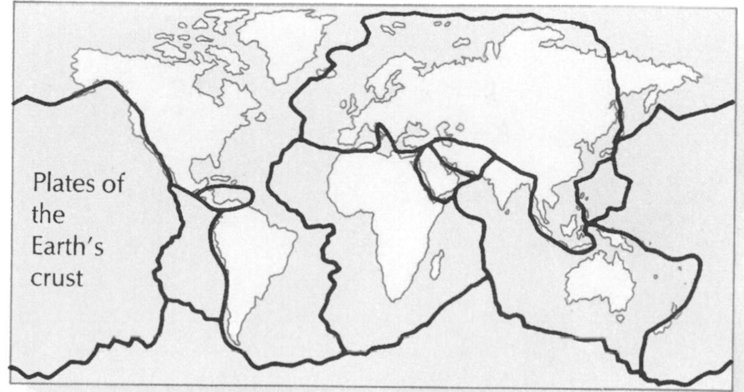

- Earthquakes are caused by the plates of the Earth's crust sliding against each other.
- The surface of the Earth is changing all the time as rocks wear down and plates move.

The Nearest Planets

The average distances from the Sun of these planets are:

Mercury
57.9 million km

The nearest planets to Earth are **Mercury, Venus** and **Mars**. They all have a solid, **rocky surface**, like Earth's.

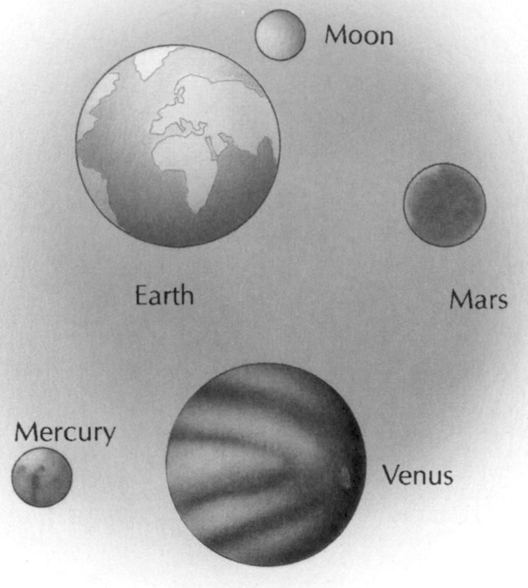

Space probes have taken photographs of Venus, Mars and Mercury and studied their surfaces. Some people thought there was a slight chance of finding **life** on Mars, but no sign of life was found on any of the planets.

Mercury facts

Mercury is the **closest planet** to the Sun. It has:

- Extremely hot days, with temperatures of 350°C, because it is so close to the Sun.
- Very cold nights, because there is no atmosphere to trap the daytime heat.
- An iron core, like the Earth's.

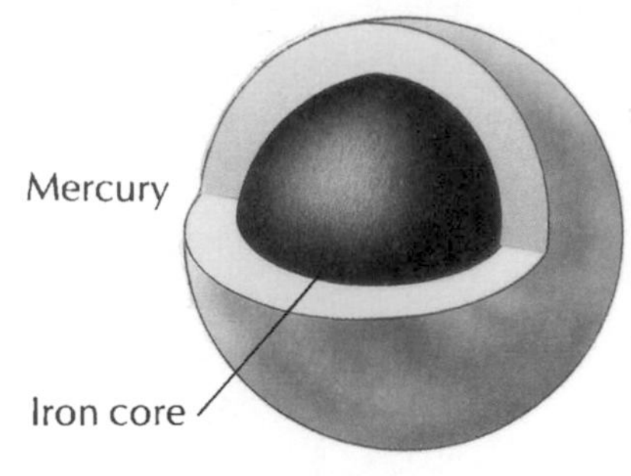

- Earth is 2½ times bigger than Mercury.

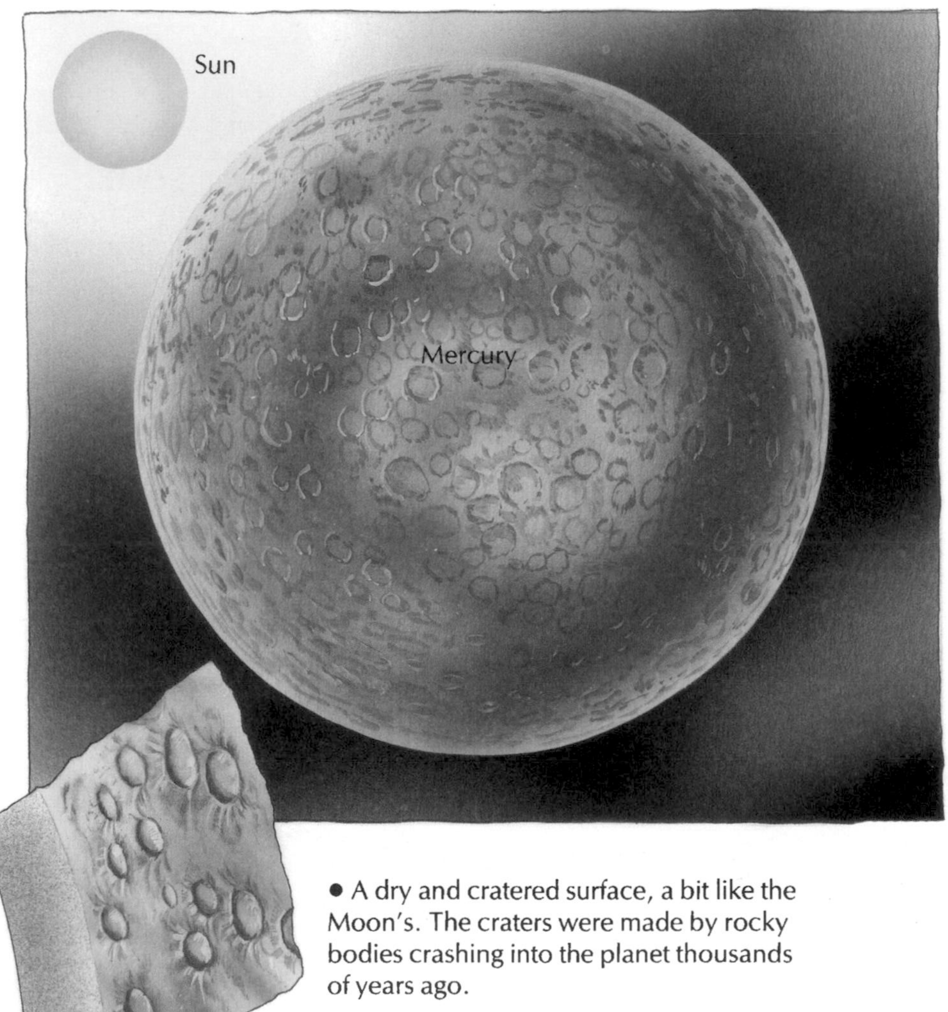

- A dry and cratered surface, a bit like the Moon's. The craters were made by rocky bodies crashing into the planet thousands of years ago.
- A day that lasts for 176 Earth days. Its year is 88 days long – about a quarter of Earth's year.
- Mercury spins round the Sun faster than any other planet. This is how it came by its name. In Ancient Roman mythology Mercury was the swift messenger of the gods.

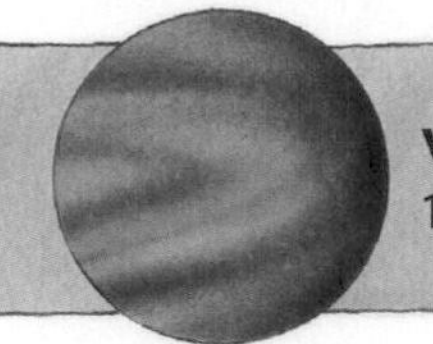
Venus
108.1 million km

Earth
150 million km

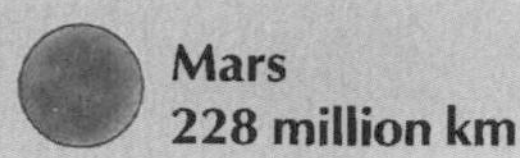
Mars
228 million km

Venus facts

Venus is the closest planet to Earth. Sunlight reflecting from it makes it the **brightest planet** in the night sky. It has:

- Heavy, swirling clouds that hide the mountains and craters on its surface. The clouds trap the Sun's heat, raising the temperature to around 480°C.
- Three large highland areas surrounded by deserts. These have been seen only by radar, as clouds cover them from view.
- An atmosphere of mainly unbreathable carbon dioxide. There are constant thunderstorms, with drops of sulphuric acid in the clouds.

Venus

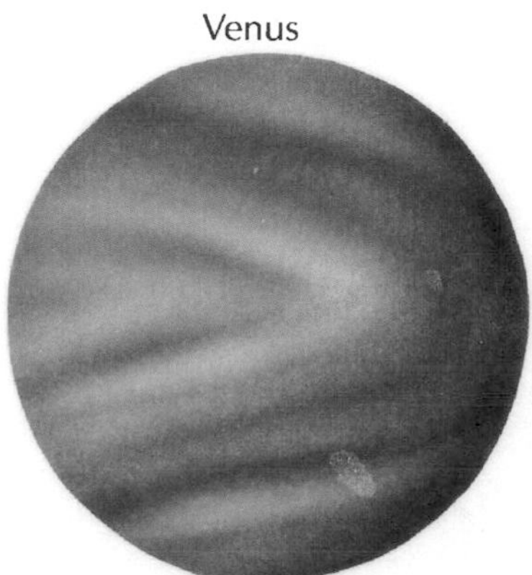

- Venus is similar in size to the Earth.
- Ishtar Terra, a highland area of Venus, is larger than the USA.

Strange but true

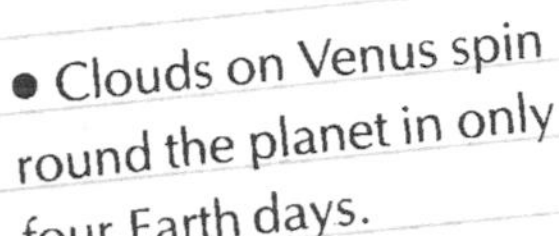

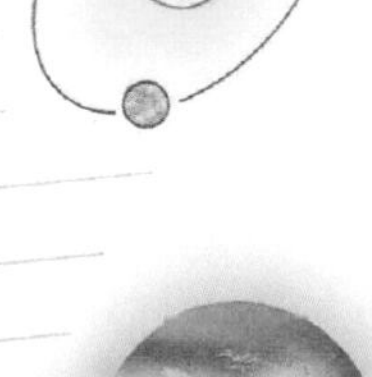

- Venus' day is longer than its year. It takes 243 Earth days to spin once, and only 225 Earth days to go round the Sun.
- Clouds on Venus spin round the planet in only four Earth days.

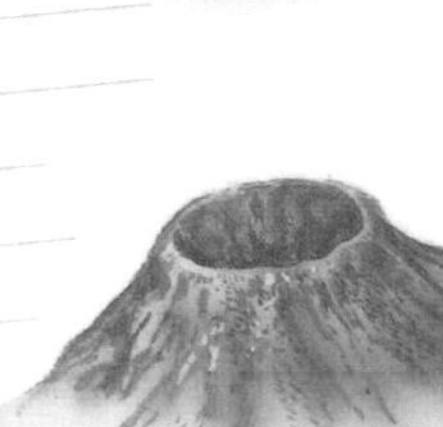

- Mars has a volcano, called Olympus Mons, that stretches 25 km above the planet's surface. It is the largest volcano in the Solar System.

Mars facts

Mars is the furthest inner planet from the Sun. It looks red from Earth, which is why it was named after Mars, the god of war. Mars has:

- A barren, dusty surface with reddish soil and rocks. There are deep canyons and high volcanoes.
- A day that lasts for 24 hours, 37.5 minutes – almost the same as Earth's. Its year, however, is nearly twice as long as Earth's – 687 Earth days.
- A thin atmosphere of carbon dioxide that does not block the Sun's harmful radiation. It is cold, with temperatures averaging –23°C.
- Occasional large dust storms that are visible through a telescope from Earth.
- Spectacular white icy caps at its north and south poles. These grow and shrink depending on the Martian seasons.
- A long time ago, some astronomers thought there might be intelligent life on Mars, because regular lines on the planet's surface looked as if they had been made by intelligent beings.

Mars' surface

- Mars has two very small natural satellites, or moons, called Phobos and Deimos. Phobos is 22 km across. Deimos is 14 km across.

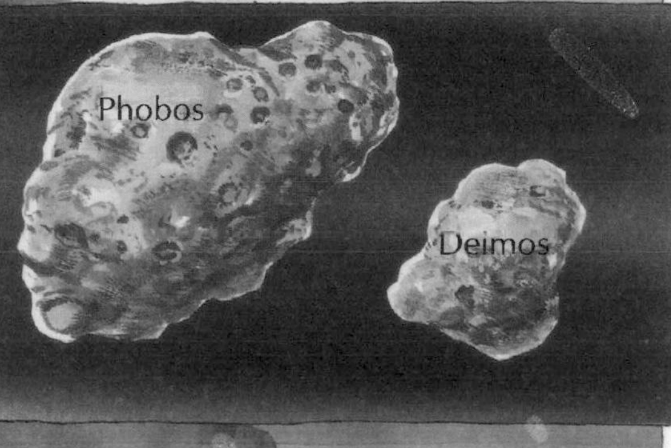

Asteroids, Comets and Meteoroids

Here are some facts about asteroids:

Asteroids are mini-planets that orbit the Sun. Most of them are less than 1 km across. **Comets** are lumps of dirty ice, dust and rock. Most of them move in long oval-shaped orbits around the Sun. **Meteoroids** are rocky fragments, mostly varying in size from a grain of sand to fragments a few centimetres across. If they enter Earth's atmosphere they usually burn up in flashes of light known as **meteors.** However, larger meteoroids are not always destroyed and may land on Earth. Then they become known as **meteorites.**

The asteroid belt

The **asteroid belt** lies between the orbits of Mars and Jupiter. It probably contains at least 40,000 **tiny planets** over 1 km across, revolving round the Sun.

- Astronomers once thought asteroids were fragments of one mini-planet that broke up. Evidence now suggests they are fragments of smaller bodies that collided with each other.

- The asteroid belt makes journeys dangerous for spacecraft, which can be destroyed if they hit even a tiny object. Fortunately, the asteroids are several kilometres apart!

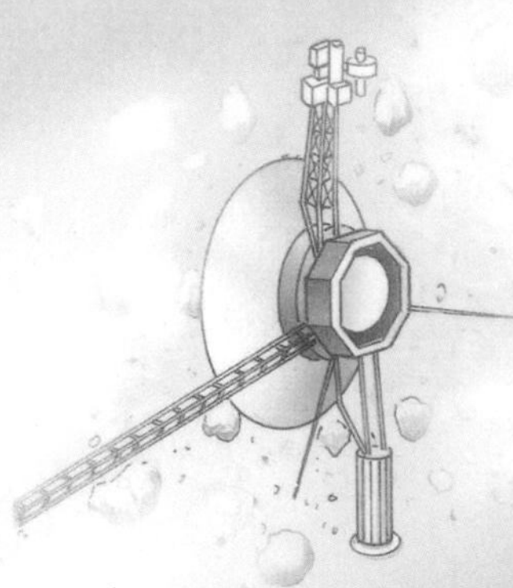

Comets

Comets are made of crumbly **rock** and **ice.** Most travel in long orbits that stretch from near the Sun to the outer part of the Solar System.

- When a comet is near the Sun, the heat turns some of the ice to gas. It streams out behind the comet's head in a glowing tail that may be tens of millions of kilometres long.

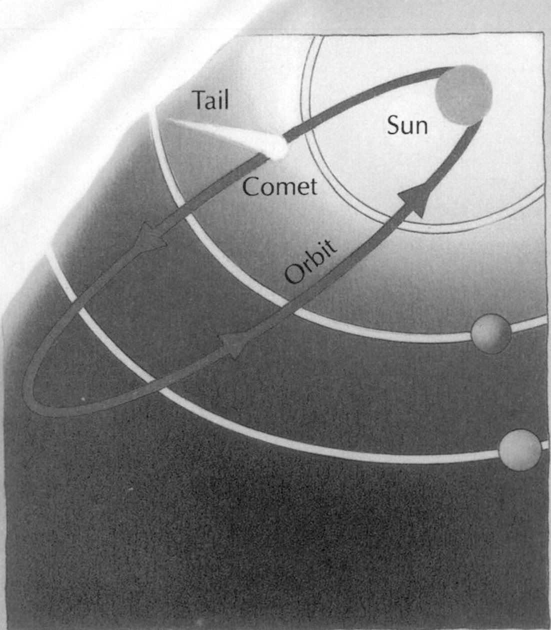

- Comets freeze down to a small, dark core when they are far from the Sun.

- Some comets go right round the Sun every few years. Others take thousands or even millions of years to do so because their orbits are so huge.

- Halley's Comet takes 76 years to orbit the Sun. It was last seen in 1986, although it was much less spectacular than on its previous appearance in 1910.

Chiron orbits between Saturn and Uranus and is the furthest asteroid from Earth

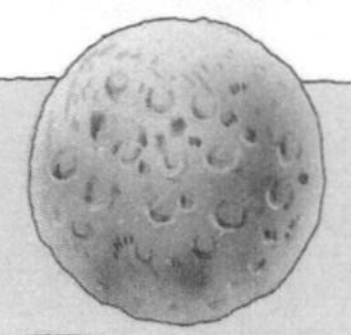

The largest asteroid is Ceres, which is 940 km in diameter

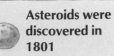

Asteroids were discovered in 1801

Strange but true

• Halley's Comet was seen in 1066, before the Battle of Hastings. William the Conqueror believed it was a sign that he would win the battle.

• In Greenland, people dig up meteorites and use the iron in them to make tools.

• In 1908, forests in Siberia were flattened by a strange explosion. It may have been caused by a small comet hitting the Earth.

Meteors

Meteors are the **bright streaks** seen when **meteoroids** burn up as they hurtle through the atmosphere at up to 50 km/sec. They are often called **shooting stars.**

• Shooting stars (meteors) are seen more often when the Earth travels through a swarm of meteoroids in its path round the Sun. This is known as a meteor shower. The most famous meteor shower is called the Perseids.

• More than 20 million meteoroids are thought to enter Earth's atmosphere every day. Most burn up.

Meteorites

Meteorites are large **meteoroids** that do not burn up completely in the Earth's atmosphere. They fall to the ground.

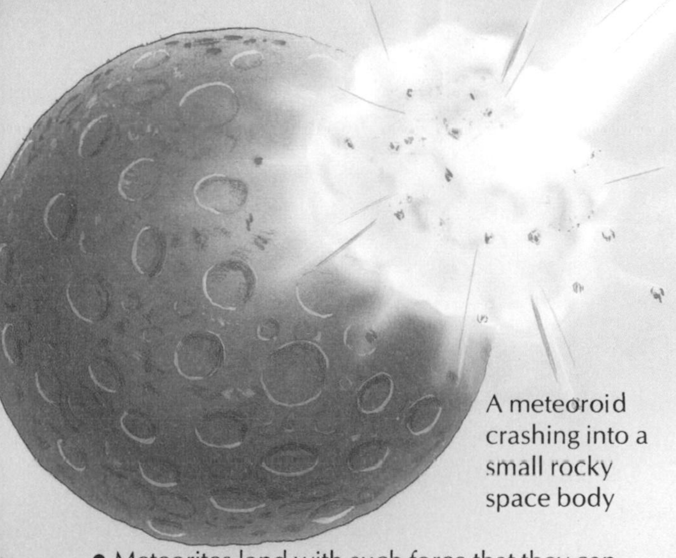

A meteoroid crashing into a small rocky space body

• Meteorites land with such force that they can make holes in the ground called craters. Craters can be seen on many planets and their satellites.

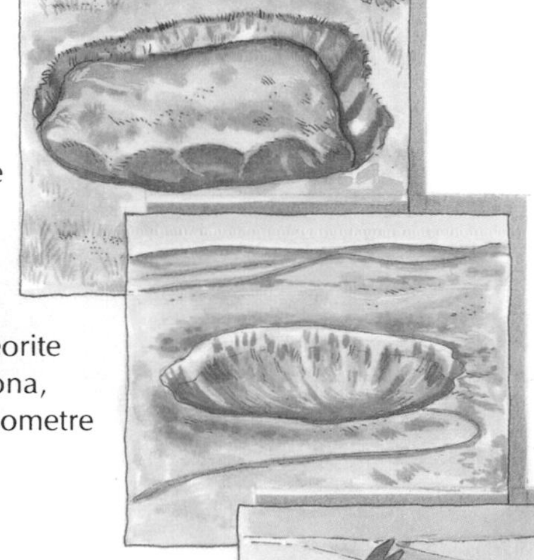

• The biggest known meteorite weighed 60 tonnes. It fell in prehistoric times in Namibia, Africa, where it still lies.

• The most famous meteorite crater on Earth is in Arizona, USA. It is more than a kilometre wide.

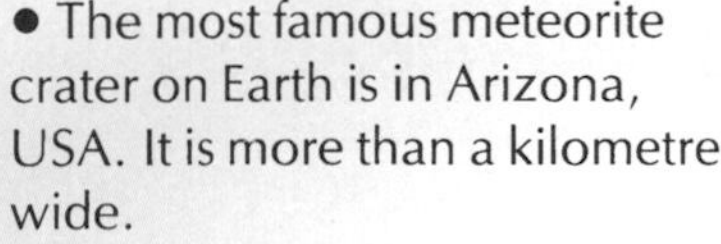

• Not all meteorites are so large. In May 1991 a meteorite weighing only 0.5 kg fell into a garden in southern England. Some meteors fall as dust onto the ground.

The Giant Planets

Here are some facts about Jupiter and Saturn:

The giant planets, **Jupiter** and **Saturn,** are the largest planets in the Solar System. Their surfaces are not solid and rocky but are made up of a mixture of turbulent, swirling **gas** and **ice**.

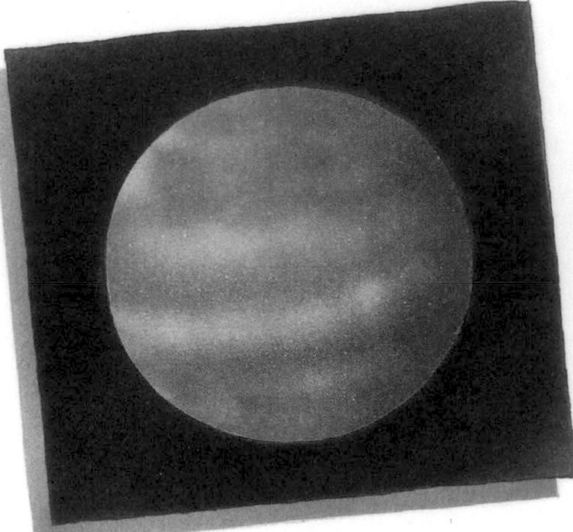

Jupiter

Jupiter, the biggest planet, is so huge that all the other planets in the Solar System could fit inside it.

Saturn

Saturn is smaller than Jupiter, but is very large. It is surrounded by brightly shining rings.

Jupiter facts

- Its day is only 9 hours 50 minutes long.
- Its year is 11.9 Earth years long.
- Its diameter (through the Equator) is about 142,800 km.
- There is a very faint ring around it, made of rocky particles. The ring is too faint to be seen from Earth.
- Its atmosphere is made of hydrogen and helium.

Strange but true

- Jupiter's gases change colour so often that the planet looks different each night when seen through a telescope.

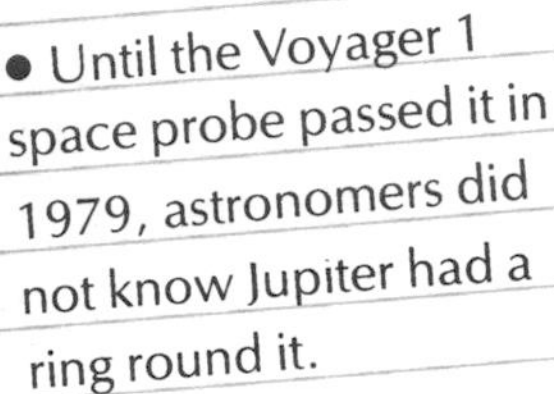

- Until the Voyager 1 space probe passed it in 1979, astronomers did not know Jupiter had a ring round it.
- Winds on Saturn blow at about 1400 km/h. Tornadoes on Earth blow at only 300-600 km/h.

The Great Red Spot

Jupiter's **Great Red Spot** is a swirling **tornado** that has been raging for at least 100 years. It is about 40,000 km long and 11,000 km wide. That is more than three times the diameter of Earth!

Inside Jupiter

Jupiter is made mainly of **hydrogen.** Its four major layers are:

- A very small rocky core
- An inner layer of hydrogen
- A shell of liquid hydrogen and helium
- A swirling surface of icy clouds

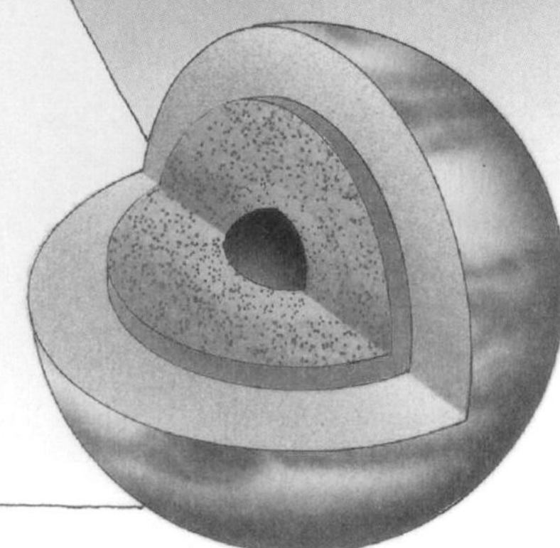

Jupiter is about 778 million km from the Sun

Jupiter shines brightly about 9 months each year

Saturn is 1427 million km from the Sun

Saturn's rings can be seen even with a small telescope

Saturn's rings

Saturn's **rings** are **bands of ice** and **rock** whirling round the planet. The largest rocks are several metres across.

- There are three main rings containing thousands of separate ringlets.

- Saturn's rings are huge but very thin. A sheet of paper 4 metres across would give you a scale model of their depth (the thickness of the paper) compared to their width (the width of the paper).

Voyager space probe

- Voyager probes photographed Saturn's rings and found new satellites.

Saturn facts

- Its day is only 10 hours 14 minutes long.
- Its year is 29.5 Earth years.
- Its diameter (through the Equator) is about 120,000 km.
- Its diameter measured from one side of the ring system to the other is 272,000 km.
- Its atmosphere is made of hydrogen and helium.
- A bright white area appeared on the surface in September 1990. It is as large as Jupiter's Great Red Spot.

The satellites

Jupiter and Saturn have natural **satellites**, or **moons,** orbiting them. Jupiter has at least 16 moons and Saturn at least 18.

Jupiter's main satellites

- Callisto, the outermost, is an icy and cratered satellite much bigger than Earth's Moon.
- Ganymede is larger than the planet Mercury. Its surface is icy, with grooves and streaks.
- Europa is smaller than Earth's Moon. It is smooth and icy with very few craters.
- Io, the innermost, is slightly larger than the Moon. It has a red, volcanic surface.

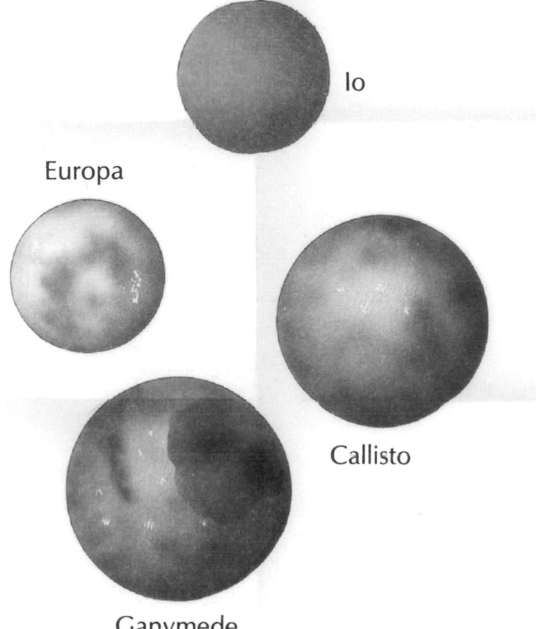

Some of Saturn's satellites

- Mimas (pictured below) is one of the innermost satellites. It has a crater on its surface over 100km wide. That is nearly two-thirds of its diameter!

- Titan, the largest satellite, is bigger than Mercury. It has a cloudy atmosphere of nitrogen gas, and may have oceans made of liquid methane.

Uranus, Neptune and Pluto

These are the distances from the Sun of the furthest planets:

Uranus, Neptune and Pluto are the **furthest planets** from the Sun. They are all icy cold. Uranus and Neptune are quite similar to each other and look greenish in colour from Earth. Pluto, the tiniest of all the planets, is a dim speck.

In 1985 and 1989, the space probe **Voyager 2** flew past Uranus and Neptune. It took spectacular pictures of the planets, showing details never seen before. It also showed the **rings** around both planets, and discovered an amazing number of new **satellites** – ten for Uranus and six for Neptune.

Uranus

Uranus was discovered in 1781 by **William Herschel**, an amateur astronomer, using a home-made telescope. At first he thought he had found a comet.

Uranus

• The diameter of Uranus is 51,000 km. Its day is about 17 hours long, and it takes 84 Earth years to travel round the Sun.

• Uranus is made up mostly of hydrogen and helium. The gas methane is also present in its atmosphere, which makes Uranus look green from Earth.

• Until 1986, only nine rings had been counted round Uranus. On its fly-past, however, Voyager 2 found four more rings, making 13 in all.

Uranus' satellites

Uranus has 15 satellites altogether. The five main ones are Miranda, Ariel, Umbriel, Titania and Oberon. The largest, Oberon and Titania, are about 1500 km across.

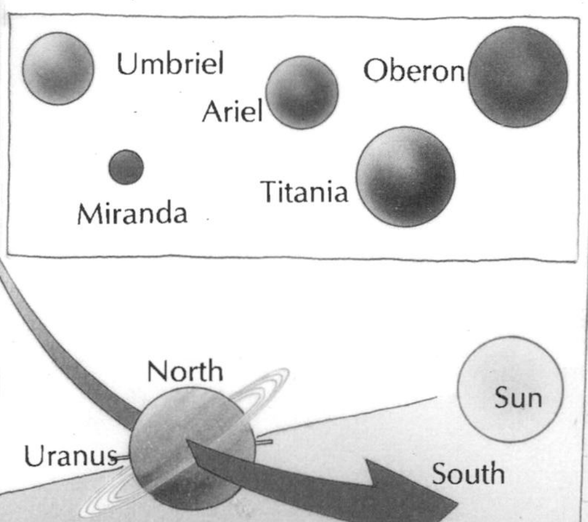

• Uranus spins on its side instead of almost upright, like the other planets. Because of this, the poles of the planet can sometimes face the Sun. When this happens, they are warmer than the planet's equator!

Strange but true

• Uranus' small satellite Miranda may have been shattered in a collision with another body. It seems to have broken up into large pieces which collected together again.

• The cycle of seasons on Triton, Neptune's largest satellite, takes 680 years.

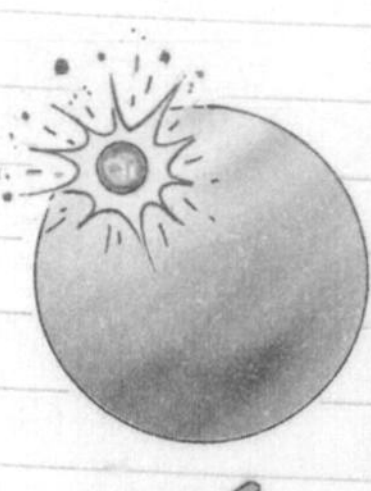

• During the 1990s, Pluto is the nearest it can get to Earth, so it is a very good time to study it. This will not happen again until the 23rd century!

Uranus
2870 million km

Neptune
4493 million km

Pluto
5898 million km

Neptune

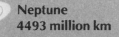

Neptune was discovered in 1846. It cannot be seen with the naked eye. Through a telescope it looks like a faint blue-green star. Like Uranus, it is surrounded by **rings**.

• Neptune is colder than Uranus. It is about −220°C.

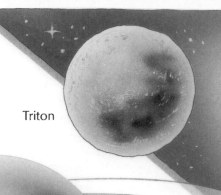

Neptune's satellites

Neptune has **eight satellites**. The two main ones are called Triton and Nereid. Triton, the larger, is smaller than Earth's Moon. Very unusually it orbits Neptune in the opposite direction from the planet's own spin.

Triton

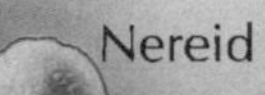

Nereid

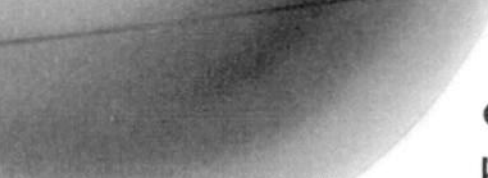

• Neptune is slightly smaller than Uranus, measuring 48,400 km across.

Neptune

• Neptune's day is about 18 hours long. Its year, however, is 164.8 Earth years long.

Pluto

Pluto is the **smallest planet**. Because of its orbit (see below) it is usually the furthest away from the Sun. It was not discovered until 1930 and is very difficult to see, even with a telescope.

Pluto

• Pluto's diameter is 2200 km which means it is smaller than our Moon.

• Pluto's day lasts for just over six Earth days, and its year lasts 247.7 Earth years.

Pluto's satellite

Pluto has **one known satellite**, Charon. It is 800 km across and was discovered in 1978.

Charon

Pluto

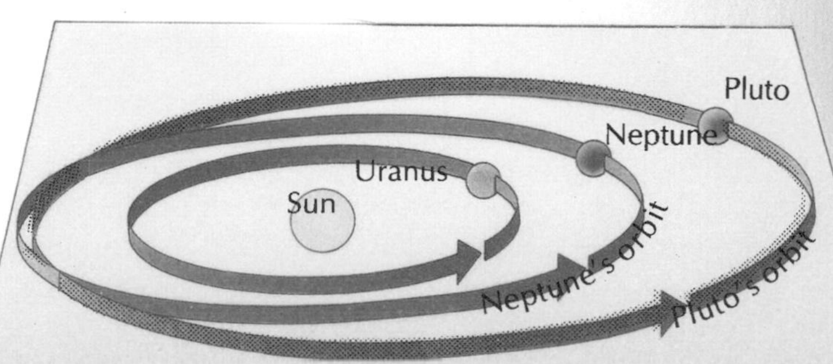

• Pluto is usually the furthest planet from the Sun. However, its orbit sometimes takes it inside Neptune's orbit. This is happening now, so from 1979 until 1999 Neptune is the 'outermost planet'.

Eris, the largest dwarf planet, sits beyond Pluto and was discovered only in 2006.

Ancient Astronomy

These ancient monuments may have been used as observatories:

From early times, people have been interested in the stars and planets. They have tried to understand Space and how it affects human life. Great **stone circles**, such as Stonehenge in England (built about 3500

years ago) may have been used to study how the Sun and Moon moved through the sky.

More than 2000 years ago, the **Chinese**, **Egyptians**, **Babylonians** and **Greeks** were all skilled astronomers.

The Babylonians

About 3000 years ago, the **Babylonians** (who used to live in what is now Iraq) studied the stars. They invented **astrology** - the belief that people's lives are influenced by the position of the stars and planets.

• This Babylonian boundary stone shows the importance of the Sun, Moon and planets to this ancient civilization.

• The Babylonians invented the twelve signs of the zodiac that are still used in astrology.

The Ancient Greeks

The **Greeks** were fine astronomers and mathematicians. In about 240 BC, Eratosthenes, a Greek mathematician, accurately worked out the **size of the Earth**.

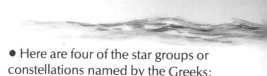

• Here are four of the star groups or constellations named by the Greeks:

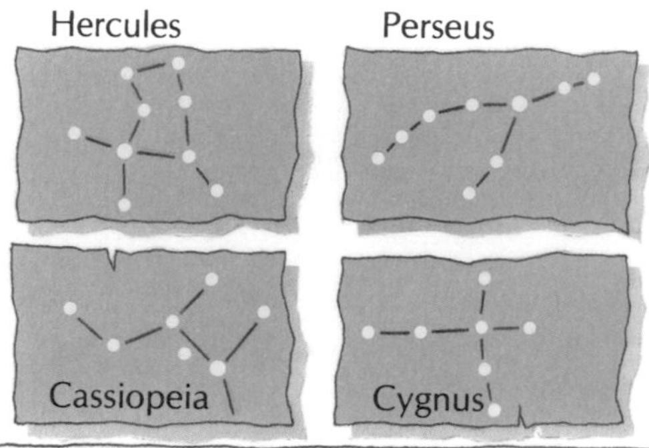

Pioneers of astronomy

Many ancient astronomers added a great deal to our understanding of Space. Some were **persecuted** for their discoveries because they went against the teachings of the Christian Church.

• Ptolemy of Alexandria was born in AD 120. He believed the Earth was at the centre of the Solar System and that the Sun, Moon and planets circled round it.

• Ptolemy's idea of the Solar System was accepted for 1300 years.

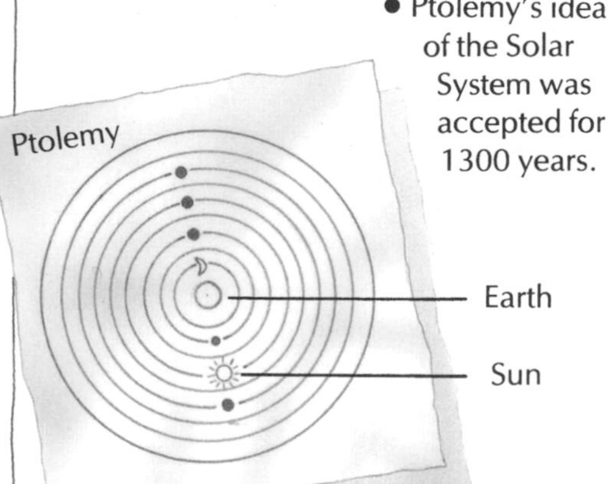

• Nicolaus Copernicus (1473-1543) was a Polish astronomer and mathematician. He published a book that said the Sun, not Earth, was the centre of the Solar System. His book was officially banned until 1835.

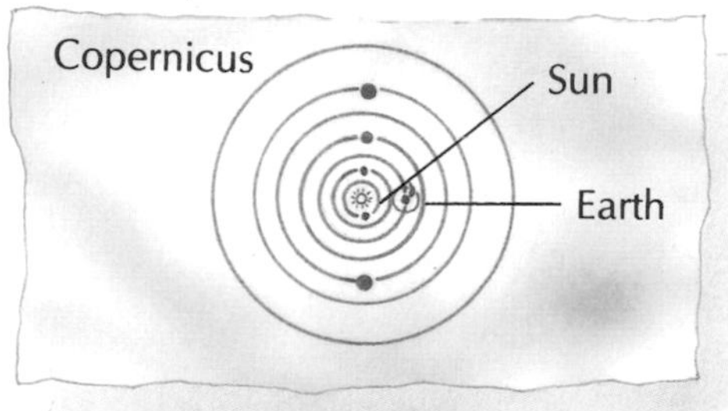

• Tycho Brahe (1546-1601) was a Danish astronomer. He wrongly placed Earth back in the centre of the Solar System but accurately observed and measured stars, planets and comets.

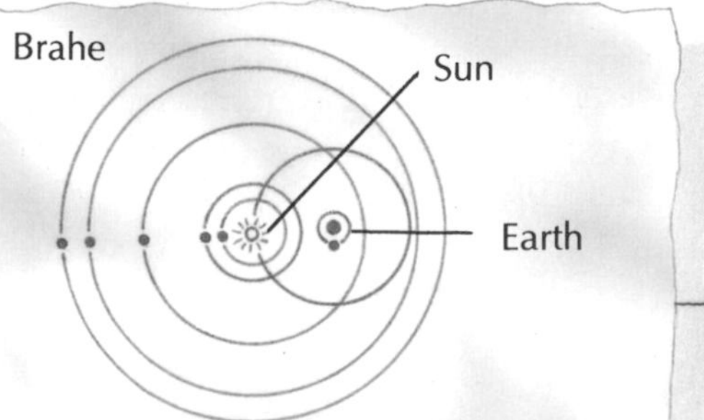

The Great Pyramid of Cheops, in Egypt

Ancient Chaldean buildings called ziggurats

Standing stones such as the Ring of Brodgar, Scotland

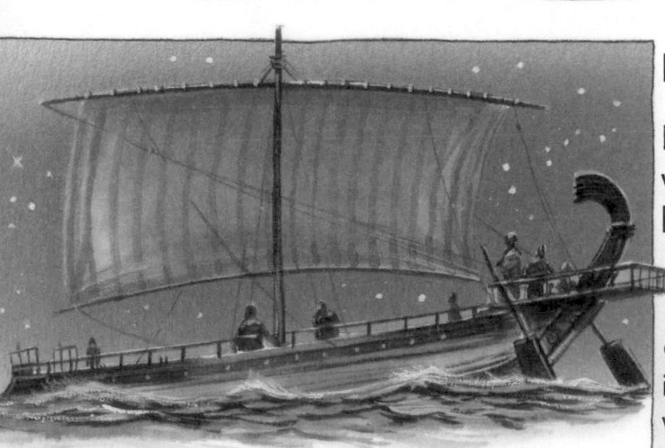

• Ancient Greek sailors studied the stars and the Sun to help them navigate.

• Ancient people knew only five planets: Mercury, Venus, Mars, Jupiter and Saturn.

Early equipment

Before the **telescope** was invented, all astronomy was done with the **naked eye.** However, there were some **instruments** to help astronomers when they studied the sky.

• Quadrants and sextants were instruments that enabled astronomers to work out the position of stars and planets.

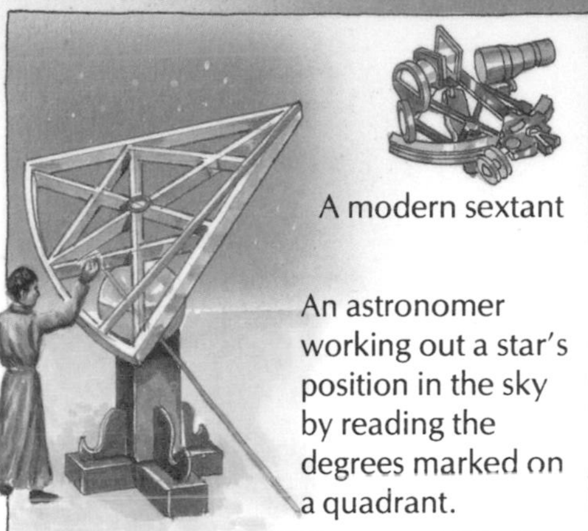

A modern sextant

An astronomer working out a star's position in the sky by reading the degrees marked on a quadrant.

• Observatories were built to study the sky. This stone-built observatory in India was designed to help people measure the movements of stars and planets, and foretell eclipses.

• Johannes Kepler (1571-1630), a German mathematician, put the Sun back in the centre of things. He drew up three Laws of Planetary Motion, which are still used today.

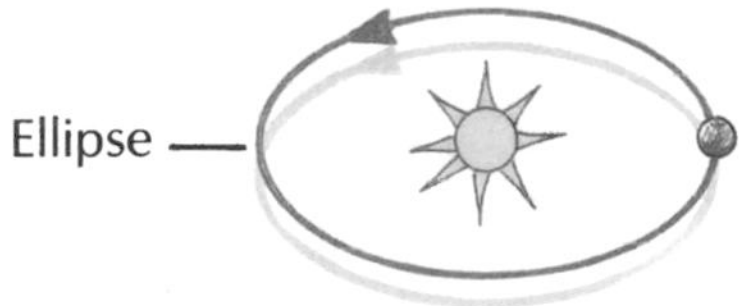

• Kepler correctly showed that a planet's orbit is an ellipse (a squashed circle) rather than a true circle.

• Galileo Galilei (1564-1642), an Italian mathematician, was persecuted for saying that the Sun, not Earth, is the centre of the Solar System. He made many discoveries, such as sunspots and Jupiter's four large satellites.

• In 1609, Galileo made one of the first drawings of the Moon's surface.

Galileo's drawing

• Galileo was one of the first to use a telescope. This is one of his instruments, which he built soon after telescopes were invented at the beginning of the seventeenth century. He even made the lenses himself. The most powerful of his telescopes magnified, or enlarged, an object thirty times.

Galileo's telescope

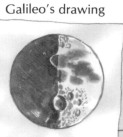

Strange but true

• The oldest observatory building still standing is in Greece. It was built in about 100 BC.

• Anaxagoras, an early Greek philosopher, was banished for saying the Sun was a red-hot stone.

• In 280 BC the Greek astronomer Aristarchus said the Sun, not Earth, was the centre of the Solar System. It was more than 1800 years before he was proved right.

Modern Astronomy

These are some space telescopes:

The invention of the telescope made it possible to see objects in Space more clearly. But the Earth's atmosphere makes them appear blurred and blocks out some important radiation coming from stars and galaxies.

Now there are space telescopes that, outside the haze of Earth's atmosphere, can 'see' much more clearly than Earth-based telescopes. They have instruments for detecting X-rays and other invisible radiations. They can tell astronomers more about such things as galaxies and black holes.

Telescopes

Telescopes make distant things seem nearer. Light from a distant object enters the tube and the image of the object is then **magnified** (made larger). There are two main kinds: reflector and refractor.

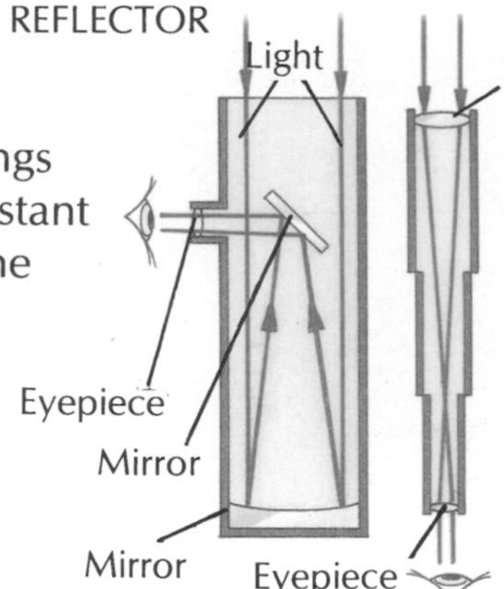

- Reflectors: Light is bounced off mirrors into an eyepiece.
- Refractors: Light is focused by lenses.
- Both types of telescope produce upside-down images.

Binoculars are good for giving a **wide, general view** of the night sky, and for tracking moving objects such as satellites.

- Binoculars make distant things look closer but do not magnify as powerfully as telescopes.

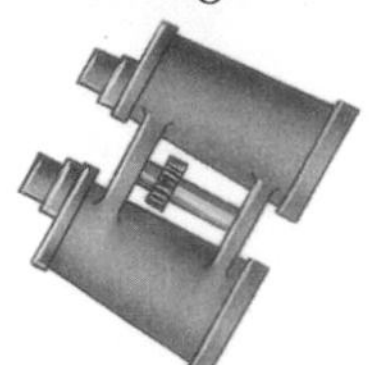

Earth-based astronomy

There are many powerful **telescopes on Earth** that provide a good view of Space.

- Large optical telescopes produce images that can be analyzed by computer. They are put in buildings on high ground so they can avoid the lights and polluted air of towns and cities.

Optical telescope

Radio telescope

- Radio telescopes pick up radio waves from Space that are usually produced by clouds of gas or dust. Radio waves are one of the few kinds of space radiation that can pass through Earth's atmosphere.

Kitt Peak observatory

- There are several telescopes on Kitt Peak in Arizona, USA, including a reflector 4 metres across. It also has the world's largest solar telescope (for observing the Sun).

- The MMT (Multiple Mirror Telescope) on Mount Hopkins, Arizona, USA, has six mirrors, all 1.8 metres wide.

MMT

- The largest single radio telescope dish in the world is at Arecibo in Puerto Rico. It is 305 metres across.

Arecibo

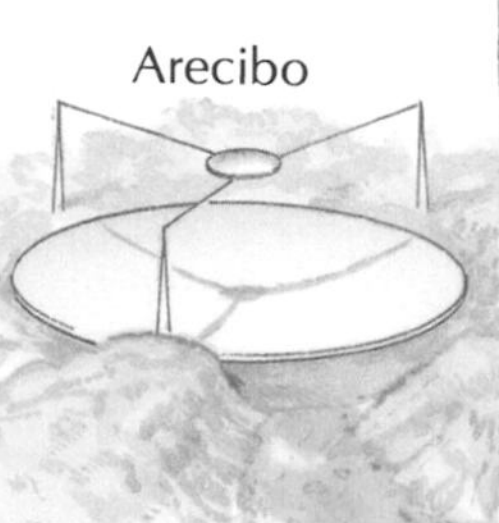

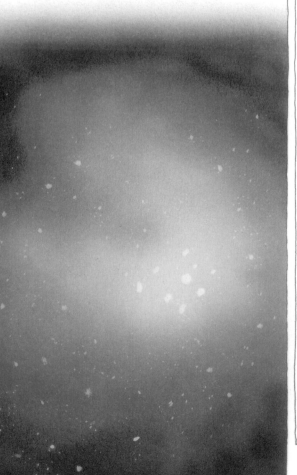

OSO satellites, first launched in 1962. They observed the Sun.

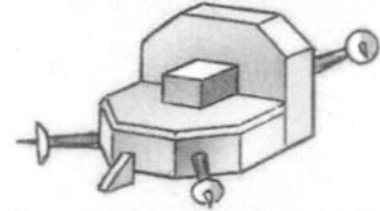

COS-B (1975) monitored gamma and X-rays.

Exosat (1983), monitored X-rays from neutron stars.

Space telescopes

Space telescopes revolutionized astronomy. They can now be launched by **Space Shuttle** and other craft.

Space telescopes have monitored the **Sun** and invisible **radiation**. They have also observed **stars** and **galaxies** that could never be studied before.

The Hubble telescope

The Hubble space telescope was launched by the USA on 24 April 1990. It can detect **ultra-violet** and **infra-red waves** as well as **visible light**.

- If all had gone well, Hubble would have transmitted pictures of distant objects never seen before, and stunningly clear images of closer objects.

Space Shuttle

- Unfortunately, Hubble does not work properly. One of its two mirrors is two-thousandths of a millimetre too flat – enough to make all its images out of focus.

Telescope

Solar panels

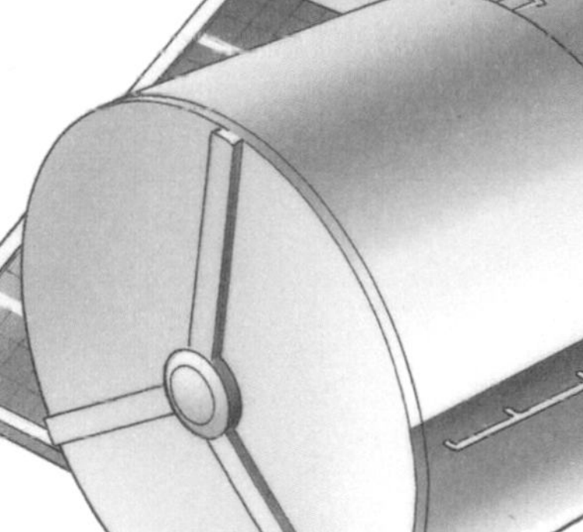

- The fault happened because the equipment used to test the mirror was out of adjustment by just one millimetre!

The Hubble space telescope

- Despite problems, some pictures have been successful. Pluto and its satellite, Charon, for instance, were seen clearly for the first time.

- The Hubble telescope had other problems after the launch. The telescope wobbles twice for several minutes in each orbit.

- Scientists hope to send astronauts to mend the Hubble telescope. Three similar space telescopes are planned for the future.

Strange but true

- The satellite IRAS discovered the closest known comet to pass Earth for 200 years.

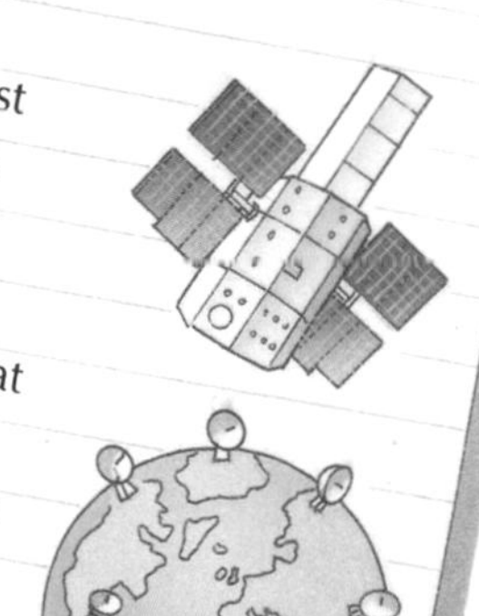

- The radio telescope at Arecibo, Puerto Rico, can pick up signals from up to 15 billion light-years away.

- An astronomer called James Lick, who died in 1876, is buried in the base of the telescope at the Lick Observatory in the USA.

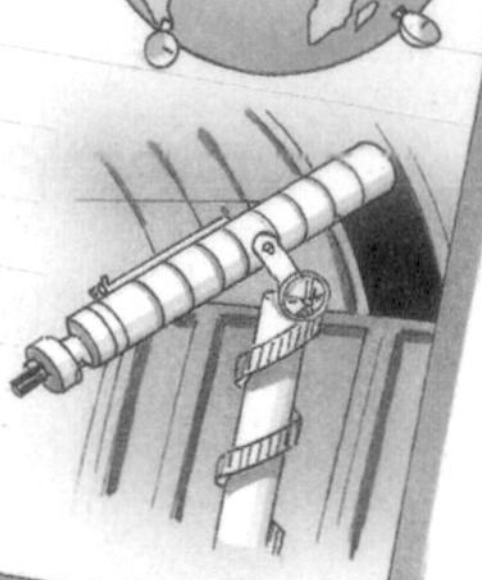

The Space Age

Here is a selection of different rocket designs:

Lambda-4S-5: the first Japanese rocket, launched in Japan in 1970

The Space Age began on 4 October, 1957, when the USSR launched the satellite **Sputnik 1**. This was a small metal sphere with four thin antennae. It contained a radio transmitter.

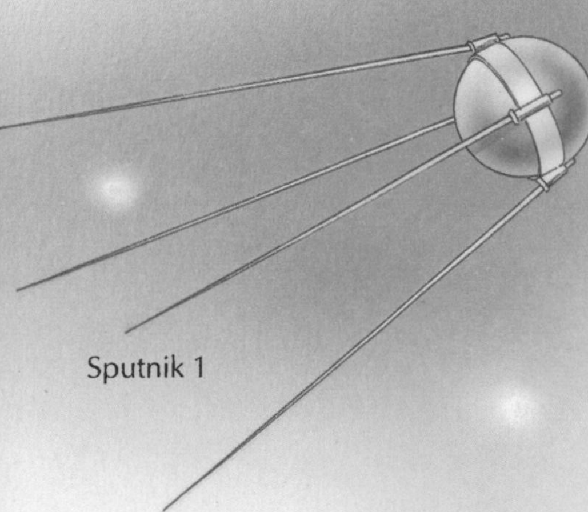

Sputnik 1

The development of **spacecraft** has moved incredibly quickly. **Probes**, **satellites**, **rockets** and **space stations** have been successfully launched and have helped astronomers learn much more about the Solar System and beyond. Satellites also have many other uses for people on Earth.

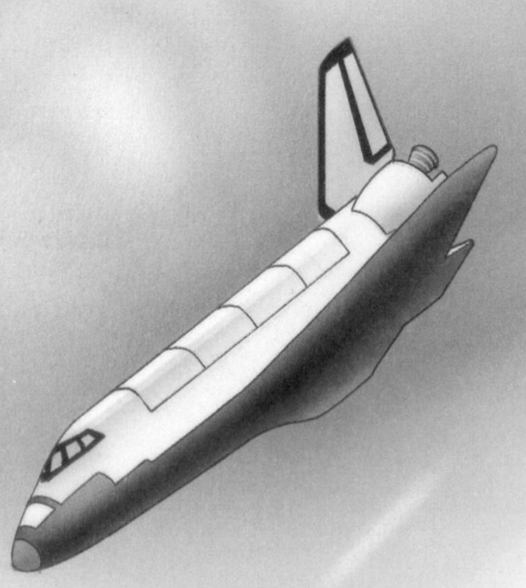

Getting off the ground

The invention of the **rocket** made space exploration possible.

V2

• As early as 1903, a Russian teacher called Tsiolkovskii suggested using liquid fuel for rockets and proposed rocket-building in separate parts, called stages.

• Weapons called V2 rockets were developed by a German research team and used near the end of World War II. Space rockets were developed from them.

Laika

• The USSR sent a small dog, called Laika, into orbit in Sputnik 2 in November 1957. She orbited Earth for a week and became the first animal in Space.

Vostock 1

• In 1961, Yuri Gagarin, a Soviet cosmonaut, became the first person in Space. He orbited Earth once in the spacecraft Vostock 1, landing safely after a 108-minute flight.

Space Shuttle

In 1981, the first **Space Shuttle**, Columbia, was launched in the USA. For the first time a spacecraft could go into Space and return to Earth, landing like a plane. It could then be used again for another flight.

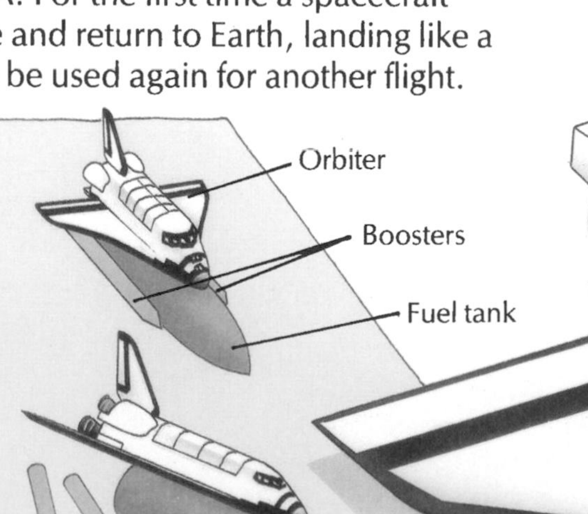

1 The Shuttle plane, called an orbiter, is launched attached to a giant fuel tank and two solid-fuel boosters.

2 The boosters drop off at a height of 43 km. They drop into the sea and are rescued for re-use.

3 At 115 km high, the fuel tank separates and burns up as it falls through Earth's atmosphere. It is the only part of the Shuttle that is not re-used.

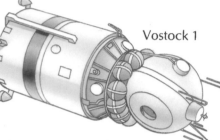

Ariane: developed in Europe and launched in French Guiana (South America)

D-1: the Soviet rocket that launched the Salyut and Mir space stations

Energiya: launcher for the proposed Soviet version of the Space Shuttle

How do rockets work?

Rockets need a great deal of **power** to escape from Earth's gravity. Most have from two to four fuel-burning parts, called **stages**, that lift the rocket into orbit. The stages separate from the rocket as their fuel runs out. Then they burn up in the Earth's atmosphere.

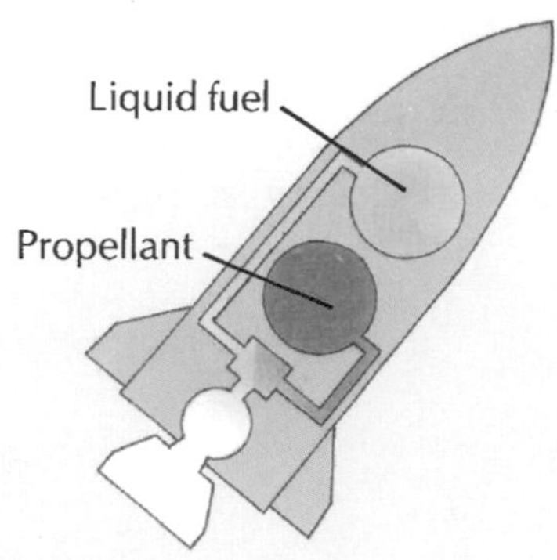

1 Liquid-fuel rockets work by burning a mixture of fuel and a propellant.

2 The propellant makes the fuel catch fire with an explosive blast that pushes the rocket upwards.

3 The rocket then builds up enormous speed – many times faster than Concorde.

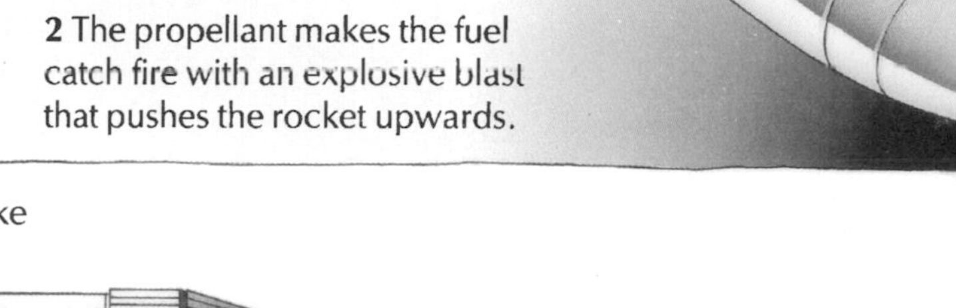

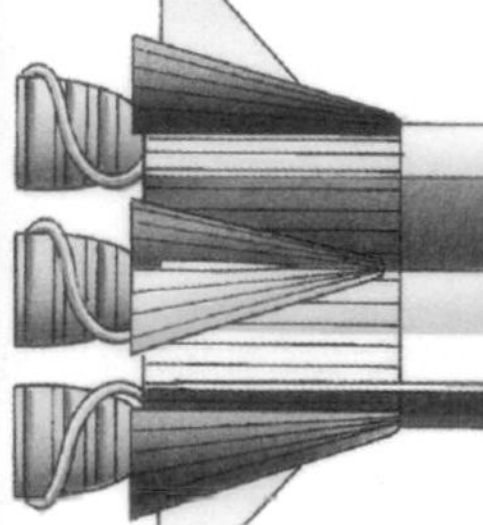

An Apollo Saturn V rocket, the one used to take people to the Moon.

Stage 1

Stage 2

Stage 3

Capsule

Stage 1 separated from the rocket at a height of about 61 km.

Stage 2 took the rocket up to about 183 km.

Stage 3 took the Apollo capsule into Earth orbit and then to the Moon.

4 The Space Shuttle carries a large cargo. Once in Space, the astronauts can repair or rescue satellites, launch new ones, or carry out experiments.

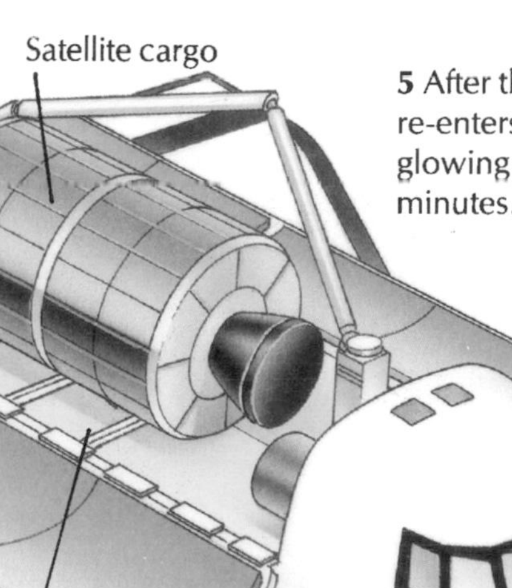

5 After the mission, the Shuttle re-enters Earth's atmosphere, glowing red-hot for about 10 minutes.

6 It glides down to Earth and lands on a long runway, like an ordinary aeroplane.

- In 1986, the Space Shuttle Challenger exploded 73 seconds after blast-off. All seven astronauts were killed. It happened because of a tiny fault in one of the solid-fuel boosters.

Strange but true

- Yuri Gagarin survived the first manned spaceflight but was killed in a plane crash seven years later.

- Astronauts become a little taller in Space! There is less gravity, so their bones are less squashed together.
- As it comes back into Earth's atmosphere, the Space Shuttle reaches a temperature of 1260°C.

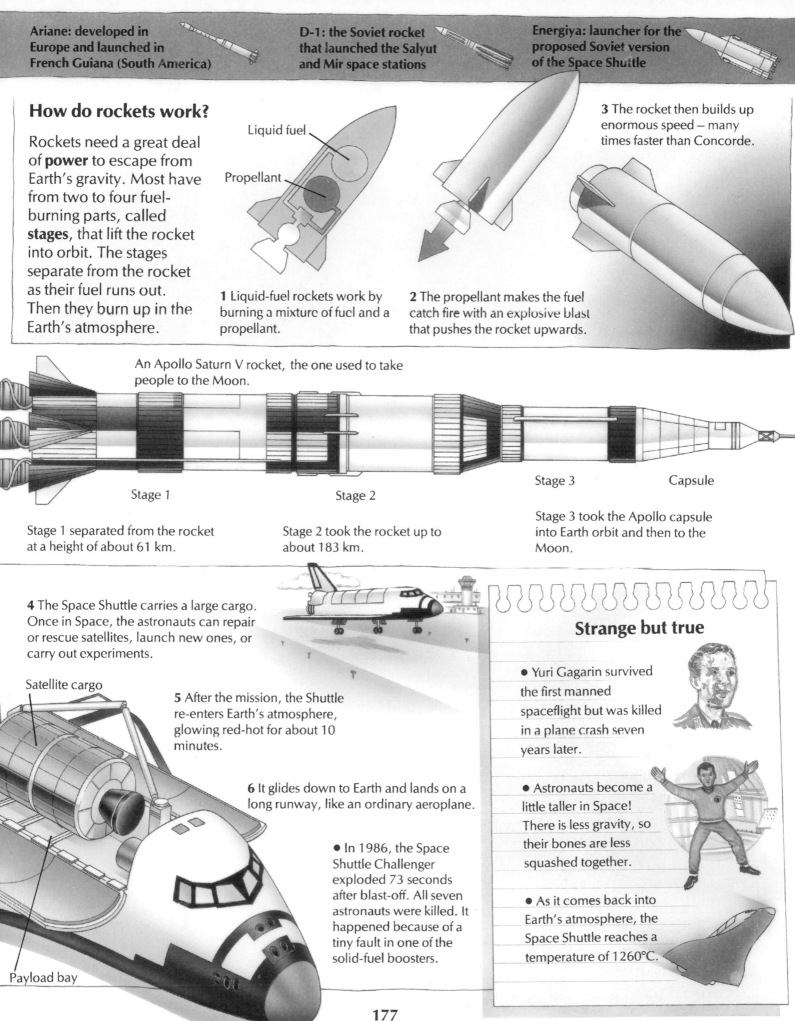

Landing on the Moon

This is some of the equipment used for experiments on the Moon:

Solar Wind Spectrometer measured the effect of solar wind

The Moon is the only place in the Universe that **people** have **visited**. The effects of the journey on the astronauts, along with their experiments and rock samples, taught scientists a great deal about the Moon.

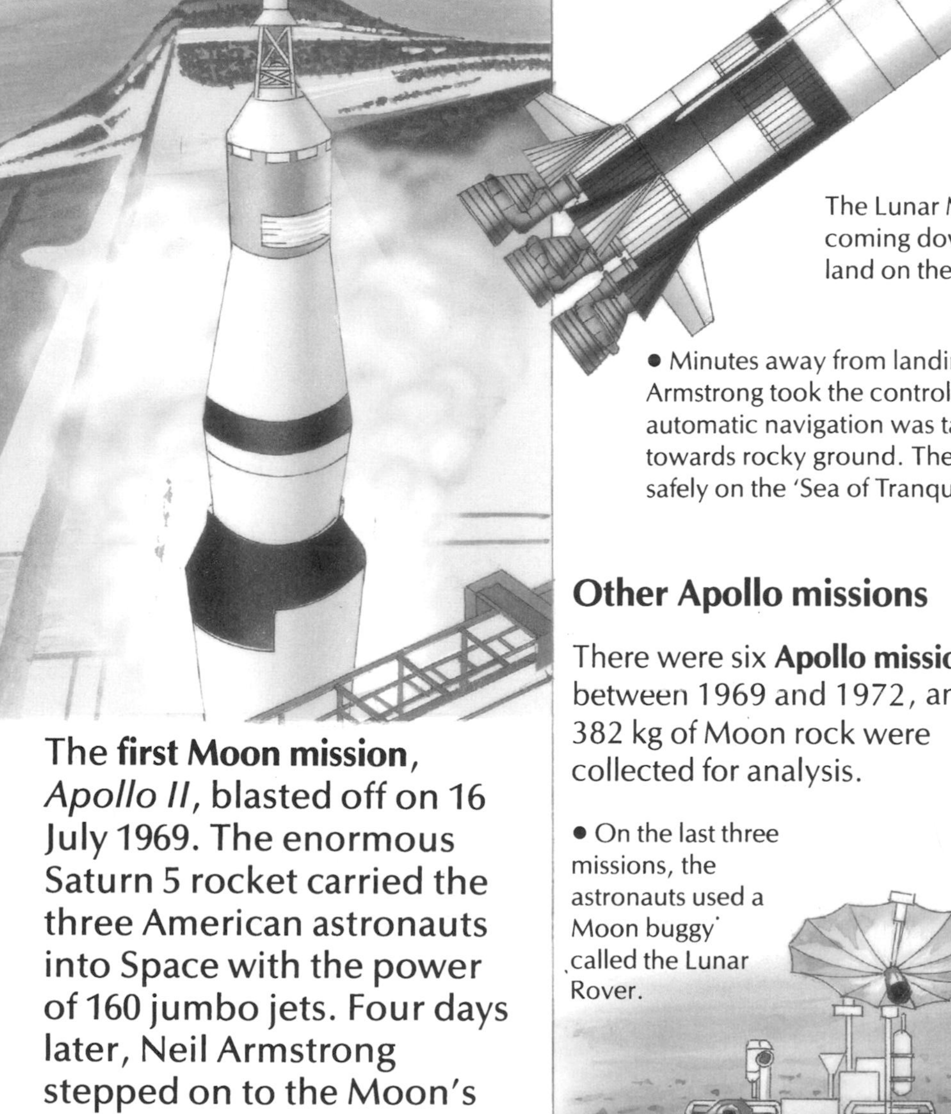

The **first Moon mission**, *Apollo II*, blasted off on 16 July 1969. The enormous Saturn 5 rocket carried the three American astronauts into Space with the power of 160 jumbo jets. Four days later, Neil Armstrong stepped on to the Moon's surface and said the famous words: "That's one small step for a man, one giant leap for mankind."

The first Moon landing

Stacked at the top of the **Saturn 5 rocket** were the **Command Module**, the **Service Module** and the **Lunar Module**. Once in orbit round the Moon, the Lunar Module separated to start its journey to the Moon's surface.

- One astronaut, Michael Collins, stayed behind in the Command Module. Neil Armstrong and Edwin Aldrin were in the cramped Lunar Module.

The rocket as it was at take-off

The Lunar Module coming down to land on the Moon

- Minutes away from landing, Neil Armstrong took the controls, as the automatic navigation was taking them towards rocky ground. They landed safely on the 'Sea of Tranquillity'.

Other Apollo missions

There were six **Apollo missions** between 1969 and 1972, and 382 kg of Moon rock were collected for analysis.

- On the last three missions, the astronauts used a Moon buggy called the Lunar Rover.

The Soviet missions

- In 1959, the Soviet unmanned probe, Luna 1, flew close to the Moon. A few months later Luna 2 was the first Earth-made object to land on the Moon.

Luna 3

- Soon after, Luna 3 flew past the far side of the Moon and took the first pictures of it.
- In 1966, Luna 9 landed on the Moon's surface and took the first close-up pictures of it.

Luna 9

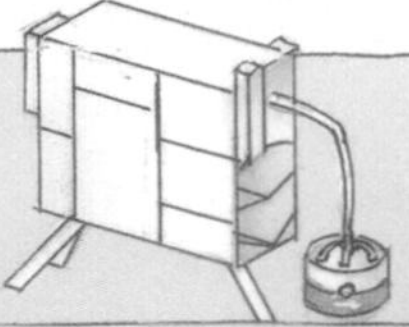

Ion detector measured the Moon's ionosphere

Magnetometer measured the magnetic field and solar wind

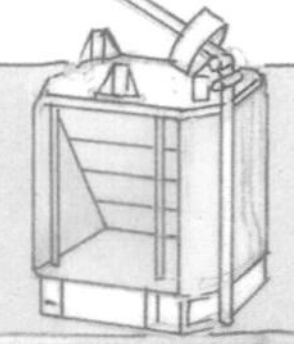

This machine sent all the experimental data back to Earth

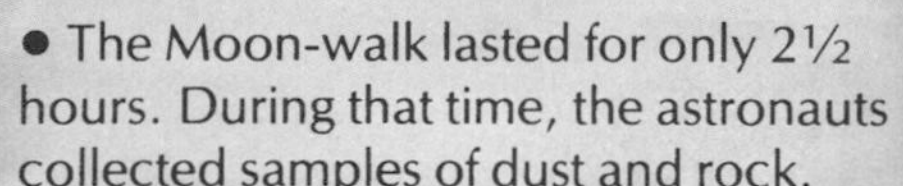

- The Moon-walk lasted for only 2½ hours. During that time, the astronauts collected samples of dust and rock.
- They also put up a US flag, which they had to stiffen with wire as there is no wind on the Moon to blow it!

- The Moon has six times less gravity than Earth. This means that on the Moon astronauts weigh only a sixth of their normal weight. They could jump and spring about with ease, but it was difficult to walk.

- The astronauts tried to sleep in the Lunar Module, but it was much too cold. At night, temperatures on the Moon reach –150°C.

- The astronauts had to use special tools to collect rock samples because they could not bend over in their spacesuits.

Moon discoveries

On Earth the surface is changing all the time. The Moon, however, is a dead place with **no atmosphere** and **no weather** to erode and change the landscape. So Moon dust and rock have lain in the same positions for millions of years. The youngest **Moon rock** analyzed was 3.1 billion years old.

Moon rock

- One sample of Moon rock was found to be about 4.6 billion years old – about the same age as Earth.

Moonquake detector

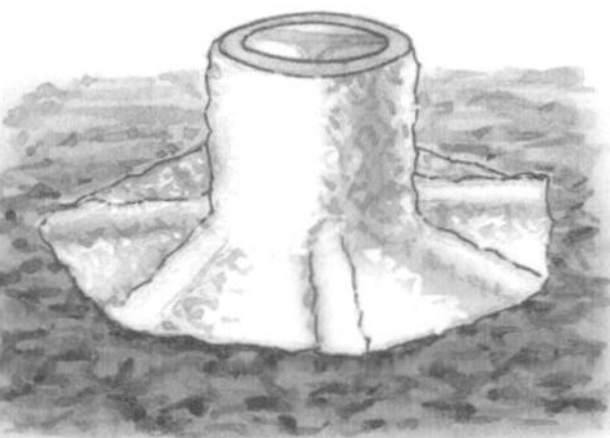

- Instruments detecting 'moonquakes' found them to be much weaker than earthquakes.

The Moon

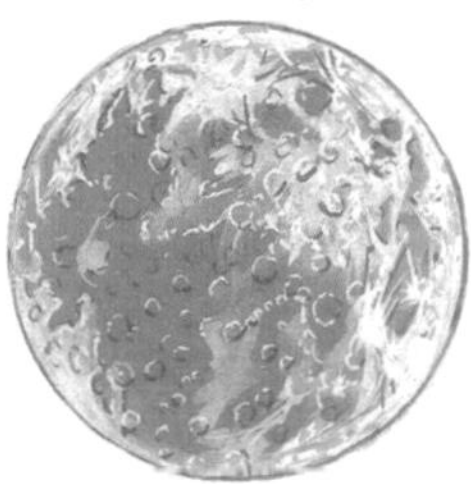

- Because of the Apollo missions, the Moon has now been mapped more accurately than before.

Strange but true

- Astronauts' footprints and Lunar Rover tyre tracks will stay on the Moon for millions of years as there is no wind to blow them away.

- The Moon is completely quiet, because there is no air to carry sound.
- Nothing can grow on the Moon, but plants did grow in Moon-soil on Earth.

Satellites

These satellites have monitored Earth and Space:

Telstar beamed the first live TV pictures between the USA and the UK in the 1960s

There are about 200 **artificial satellites** whirling round the Earth. There is also lots of junk in Space, such as the remains of old satellites. Thousands have been launched and worked for a while before being replaced.

Satellites do all sorts of different jobs. Some can study Earth's **land** and **weather**, or beam **television pictures** and **telephone calls** around the world. Others can analyze **space radiation** that cannot penetrate the Earth's atmosphere. Some are used to **spy** on other countries.

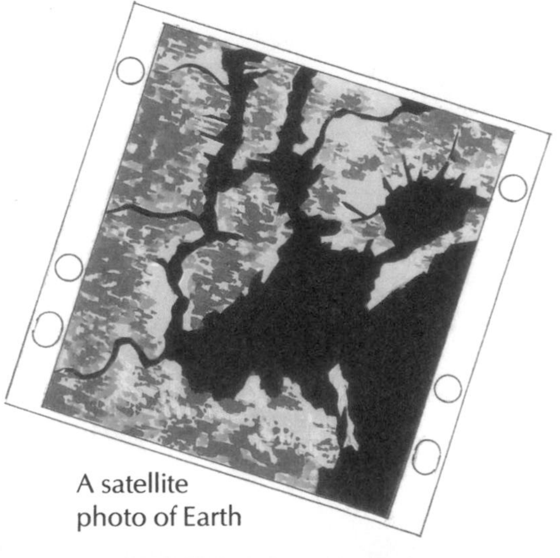

A satellite photo of Earth

Getting into orbit

Satellites are taken into Space by **rockets** or by **Space Shuttle**. They are carried in the Shuttle's cargo, or payload, bay and then launched into orbit in Space.

- Sometimes a robot arm, controlled by a Shuttle astronaut, lifts a satellite out of the payload bay and launches it.

- Most satellites have their own rocket launchers that boost them into orbit when they are at a safe distance from the Shuttle.

- These are some of the kinds of orbit a satellite might use:

Geostationary orbit: the satellite orbits at the same speed as Earth's spin. It is always above the same point over the Equator, at a height of about 36,000 km.

Polar orbit: the satellite orbits Earth from north to south, and can cover most of the Earth within a day. This orbit is usually at a height of about 1000 km.

Eccentric orbit: the satellite flies low over parts of the Earth before swinging out to complete the orbit.

Different kinds of satellites

Communications satellites (comsats) beam telephone calls and television pictures from one part of the world to another. They receive a picture from Earth and send it on to its destination.

A Molniya satellite

Intelsat 6

- In 1965, Russian Molniya satellites began the world's biggest network of comsats.

- Intelsat 6 carries 120,000 telephone circuits and three television channels.

Power from Space

Satellites have large **solar panels** to trap energy from the Sun.

- Satellites store the Sun's energy in batteries and use it to power their equipment.

Meteosat takes pictures of Earth and monitors its weather
IMEWS can give early warning of a nuclear explosion
GMS-2 is a weather satellite launched by Japan

Space stations

Space stations are also called satellites, because they orbit the Earth. The Mir station was launched by the USSR in 1986. It now has three other sections added to the main station.

- Astronauts live and work for a few months at a time on space stations.

Strange but true

- To run their equipment, satellites need only about the same amount of power as a one-bar electric fire.
- Space rubbish, such as bits of old satellite, are a hazard for spacecraft. Space Shuttle has already been hit.
- Some people think that one day there may be huge space stations with many people living on them. They could travel far from Earth.

- Astronauts on space stations can use the lack of gravity to do experiments such as crystal-growing or making lenses and new kinds of medicines.
- Space stations have laboratories, living quarters and docking ports for other spacecraft.

- ERTS (Earth Resources Technology Satellites) were launched to monitor sea and land. Landsats gave information on crops, forests and changing coastlines. Seasat studied the sea and provided information about such things as the sea bed, ocean currents, storms and the movement of fish shoals.
- SAGE (Stratospheric Aerosol and Gas Experiment) was launched to monitor the ozone layer and the effects of pollution on it.
- IRAS (Infra-red Astronomy Satellite) was launched in 1983. During the 10 months that it operated it taught scientists a great deal about space objects. It could pick up infra-red radiation from galaxies hundreds of millions of light-years away. IRAS discovered a cloud of dust round the bright star, Vega, which could possibly turn into a new Solar System.

Space Probes

This is what the Magellan probe achieved in 1990-91, its first year of orbiting Venus:

Space probes have been some of the most successful developments of the Space Age. They have taught astronomers a great deal about the **Solar System** by visiting all the planets except Pluto. Scientists now have much more information about **planets** and their **satellites**, as well as amazing pictures.

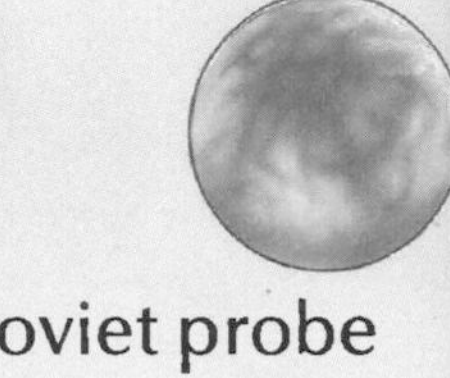

In 1959, the Soviet probe **Luna 1** was the first to bypass the Moon. Thirty years later, in 1989, **Voyager 2** sent back the first detailed pictures of Neptune. The US probe **Galileo**, launched in 1989, will reach Jupiter in 1995. It will orbit the planet and send a probe into its deadly atmosphere.

Probes to the nearest planets

In 1974-5 the US probe **Mariner 10** flew past Mercury three times. It took 8000 pictures, all showing the same side of the planet. These are some other probes and their achievements:

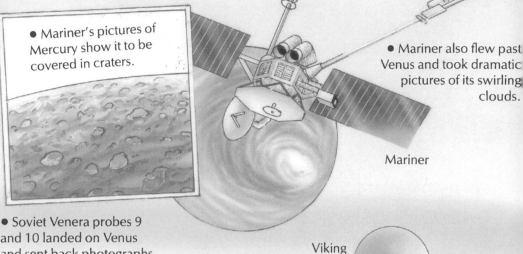

• Mariner's pictures of Mercury show it to be covered in craters.

• Mariner also flew past Venus and took dramatic pictures of its swirling clouds.

Mariner

• Soviet Venera probes 9 and 10 landed on Venus and sent back photographs.

Viking

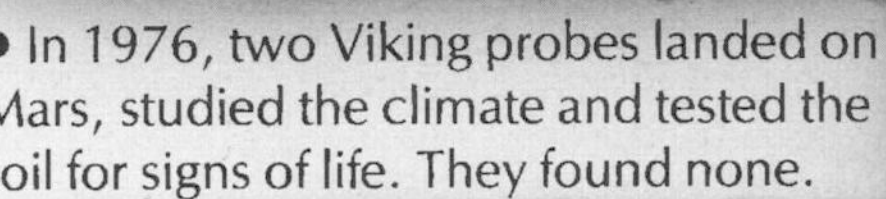

• In 1976, two Viking probes landed on Mars, studied the climate and tested the soil for signs of life. They found none.

• More Mars probes are planned. They may lead to people landing on Mars within the next 50 years.

Pioneer probes

• Pioneers 10 and 11 were the first probes to brave the dangers of the Asteroid Belt on their journey to Jupiter and Saturn.

• Pioneer 10 flew past Jupiter in 1973, sending information back to Earth by radio signals. It is now further than Pluto from the Sun.

• Giotto found that the comet's solid nucleus was 15 km wide.

• The Giotto probe intercepted Halley's comet in 1986. It flew right into the comet's tail. Despite being damaged, it was able to send back information.

Mapped 84 per cent of Venus' surface

Photographed swellings, called coronae, some of them 200 km wide

Discovered that Venus is volcanic and covered in lava flows

Voyager probes

The two **Voyager** probes, launched in 1977, have given stunning new information about the **outer planets**. Both probes flew past Jupiter and Saturn, and Voyager 2 sent back the first detailed pictures of Uranus, Neptune and their satellites.

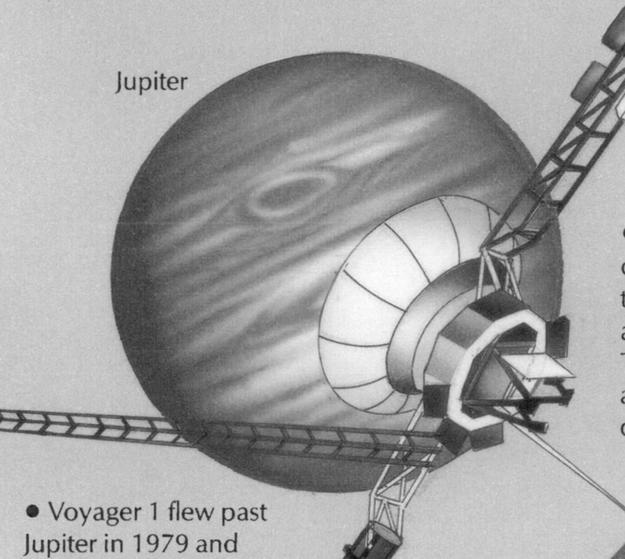

• Voyager probes carried TV cameras and special equipment to measure such things as heat and magnetic fields on planets. They each had a large radio antenna and carried experiments on a central work ring.

• Voyager 1 flew past Jupiter in 1979 and Saturn in 1980 before flying out of the Solar System.

Voyager messages

Both Voyagers carry **messages** in case they are intercepted by **aliens**. They include:

• Pictures of a man, woman and child and a map of the Solar System, showing where Earth is.

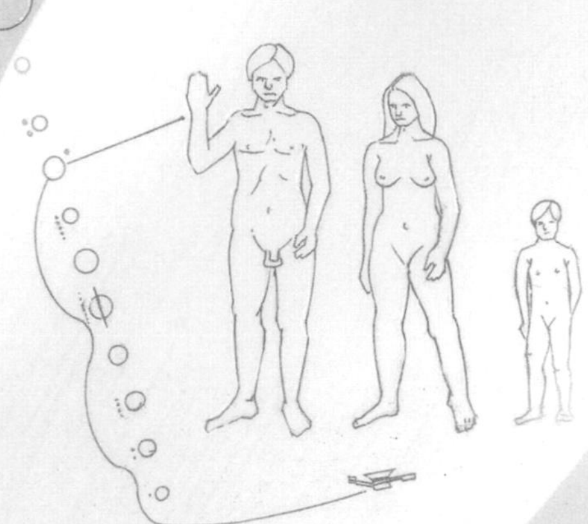

• A record containing music and greetings in various languages. There are 118 pictures of Earth stored on the record.

Strange but true

• Pioneer and Voyager probes may survive for millions of years, drifting in Space.

• Voyager 2 discovered huge 5 km-high ice cliffs on Miranda, Uranus' satellite.

• If Voyager had existed a few years earlier, it might have been possible to send it to visit Pluto as well, when Pluto was nearer the other outer planets.

• Voyager 2 flew past Jupiter in 1979, Saturn in 1981, Uranus in 1986 and Neptune in 1989. It discovered ten satellites of Uranus and six of Neptune.

• Voyager probes could visit so many planets because between 1979 and 1989 the planets furthest from the Sun were lined up together. This happens only once every 175 years.

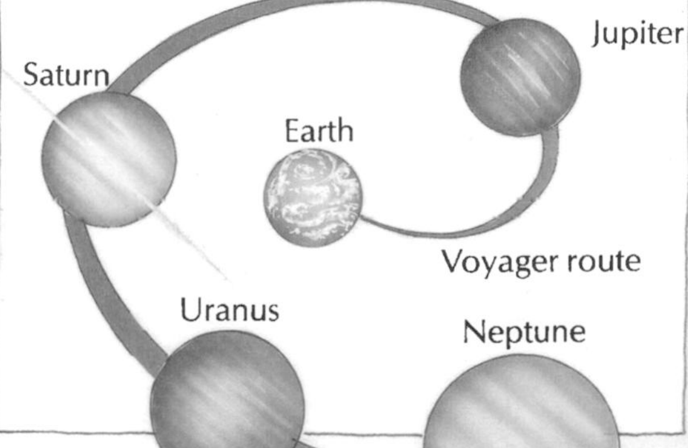

Uranus

Neptune

• Voyager photographed Neptune's Great Dark Spot – a storm similar to Jupiter's Great Red Spot.

The Future

These are some ideas for future spacecraft:

Space exploration is hugely expensive. Nevertheless, plans are underway for large orbiting **space stations** and **permanent bases** on the Moon and Mars. Eventually, people may live on a planet other than Earth. It might even be possible to travel to other stars and set up bases in their solar systems.

Materials from outside Earth would be used to build bases on nearby planets. Rocks from the Moon and asteroids, for example, could be used for building materials. Astronauts would be sent to work on these projects.

Moon base

A Moon base could become a reality in the fairly near future, with astronauts living and working there for long periods.

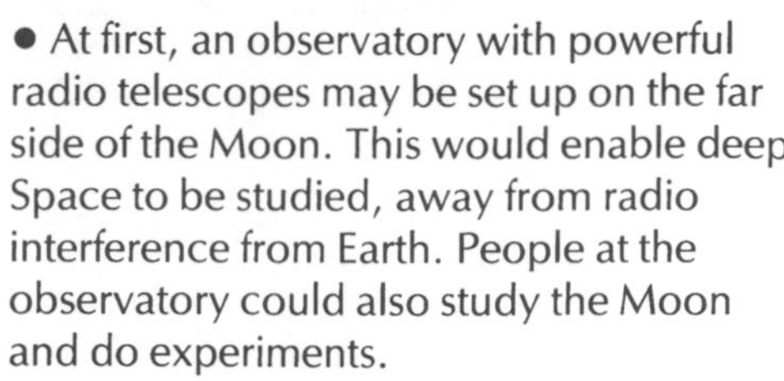

- At first, an observatory with powerful radio telescopes may be set up on the far side of the Moon. This would enable deep Space to be studied, away from radio interference from Earth. People at the observatory could also study the Moon and do experiments.
- Eventually, a permanent base could be set up on the Moon. The main industry would be mining Moon rock.
- A Moon base could help scientists plan manned landings on Mars. This is why the Moon was called a 'bridge between two worlds' by the US National Commission on Space.

Mars base

Within the next 50 years or so, people may have walked on Mars. They may even have started building the first **Mars base**.

- A base on Mars would be slow to build. It would take many missions, and many years, for astronauts to complete the work. They would have to spend eight months travelling in Space before they reached the planet.
- Some scientists believe that it may be better to set up a base on Phobos, Mars' larger satellite. Because of Phobos' weak gravity, it would be easier for spacecraft to approach and land there.

The cost of exploration

How much new space exploration takes place will depend on whether governments can afford the **cost**:

- From 1961-72, the USA spent about 25.5 billion dollars on getting astronauts to the Moon.
- From 1958-73, the USSR spent about 45 billion dollars on its space programme.

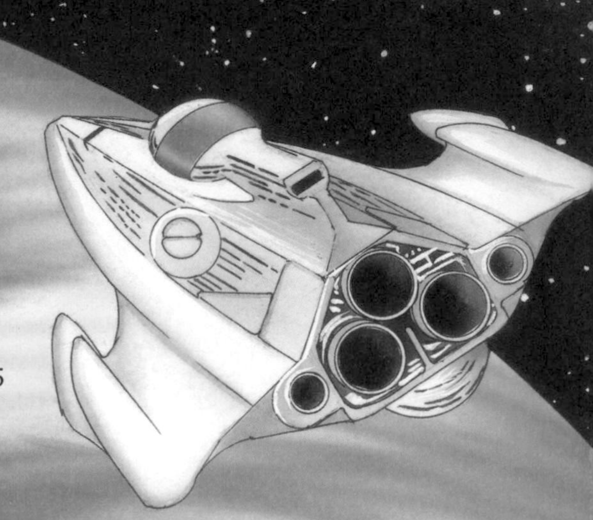

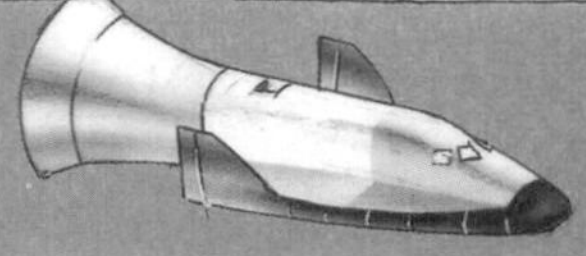
Hermes (Europe)

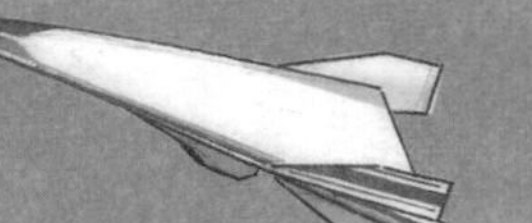
National Aero-Space Plane (USA)

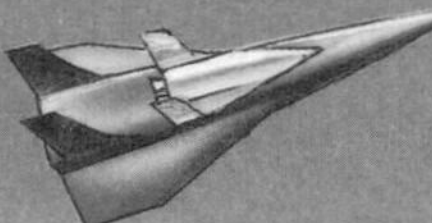
Sanger project (Germany)

Near-future spaceflight

Britain, the USA, Japan and Germany all have plans for a new hypersonic **aerospace plane**. It would take off rather like a jet fighter, burning **oxygen** from the atmosphere rather than propellant. Rockets would then fire to take it into orbit.

- The new space planes could carry three times more than the Shuttle, either as passengers or as cargo. The planes would also be completely reusable.

Power from Space

New sources of power for people on Earth could be found in Space. **Space power stations** would be built to do this.

- A gigantic solar panel could be sent into orbit to capture the Sun's energy and beam it back to Earth.

An artist's impression of what the space power station might look like

- The power station would probably have to be built in Space.
- One idea is to set up a 'factory' in a low orbit. Completed parts would then be moved into a higher orbit and used to build the station, which would orbit above one place on Earth.

International space station

The International Space Station (ISS) is a research facility currently being assembled in outer space. The station is in a low Earth orbit: its altitude varies from 319.6 km to 346.9 km above the surface of the Earth.

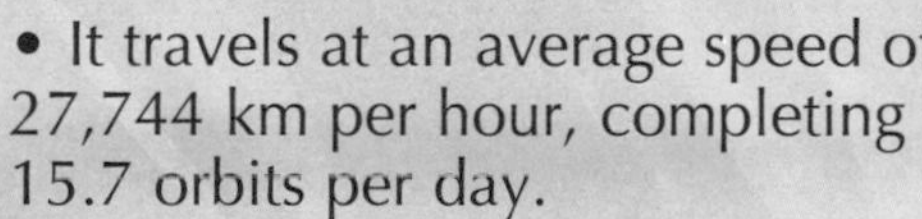

- It travels at an average speed of 27,744 km per hour, completing 15.7 orbits per day.
- The ISS is a joint project between space agencies of the USA, Russia, Japan, Canada, and the European Space Agency.

- Russia has cancelled some space projects because political changes have made space exploration too expensive.

Strange but true

- One idea for a space power station includes an orbiting solar panel that would be 21 km long and 5 km wide!
- In 1865 the French writer Jules Verne wrote a story about people travelling to the Moon from a launch site in Florida. A hundred years later, Apollo astronauts did exactly that!
- There could be millions of inhabited planets like Earth. Nobody knows what the inhabitants might look like!

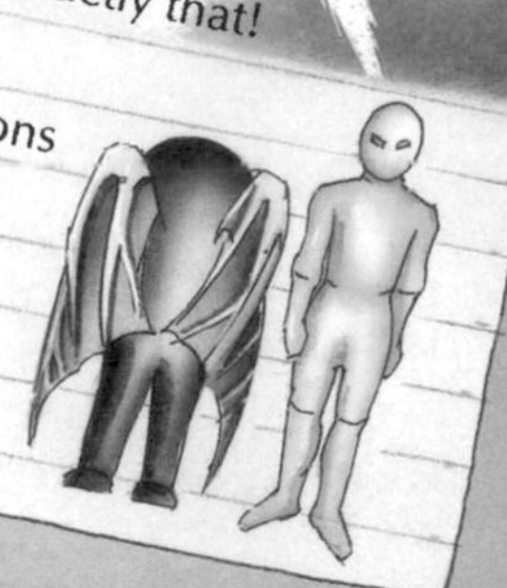

Space Facts and Lists

Stars

• About 1500 stars are visible at night with the naked eye in a clear, dark sky.

• There are 88 constellations altogether.

• The smallest star measures about 1700 km across. It is a white dwarf called LP 327-16.

Supernovae

Supernovae are exploding stars. Here are four recorded supernovae explosions seen with the naked eye. The first one was recorded by the Chinese, who said that the supernova was visible for two years.

Date	Constellation	Brightness
1006	Lupus (Wolf)	−9.5 (very bright)
1054	Taurus (Bull)	−4
1572	Cassiopeia	−4
1604	Ophiuchus (Serpent-Bearer)	−3

• At its brightest, a supernova can be 500 million times as bright as the Sun.

• There was a supernova in 1987 in the Large Magellanic Cloud – our closest galaxy.

• A cloud of dust and gas called the Crab Nebula is the remains of the supernova seen in 1054.

Galaxies

These are the nearest galaxies to the Milky Way.

Name	Distance (Light-years)	Diameter (Light-years)
Large Magellanic Cloud	180,000	30,000
Small Magellanic Cloud	190,000	16,000
Ursa Minor dwarf	250,000	2000
Draco dwarf	250,000	3000
Sextant dwarf	280,000	6000
Sculptor dwarf	280,000	5000
Fornax dwarf	420,000	7000
Carina dwarf	550,000	3000
Leo I	750,000	2000

Solar eclipses

• The longest total eclipse of the Sun was recorded on 20 June 1955. It lasted for 7 minutes, 8 seconds.

• The first recorded eclipse of the Sun was in China on 22 October 2136 BC.

• There are usually two to four solar eclipses each year. However, occasionally there are five. This last happened in 1935.

Here are the dates of the eclipses of the Sun between 1992-2000.

Year	Visible in	Kind of eclipse
1992		
4/5 January	Central Pacific	Annular
30 June	S.Atlantic	Total
24 December	Arctic	Partial
1993		
21 May	Arctic	Partial
13 November	Antarctic	Partial
1994		
10 May	Pacific, Mexico USA, Canada	Annular
3 November	Peru, Brazil S.Atlantic	Total
1995		
29 April	S.Pacific, Brazil Peru, S.Atlantic	Annular
24 October	Iran, India, E.Indies, Pacific	Total
1996		
17 April	Antarctic	Partial
12 October	Arctic	Partial
1997		
9 March	Russia, Arctic	Total
2 September	Antarctic	Partial
1998		
26 February	Pacific, South of Panama, Atlantic	Total
22 August	Indian Ocean E.Indies, Pacific	Annular
1999		
16 February	Indian Ocean Australia, Pacific	Annular
11 August	Atlantic, England, France, Turkey, India	Total

• An annular eclipse happens when the Moon is too far away to cover the Sun completely. A ring of light appears round the Moon.

The Moon

• The biggest 'sea' on the Moon is the Mare Imbrium (Sea of Showers), which is 1300 km across.

• The biggest Moon crater visible from Earth is Bailly, which is 295 km wide and 4 km deep.

• The deepest Moon crater is Newton, which is over 8 km deep.

• There are about 1500 moonquakes a year. They are usually 700-1100 km below the surface and are much weaker than earthquakes.

Lunar eclipses

These are the dates of Lunar eclipses between 1992 and 2000.

Date	Type	Mid-point of eclipse
1992		
15 June	Partial	4.58 am
9 December	Total	11.45 pm
1993		
4 June	Total	1.02 pm
29 November	Total	6.26 am
1994		
25 May	Partial	3.32 am
1995		
15 April	Partial	12.19 pm
1996		
4 April	Total	12.11 am
27 September	Total	2.55 am
1997		
24 March	Partial	4.41 am
16 September	Total	6.47 pm
1999		
28 July	Partial	11.34 am
2000		
21 January	Total	4.45 am
16 July	Total	1.57 pm

Comets

• Halley's Comet is the brightest comet seen regularly. It passes the Sun every 76.1 years.

• People used to believe that a comet's appearance signalled an important event about to happen on Earth.

• Comet West, which was visible in daylight in 1976, may take a million years to orbit the Sun.

• The comet with the shortest orbit is Encke's. It takes 3.3 years to travel round the Sun.

• The biggest comet was recorded in 1811. The head was 2 million km in diameter and the tail was 160 million km long.

• The Great Comet of 1843 had the longest recorded tail – 330 million km.

These are some comets that have been observed more than once:

Name	Years taken to circle the Sun
Enke	3.3
D'Arrest	6.2
Wolf-Harrington	6.6
Shajn-Schaldach	7.3
Smirnova-Chernykh	8.5
Slaughter-Burnham	11.6
Temple-Tuttle	32.9
Pons-Brooks	71
Halley	76.1
Herschel-Rigollet	156

Meteors

• Every year the Earth passes through groups of meteoroids. As Earth passes through them, showers of meteors can be seen in the sky.

• To see meteors, you need patience and a clear night sky, away from city lights and with no moonlight.

• The most spectacular meteor shower that takes place each year is called the Perseids. They are visible around 12 August.

• During the Perseids meteor shower, several dozen meteors can be seen every hour for several hours.

Meteorite craters

These are the names and sizes of some meteorite craters on Earth:

Name	Diameter (metres)
Meteor Crater, Arizona, USA	1265
Wolf Creek, Australia	850
Henbury, Australia	200
Boxhole, Australia	175
Odessa, Texas, USA	170
Waqar, Arabia	100
Desel, Estonia	100
Campo del Cielo, Argentina	75
Dalgaranga, Australia	70
Sikhote-Alin, Siberia	28

These are the weights of some of the biggest meteorites ever found:

Meteorite	Weight
Hoba west, Grootfontein, South Africa	60 tonnes
Armanty, Outer Mongolia	20 tonnes
Willamette, Oregon, USA	14 tonnes
Campo del Cielo, Argentina	13 tonnes
Mundrabilla, Australia	12 tonnes
Magura, Czechoslovakia	1.5 tonnes

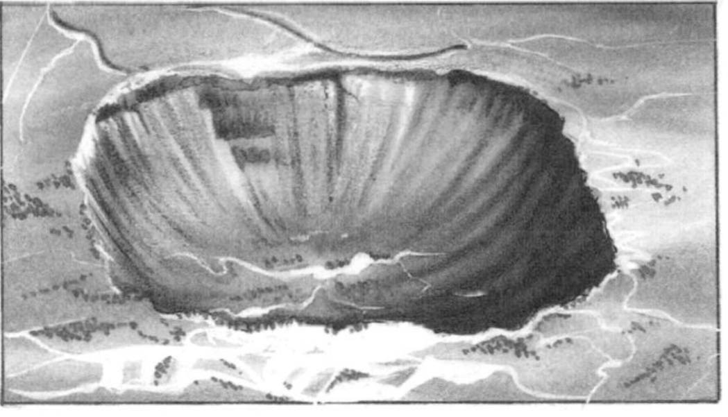

Asteroids

• The biggest asteroid is Ceres, with a diameter of 940 km.

• The smallest known asteroid is probably Hathor. Its diameter is about 0.5 km.

• Vesta is the brightest asteroid. Arethusa is the darkest.

• The asteroid Hermes came within 800,000 km of Earth on 28 October 1937.

• An asteroid called the NORC was named after an electronic calculator. Most asteroids are named by their discoverers, who can choose any name they like.

Space Facts and Lists

Astronomy dates

1543
Copernicus published the book in which he stated that the Sun, not Earth, was the centre of the Solar System.

1576-1596
Tycho Brahe drew up the most accurate star catalogue ever made without a telescope.

1600
Giordano Bruno was burned at the stake for publicly stating that the Earth goes round the Sun.

1604
Kepler's Star was the last supernova to be seen in our galaxy, to date.

1608
The telescope was invented in Holland by Hans Lippershey.

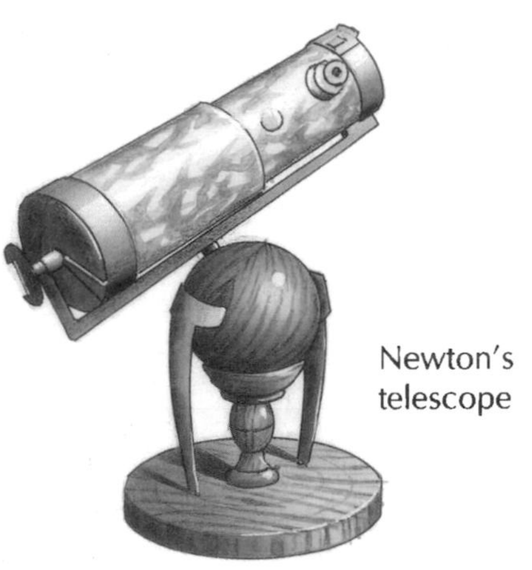

Newton's telescope

1668
Isaac Newton made the first reflecting telescope.

1758
Halley's Comet returned, as had been predicted for the first time.

1781
The astronomer William Herschel discovered Uranus.

1801
Ceres was the first asteroid to be discovered.

1846
Neptune was discovered, using the predictions of its position made by John Adams and Urbain Leverrier.

1850
The first successful photograph of a star (Vega) was produced.

1908
There was a mysterious explosion in Tunguska, Siberia, which was thought to be caused by a meteorite landing.

1930
Astronomer Clyde Tombaugh discovered Pluto.

1937
The first radio telescope dish was built. It measured 9.4 metres across.

1963
Quasars were identified for the first time.

1967
Pulsars were discovered.

1986
Halley's Comet returned as predicted. The probe Giotto passed through the comet's tail and sent back information about the comet's head.

1990
The Hubble space telescope was launched.

Space Age firsts

- The first object to orbit Earth was Sputnik 1, launched by the USSR in October 1957.
- The first animal in Space was the Soviet dog, Laika, in November 1957. It died on the flight.
- The first animals to survive an orbital spaceflight were the Soviet dogs, Strelka and Belka, launched in Sputnik 5 in August 1960.
- The first person to orbit Earth was Yuri Gagarin, from the USSR, in April 1961.
- The first American to orbit Earth was John Glenn in February 1962.
- The first woman in Space was Valentina Tereshkova, from the USSR, in June 1963.

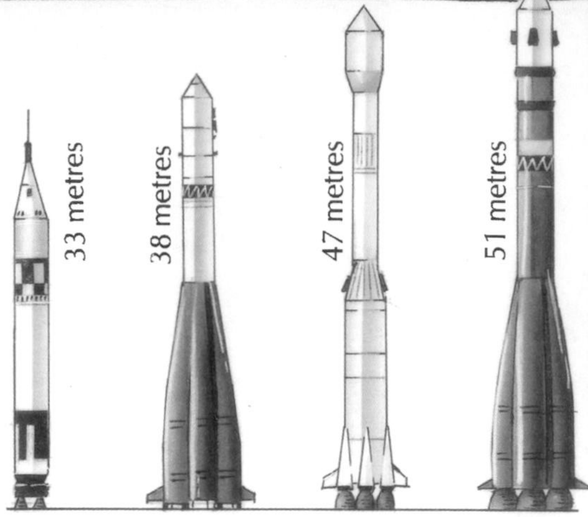

Some space rockets and their heights

- The first docking in Space of two manned spacecraft was in January 1969. The spacecraft were the Soviet Soyuz 4 and 5. Two cosmonauts spacewalked to Soyuz 4.
- The first person to walk on the Moon was Neil Armstrong in July 1969.
- The first vehicle on the Moon was the unmanned Soviet Lunokhod Rover in November 1970.
- The first landing on Venus was by the Soviet Venera 3 probe in March 1966.
- The first space station to be launched was the Soviet Salyut 1 in April 1971.
- The first space probe sent to the outer planets was Pioneer 10, launched in March 1972. It passed out of the Solar System after its mission.
- The first US space station, Skylab 1, was launched in May 1973.
- The first Space Shuttle, Columbia, was sent into orbit by the United States in April 1981.
- The first US woman in Space was Sally Ride in 1983.
- The first astronaut to fly untethered in Space, using a self-propelling backpack called a Manned Manoeuvring Unit (MMU), was American Bruce McCandless in February 1984.
- The first British person in Space was Helen Sharman in May 1991.

Rocket launch centres

Here are the world's main rocket launch centres:

USA:
- Cape Canaveral, Florida
- Vandenberg Air Force Base, California
- Wallops Station, Virginia

Former USSR
- Baikonu Cosmodrome
- Plesetsk
- Kapustin Yar

JAPAN:
- Kagoshima Space Centre
- Tanegashima, Osaki

CHINA:
- Jiuquan Satellite Launch Centre
- Xi Chang Satellite Launch Centre
- Taiyuan Satellite Launch Centre

ESA (European Space Agency):
- Guiana Space Centre, Kourou, French Guiana

ITALY:
- San Marco Launch Platform, Formosa Bay, Kenya

INDIA:
- Sriharikota Launching Range (SHAR)

ISRAEL:
- Palmachim Air Force Base

Giant telescopes

These are the biggest telescopes in the world:

Reflectors

Name	Aperture
Keck Telescope, Hawaii	982 cm
Mount Semirodriki, USSR	600 cm
Palomar, California, USA	508 cm
Mount Hopkins, California	440 cm
La Palma, Canary Islands	420 cm
Cerro Tololo, Chile	401 cm
Kitt Peak, Arizona, USA	401 cm
Siding Spring, Australia	389 cm

Refractors

Name	Aperture
Yerkes, Williams Bay, USA	102 cm
Lick, California, USA	91 cm
Meudon, France	83 cm
Potsdam, Germany	81 cm
Alleghany, Pittsburgh, USA	76 cm
Nice, France	76 cm

Radio telescopes

- The biggest non-steerable radio dish is in Arecibo, Puerto Rico. It measures 305 metres across.
- The biggest steerable radio dish is in the Max Planck Institute, Bonn, Germany. It is 100 metres across.
- The biggest group, or array, of radio antennae is in New Mexico. There are 27 antennae, all 25 metres wide. The array is Y-shaped and each arm measures 20.9 km.

Manned Moon missions

All manned missions to the Moon to date were made by US astronauts in Apollo spacecraft during the late 1960s and early 1970s.

Date	Mission	Astronauts
July 1969	Apollo 11	Neil Armstrong Edwin Aldrin Michael Collins
Nov 1969	Apollo 12	Charles Conrad Richard Gordon Alan Bean
April 1970	Apollo 13 (abandoned)	James Lovell John Swigert Fred Haise
Feb 1971	Apollo 14	Alan Shepard Stuart Roosa Edgar Mitchell
July 1971	Apollo 15	David Scott James Irwin Alfred Worden
April 1972	Apollo 16	John Young Thomas Mattingly Charles Duke
Dec 1972	Apollo 17	Eugene Cernan Ronald Evans Harrison Schmitt

Space probes

Here are some of the main space probes that have been launched:

1959
Luna 1, 2 and 3 (USSR) became the first successful probes to the Moon.

1965
Mariner 4 (USA) took pictures of Mars.

1966
Luna 9 (USSR) landed on the Moon.

1967
Venera 4 (USSR) landed on Venus ·

1971
Mariner 9 (USA) was put into orbit round Mars and took photographs of the surface.

1976
Vikings 1 and 2 (USA) landed on Mars.

1978
Veneras 11 and 12 (USSR) and two Pioneer probes (USA) visited Venus.

1979
Voyager 1 (USA) by-passed Jupiter.

1980
Voyager 1 (USA) by-passed Saturn.

1986
Voyager 2 (USA) by-passed Uranus. Five probes, including Giotto (USA), were sent to intercept Halley's Comet.

1989
Voyager 2 (USA) by-passed Neptune. Phobos 2 (USSR) entered orbit round Mars. Galileo (USA) was launched, eventually bound for Jupiter.

1991
Magellan (USA) sent back detailed information about Venus after mapping most of its surface by radar.

INDEX

Indexes to other sections are on pages 46, 94 and 142.

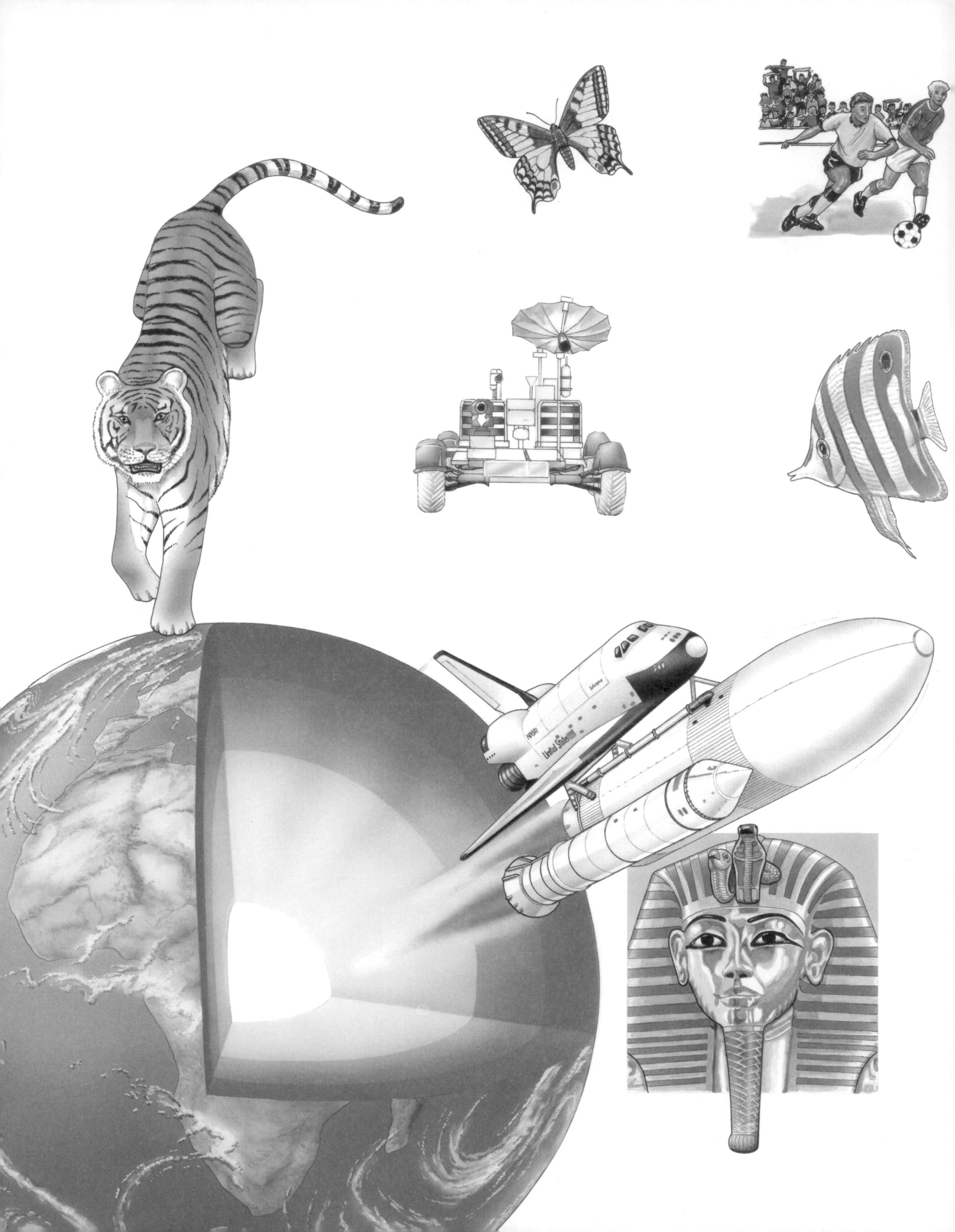
NASA
United States